READINGS IN THE
METHODS OF EDUCATION

$2.50

COMPLIMENTS OF

THE ODYSSEY PRESS · INC ·

55 FIFTH AVENUE   NEW YORK 10003

READINGS IN THE METHODS OF EDUCATION

FRANK L. STEEVES THE UNIVERSITY OF VERMONT

THE ODYSSEY PRESS · INC · *New York*

COPYRIGHT © 1964 BY THE ODYSSEY PRESS, INC.

ALL RIGHTS RESERVED

PRINTED IN THE UNITED STATES

LIBRARY OF CONGRESS CATALOG CARD NUMBER: 64–19195

A 0 9 8 7 6 5 4 3 2 1

PREFACE

A problem confronting the teacher of educational method is the determination of the role the textbook should play in his course. Do the words in the text determine the official opinion of the course? Does the organization of the text constitute the course outline? Are the facts in the book those that the students are expected to learn to the exclusion of equally important facts that the text does not contain? Does the book, in fact, limit the boundaries of the course, furnish the basis for examinations, set the pattern for class activities, and leave the professor with little defense of his teaching as an example of good methods?

Without doubt, most professors of education who teach methods courses would respond with a resounding "No!" to all of these questions, and would hold that they are well acquainted with the pitfalls of textbook teaching and would not permit a textbook to teach their courses. They treat all textbooks, even the so-called "basic" text, only as supplements to the course itself, which is a series of lectures, readings, discussions, audio-visual experiences, and other activities designed to achieve predetermined objectives. The "course" is something planned and taught by the instructor. It has meaning because of the instructor's emphases and direction, because of his guidance and interest, because of his skill in motivating and leading others, because of his manner of speech, because of his personality, indeed, because of his very presence.

Without the instructor there could be no course as such. Without students and the interchange of their opinions, their reactions to each other, and their contributions as human beings, there could be no course. Hence, reading a textbook is not the same thing as taking a course. The "course" becomes a reality only when more than one person is involved in the acts of guided teaching and learning. At this point it might be suggested that if reading a textbook is not the same as taking a course, neither is working through the steps of a learning program the same as taking a course. The "teaching machine" cannot teach a course of study any more than courses are taught by any other tool used by teachers.

Yet, even though the textbook does not teach the course of study, and, by extension of this idea, neither does the teaching machine, the motion picture, the television set, or any other teaching device, it would be admitted readily by teachers at all levels that pupils do learn from all of these tools. The power of the television to teach is well understood by the parents whose four-year-old son or daughter chants all the television commercials a split second before the announcer can form the words. Fear of the motion picture and the book as effective teaching instruments is one of the motivations of those who would censor books and motion pictures.

Because of its many advantages the textbook became the most widely used single teaching tool in American schools during the latter part of the nineteenth century and continues into the second half of the twentieth century to be the one tool that is found as part of nearly all courses of study. The elementary-school teacher relies on series of textbooks and workbooks in all subjects. Junior and senior high school teachers expect that textbooks in their courses will be available and will be studied by pupils. College professors, those in education included, search for appropriate textbooks to supplement course lectures and other activities. Despite increasing competition from newer technological devices, the textbook remains firm in its leading position as a tool that is known, used, and understood by all teachers; not to teach the course, but to give direction; not to limit the learning of pupils, but to facilitate it; not to control thought, but to stimulate it.

THE USES FOR THIS BOOK

Instructors of methods courses face additional questions which teachers in other areas may safely ignore. Even though students do learn by reading, can teachers and prospective teachers learn how to teach by reading a book? Is the act of teaching something that must be performed in order to be learned? Is the art of teaching something that would be better demonstrated than talked about by education professors? Surely, questions such as these must nag at the minds of those who select textbooks for courses in the methods and principles of teaching. Because of the validity of such questions the textbook becomes even more of a supplemental device in the methods course than it might be, for example, in the course in European history.

This anthology, therefore, should be at least as useful in the principles or methods course as the standard logically organized textbook and may, in fact, be preferred by instructors who believe that none of the available textbooks on teaching is an adequate supplement to their courses. On the other hand, there are a number of well-written, comprehensive books on the methods of teaching, and those instructors who have found a satisfactory textbook may be inclined to use the present volume as an adjunct to the standard textbook adopted for the course of study. Either use would seem to be appropriate, the decision depending on the needs and desires of particular instructors. And, although the book was designed to be used more specifically in courses in teacher preparation, it is quite possible that experienced teachers may find it a useful source of reference.

CORRELATION WITH EXISTING TEXTS

It would be possible to prepare a chart showing the page numbers from leading textbooks where are treated the many topics included in the readings in this book. The present writer has not undertaken this clerical chore for several reasons. Such a chart would add little real value for those using the book. It would illustrate little except that the writer had consulted the indexes and tables of contents of a number of textbooks assumed to be the leading ones. This task, if appropriate at all, is more appropriate for those using the book, namely the students who consult it as part of their course of study. The typical college student and teacher are well able to use indexes and tables of contents and do not need specific page references to textbooks in order to locate topics included in them. In fact, it might be argued that this type of spoon feeding retards progress toward one of the major aims of a college education, the goal that finds the mature student cross-checking his own information and expanding his own intellectual horizons.

Actually, all well-known textbooks in educational methods cover all of the major topics included within the readings contained in Parts Two and Three of this book. Words such as "discussion," "questioning," "homework," "field trip," "discipline," "evaluation," "textbooks," "workbook," "television," and so on, are standard to the field and form part of the content of all leading textbooks.

The readings in Part One encompass both historical and contemporary sources, all of which may not be found in some current textbooks. However, they were included here because it is essential that both those preparing to be teachers and teachers in service understand that the general principles of teaching are more fundamental to good teaching than are the classroom tricks of the trade. Technical competence without philosophical conviction is of little value. Of course, competent teachers know how to conduct discussions, organize and lead field trips, show filmstrips, conduct demonstrations, prepare charts, lay out bulletin boards, adopt textbooks, as well as direct a host of additional class activities that might be listed. But it is more important that teachers understand why this variety of activity is, in itself, valuable in learning, that they know something about the historical developments that have contributed to today's wide choice of activities for pupils, and that they formulate some systematic procedure for organizing class work.

ORGANIZATION OF THE BOOK

The sixty-six readings in this book are grouped into three parts. Part One, "Developmental Contributions to Modern Teaching Method," includes twenty-seven readings encompassing a number of general theories and practices in teaching set forth during the nineteenth and twentieth centuries. Part One also includes selections which discuss some of the factors which influence classroom procedures. The environment in which teaching is done, the nature of the learners being taught, and the influence of the teacher's personal characteristics on his teaching method, for example, are key concerns of one or more of the readings in Part One.

Part Two, "Classroom Procedures: Widely-Used Activities for Teaching and Learning," contains twenty-seven readings which, by contrast with those in Part One, are very specific in nature. These readings concern the methods of teaching, the specific techniques of classroom instruction, the tools which are part of the equipment of all capable teachers.

Part Three, "Professional Activities and Problems," includes twelve readings covering some of the major problems and activities of teachers which exert a direct influence on their classroom work. Discipline, for example, as an aspect of method, and measurement as a tool for learning, are basic ideas treated in Part Three. This Part is also concerned with the out-of-class and professional obligations of teachers as well as with certain proposals for school and staff organization which have an influence on methods of teaching.

The readings have not been edited or abridged in any way. Nor have questions or bibliographies been added to those that may be included in some of the readings. The discerning reader will perceive the fundamental questions and problems that concern each writer. The serious student will seek out additional opinions and facts to compare and contrast with those given in any reading in which he is particularly interested. There is a brief introduction to each Part. These introductions suggest some of the general questions which the student may keep in mind as he studies the readings.

CRITERIA FOR SELECTING READINGS

The readings in this book, so far as possible, were selected because of their pertinence to the work of all teachers rather than to the work of teachers at a particular grade level or in a particular subject. Hence, the emphases are neither elementary nor secondary but rather are directed to the problems, activities, and skills which, properly, are the concerns of all teachers, elementary school through college. Naturally, some of the selections are written from a specific viewpoint. An elementary-school experience may be reported, or a high-school project outlined, or the details given for a successful plan for teaching in a specific subject. However, even in these instances the principles of teaching that are illustrated enable the alert reader to make ready applications to his own subject and grade level. It seems to the present writer that many of the lines drawn between elementary and secondary education are artificial at best. The ideas of Pestalozzi are not exclusively those of elementary education merely because Pestalozzi worked with small children. Depth of exploration in subject matter is not an exclusive prerogative of the high-school or college instructor. With due allowance, of course, for variations in the maturity of learners, many methods are appropriate for all grade levels.

An effort was made to secure a reasonable balance among historical and contemporary sources, among research reports and informed opinions, and among the many sources that sponsor professional publications in education. The size of the literature in professional education, of course, poses a formidable problem for anyone who attempts to prepare an anthology in any of its branches, and the methods of education are no exception. It is only a factual recognition of the size of the literature to state that a collection of readings in the methods of education could be built around the contents of any one of several leading professional journals through the years. A collection could be devised consisting entirely of selections appearing in all journals for a single month of almost any year. An anthology could be prepared devoted entirely to a given teaching technique, for example, the field trip or the bulletin board, because hundreds, perhaps thousands, of articles have been published and continue to appear on every conceivable topic in educational method.

It is no reflection on the merit of the selections in this book to say that no effort was made to find the "best" article or report ever published on each topic. This would have been an impossible goal even if criteria for identifying the "best" could have been formulated. It is sufficient to say that each of these readings is well written and possesses a merit of its own that renders it of value to those interested in the improvement of teaching. In general, two types of readings are included: (1) Those that introduce one or more broad concepts and general problems and which touch upon many specific questions which may or may not be answered, and, (2) Those which discuss a very specific activity or problem and which include appropriate procedures for directing the activity or solving the problem. As might be expected in the organization of the book, the readings in Part One tend to be those that are broad in scope and general in nature, while those in Parts Two and Three, generally, deal with specific topics.

A NOTE OF CAUTION

Anyone who prepares a new anthology in education when so many are already available should be expected to justify his act. To some degree the preceding paragraphs constitute a justification for either the textbook or the anthology in methods courses and suggest uses which may be found for the present collection. However, it should be noted that the anthology itself is open to the criticism that it can become a superficial device by means of which students are fed excerpts from a number of authorities when they ought to be doing their own research and searching out their own sources of information. The enormous quantity of professional writing previously noted cannot be read in its entirety, but it should be probed and investigated by all serious students of education. Neither this collection nor any other should leave students satisfied with the extent of their reading or be accepted as a substitute for personal research.

This caution, however, relates more to the use which is made of the collection than to the discrimination with which it is assembled. Wisely used, the anthology does possess positive virtues. First, the vast content of educational literature, as many critics have noted, is heavily repetitive and is loaded with contradictory opinions and conflicting research findings. The student who is turned loose in a professional library without guidelines for his study is just as likely to become lost and confused as he is to be enlightened. If the anthology does no more than furnish examples of good writing and clarity of thought, it accomplishes a worthwhile purpose. At least, the student will have standards by which to judge his further reading. Second, the selective anthology stands as an example of the contributions of many people and within a consistent framework illustrates a wide variety of serious thought and opinion. Third, it is unfortunate but true that many libraries simply do not contain all of the sources that are brought together in the collection. The argument that each student should complete his own original research is meaningless to the student whose carefully prepared list of titles for investigation is found to contain magazines to which his library does not subscribe, books which are out of print and unavailable, and monographs which cannot be located. Fourth, the ideal of the teacher culling professional articles for information is an ideal which is not often realized during the press of an already overloaded schedule. Too often trial and error take over when time is lacking. Any device is of value which provides accurate and readable information when it is needed. For these reasons and probably for others that might be listed, the collection of selected readings may be successfully defended.

Perhaps with some optimism, it is hoped that these selections will meet important needs of students and teachers and will also stimulate readers to pursue further thought, reading, and study in the methods of education.

The editor is grateful to the authors and publishers who generously granted permission to reprint their materials in this volume.

CONTENTS

PART TWO: Classroom Procedures: Widely-Used Activities for Teaching and Learning

PART THREE: Professional Activities and Problems

READINGS IN THE
METHODS OF EDUCATION

PART
ONE

DEVELOPMENTAL CONTRIBUTIONS TO MODERN TEACHING METHOD

Introduction

The dimensions of method.—It is doubtful that any collection of only twenty-seven readings, no matter how carefully selected, can do more than to point the way to a full understanding of the complexities of teaching. Perhaps it is sufficient if the broad dimensions of educational method can be appreciated and if it can be seen that the boundaries of method encompass whatever the teacher is and include whatever the pupils are. The limits of method reach into and are influenced by the environment, natural, technological, social, and political, within which teaching and learning are done. The perimeters of method are intertwined with the borders of the subjects which are taught and learned. Method, therefore, is influenced by all of these factors: the personal qualities of teachers, the nature of pupils, all aspects of the environment, and the demands of the subjects studied.

The teacher who is not aware that all of these factors share in the determination of his teaching method is bound to be deficient in his knowledge of how to teach. For example, it is not sufficient to argue that a knowledge of the subject alone is adequate preparation for the methodology of the classroom. Knowledge of the subject, of course, is an essential part of the equipment of all qualified teachers, but subject knowledge, in itself, proves merely that the teacher has been able to learn and not that he is capable of teaching. Learning the subject suggests that some of the techniques appropriate to teaching that subject may have been learned as an incidental aspect of the subject course, but does not prove that the teacher can use the pertinent techniques, nor, if he can use them, that he can use them within the systematic, orderly framework of a valid, general approach to teaching. By the same token,

3

the teacher whose concept of teaching is limited to the cultivation of his own personality may turn out to be a genial type of chap from whom pupils learn little of value. He may be well liked as a person but not respected as a teacher. The old saying that good teachers are born, not made, is a partial truth which, if taken seriously by the would-be teacher, can lead to endless difficulty before he finally perceives that there is much to be learned about the art and science he has chosen to practice. Similarly, we can know a great deal about the ways by which children learn, or about the nature of our communities, or about twentieth-century technology, and still have an incomplete understanding of educational method because it is all of these things in varying proportions that contribute to the orderly process of classroom teaching. The method of the teacher is what results when he organizes what he knows about all of these factors into some kind of coherent arrangement for teaching and learning and follows through with a systematic classroom process. And in this organization for teaching, as well as during the systematic process of teaching, all constituent influences on method are given due consideration, and none is allowed to predominate. Teachers who understand this are not likely to become identified as "subject-centered" teachers, nor as "pupil-centered" teachers, nor as "textbook" teachers, nor even as "television" or "machine" teachers, as could well happen with any who accept uncritically all that is claimed by the sponsors of current technology. Teachers who comprehend the dimensions of method can be known only as teachers, master teachers in the truest and purest sense of the phrase, and there is no need for limiting adjectives to describe the kind of teachers they are.

The selections that follow touch upon these matters and, in addition, raise a number of serious questions about teaching which, in the long run, each teacher must think through for himself. What is teaching? To what extent is telling part of teaching and in what ways does teaching differ from telling? Is teaching a process whereby facts to be learned are presented to pupils, or is it a means by which pupils are guided and directed to develop their own powers? Is there a best method of teaching, a body of fixed principles underlying the teaching-learning process? Or are the principles of teaching an illusion created and promoted by professors of education as a means of earning an easy living? Is it a fact that there are no principles of teaching which, collectively, constitute an appropriate method? What are the goals of education? Are definite ends worth stating, or is the labor of defining educational objectives a waste of valuable teaching time? Who are some of the people who have thought about questions such as these, both in the past and today? What are the essential features of some of the broad, general movements in educational method and in school organization that have contributed to the development of modern teaching method? It is the answers that teachers accept to questions such as these that inevitably determine the kind of teaching they do and the kind of teachers they are.

Theory and practice in general teaching method.—Theory in educational method does not mean speculation about how to teach as opposed to the techniques actually practiced by the majority of teachers. Educational theory consists of general principles which have been derived from the observations and experiences of successful teachers through the years as well as from experimental evidence and reason. The only conflict between theory and practice in education is between ineffective or uninformed practice and the accumulated wisdom of effective teachers as expressed in principles of teaching.

Of course, it is a part of educational history that individual, outstanding teachers, working alone in their own schools, have tried out ideas in teaching that were at the time novel and strange to most other teachers. This is as true today as it was hundreds of years ago, and the pattern of action that follows is happening today, has happened in the past, and most probably will continue happening for as long as men maintain schools. In brief, the pattern includes about five major steps: (1) The new idea or experiment is tried out by the innovating teacher or teachers. (2) If successful, it is reported to other teachers and administrators in professional journals, at professional conferences, in special reports or monographs, or, if newsworthy enough, by way of general magazines and newspapers. It is given a name, a convenient label for quick identification. (3) The interest generated by these early reports, all of which, of course, are affirmative, leads to considerable interest and tryout of the idea in additional schools. During the period of peak interest teachers and administrators from other schools may visit the original schools where the idea was first practiced. The principles underlying the new practice are explained carefully by educators. Thus, educational theory is born. (4) Widespread tryout, of course, brings a certain amount of disillusionment because as environments, pupils, and teachers change, so also must the specific practice. Consequently, the original practice is modified in the programs of many schools. Some would say that it is distorted in later practice. Critical articles begin to appear. Some say that the general theory behind the new method is not practical and that it does not work nearly so well in practice as was first reported. Others maintain that the original concept is not understood by those who came later. (5) After a more-or-less prolonged debate in professional journals, one of two things happens. Either the new practice comes to be part of the equipment of all competent teachers, taking its place for routine use under certain conditions and within certain limits imposed by the local teaching situation. Or, the new idea is found to be unworkable by most teachers over a period of time, and it passes from the educational scene. The former result occurs if the theory is sound, the latter if the theory is unsound. Sound theory is little more than the distillation and generalization of that which does work in practice.

The readings in Part One, if not concerned with what was described in the preceding comments on "The Dimensions of Method," consist of descriptions of general theories and practices in education, designs for classroom teaching which for the most part have contributed significantly to our present knowledge about the nature of teaching and learning.

1. The Nature of Teaching Method

JOHN A. BARTKY

All through the history of education, theory and practice have defined varying roles for the teacher in interaction with pupils. Some of these roles suggested that the teacher be directive; others, that he adopt a permissive attitude; and still others that he abandon himself to a laissez faire policy. There almost seems to have been an alternation between the extremes of direction and laissez faire in teaching, as education developed its methodology. For example, the ancient Greek philosophers were often directive in their teaching, though the Socratic method is permissive. The teaching method advocated in Rousseau's *Émile* is laissez faire.

My generation has seen a complete swing from the authoritarian directive role for the teacher to the laissez faire role, plus a partial swing back to the permissive approach—from the teacher-directed assignment through pupil-teacher planning to the child-centered school and now

From John A. Bartky, "The Nature of Teaching Method," *The Elementary School Journal*, LVIII (January, 1958), 199–203. Now Professor of Education at Stanford University, John A. Bartky has served in many responsible teaching and administrative positions. He is a former Dean of the School of Education at Stanford, past District Superintendent of Schools in Chicago, and past President of the Chicago Teachers College. He is the author of many articles and books on teaching method, supervision, and school administration. Professor Bartky is eminently qualified to write on the many facets of method that are described in the introductory article to Part One of this volume. Reprinted from *The Elementary School Journal* by permission of The University of Chicago Press. Copyright 1958 by The University of Chicago.

back to the planned experience. It is my thesis that such alternations are essentially reflections of fashion in philosophy and that the true role of the teacher must be determined by the situation in which he finds himself—that it may be directive, permissive, or laissez faire, depending upon the variables involved in that situation. I contend that failure to recognize this fact results in teacher and pupil frustration and produces ineffective instruction.

Education prior to the thirties concerned itself with a directive method of instruction called the "administration of the assignment." "Assignment" is a comparatively old term that reflects those methods in which the teacher operates as a dominating force. "Assignment," therefore, is hardly a respectable term for use by the child-centered teacher, who looks upon a teacher-dominated method as autocratic and threatening to democratic values.

"Assignment" developed out of the concept that teachers "assigned" learning tasks to children and then heard recitations on that assignment. In a curriculum which accepts teacher direction, the word "assignment" is used to include the process of considering all the variables in a learning experience and communicating the resulting plan for that experience to the children for their action upon it.

Three possible concerns confront the teacher who would administer an assignment properly: (1) Is the assignment properly planned? (2) Is the assignment understood? (3) Is the assignment motivated? The educational theory which centers on the assignment considers these questions.

There are, however, those who feel that the assignment is excessively teacher-directed and that teachers should be more permissive in interacting with pupils. These teachers employ a method in which the child has a strong voice in the determination and planning of his learning experience and in which the child and teacher co-operatively evaluate the success of that learning experience. This method is called "pupil-teacher planning." Pupil-teacher planning, thus, is the co-operative determination of curricular experiences by pupils and teachers alike. It is a permissive approach to teaching.

In the pupil-teacher planning method the teacher is primarily concerned with the group dynamics of a situation. Like the teacher who uses the assignment method, he is also concerned with planning the learning experience, but he need not attend to such things as communicating the assignment or motivating it. These are assumed to be innate to the planning experience itself.

There are some educational philosophers who would place the teacher in the non-participating role of a catalytic agent that facilitates the learning but does not enter too actively into the learning experience.

The teacher is considered nothing more than part of the environment to which the child must adjust, and learning emerges from the experience resulting from environmental adjustment. We call the method of these educators "child-centered," and we speak vaguely of it as being the technique which meets the needs of the children.

"Meet the needs of the children," as a matter of fact, has become one of the many clichés that provide shelter for the professor in the school of education who must hide behind something when he cannot provide teachers with a more realistic answer. For the child-centered teacher, "meeting the needs of the children" means meeting those needs which emerge as the child is confronted with a challenging environment to which he must respond. The child-centered teacher is concerned neither with planning the learning experience nor with motivating it. These take care of themselves as the child strives to meet his needs. The teacher's worry is with the environment which he recognizes must stimulate needs.

Within my lifetime I have been bombarded by the propaganda of proponents for the assignment, pupil-teacher planning, and felt-needs methods, and I have fallen victim to all three. If I had it to live over again, when I was faced by a change in educational approach, I would lie down and wait for the pendulum to return to its original position. As it was, I was always a victim of methodological change and a "sucker" for a new method.

As a very young principal, I learned that the proper administration of the assignment was the goal of all educational method. Hence I strove for competency in this area. I arranged with the teachers with whom I worked to take over their rooms every day for a few hours of practice teaching to learn my business. I was too naïve to recognize that it would take the poor teacher a week to undo the damage I could cause in an hour.

My first attempt at learning how to administer the assignment was undertaken, innocently enough, in a first grade. The children informed me that they were all birds. "A" class were "bluebirds"; "B" class, "robins"; and I renamed "C" class "crows" because it never ceased to cackle. It took me until almost 9:30 A.M. to get the aviary on its roosts. (Whatever one may think of workbooks, without them I would still be trying to calm down "A" class.) To "B" class I gave clay, upon which some of the members dined. Then I was ready to have the crows come to the reading circle. Not knowing that there is a trick to communicating an assignment, I merely said, "O.K., crows, come up to the little chairs."

This was the cue for a violent game of musical chairs. Three children sat down on the same chair. Two children fought over one chair until they pulled the back off. My assignment degenerated into chaos and violence, which I could not control. I sent for the teacher. She gave me the magic formula. It seemed that you proceed as follows. You say: "Children, we are going to see how orderly and quietly the crows can pass up to the reading circle. When I say 'Move,' each one of us will go on tiptoes to his chair. I don't want to hear a single loud step. Do you all know which chair is yours? Very well, on tiptoe. Let me hear a pin drop. Move."

I never did manage satisfactorily the technique of administering the assignment. So when pupil-teacher planning came into vogue, I grasped at it because it promised that communication of the assignment no longer would be a problem for me. Also, the proponents for pupil-teacher planning waxed so romantic about their method that I could not resist. Here is a typical propaganda account of pupil-teacher planning.

Mrs. Brown's fourth-grade class came to her full of enthusiasm. "Mrs. Brown," said the children, "we have decided to have a picnic. Will you join us in our planning?" Ever alert to the opportunity for using children's emergent needs as a motivating force, and seeing that in the planning experience children would practice and learn real democracy, Mrs. Brown concurred. In her wonderfully permissive way she suggested that the children divide their work among committees. The children were delighted with the idea and created, first, a refreshment committee, then an entertainment committee, and finally a finance committee.

After considerable discussion the refreshment committee decided on having "cokes" and referred the question of cost to the finance committee, in true democratic fashion. The finance committee deliberated over the problem and concluded that the money could be obtained by collecting old newspapers and selling them to the junkman. This meant organizing a canvass of the neighborhood for old papers. The children drew a map of the school district. They divided the district into areas to be canvassed, and they assigned each child a district—a wonderful experience in local geography and map-making. The project netted ten dollars. The refreshment committee divided the ten dollars by the price of a "coke" and found this would provide each child with ten bottles. Even they recognized that this was a little beyond most children's capacity, so they considered the problem of how better to spend the money. This taught them arithmetic and even introduced the subject of health and nutrition. They had their picnic, and everyone (including Mrs. Brown?) had a wonderful time. This despite the fact that the children had learned geography, arithmetic, health, and democratic action in the process of pupil-teacher planning of the picnic.

When I was a teacher in a high school, I read many such intriguing accounts of this method and hoped that I, too, could introduce pupil-teacher planning. I was teaching civics at the time, and the newspapers were filled with accounts of gambling in Chicago. My students, impressed with these accounts, came to me and said, "Mr. Bartky, we would like to study gambling in the city. Will you join us in our investigation of bookmaking in the school area?"

What could I say? I had to be permissive and alert to emergent needs, so I reluctantly muttered, "O.K., but take it easy."

An investigating committee was formed, and its members went on a tour of the cigar stores in the neighborhood. This committee exhibited far more zeal than I had ever noticed in my class before. It made a map of the school district and upon it located every "bookie joint." This map was mimeographed and distributed. Copies were sent to the mayor and the local police captain.

Unfortunately, in labeling a tobacco store a "bookie joint," the only criterion used was whether that store contained a backroom that was not open for student inspection. Consequently many perfectly honest storekeepers who lived in quarters behind their stores were identified as "bookies." They were by no means only moderately indignant at our map. They violently protested to principal, superintendent, and mayor and said many unkind things about my pupil-teacher planning enterprise. To climax the situation, the police raided one joint that really made book and picked up two boys from my class. When these boys were asked how they had found out about the place, they generously pointed out that they had learned about it in my class. The project, however, must be considered a great success. The children learned how to make maps, how to get along together, and how to tell a "bookie joint" from an innocent cigar store, I, too, benefited. I was fired and became an administrator.

As an elementary-school principal, I saw the advertising possibilities in the child-centered school. The propaganda for that school just oozed with the sentimentality, love, and respect for the child that makes good copy. All teachers except child-centered teachers were sadists, brutes, and perverts. Also, the neighboring university preached child-centered methods, and, needing a Doctor's degree, I ran with the mob.

I completely frustrated my teachers by prating about "felt needs," "whole child," "emergent experiences," and "learning environments" without interpreting these phrases into realities for them. I insisted that the child be allowed to grow. The combination of frustrated children, who "growed" like Topsy and who became uncontrollable "monsters," and frustrated teachers caused my eventual demise as a school administrator but qualified me for the role of college professor.

I would hate to admit that all of my thirty years of experience with method have been unproductive. Therefore I have striven for some functional conclusion about method. Are all methods bad? Is there one best method? Are all methods good?

The administration of the assignment, pupil-teacher planning, and the child-centered school are each an *aspect* of method. (You note I insist that they are *aspects* of method and not methods in themselves!)

If it is essential that a child experience an activity to meet a need which he himself does not feel immediately, the assignment is the course of action for a teacher to follow. The administration of the assignment, however, is an aspect of method that is too remote from a child's emergent and felt needs to be functional. These needs can better be satisfied by a more permissive attack.

Pupil-teacher planning, on the other hand, only partially does what it pretends to do. For example, pupil-teacher planning says (1) that, having been invited to choose and plan an educational activity, the pupil will be better motivated to indulge in it and (2) that pupil-teacher planning is typical of all democratic action and hence that the method teaches the democratic process.

I both agree and disagree with these assumptions. Pupil-teacher planning when a child's educational need is intense and emergent is a very effective motivating force for an educational experience. But, when a need is not apparent and it is necessary to create one, the assignment is more functional. For example, I have tried for years to get my own children involved in the consideration of the problem of cutting the grass at home. Not only have I failed to encourage them to participate with a lawn mower, I have even failed to get them to enjoy the joint planning necessary to determine who shall do the job.

With respect to the contention that pupil-teacher planning teaches the democratic process, I am amazed that its proponents have such a naïve and limited concept of democracy. Democracy is not solely a matter of participation; the democratic process calls for a nice balance between participation and forbearance on the part of each individual. Functional instruction in democracy will teach the child both when he should participate and when he should refrain from participation and permit the expert to take over. America became great because of its judicious use of expertness and specialization. The person who insists on the right to participate when he cannot contribute is a meddler, and we have far too many of these without encouraging more. The democratic process involves a paired right and obligation—the right to participate and the obligation to refrain from participation when one is not qualified to make a contribution. Teacher-pupil planning can overemphasize the right while it ignores the obligation.

The child-centered school assumes that the school is a place for child living. It is the situs where the challenge to meet the environment initiates learning experiences. But the school has more responsibility than that of just providing a place for living, where the child eventually learns all he needs to know about life through random experience. The job of the school is to hurry the learning process. I will admit that eventually, through living experiences, the child might accidentally meet all those necessary to make him a well-rounded person. But what assurance have we that this condition will not take longer than a generation to accomplish? The success of the child-centered school seems to be a function of the child's longevity.

The assignment, pupil-teacher planning, and the child-centered school came into being as fashions in education. At one time it was chic to use the assignment; at other times, la mode called for pupil-teacher planning; and at still another time, a teacher could not be seen in the classroom except in child-centered garb. But these fashions are like the fashions in ladies' dresses. They do not alter the basic garment; they are merely the new neckline, the new sleeves, and the new hemline. Any teacher who takes the fashion so seriously that she wears only a neckline, a sleeve, or a hemline is pedagogically naked. The task of teaching calls for all natures of approach. As aspects of a complete method, the approaches described are parts of a whole, not separate wholes, as some educators would have them.

Direction, permissiveness, and laissez faire—all are portions of the same continuum. One helps to define the other, and hence one cannot stand alone and have meaning. The degree of direction is measured in terms of permissiveness, and permissiveness is bounded on two sides by direction and laissez faire. There are as many possible educational approaches as there are points on the continuum between direction and laissez faire. Each of these has its own unique use. The adequate teacher employs all.

2. *Monitorial Teaching*

PHIL E. HAGER

In early nineteenth century England rudimentary school education for many children consisted of learning facts shared by monitors, youngsters of their own age who had but recently—often the same hour—acquired their information from adults. Today some school adminis-

From Phil E. Hager, "Nineteenth Century Experiments with Monitorial Teaching," *Phi Delta Kappan*, XXXX (January, 1959), 164–167. Phil E. Hager is Associate Professor of English at the University of Puget Sound, Tacoma, Washington. Reprinted by permission of the *Phi Delta Kappan*.

trators, contemplating the student flood that will presently be surging at our college doors, are reëxamining monitorial instruction potentialities. This article will describe briefly the monitorial system used in nineteenth-century England,[1] establish causes of its decline and abandonment there, and trace its spread to other parts of the world.

I

An account of monitorial instruction in the nineteenth century[2] can begin with an introduction to the work of Andrew Bell (1753–1832), a St. Andrew's University divinity school graduate. While superintending the Egmore Male Military Academy in Madras, India, Bell observed native children sand-writing with their fingers. Sensing teaching possibilities in the activity, he had sand brought into his classrooms and drilled the older boys to teach younger students the alphabet by tracing the figures on their individual sand "slates."

Andrew Bell's report (1796) to the Egmore Academy directors on his nine years' superintendency was called, elaborately: *An Experiment in Education, made at the Male Asylum of Madras. Suggesting a System by which a School or Family may teach itself under the Superintendance* [sic] *of the Master or Parent.*[3] Copies reached England and by 1798 the Bell system had been adopted by Saint Botolph's School (the oldest charity school and oldest Protestant parochial school in London), at the parochial schools of White Chapel and Lambeth, at the Royal Military Asylum in Chelsea, and at Kendal in Westmoreland.

In 1800 Bell's *Experiment* was examined by a Quaker schoolmaster, Joseph Lancaster (1778–1838), who since 1797 had been providing

[1] In England the monitorial system was often called "mutual instruction" or the "new system" of education. Some writers referred to it as the Lancaster-Bell system of monitorial education, in recognition of the work of its two most famous popularizers. Often, in deference to the educator Andrew Bell, it was termed the Bell system or the Madras system.

[2] The system had been used in England as early as the sixteenth century, by John Brinsley (*c.* 1570–*c.* 1630), and monitors had been prescribed in the statutes of several Elizabethan grammar schools. Abbé Gaultier, a French refugee of the 1770's, had established a successful school in London for children of other French refugees and used the monitorial scheme once to remedy a wholesale desertion by his school staff.

The French historian and educator Charles Rollin (1661–1741) was familiar with the technique, Herbault had employed it in the Paris Hospice de la Pitié in 1747, Madame de Maintenon used the system in her school for girls at Saint-Cyr, and it had been an integral part of school programs of the Jesuits. Comenius speaks of the plan in the *Great Didactic*.

[3] Between 1797 and 1814 this book reappeared under several titles, was expanded from 60 pages to over 900.

rudimentary schooling for hundreds of boys in his Southwark, London, school.[4] Bell's plan received Lancaster's immediate, warm support.

> . . . I lie under [obligation] to Dr. Bell of the Male Asylum at Madras. . . . From [Dr. Bell's] publication I have adopted several useful *hints;* I beg leave to recommend it to the attentive perusal of the friends of education and of youth. . . . I much regret that I was not acquainted with the beauty of his system till somewhat advanced in my plan; if I had known it, it would have saved me much trouble and some retrograde movements.[5]

Lancaster's plan, appearing in print in 1802, was more elaborate than Bell's.[6] Bell had considered twenty-four to thirty pupils or in large schools twenty-four to forty to be the ideal number; Lancaster thought ten to be an ideal "draft" (class) and urged in a favorite motto, "Let every child at every moment have something to do and a motive for doing it." He employed many monitors, for many duties.

> When a child was admitted, a monitor assigned him his class, . . . when he was absent one monitor ascertained the fact and another found out the reason; a monitor examined him periodically and when he made progress a monitor promoted him; a monitor ruled the writing paper; a monitor made or mended the pens; a monitor had charge of the slates and books; and a monitor-general looked after all the other monitors.[7]

Monitorial instruction required little more than a bare room, since for most lessons pupils stood, grouped about "stations" along the schoolroom walls where they learned by rote the information their monitors had earlier received. Administrators generally taught the monitors a lesson from a printed card. Lancastrian schools used dictation extensively, slates instead of paper, and wall sheets for reading rather than books. (A chapter of Lancaster's manual was headed, "A Method of teaching to spell and read, whereby one Book will serve instead of Six Hundred Books.") Pupils enrolled as early as age 7 and could remain until 13 or 14. At Lancaster's Borough Road School children were to have learned to read in twelve months, to write and learn simple arithmetic, geometry, and geography in three or four years; but the average attendance

---

[4] In June, 1801, Lancaster moved into new quarters for 350 boys in Belvedere Place, Borough Road, Southwark. This school was the one for which he became best known.

[5] David Salmon, editor, *The Practical Parts of Lancaster's "Improvements" and Bell's Experiment.* Cambridge, England: 1932, p. xxiii.

[6] Complete title: *Improvements in Education, as it respects the Industrious Classes of the Community: containing, a short account of its present state, hints towards its improvements, and a detail of some practical experiments conducive to that end.*

[7] David Salmon, "Monitorial System," *A Cyclopedia of Education,* edited by Paul Monroe (New York, 1913), IV, 296.

was about a year.[8] Promotion was possible in one subject a pupil was learning while not necessarily in any others. Rewards and punishments varied greatly in monitorial schools.

By 1805 Lancaster's plan had been carefully formulated,[9] and that year Lancaster increased his school accommodations to care for 700 boys and soon afterward for an additional 200 girls. The same year he was received by King George III, who visited the Borough Road School. Lancaster presented the monarch a copy of his *Improvements*, an account of his work, and a petition for support. The King was enthusiastic: "I highly approve of your system and it is my wish that every poor child in my dominions should be taught to read the Bible; I will do anything you wish to promote this object." Royal patronage was unusually personal. It is reported that George III declared, "Lancaster, I will subscribe £100 annually," and that, turning to the Queen, he added, "You will subscribe £50, Charlotte, and the Princesses £25 each."[10]

Lancaster had meanwhile (1804) visited Bell and the two had become fast friends. Gradually this friendship was undermined, however, by a Mrs. Sarah Trimmer, self-appointed spiritual watchdog of the Established Church, who managed to convince Bell that the Quaker Lancaster was appropriating his "invention." The formal break had significant repercussions. The Bellites formed the National Society for Promoting the Education of the Poor in the Principles of the Established Church in England and Wales (1811),[11] and the Lancastrians organized to become The British and Foreign School Society.[12] For many years religious and factional considerations would determine the direction of English school education.

[8] *S. C. in Education, Parliamentary Papers*, 1834, ix, 20, Q. 262–267; and Frederic Hill, *National Education* (London, 1836), i, 72, 90, as quoted in R. K. Webb, *The British Working Class Reader* (London, 1955), p. 17.

[9] In this year appeared the third edition, entitled *Improvements in Education, as it respects the industrious Classes of the Community, containing, among other important particulars, An Account of the Institution for the Education of One Thousand Poor Children, Borough Road, Southwark; and of the New System of Education on which it is conducted.*

[10] W. O. Lester Smith, *Education in Great Britain.* (London, 1949), p. 101.

[11] *National* was a term adopted against much protest. Since it was of French origin, it had a Jacobin taint.

Bell was appointed superintendent of the Society's schools and soon after was made an honorary member of the General Committee.

[12] Founded in 1814, the Society was the successor of "The British System," in turn the successor of the "Royal British (or Lancasterian) System" (1810), in turn the successor of the Royal Lancasterian Institution (1808), which grew out of a committee of three (formed in 1808 by Joseph Lancaster, William Corston, and Joseph Fox). The Committee was elaborately called "Society for the purpose of affording education, procuring employment, and as far as possible to furnish clothing to the children of the poorer subjects of King George III."

Thereafter monitorial instruction spread quickly in England. It was incorporated into grammar schools, private boarding schools, the public schools of Charterhouse and Christ's Hospital, and wealthy London families cooperatively formed their own small monitorial schools.[13] National Society figures reflect the popularity of the system:

	Number of Schools	*Number of Pupils*
1812	52	8,620
1813	230	40,484
1820	1,614	c. 200,000
1830	3,670	c. 346,000[14]

Similarity between the repetitive pattern of the new teaching scheme and the mechanical operation of efficient machinery in English factories recommended monitorial instruction to nineteenth-century, industry-conscious England. "The principle in schools and manufactories is the same," declared Sir Thomas Bernard, a founder of the Society for Bettering the Condition and Increasing the Comforts of the Poor. "The grand principle of Dr. Bell's system is the division of labour applied to intellectual purposes."[15]

The overlooking teacher, the minding monitors, and the repetitive processes of learning the Catechism and the rules of arithmetic had their parallels within the factories throbbing with the new machinery; and too often the school buildings erected with such pride bore a family resemblance, both externally and internally, to "the dark satanic mills" of the period.[16]

II

The decline and abandonment of the monitorial system were developments of an increased interest in education. One development was that instructors needed by sponsors establishing additional monitorial schools came increasingly from teacher-training schools and steadily replaced monitors. The National Society and The British and Foreign School Society trained *teachers* and assistants to meet the demand for instructors,[17] and when the government became interested in education,

[13] Jeremy Bentham backed a scheme for founding the Chrestomathic (useful knowledge) Day School to teach a thousand boys and girls the sciences by "the New Instruction System." His prospectus was entitled *Chrestomathic Day School, or Chrestomathic School, for the extension of the new system of instruction to the higher branches of learning for the use of the middling and higher ranks in life.*

[14] David Salmon, "National Society, England," *A Cyclopedia of Education*, edited by Paul Monroe (New York, 1913), IV, 384, and M. E. Sadler and J. W. Edwards, *Special Reports on Educational Subjects* (London, 1898), II, 446.

[15] Sir Thomas Bernard, *Of the Education of the Poor* (London [?], 1809), pp. 35–36, as quoted in M. G. Jones, *The Charity School Movement* (Cambridge, England, 1938), p. 337.

[16] Smith, *op. cit.*, p. 102.

[17] Monitorial schools' most intelligent graduates could seldom be induced to remain as monitors for the pittance they received.

grants were made to train teachers, not monitors.[18] The other development was that the government's report (*circa* 1842)[19] that British elementary education was shockingly bad awakened school administrators to the deficient quality of the basically unimaginative and inelastic monitorial instruction and provoked improvement. The British and Foreign School Society, through a report of one of its committees, had earlier recognized the disadvantages of the mechanical instruction by monitors and in 1839 reported that they were "by no means disposed to bind themselves exclusively" to the monitorial system of instruction. Two years later the Society reported that "the British System as now practiced in the Central School may properly be denominated mixed, simultaneous teaching being satisfactorily united with that which is monitorial."[20] By 1847 The British and Foreign School Society replaced its monitors entirely with teachers and established, between 1855 and 1880, five schools to provide professional instructors.[21]

III

The monitorial system also became quickly and firmly established in Europe.

France adopted the technique eagerly. In 1814 the French Society for the Encouragement of National Industry sent four of its members to England to learn about the system. They visited Lancaster's Borough Road School, the National Society's Central School, and others. Within months after the deputation's report, the Society for the Encouragement of National Industry formed the Society for Elementary Instruc-

---

To provide its necessary teachers, the National Society established a model school at Holborn Hill, soon supplanting it with a much larger one in Baldwin's Gardens, Gray's Inn Lane. Prospective teachers in these schools did little more than master the mechanics of the monitorial system, however, and the Society, acutely aware of the need for more thorough training, soon opened five other colleges—of which three were still in existence in this century.

At Lancaster's Borough Road School a normal school was established which trained teachers from all over the world. (About 1814 it became the property of The British and Foreign School Society.)

[18] In 1833 Parliament voted £10,000 for the erection of model schools and, though the money was not forthcoming until 1839, it was used by The British and Foreign School Society and the National Society equally to erect teacher-training colleges. In 1842 the government granted money to rebuild the Borough Road teacher-training school and in 1846 (and 1853) gave grants for the maintenance of other teacher-training colleges. In 1846 Parliament also provided competent monitors with fair wages from the government and promised them teaching apprenticeships for five years and two- and three-year scholarships in a teacher-training college.

[19] Lord Brougham's Charity Commission published (1819–1840) thirty-seven folio volumes of reports on British schools.

[20] David Salmon, "Monitorial System," *A Cyclopedia of Education*, edited by Paul Monroe (New York, 1913), IV, 297.

[21] At Bangor, Stockwell, Darlington, Saffron Walden, and Swansea.

tion[22] and established an experimental monitorial school in Paris.[23] The French government appointed a primary education committee for every canton and granted 50,000 francs annually to aid primary instruction. Within five years 1,500 monitorial schools were opened![24]

Sweden, following the report of observers sent to England by the king, established a society in 1822 to promote monitorial instruction, and by 1841 had founded nearly 500 schools. In Denmark the system was being used in nearly 3,000 schools by 1831, and a knowledge of the system was made a teaching diploma requisite.

In Russia Alexander I commissioned (1813) an observer to report on the English monitorial schools, four students were sent to Lancaster's Borough Road School to study the system, and the czar himself went to England (1814) and observed monitorial schools in action. The monitorial plan was soon introduced into Russian military schools, and many nobles established monitorial schools on their estates. Some of these schools survived long after Russia's principal supporter, the czar, died.

Monitorial instruction was incorporated in elementary schools in Switzerland,[25] Italy, Spain, even in the West Indies and South America.[26]

In the United States the first monitorial (Lancastrian) school was opened in 1806 in New York City. The system spread rapidly over much of the eastern part of the U.S., especially in the cities, and particularly in New York State. In many cities the first free schools established were monitorial. The academy systems of the states of New York, Indiana, and Maryland (1826) adopted monitorial instruction. Mexico instituted higher Lancastrian schools for the Mexican State of Texas (1829), and North Carolina in 1832 proposed a state system of Lancastrian schools.

In 1818 New York City's Public School Society, which published *A Manual of the Lancasterian System* and greatly helped to popularize the monitorial system in the United States, invited Joseph Lancaster to lecture in America. Lancaster's welcome was enthusiastic and he assisted New York City, Brooklyn, and Philadelphia schools. In Baltimore he established a monitorial institute.[27]

[22] The Society still exists in France.

[23] The master was the Rev. Francis Martin, trained in Lancaster's Borough Road School.

[24] The best known was probably the Duchesse de Duras' school in Paris.

[25] The most famous schools to employ the method in Switzerland were Froissard's school at Lausanne and Père Girard's school at Fribourg.

[26] In South America monitorial instruction was unusually successful under the direction of James Thomson, a British and Foreign Bible Society agent.

[27] In 1825, while in the United States, Lancaster accepted an invitation from

Monitorial instruction began to decline in the United States in the 1820's and by 1830 few monitorial schools remained, although at least one school existed (in St. Louis) as late as 1850.

The far-reaching influence of American Lancastrian schools is glowingly summarized by Ellwood Cubberley in his *History of Education:*

> The Lancasterian schools naturally hastened the adoption of the free school system in all the Northern States by gradually accustoming people to bearing the necessary taxation which free schools entail. They also made the common school common and much talked of, and awakened thought and provoked discussion on the question of public education. They likewise dignified the work of the teacher by showing the necessity for teacher-training. The Lancasterian Model Schools, first established in the United States in 1818, were the precursors of the American normal schools.[28]

3. *A Commentary on* Leonard and Gertrude

G. STANLEY HALL

This homely tale was not written for the modern novel-reader. It is a story of deep and ardent love, not for an individual, but for the wretched, the weak, and for children. Though he wrote much, the author could tell no tale but this. Its purpose was his earnest inner life, and its details a picture of his own surroundings, as humble and as realistically depicted as anything in Heyse or Auerbach. It is of peasants who kick their wives, of hungry children who steal a handful of raw potatoes, and who only on gala-days have the cream left on their milk; of literal dunghills and stable-drains. It is, moreover, fairly packed with

---

Simon Bolivar to organize schools in Bolivia. In 1829 he went to Canada where the Canadian Parliament made several grants to further Lancasterian school experimentation.

Lancaster settled in Philadelphia. He died in New York City in 1838.

[28] Ellwood P. Cubberley, *The History of Education* (Boston, 1920), p. 664.

From G. Stanley Hall, the Introduction to Pestalozzi's *Leonard and Gertrude,* translated and abridged by Eva Channing (Boston: D. C. Heath and Company, 1885, 1906). G. Stanley Hall was an eminent American psychologist, philosopher, and educator during the three decades including roughly the years 1890 to 1920. This was one of his earliest writings, having been prepared in 1885 for the original edition of Channing's translation. Yet by 1888 Hall was recognized as one of the foremost critics of American education. At the time of writing this essay he was Professor of Psychology and Pedagogics at Johns Hopkins University.

incident and character. The hypocrite, the fool, the gossip, the miser, the sot, the sycophant, the schemer, the just judge, the good parson, the intriguing woman from the court, the old schoolmaster enraged at a new departure in education, the quack doctor sentenced to dig the graves of those he kills, and many more, stand out from these pages in as sharp relief as words can well paint them. The action is all intense. The bailiff's wife runs home from church as fast as her legs can carry her; her husband is repeatedly so terrified he cannot speak; and his accomplice rolls on the floor in his remorse, and beats himself with his fists. The death of Rudy's mother is full of pathos. The pursuit of Hummel by the devil is extremely humorous; the scene under the gallows, where he confesses himself willing to die, and where his fingers are indelibly stained, is very impressive.

Moreover, as a picture of a somewhat primitive village community, the story is replete with interest and instruction. The large public square where the people assemble; the extensive common, the division of which among individual proprietors is one thread of interest throughout the book; the public hangman's tree; the bailiff beer-house keeper, with everybody in his debt, listening at the windows, extracting the domestic secrets of all his customers; the petty thieveries and deceits and superstitions; the intrigues, scandals, lies, amidst which nothing thrived but the beer-house; and lastly the great, beneficent magistrate in the old manor-house in the distant background, watching like a good Providence over all the affairs of the hamlet, and meting out justice in the market, and whom no one could deceive or thwart,— these scenes are all as strange to us as they were real to Pestalozzi. The art, in a word, reminds one of that of the large, colored charts, for combined language and object teaching, on the walls of so many German schoolrooms,—masses of strong colors, a crowd of things and persons, without attempted art or unity, but far truer to and richer in life, for a child's eye, than anything in the art galleries. Unlike these charts, however, it has a purpose which lifts it far above these details to a moral plain, the highest to which literary art can attain.

There was one good woman in this dismal hamlet,—Gertrude, the mason's wife, who trudged many miles one day to see the county magistrate, and beg work for her husband, and to complain of the bad arts of the wicked bailiff, whose beer made her husband drunk. Her faltering story was heard, and her husband obtained the job of building a new church; and at length, after a long struggle, the bailiff was exposed and fell. Gertrude had taught her own children home industries and maxims, hymns, prayers, and cleanliness and courtesy, and finally allowed the children of a neighbor to come in. An idle man of a noble but decayed family witnessed her home-school, and at length resolved to be a schoolmaster himself. Gertrude could not tell him much of her secret, though occasionally she let fall a "key-word." She felt that the school should stand in the closest relation with home life, and not in opposition to it; that it should be a larger circle drawn about the fireside hearth; that verbal instruction should vanish in the spirit of real activity. The schoolmaster's establishment flourished. The preacher was interested, and realized that his sermons were too refined and doctrinal, and not practical, and changed his style. The whole spirit of home life and of industry gradually revived. A few of the best citizens met weekly to discuss the larger educational question of commercial prosperity. The royal cabinet became interested, studied Bonnal,—which had become the thriftiest hamlet in Switzerland,—and at length concluded, that, if the ministry of a realm should seriously and deeply desire reform, they could set about it in no better or more radical way than by imitating Bonnal. Here was, in fact, the principle of universal government.

Thus Bonnal is the world; the bailiff is intemperance, intrigue, and all influences which degrade society; and Gertrude is the Good Teacher by whom alone the world is to be saved, if it is to be saved at all. We shall not read this story as we ought if we forget that there are hundreds of communities in our land to-day in the same need as was Bonnal of a regeneration so radical that only these same slow methods of practical, ethical education can ever accomplish it. Such a regeneration is not to be effected by endowments, legislation, or by new methods, important as these are, but, as Pestalozzi thought, by the love and devotion of noble women overflowing from the domestic circle into the community, by the good Gertrudes of all stations in life, the born educators of the race, whose work and whose "key-words" we men-pedagogues must ponder well if our teaching is to be ethically inspired.

This book represents the culmination of Pestalozzi's influence. Royal personages came to see him, and gave him presents. Herbart, Fichte, and many others, lit their torches at the fire he kindled here. This is a book which all good teachers should read with care, and, having read it, will thank the translator for the great and discriminating labor she has spent upon the very voluminous and intractable original in converting it into the present pleasing form.

4. Gertrude's Method of Instruction

JOHANN HEINRICH PESTALOZZI

It was quite early in the morning when Arner, Glülphi and the pastor went to the mason's cottage. The room was not in order when they entered, for the family had just finished breakfast, and the dirty plates and spoons still lay upon the table. Gertrude was at first somewhat disconcerted, but the visitors reässured her, saying kindly: "This is as it should be; it is impossible to clear the table before breakfast is eaten!"

The children all helped wash the dishes, and then seated themselves in their customary places before their work. The gentlemen begged Gertrude to let everything go on as usual, and after the first half hour, during which she was a little embarrassed, all proceeded as if no stranger were present. First the children sang their morning hymns, and then Gertrude read a chapter of the Bible aloud, which they repeated after her while they were spinning, rehearsing the most instructive passages until they knew them by heart. In the mean time, the oldest girl had been making the children's beds in the adjoining room, and the visitors noticed through the open door that she silently repeated what the others were reciting. When this task was completed, she went into the garden and returned with vegetables for dinner, which she cleaned while repeating Bible-verses with the rest.

It was something new for the children to see three gentlemen in the room, and they often looked up from their spinning toward the corner where the strangers sat. Gertrude noticed this, and said to them: "Seems

From Eva Channing (Translator), chap. XXV, "Gertrude's Method of Instruction," Pestalozzi's *Leonard and Gertrude* (Boston: D. C. Heath and Company, 1885, 1906). Pestalozzi's *Leonard and Gertrude* was first published in a series of four volumes during the years 1781–1787. Pestalozzi is generally credited as the first educator to base his teaching method upon the nature of learners rather than upon subject matter. Because of this he placed great emphasis on plans for teaching which appealed to all of the senses of the learner and which utilized models and real objects to a maximum degree. His school at Yverdun, Switzerland, became a focal point for students from throughout the world and his teachings continue to influence school organization and practice, especially in elementary education.

to me you look more at these gentlemen than at your yarn." But Harry answered: "No, indeed! We are working hard, and you'll have finer yarn to-day than usual."

Whenever Gertrude saw that anything was amiss with the wheels or cotton, she rose from her work, and put it in order. The smallest children, who were not old enough to spin, picked over the cotton for carding, with a skill which excited the admiration of the visitors.

Although Gertrude thus exerted herself to develop very early the manual dexterity of her children, she was in no haste for them to learn to read and write. But she took pains to teach them early how to speak; for, as she said, "of what use is it for a person to be able to read and write, if he cannot speak?—since reading and writing are only an artificial sort of speech." To this end she used to make the children pronounce syllables after her in regular succession, taking them from an old A-B-C book she had. This exercise in correct and distinct articulation was, however, only a subordinate object in her whole scheme of education, which embraced a true comprehension of life itself. Yet she never adopted the tone of instructor toward her children; she did not say to them: "Child, this is your head, your nose, your hand, your finger;" or: "Where is your eye, your ear?"—but instead, she would say: "Come here, child, I will wash your little hands," "I will comb your hair," or: "I will cut your finger-nails." Her verbal instruction seemed to vanish in the spirit of her real activity, in which it always had its source. The result of her system was that each child was skilful, intelligent and active to the full extent that its age and development allowed.

The instruction she gave them in the rudiments of arithmetic was intimately connected with the realities of life. She taught them to count the number of steps from one end of the room to the other, and two of the rows of five panes each, in one of the windows, gave her an opportunity to unfold the decimal relations of numbers. She also made them count their threads while spinning, and the number of turns on the reel, when they wound the yarn into skeins. Above all, in every occupation of life she taught them an accurate and intelligent observation of common objects and the forces of nature.

All that Gertrude's children knew, they knew so thoroughly that they were able to teach it to the younger ones; and this they often begged permission to do. On this day, while the visitors were present, Jonas sat with each arm around the neck of a smaller child, and made the little ones pronounce the syllables of the A-B-C book after him; while Lizzie placed herself with her wheel between two of the others, and while all three spun, taught them the words of a hymn with the utmost patience.

When the guests took their departure, they told Gertrude they would come again on the morrow. "Why?" she returned; "You will only see the same thing over again." But Glülphi said: "That is the best praise you could possibly give yourself." Gertrude blushed at this compliment, and stood confused when the gentlemen kindly pressed her hand in taking leave.

The three could not sufficiently admire what they had seen at the mason's house, and Glülphi was so overcome by the powerful impression made upon him, that he longed to be alone and seek counsel of his own thoughts. He hastened to his room, and as he crossed the threshold, the words broke from his lips: "*I* must be schoolmaster in Bonnal!" All night visions of Gertrude's schoolroom floated through his mind, and he only fell asleep toward morning. Before his eyes were fairly open, he murmured: "I will be schoolmaster!"—and hastened to Arner to acquaint him with his resolution.

5. *Observations on Teachers and Teaching from Hard Times*

CHARLES DICKENS

CHAPTER I   THE ONE THING NEEDFUL

'Now, what I want is, Facts. Teach these boys and girls nothing but Facts. Facts alone are wanted in life. Plant nothing else, and root out everything else. You can only form the minds of reasoning animals upon Facts: nothing else will ever be of any service to them. This is the principle on which I bring up my own children, and this is the principle on which I bring up these children. Stick to Facts, Sir!'

The scene was a plain, bare, monotonous vault of a schoolroom, and the speaker's square forefinger emphasized his observations by underscoring every sentence with a line on the schoolmaster's sleeve. The emphasis was helped by the speaker's square wall of a forehead, which had his eyebrows for its base, while his eyes found commodious cellarage in two dark caves, overshadowed by the wall. The emphasis was helped

---

Hard Times was originally printed as a serial in *Household Words* from April to August, 1854, Nos. 210–229. It was first published in a single volume in 1854. These passages constitute the first two chapters of the novel.

by the speaker's mouth, which was wide, thin, and hard set. The emphasis was helped by the speaker's voice, which was inflexible, dry, and dictatorial. The emphasis was helped by the speaker's hair, which bristled on the skirts of his bald head, a plantation of firs to keep the wind from its shining surface, all covered with knobs, like the crust of a plum pie as if the head had scarcely warehouse-room for the hard facts stored inside. The speaker's obstinate carriage, square coat, square legs, square shoulders,—nay, his very neckcloth, trained to take him by the throat with an unaccommodating grasp, like a stubborn fact, as it was,—all helped the emphasis.

'In this life, we want nothing but Facts, Sir; nothing but Facts!'

The speaker, and the school master, and the third grown person present, all backed a little, and swept with their eyes the inclined plane of little vessels then and there arranged in order, ready to have imperial gallons of facts poured into them until they were full to the brim.

CHAPTER II   MURDERING THE INNOCENTS

Thomas Gradgrind, Sir. A man of realities. A man of facts and calculations. A man who proceeds upon the principle that two and two are four, and nothing over, and who is not to be talked into allowing for anything over. Thomas Gradgrind, Sir—peremptorily Thomas—Thomas Gradgrind. With a rule and a pair of scales, and the multiplication table always in his pocket, Sir, ready to weigh and measure any parcel of human nature, and tell you exactly what it comes to. It is a mere question of figures, a case of simple arithmetic. You might hope to get some other nonsensical belief into the head of George Gradgrind, or Augustus Gradgrind, or John Gradgrind, or Joseph Gradgrind (all supposititious, non-existent persons), but into the head of Thomas Gradgrind—no, Sir!

In such terms Mr. Gradgrind always mentally introduced himself, whether to his private circle of acquaintance, or to the public in general. In such terms, no doubt, substituting the words 'boys and girls,' for 'Sir,' Thomas Gradgrind now presented Thomas Gradgrind to the little pitchers before him, who were to be filled so full of facts.

Indeed, as he eagerly sparkled at them from the cellarage before mentioned, he seemed a kind of cannon loaded to the muzzle with facts, and prepared to blow them clean out of the regions of childhood at one discharge. He seemed a galvanizing apparatus, too, charged with a grim mechanical substitute for the tender young imaginations that were to be stormed away.

'Girl number twenty,' said Mr. Gradgrind, squarely pointing with his square forefinger, 'I don't know that girl. Who is that girl?'

'Sissy Jupe, Sir,' explained number twenty, blushing, standing up, and curtseying.

'Sissy is not a name,' said Mr. Gradgrind. 'Don't call yourself Sissy. Call yourself Cecilia.'

'It's father as calls me Sissy, Sir,' returned the young girl in a trembling voice, and with another curtsey.

'Then he has no business to do it,' said Mr. Gradgrind. 'Tell him he mustn't. Cecilia Jupe. Let me see. What is your father?'

'He belongs to the horse-riding, if you please, Sir.'

Mr. Gradgrind frowned, and waved off the objectionable calling with his hand.

'We don't want to know anything about that, here. You mustn't tell us about that, here. Your father breaks horses, don't he?'

'If you please, Sir, when they can get any to break, they do break horses in the ring, Sir.'

'You mustn't tell us about the ring, here. Very well, then. Describe your father as a horsebreaker. He doctors sick horses, I dare say?'

'Oh yes, Sir.'

'Very well, then. He is a veterinary surgeon, a farrier, and horsebreaker. Give me your definition of a horse.'

(Sissy Jupe thrown into the greatest alarm by this demand.)

'Girl number twenty unable to define a horse!' said Mr. Gradgrind, for the general behoof of all the little pitchers. 'Girl number twenty possessed of no facts, in reference to one of the commonest of animals! Some boy's definition of a horse. Bitzer, yours.'

The square finger, moving here and there, lighted suddenly on Bitzer, perhaps because he chanced to sit in the same ray of sunlight which, darting in at one of the bare windows of the intensely whitewashed room, irradiated Sissy. For, the boys and girls sat on the face of the inclined plane in two compact bodies, divided up the centre by a narrow interval; and Sissy, being at the corner of a row on the sunny side, came in for the beginning of a sunbeam, of which Bitzer, being at the corner of a row on the other side, a few rows in advance, caught the end. But, whereas the girl was so dark-eyed and dark-haired, that she seemed to receive a deeper and more lustrous colour from the sun, when it shone upon her, the boy was so light-eyed and light-haired that the self-same rays appeared to draw out of him what little colour he ever possessed. His cold eyes would hardly have been eyes, but for the short ends of lashes which, by bringing them into immediate contrast with something paler than themselves, expressed their form. His short-cropped hair might have been a mere continuation of the sandy freckles on his forehead and face. His skin was so unwholesomely deficient in the natural tinge, that he looked as though, if he were cut, he would bleed white.

'Bitzer,' said Thomas Gradgrind. 'Your definition of a horse.'

'Quadruped. Graminivorous. Forty teeth, namely twenty-four grinders, four eye-teeth, and twelve incisive. Sheds coat in the spring; in marshy countries, sheds hoofs, too. Hoofs hard, but requiring to be shod with iron. Age known by marks in mouth.' Thus (and much more) Bitzer.

'Now girl number twenty,' said Mr. Gradgrind. 'You know what a horse is.'

She curtseyed again, and would have blushed deeper, if she could have blushed deeper than she had blushed all this time. Bitzer, after rapidly blinking at Thomas Gradgrind with both eyes at once, and so catching the light upon his quivering ends of lashes that they looked like the antennæ of busy insects, put his knuckles to his freckled forehead, and sat down again.

The third gentleman now stepped forth. A mighty man at cutting and drying, he was; a government officer; in his way (and in most other people's too), a professed pugilist; always in training, always with a system to force down the general throat like a bolus, always to be heard of at the bar of his little Public-office, ready to fight all England. To continue in fistic phraseology, he had a genius for coming up to the scratch, wherever and whatever it was, and proving himself an ugly customer. He would go in and damage any subject whatever with his right, follow up with his left, stop, exchange, counter, bore his opponent (he always fought All England) to the ropes, and fall upon him neatly. He was certain to knock the wind out of common sense, and render that unlucky adversary deaf to the call of time. And he had it in charge from high authority to bring about the great public-office Millennium, when Commissioners should reign upon earth.

'Very well,' said this gentleman, briskly smiling, and folding his arms. 'That's a horse. Now, let me ask you girls and boys, Would you paper a room with representations of horses?'

After a pause, one half of the children cried in chorus, 'Yes, Sir!' Upon which the other half, seeing in the gentleman's face that Yes was wrong, cried out in chorus, 'No, Sir!'—as the custom is, in these examinations.

'Of course, No. Why wouldn't you?'

A pause. One corpulent slow boy, with a wheezy manner of breathing, ventured the answer, Because he wouldn't paper a room at all, but would paint it.

'You *must* paper it,' said the gentleman, rather warmly.

'You must paper it,' said Thomas Gradgrind, 'whether you like it or not. Don't tell *us* you wouldn't paper it. What do you mean, boy?'

'I'll explain to you, then,' said the gentleman, after another and a dismal pause, 'why you wouldn't paper a room with representations of horses. Do you ever see horses walking up and down the sides of rooms in reality—in fact? Do you?'

'Yes, Sir!' from one half. 'No, Sir!' from the other.

'Of course, No,' said the gentleman, with an indignant look at the wrong half. 'Why, then, you are not to see anywhere, what you don't see in fact; you are not to have anywhere, what you don't have in fact. What is called Taste, is only another name for Fact.'

Thomas Gradgrind nodded his approbation.

'This is a new principle, a discovery, a great discovery,' said the gentleman. 'Now, I'll try you again. Suppose you were going to carpet a room. Would you use a carpet having a representation of flowers upon it?'

There being a general conviction by this time that 'No, Sir!' was always the right answer to this gentleman, the chorus of No was very strong. Only a few feeble stragglers said Yes: among them Sissy Jupe.

'Girl number twenty,' said the gentleman, smiling in the calm strength of knowledge.

Sissy blushed, and stood up.

'So you would carpet your room—or your husband's room, if you were a grown woman, and had a husband—with representations of flowers, would you?' said the gentleman. 'Why would you?'

'If you please, Sir, I am very fond of flowers,' returned the girl.

'And is that why you would put tables and chairs upon them, and have people walking over them with heavy boots?'

'It wouldn't hurt them, Sir. They wouldn't crush and wither, if you please, Sir. They would be the pictures of what was very pretty and pleasant, and I would fancy——'

'Ay, ay, ay! But you mustn't fancy,' cried the gentleman, quite elated by coming so happily to his point. 'That's it! You are never to fancy.'

'You are not, Cecilia Jupe,' Thomas Gradgrind solemnly repeated, 'to do anything of that kind.'

'Fact, fact, fact!' said the gentleman. And 'Fact, fact, fact!' repeated Thomas Gradgrind.

'You are to be in all things regulated and governed,' said the gentleman, 'by fact. We hope to have, before long, a board of fact, composed of commissioners of fact, who will force the people to be a people of fact, and of nothing but fact. You must discard the word Fancy altogether. You have nothing to do with it. You are not to have, in any object of use or ornament, what would be a contradiction in fact. You don't walk upon flowers in fact; you cannot be allowed to walk upon flowers in carpets. You don't find that foreign birds and butterflies come and perch upon your crockery; you cannot be permitted to paint foreign birds and butterflies upon your crockery. You never meet with quadrupeds going up and down walls; you must not have quadrupeds represented upon walls. You must see,' said the gentleman, 'for all these purposes, combinations and modifications (in primary colours) of mathematical figures which are susceptible of proof and demonstration. This is the new discovery. This is fact. This is taste.'

The girl curtseyed, and sat down. She was very young, and she looked as if she were frightened by the matter-of-fact prospect the world afforded.

'Now, if Mr. M'Choakumchild,' said the gentleman, 'will proceed to give his first lesson here, Mr. Gradgrind, I shall be happy, at your request, to observe his mode of procedure.'

Mr. Gradgrind was much obliged. 'Mr. M'Choakumchild, we only wait for you.'

So, Mr. M'Choakumchild began in his best manner. He and some one hundred and forty other schoolmasters, had been lately turned at the same time, in the same factory, on the same principles, like so many pianoforte legs. He had been put through an immense variety of paces, and had answered volumes of head-breaking questions. Orthography, etymology, syntax, and prosody, biography, astronomy, geography, and general cosmography, the sciences of compound proportion, algebra, land-surveying and levelling, vocal music, and drawing from models, were all at the ends of his ten chilled fingers. He had worked his stony way into Her Majesty's most Honourable Privy Council's Schedule B, and had taken the bloom off the higher branches of mathematics and physical science, French, German, Latin and Greek. He knew all about all the Water Sheds of all the world (whatever they are), and all the histories of all the peoples, and all the names of all the rivers and mountains, and all the productions, manners, and customs of all the countries, and all their boundaries and bearings on the two-and-thirty points of the compass. Ah, rather overdone, M'Choakumchild. If he had only learnt a little less, how infinitely better he might have taught much more!

He went to work in this preparatory lesson, not unlike Morgiana in the Forty Thieves: looking into all the vessels ranged before him, one after another, to see what they contained. Say, good M'Choakumchild. When from thy boiling store, thou shalt fill each jar brim full by-and-by, dost thou think that thou wilt always kill outright the robber Fancy lurking within—or sometimes only maim him and distort him!

6. Self-Development Versus Telling

HERBERT SPENCER

A second corollary from the foregoing general principle, and one which cannot be too strenuously insisted upon, is, that in education the process of self-development should be encouraged to the fullest extent. Children should be led to make their own investigations, and to draw their own inferences. They should be *told* as little as possible, and induced to *discover* as much as possible. Humanity has progressed solely by self-instruction; and that to achieve the best results, each mind must progress somewhat after the same fashion, is continually proved by the marked success of self-made men. Those who have been brought up under the ordinary school-drill, and have carried away with them the idea that education is practicable only in that style, will think it hopeless to make children their own teachers. If, however, they will call to mind that the all-important knowledge of surrounding objects which a child gets in its early years is got without help—if they will remember that the child is self-taught in the use of its mother tongue —if they will estimate the amount of that experience of life, that out-of-school wisdom, which every boy gathers for himself—if they will mark the unusual intelligence of the uncared-for London *gamin,* as shewn in all directions in which his faculties have been tasked—if further, they will think how many minds have struggled up unaided, not only through the mysteries of our irrationally-planned *curriculum,* but through hosts of other obstacles besides; they will find it a not unreasonable conclusion, that if the subjects be put before him in right order and right form, any pupil of ordinary capacity will surmount his successive difficulties with but little assistance. Who indeed can watch the ceaseless observation, and inquiry, and inference going on in a child's mind, or listen to its acute remarks on matters within the range of its faculties, without perceiving that these powers which it mani-

From Herbert Spencer, *Education, Intellectual, Moral, and Physical* (New York: D. Appleton and Company, 1912), pp. 120–122. Herbert Spencer, the leading British utilitarian philosopher of the nineteenth century, published his volume on education in 1861. Meredith Press, New York, a division of the Meredith Publishing Company, now publishes Appleton-Century books.

fests, if brought to bear systematically upon any studies *within the same range,* would readily master them without help? This need for perpetual telling is the result of our stupidity, not of the child's. We drag it away from the facts in which it is interested, and which it is actively assimilating of itself; we put before it facts far too complex for it to understand, and therefore distasteful to it; finding that it will not voluntarily acquire these facts, we thrust them into its mind by force of threats and punishment; by thus denying the knowledge it craves, and cramming it with knowledge it cannot digest, we produce a morbid state of its faculties, and a consequent disgust for knowledge in general; and when, as a result partly of the stolid indolence we have brought on, and partly of still continued unfitness in its studies, the child can understand nothing without explanation, and becomes a mere passive recipient of our instruction, we infer that education must necessarily be carried on thus. Having by our method induced helplessness, we straightway make the helplessness a reason for our method. Clearly then the experience of pedagogues cannot rationally be quoted against the doctrine we are defending. And whoever sees this will see that we may safely follow the method of nature throughout—may, by a skilful ministration, make the mind as self-developing in its later stages as it is in its earlier ones; and that only by doing this can we produce the highest power and activity.

7. *The Importance of the Theory and Practice of Education*

HERBERT SPENCER

Strangely enough, the most glaring defect in our programmes of education is entirely overlooked. While much is being done in the detailed improvement of our systems in respect both of matter and manner, the most pressing desideratum has not yet been even recognised as a desideratum. To prepare the young for the duties of life is tacitly admitted by all to be the end which parents and schoolmasters should have in view; and happily the value of the things taught, and the goodness of the method followed in teaching them, are now ostensibly

From Herbert Spencer, *Education, Intellectual, Moral, and Physical* (New York: D. Appleton and Company, 1912), pp. 162–164.

judged by their fitness to this end. The propriety of substituting for an exclusively classical training a training in which the modern languages shall have a share, is argued on this ground. The necessity of increasing the amount of science is urged for like reasons. But though some care is taken to fit youth of both sexes for society and citizenship, no care whatever is taken to fit them for the still more important position they will ultimately have to fill—the position of parents. While it is seen that for the purpose of gaining a livelihood, an elaborate preparation is needed, it appears to be thought that for the bringing up of children, no preparation whatever is needed. While many years are spent by a boy in gaining knowledge, of which the chief value is that it constitutes 'the education of a gentleman;' and while many years are spent by a girl in those decorative acquirements which fit her for evening parties; not an hour is spent by either of them for that gravest of all responsibilities—the management of a family. Is it that this responsibility is but a remote contingency? On the contrary, it is certain to devolve on nine out of ten. Is it that the discharge of it is easy? Certainly not: of all functions which the adult has to fulfil this is the most difficult. Is it that each may be trusted by self-instruction to fit himself, or herself, for the office of parent? No: not only is the need for such self-instruction unrecognised, but the complexity of the subject renders it the one of all others in which self-instruction is least likely to succeed. No rational plea can be put forward for leaving the Art of Education out of our *curriculum*. Whether as bearing upon the happiness of parents themselves, or whether as affecting the characters and lives of their children and remote descendants, we must admit that a knowledge of the right methods of juvenile culture, physical, intellectual, and moral, is a knowledge second to none in importance. This topic should occupy the highest and last place in the course of instruction passed through by each man and woman. As physical maturity is marked by the ability to produce offspring, so mental maturity is marked by the ability to train those offspring. *The subject which involves all other subjects, and therefore the subject in which the education of every one should culminate, is the Theory and Practice of Education.*

8. What Pestalozzi Left for Herbart To Do

CHARLES DE GARMO

What the labors of Pestalozzi have done for German education were long to tell. It concerns us more for present purposes to know what he left undone. The world has read the history of Germany's brilliant educational development, whose initial stages are found in the work of the Swiss Reformer, his disciples and successors. The story need not be retold. The schools of the United States, so far as educational theory is concerned, trace their origin in large part to the same primal sources. But because these men did so much, it does not follow that they did everything. Like all great reforms, that begun by Pestalozzi was emotional rather than scientific in its initial stages. Exact and logical thought does not stir a nation into a great movement for the educational uplifting of the masses, but serves rather to give direction and efficiency to what has been set in motion by moral forces. Pestalozzi was a true reformer. He could see the end to be reached, he could rouse all Europe to the sore need of the people, he could expose the barrenness of formal teaching, he could announce universal principles; but in directing his pupils over the long road that leads from ignorance to knowledge, from untutored natural disposition to moral freedom, he could indeed rely upon the guidance that comes of faith, but not so surely upon that which comes from sight. This for him was doubtless best, but for the generations of teachers to follow, who could not be fired with his divine enthusiasm, it became as necessary to see as to believe.

For a very good reason, however, Pestalozzi is excusable for not establishing his instruction upon a firm psychological basis. At that time, no psychology in the modern sense of the term existed. It is true that Immanuel Kant had developed his system of the rational presuppositions

From Charles De Garmo, "What Pestalozzi Left for Herbart To Do," chap. I, *Herbart and the Herbartians* (New York: Charles Scribner's Sons, 1895, 1912). Charles De Garmo was a leader in the Herbartian Movement which influenced American education from about 1890 to the present. He was the author of several textbooks on method emphasizing the principles of the recitation. President of Swarthmore College, Pennsylvania, at the time he wrote this book, De Garmo later became Professor of the Science and Art of Education at Cornell University.

that make mind and experience possible, but he had studiously neglected experience itself, so that his work had little or no effect in determining how the mind of the child shall be trained. The current psychology of the day was, for the most part, that of Aristotle plus a good many misconceptions that had gradually accumulated in the common mind. This, added to the fact that Pestalozzi's reform had its sources in the heart rather than in the head, enables us to understand that there was something left for Herbart to do; namely, to give scientific precision to instruction and moral training by founding them upon an adequate system of psychology and ethics.

Bacon describes three classes of thinkers, comparing them to three insects, the spider, the ant, and the bee. Some men, like the spider, he says, spin all their knowledge out of themselves; some collect it indiscriminately like the ant; while others gather facts wherever they can find them, and from these facts bring forth new products by means of their own thoughtful elaboration, just as the bee produces honey from the sweets he has gathered from the flowers. Pestalozzi's method of investigation seems to have been the kind mentioned first. He looked into his own heart and mind for the laws of mental growth, formulated them, and forthwith began to spin his theories of instruction. Thus, in one place he says: "In these laws I believe I shall certainly find the threads out of which a universal psychological method of instruction can be spun. Man! say I to myself, in dreamy search for these threads, in the ripening of every species of fruit, you recognize in all its parts the result of the wholly perfected product, and you must regard no human judgment as ripe that does not appear in all its parts as the result of complete observation of the object considered."

The following are examples of these general principles of instruction, empirically received, from which Pestalozzi seeks to evolve the methods of teaching:—

1. "Learn, therefore, to arrange thy perceptions, and to complete the simple before proceeding to the complex.

2. "Further, bring together in thy mind all those things which essentially belong together, in the same connection in which they are actually found in nature.

3. "Strengthen and intensify thy impression of important objects by bring them nearer through art, and by making them act upon these through the different senses.

4. "Regard all the effects of physical nature as absolutely necessary, and recognize in this necessity the result of the power with which they unify their apparently hetereogeneous elements to the realization of their purpose; and let the art with which thou, through instruction, workest upon thy race, as well as the results which it effects, be elevated

to a like physical necessity, so that in all of thy doing, all means, however heterogeneous in appearance, work together for the accomplishment of their great purpose.

5. "But richness and variety in environment and excitation cause the results of physical necessity to bear the impress of freedom and independence."

"From these individual principles," he again remarks, "we may spin out the threads of a universal and psychological method of instruction."

Like an impetuous leader with an army before a river, Pestalozzi does not wait to build a bridge, but bids all rush in. Many get over; yet some are lost, and all are wet.

Looking at the query, What was left for Herbart to do? from another standpoint, we shall see that one of the main results of the labors of Comenius, Rousseau, and Pestalozzi is the firmly fixed conviction that observation, or the use of the senses, and in general the consideration of simple concrete facts in every field of knowledge, is the sure foundation upon which all right elementary education rests. This truth is now the acknowledged starting-point of all scientific methods of teaching, yet the fact of the importance of observation in instruction does not carry with it any information showing how the knowledge so obtained can be utilized, or what its nature, time, amount, and order of presentation should be. In short, it does not show how mental assimilation can best take place, or how the resulting acquisitions can be made most efficiently to influence the emotional and volitional side of our nature. Perception is, indeed, the first stage in cognition, but its equally important correlative is apperception, or mental assimilation. It is Herbart and his successors who have made us distinctly conscious of this fact. The following paragraph from Dr. William T. Harris confirms the view here taken: "The progress of education is in a zigzag line, from extreme to extreme. This appears throughout all history. But were it not that succeeding times profit by the experience of their forerunners, the progress would not be assured. The history of the good and bad incident to one extreme is sufficient to prevent its repetition. The extremes are new ones at least in substantial features, and not a discouraging survival of past issues. At one time the schools have tended almost exclusively to memory-culture, with very little attempt at verification by original research and observation. This was the case with what is called the old education, and if we are to believe the critics, this ought to be called the prevailing system of our time also. But Pestalozzi exploded the theory on which it rests and substituted another. He laid stress on sense-perception, verification, and original research. The practice of our time may not correspond to its theory, but certainly all writers uphold the Pestalozzian doctrine of instruction by object-lessons. But while this reform is progressing towards its extreme, another tendency has begun within a few years, and it promises to force a new departure on our zigzag line. This is the doctrine of Herbart, which holds that it is not so much sense-perception that is wanted in education as apperception—not so much seeing and hearing and handling things, as recognizing them and understanding them. The Herbartian trend on our zigzag of progress helps to reënforce sense-perception by the memory, through the use of the causal series of ideas. It therefore combines the two former trends in a higher. Doubtless there will be new trends on the zigzag of progress to correct the extremes and errors of Herbartianism, but, compared with Pestalozzi's theory of intellectual instruction, or with that other and older theory of memory as the sole intellectual faculty, there can be no doubt that the Herbartians are right."[1]

Closely allied to the fact that Herbart gave the initial impulse to this combination of memory and perception in apperception, is another of almost equal importance. "The natural harmonious development of all the powers of a human being for the sake of his true moral nature" is a principle to which Pestalozzi ever recurs. "It is," says Vogel, "the new principle of Pestalozzi's pedagogics. True, Comenius and Rousseau declared for an education in accordance with nature. But whereas Comenius by 'nature' understood the external world of plants and animals and physical forces, and Rousseau meant nature as opposed to art, Pestalozzi penetrated to the depths of human nature, since he found this principle in moral feeling, in the freedom that is guided by duty."[2]

Herbart fully accepts Pestalozzi's statement of the ultimate end of education, but attempts to show how the daily activity of the school may bring about this desirable result,—a problem that Pestalozzi never solved for others. It is a cardinal doctrine with all followers of Herbart, that instruction itself should consciously work toward moral ends. The watchword upon their banner is *Erziehender Unterricht*; that is, instruction that makes for character. It is to a scientific study of psychology and ethics in their application to teaching that they look for guidance in the matter.

Briefly summarizing, Pestalozzi, his contemporaries, and successors, left a threefold work for Herbart to do, as follows: 1. The development of a psychology capable of immediate bearing on the problems of teaching; 2. The scientific application of this psychology to education; and 3. The revelation of the possibility of making *all* the activities of the

[1] Dr. William T. Harris, U.S. Commissioner of Education, *Educational Review*, May, 1893.

[2] Dr. August Vogel, *Geschichte der Pädagogik als Wissenschaft*, p. 161.

schoolroom, including especially instruction, bear directly upon the development of moral character.

We should not regard Herbart's contributions as additions, however important, to an educational mosaic already existing. Such a view would be most misleading. His work is fundamental, compelling a new elaboration of the whole theory of education. Whenever the world has discovered a new principle or method of thought, all its work has been done over again. Bacon's revival of the inductive method was not an addition to science, but a revolution in science. The results wrought out in the Middle Ages were discarded or wholly revised. Since Darwin and his fellow-workers established the theory of evolution as a standpoint in thinking, the whole field of knowledge has been reëxamined in accordance with the new principle. Not only the natural sciences, but ethics, religion, psychology, and even metaphysics, have felt the leavening influence of the evolutionist. It takes a large volume to record the progress of the last ten years in bacteriology. No student of this science regards it as a mere addition to the sum of medical knowledge, but it is to him a new standpoint from which to reëxamine all medical and surgical science. The psycho-physicist does not dream of restricting his investigations to the interaction between mind and body, but claims the whole dominion of psychology, if not of metaphysics, for the applicaton of his method; that is, he too must open up again in a new way all that other methods claim to have settled. Copernicus did not add new circles to the already complicated system of Ptolemy; he wrought out a new astronomy with the old stars. In a similar way, Herbart, using the same facts of human nature and experience, the same materials and means of instruction and training, brings forth new products through the application of new principles. As Dr. Harris says, the two old stages of education, memory and perception, are united by him into the higher one of apperception, or mental assimilation. The laws of mental development are examined anew; each branch of instruction is studied in its relations to the pupil's needs, understanding, and interests, and all the studies of the curriculum are considered in their double relations to one another and to the apperception of the pupil. Finally, the truest and best methods of uniting these two factors, the mind of the child and the materials of instruction and training, are investigated. This treatment is comparable in kind to that of the modern astronomer, bacteriologist, psycho-physicist, or evolutionist; it is creative work.

9. Self-Activity in the Recitation

CHARLES A. McMURRY
AND
FRANK M. McMURRY

But there is a more fundamental fault still in the ordinary use of texts. When a lesson is assigned in a book and then carefully discussed in class, the tacit assumption is that the work of the pupil is to receive. He gets what he can by his own study of the text, then the instructor quizzes him in regard to it to make sure that he receives it correctly and that he receives all of it. Now, is it true that the one who is being educated is chiefly a receiver? Is that a high conception of education? Is not the child normally also a discoverer, a producer? And should not the *best method* make abundant provision for self-expression, for outgoing, originating activity, as well as for passive impression?

Certainly before he enters school the child is exceedingly active as a thinker; he conceives an abundance of questions and as many answers; it often seems, at least, that he divides his time about equally between questions and answers. To be sure, he receives suggestions of all sorts from persons about him, but this help is a minor factor in his mental life; he is primarily a producer of thought. The kindergarten is based upon this truth, and the mission of the instructor there is not to tell the child facts, so much as to prompt him to produce thoughts that are facts. Thus we see one's employment before he enters school proper.

After one leaves school and enters upon adult life, the situation is not changed. No matter what the position may be that he takes, he is still not mainly a receiver. Whether he becomes a teacher or a manufacturer or something else, his first duty is to conceive clearly what

From Charles A. McMurry and Frank M. McMurry, *The Method of the Recitation* (New York: The Macmillan Company, 1897, 1903), pp. 134–139. Charles A. McMurry was author or co-author of more than a dozen textbooks setting forth Herbartian ideas in education. He was also editor of the yearbooks of the National Herbart Society for many years. His brother, Frank M. McMurry, was also a prolific writer and leader in the dissemination of Herbartian teachings. At the time they co-authored *The Method of the Recitation* Charles A. McMurry was Director of the Practice Department, Northern Illinois Normal School, De Kalb (now Northern Illinois State University). Frank M. McMurry was Professor of Theory and Practice of Teaching, Teachers College, Columbia University.

the problems are that confront him. Much of the time must still be occupied in thinking questions. The teacher must ask himself what his
duties are toward the parents of his children, toward the children themselves outside of school, toward religious work in his community. He
must ask himself if he intends to be a real student, and, if so, how he
can best arrange to carry on study, etc. The manufacturer must go over
his field in the same way, mapping out the problems. No one is on hand
to tell either of them just what questions are involved in his peculiar
situation. He may receive help on particular points from various quarters. Now and then an angry parent brings unexpected light as to a teacher's duty in a certain direction. But, in the main, each individual must
depend upon himself to know when he has covered the field and has
seen all of the important problems involved in his work. If some of them
are omitted, he must suffer in consequence. Many a business man discovers too late that he did not ask himself questions enough in regard to a proposed project; he did not see all sides of it.

After the problems have thus been marked out in thought, the solution of the same must be reached. Again, each one must depend upon
himself; he may receive help and advice, but he himself must decide
whether the advice is good or not; he must do his own thinking all the
time, and his success is dependent upon the care and completeness
with which it is done.

So far, then, as the thought side of adult life is concerned, it is not
essentially different from that of the child: each spends his time upon
problems and their answers; each, though he receives valuable facts
from many sources, must conceive his own problems and his own answers. We find, then, that originality is natural to childhood and a necessity in adult life; each human being is by nature, and also *must* be,
a discoverer, a producer of thought.

Now, proper preparation for life requires that those good qualities,
that are natural and necessary, be encouraged by training. Does the
school now lead children to conceive questions and answers abundantly? And, if not, how should it improve its methods?

Suppose that a boy has passed through many textbooks in the grades,
the high school, and college. Suppose, even, that thorough discussion
followed the study of the texts. Has he received abundant practice in
mapping out the chief problems necessary to a certain topic? Has he
had the same practice in reaching their solutions? And is he, in consequence, an independent thinker? Ordinarily the answer must be, *No!*
Books are not planned with reference to this thought. The ordinary conception is that if one knows plenty of facts, he will naturally do the
thinking necessary to their proper use; hence, the books offer these
facts. But the result is that the learner occupies his time in accepting ideas of other people rather than in giving forth ideas that have orig-

inated with himself. In that way education, viewed from the teacher's side, comes to mean putting in, pouring in, while the derivation of the word *e* and *ducere,* means to draw forth, draw out. The learner, then, becoming a receiver, is made relatively passive, while his nature and the needs of life require that he be intensely active.

A hint as to a better method is given by the children themselves. When they are taken to a museum to see Indian relics, or when they are allowed to witness simple experiments in physics, they dislike having to stand back and merely look on; they have an insatiable desire to touch and handle the relics, to help arrange the apparatus. They are so constituted that they can learn better if they are allowed this activity.— They show the same attitude toward thought materials. That is, when there are no relics or apparatus present, and when they are dealing only with thoughts in the presence of their teacher, it is still unnatural for them to stand back and merely behold the thoughts that she or the book presents; they want to join in and help in the production of thought, and if this liberty is denied them, while they may learn a great deal, the amount is not what it might be, and is not welded to their personalities as it should be.

Hence the conclusion is reached that even the textbook method that provides for much discussion is seriously at fault; it contains mainly answers, thereby largely omitting questions. And these answers, many of which the child could discover for himself, are furnished to him before he has been allowed time to think them out himself; it is, therefore, a systematic violation of the *law of self-activity.* But in order to comprehend thoughts, or to adjust the new to the old properly, one must conceive clearly the problems involved, and must reach these problems and their answers largely through his own effort, i.e. through his own self-activity. Inasmuch as the text-book method does not fulfil these requirements, it does not secure a high degree of adjustment of the new to the old.

The third method under discussion, that of development, avoids these errors. It makes both problems and answers prominent, and it puts the questions to the child before their answers have been presented. More than that, the child is expected to *conceive these answers himself;* he is systematically required to make discoveries, to judge what might reasonably follow from a given situation, to put two and two together and declare the result. Often, too, he finds it possible to *discover the leading questions* involved, as well as their answers; he must often state what should be the next question to be considered, and by practice in such thinking he becomes skilled in *conceiving both problems and their solutions.* Thus provision is made for adjustment of the new to the old by the large amount of self-activity allowed.

10. Principles Underlying the Recitation

CHARLES A. McMURRY
AND
FRANK M. McMURRY

If the leading thoughts thus far presented are true, there are certain steps in instruction that are universal. No matter what the study be, whether Latin, mathematics, science, or some other, there is a certain order that the mind must follow in acquiring knowledge. Through the old related experiences (first step, preparation) new individual notions are reached (second step, presentation); these are compared and their essential characteristics abstracted (third step, comparison), and the resulting general truth is worded (fourth step, generalization); this generalization finally receives application (fifth step, application). Since these steps are passed through in this order without reference to the nature of the subject-matter presented, they are rightly called the Formal Steps of Instruction. They indicate the order of the movements of the mind, or of the forms through which thought must pass in reaching full maturity.

Now, law is reached the moment that a certain order is shown to be uniform; for a law is nothing more than a statement of a uniform sequence, and a law of teaching, the statement of a uniform sequence in the process of learning. Hence, it is clear that these natural or Formal Steps of Instruction simply embody the laws of teaching.

I. The most prominent one, often known as the *law of induction* and discussed particularly in Chapter V, may be stated thus: The order of steps in the acquisition of knowledge is: (*a*) individual notions; (*b*) general notions. Eminent authorities on teaching now generally agree upon this law, and it is stated by Huxley in these words:[1]—

"The subject-matter of biological science is different from that of other sciences, but the methods of all are identical.

"And these methods are:—

From Charles A. McMurry and Frank M. McMurry, *The Method of the Recitation* (New York: The Macmillan Company, 1897, 1903), chap. XII, "Laws Underlying Processes in Teaching."

[1] Lay Sermons, p. 83.

"1. Observation of facts—including under this head that artificial observation which is called experiment.

"2. That process of tying up similar facts into bundles ticketed and ready for use, which is called comparison and classification, the results of the process, the ticketed bundles, being named general propositions.

"3. Deduction, which takes us from the general proposition to facts gained—teaches us, if I may so say, to anticipate from the ticket what is inside the bundle. And finally,—

"4. Verification, which is the process of ascertaining whether in point of fact our anticipation is a correct one.

"Such are the methods of all science whatsoever."

Considering 3 and 4 as belonging to step 5, the essential agreement of the preceding statements with this quotation is evident. It is well to ask what other method there is that could better be followed than this.

II. Another law discussed especially in the first part of Chapter VI is commonly known as the *law of apperception,* and may be stated in these words: New thoughts can be comprehended only by the help of old thoughts; also, new emotions (and volitions) are dependent both in quality and in strength upon old emotions (and volitions). The same general thought is expressed by Dr. W. T. Harris as follows:[2]—

"Inasmuch as instruction is the leading of the ignorant into knowledge by translating the unknown into the known, there are two factors involved: (*a*) the unknown subject; (*b*) the stock of knowledge already possessed by the pupil. The knowledge already possessed is the means by which the unknown can be grasped and retained. All learning is a translating of an unknown into a known, just as the learning of a foreign language proceeds by translating the unfamiliar words into familiar words, and thereby changing the strange into the familiar. This being so, unless constant reference is had by the teacher to the stock of familiar ideas belonging to the pupil, there is imminent danger to instruction. It may pass off into the process of exchanging unknown words for unknown words—a movement entirely within the realm of the unfamiliar. Such a process is not instruction, whatever else it may be."

III. *The law of aim,* discussed in Chapter VI, is one practically agreed upon in daily life, but until recently it has not been dignified by teachers as a law affecting their instruction. Nevertheless, they are coming rapidly to agree that a definite and attractive aim is a condition of the most effective work of any kind, and hence that a clear aim should be daily fixed in each recitation as elsewhere. Upon this point Dr. Wilhelm Rein says:[3]—

---

[2] Rosenkranz, "Philosophy of Education," p. 99.

[3] "Theorie und Praxis des Volksschulunterrichts. Das erste Schuljahr," p. 103.

"The pupil should know beforehand what is coming if he is to bring all his powers to bear upon the work of learning; and it is easier to call out all his effort if he knows beforehand what is to be gained. To conduct a child along an unknown road, toward an unknown object by means of questions and hints, the purpose of which he does not see, to lead him on imperceptibly to an unknown goal, has the disadvantage that it develops neither a spontaneous mental activity nor a clear insight into the subject. Having reached the end of such a line of thought, the pupil looks about himself bewildered. He cannot survey the road which he has just gone over, he does not comprehend what has happened to him. He stands at the goal but does not see the relation that the result bears to the labor performed. He does not rise to that satisfactory mental activity and favorable disposition of mind which are stimulated by the pursuit of a clearly set purpose."

IV. *The law of self-activity* has been insisted upon by all great educators in modern times, particularly, however, by Froebel. It may be briefly stated thus: proper development is possible only through a high degree of self-activity. The law was discussed especially in reference to the development method of teaching in the latter part of Chapter VI. Herbert Spencer's opinion is shown in the following quotation[4]—

"In education the process of self-development should be encouraged to the fullest extent. Children should be led to make their own investigations and to draw their own inferences. They should be told as little as possible, and induced to discover as much as possible. Humanity has progressed solely by self-instruction, and that to achieve the best results each mind must progress somewhat after the same fashion, is continually proved by the marked success of self-made men."

As indicated in connection with the discussion of the text-book method, there is abundant room for improvement in the application of this law.

V. *The law of absorption and reflection* was briefly discussed in the latter part of Chapter VI. According to it, absorption in details and reflection in regard to them, regularly alternate in effective thinking. Herbart's own words are as follows:[5]—

"Absorption and reflection, like a mental breathing, should continually alternate with each other. Absorption takes place when ideas are brought to consciousness one after another with proper clearness and accuracy; reflection takes place when they are collected and combined. The more fully and carefully these operations are provided for, the more effective proves the instruction."

Any good instructor unconsciously applies this law when he stops

[4] Herbert Spencer, Chapter II, in "Education."
[5] Herbart, "Paedagogische Schriften," I, p. 417.

to summarize and take a bird's-eye view of ground covered, ranking the facts according to their relative worth.

VI. In Chapter VI the importance of physical action, or *motor activity*, was urged, and it was practically declared to be a law that ideas must find expression, must be realized in action, before they can be conceived with the greatest clearness and accuracy. The kindergarten, especially, has always stood for this thought; in its plan of study more time each day is devoted to carrying out ideas into action than to the presentation of the ideas themselves—a practice that has been by no means characteristic of instruction above the kindergarten. But in recent years several distinguished psychologists and educators have declared themselves in favor of accepting this statement as a law, and its marked influence on education in the near future seems certain.

VII–VIII. Other possible laws have been occasionally referred to in the preceding pages, but they are not here enumerated, either because of some doubt as to their universality, or because they are commonly thought of as affecting rather the selection and arrangement of subject-matter in studies than its method of presentation in the class room. Two of these are known as the *laws of interest and of correlation*. According to the former a deep interest must be aroused in thoughts before they can exert the strongest influence upon mental life and character; according to the latter, the ultimate value of facts depends as well upon the number and closeness of relations into which they enter as upon the clearness and accuracy with which they are conceived.

The law of interest expresses one great condition of effective instruction; it makes a demand that the teaching accomplish a certain end, but does not itself give any hint as to how this end can be attained. It affects first of all the selection of subject-matter, but furnishes a daily test of method as well, by requiring that there be a healthy stimulation of the emotions as well as of the intellect in all instruction. The law of correlation was involved in the insistence (in Chapter VI) upon a close sequence in the facts of a lesson, in the demand that they be arranged in a series or network, and that even the teacher's questions reveal a close connection.

Both of these laws, therefore, have a direct influence upon method, although not limited to that field.

Undoubtedly there are other laws of teaching besides the eight that are here mentioned, but these are at least some of the broadest and most important. The law of apperception alone includes and interprets most of the so-called principles of teaching that have often been mentioned in times past; for example, from the near to the remote; from the simple to the complex; from the easy to the difficult; from the whole to the parts. These sayings are sometimes true, sometimes not.

The law of apperception is deeper than they and shows where they are applicable.

These eight laws should be guides to the teacher in the fullest sense. It would scarcely be possible to conduct a single thirty-minute recitation without applying all of them several times, with the possible exception of the law of induction.

Thus we see a most intimate connection between theory and practice when skilful instruction is imparted. The fact that these are general laws and not specific devices prevents them from cramping the teacher's freedom and individuality, for a general law is always capable of infinite variety in application.

To the extent that laws of instruction are developed and brought into a system, there is a science of method; consequently these eight laws being as deep and broad as they are, and being intimately related to one another, furnish a fair basis for the assertion that there is a scientific method of teaching.

11. *Monitorial, Pestalozzian, and Herbartian Contributions to the Recitation*

V. T. THAYER

When the historians of education do equal and exact justice to all who have contributed toward educational progress they will devote several pages to those revolutionists who invented steel pens and blackboards. They will tell us that these men were the indispensable instruments in the substitution of group recitations for individual instruction.

Prior to 1800 instruction in both elementary and grammar schools was prevailingly individual. The master's chief occupation seems to have been that of whittling goosequills, and while school legislation

From V. T. Thayer, "The Origin of the Recitation," chap. I, *The Passing of the Recitation* (Boston: D. C. Heath and Company, 1928). Reprinted by permission of D. C. Heath and Company. Vivian Trow Thayer was Professor of Education at The Ohio State University when this book was published. This was the first of many contributions to education authored or co-authored by Dr. Thayer. His latest book, *The Role of the School in American Society*, was published by Dodd, Mead, and Company, New York, in 1960. A forthcoming book, *Ideas in American Education*, is in preparation for Dodd, Mead, and Company.

usually provided that at twelve or thirteen years of age the pupil should whittle his own pens, we are told that, like many laws of today, these regulations were seldom enforced. The results of this procedure were, of course, wasteful in the extreme. Not only was the master unable to give attention to the pupils' study habits, but the practice of calling pupils to the master's desk, there to recite individually, severely limited the amount and the character of attention devoted to each pupil. Henry K. Oliver describes as follows his experiences as a pupil in the Boston reading school of 1800: "I received about twenty minutes of instruction each half day, and as school was kept three hundred and sixty minutes daily, I had the privilege of forty minutes' worth of teaching and three hundred and twenty minutes' worth of sitting still, if I could, which I could not, playing, whispering, and generally wasting time, though occasionally a picture book relieved the dreary monotony."[1]

This system of individual teaching persisted much later than is generally supposed, much later than the inventions we have mentioned or the contributions of the monitorial system necessitated. Grimshaw, writing in *Barnard's Journal* as late as 1855, "deplored the time wasted by the old-fashioned and false method of teaching individuals instead of classes. 'I notice,' he says, 'in my visits to the schools many pupils sitting idle; sometimes part of the school is asleep, or what is worse, making a noise and disturbing the remainder who desire to be industrious.' "[2]

These illustrations of early methods of teaching will throw light upon the disciplinary problems of the teacher, and we can well understand why it was advisable for Mr. Means, in the *Hoosier Schoolmaster,* to address the new applicant for the position at Flat Creek schoolhouse in these words:

"You can begin right off a Monday. They ain't been no other applications. You see, it takes grit to apply for this school. The last master had a black eye for a month. But, as I wuz sayin', you can jist roll up and wade in."

The invention of steel pens freed the master from the deadly routine of preparing pens for his pupils and made it possible to supervise and direct their writing. But the invention of blackboards was an additional step forward. He could now gather together a few pupils who were at the same stage of progress and present to them new materials and clear up common difficulties. He could, in short, teach them in groups. Barnard tells of his surprise upon viewing a blackboard for the first time.

[1] Parker, S. C., *History of Elementary Education,* Ginn and Co., 1912, p. 88.
[2] Quoted by Breslich in the Thirteenth Yearbook of the National Society for the Study of Education, p. 34, from Holmes's *School Organization and the Individual Child,* p. 13.

It was in the winter of 1813–1814, during his student days at Harvard. While on a vacation trip to Boston he visited a mathematical school and there saw a group of pupils gathered about a blackboard. It was his first experience with what he called "analytical and inductive teaching."

These two reforms were indispensable for a more vital teaching method, but they provided merely the raw materials for the organization of class instruction. If we would adequately understand the evolution of teaching procedure, we should study in some detail the creative work of Joseph Lancaster and his fellow monitorians. We have only to read their manuals in order to appreciate how fully the general characteristics of classroom method were worked out by these predecessors of job analysis. It is to Lancaster that we must attribute the saying, "A place for everything and everything in its place." The most insignificant detail did not escape him. Most of us have seen pictures of the monitorial school and we may have noticed the children's hats attached with cords to their shoulders in order to save both time and cloakroom space. The children were organized into small groups, usually of ten, and each in charge of an older pupil monitor. They marched to and from their classes in military fashion; they recited in unison on command, and they responded as a group to such instructions as, "hats off," "show slates," etc. David Salmon writes: "To avoid, for instance, the waste of time involved in calling the name of the whole school to discover the two or three absentees, each boy was given a fixed number. Corresponding numbers were printed in a row on the wall; the class was marched into position; each boy took his place under his own number, and the vacant numbers instantly showed who were missing."[3]

Not only were the details of class organization and management worked over in detail but subject matter was likewise given a carefully graded organization for purposes of class instruction. Thus, in arithmetic, "Lancaster had the following plan: The basis of progress was placed in a thorough knowledge of the tables. In every new rule the examples were at first short and easy, increasing in length and difficulty with the power of the learner. Each class had a definite number of examples which were written in a book kept by the monitor; others were worked over and over again until they could be worked with facility and dispatch. In teaching a new rule, a monitor dictated an example; he then worked it out, the scholars following him on their slates; then the slates were cleaned, the example written on the blackboard, and each boy in turn took a part of the operation. This was persisted in until the mode of working was understood."[4]

The teaching results under this system, when contrasted with the

[3] Salmon, David, *Joseph Lancaster*, Longmans, Green and Co., 1904, p. 9.
[4] Gill, John, *Systems of Education*, D. C. Heath and Co., 1887, pp. 192–193.

methods of individual instruction, were startling. David Salmon, in his book on Joseph Lancaster, relates an incident in which an anxious and perhaps an embarrassed father called upon his local pastor to protest against the practices of the monitorial school. This parent objected to the rapid school progress of his boy. Since he recalled with what difficulty and delay he himself had learned his arithmetic, he was convinced that the master of the monitorial school must be exercising an evil magic in teaching the same operations so rapidly.

To be sure, from a modern standpoint, the method was not without fault. Instruction was mechanized. Mere performance and the memorization of facts were commonly confused with genuine learning. Frequently the processes mastered were mastered as forms without being understood by either the pupil or the monitor. The monitor's manual in arithmetic consisted of examples and a key which revealed not merely the complete solution of a problem but the detailed steps by means of which the answer was obtained. Thus, "If the question were one of simple addition, for instance, the monitor might read from the key: 'First column: 7 and 9 are 16, and 3 are 19, and 5 are 24. Set down 4 under 7 and carry 2 to the next column'; and the class would thereupon set down 4 as told. It is doubtful whether monitor or pupils would understand the reasons for them."[5]

If one were to attempt to characterize in a phrase the monitorial system, in contrast with the method of teaching it displaced, he might say that it attempted to have ten little voices chirrup where one voice chirruped before. Such a characterization, however, while accurate in the main, is nevertheless in danger of blurring the monumental contributions of the monitorial system. Parker[6] has described how Lancaster studied in detail not only such matters as the mechanics of instruction and elimination of waste in school routine, but also the effective construction of schoolrooms and teaching apparatus, the flexible classification of children, and the motivation of school work, largely through incentives of competition.

For all these things teachers are more heavily obligated than they usually appreciate. Were we to discuss adequately the contributions of the monitorial system, we should indicate not only the fact that it gave to the recitation system the structural outlines which it still retains, but it laid as well the basis for a free public education with professionally trained teachers. Under no other method could universal and free education have been envisaged; the expense would have seemed prohibitive. Thus in 1819 there were ten monitorial schools in Philadelphia, each with one teacher in charge and an average of 284 pupils per teacher. As late as 1834 in the same city the average num-

[5] Salmon, David, *op. cit.*, p. 12.
[6] *The History of Modern Elementary Education*, Ginn and Co., 1912, pp. 101–107.

ber of pupils per teacher was 218. The monitorial system alone made it economically feasible to undertake the public education of children.

But such a huge per teacher enrollment also made clear the necessity for training both teachers and monitors. It was clearly recognized under these conditions that teaching required skill and a resourcefulness that could not spring unaided out of a knowledge of subject matter or a "natural gift" for teaching. No longer would it do for a writer of a textbook to preface it with the remark which Edmund Coote inserted in the introduction to his *Text Book for Elementary Schools:*

> "To the unskillful, which desire to make use of it for their own private benefit, and to *such men and women of trade as Tailors, Weavers, Shopkeepers, Seamsters, and such others as have undertaken the charge of teaching others* (with this textbook) *thou mayest sit on thy shopboard, at thy books or thy needle, and never hinder any work to hear thy scholars,* after thou hast made this little book familiar to thee."[7]

To the monitorial system, then, must we give major credit for originating and developing the fundamental structure of the recitation. It is true, of course, that the Pestalozzian and Herbartian influences have profoundly modified education since Lancaster, but when we give attention to the essential outlines of the recitation system, Pestalozzian and Herbartian contributions will seem chiefly to have flowed into molds already prepared and to have adjusted themselves to these characteristics.

Take, for example, Pestalozzian methods. In this country these date from their introduction in Oswego, N.Y., in 1860. Two outstanding features of Pestalozzian procedure were: (1) to start with the experiences of children, observation and clear ideas; (2) to proceed by means of carefully graded oral instruction to systematic and organized knowledge. In this process the laws of child development were to constitute the criteria for selecting and presenting the materials for learning. Thus child experience was intended to replace exclusive dependence upon books, and the teacher's direction of learning activity to replace a passive method of hearing recitations.

These ideals effected profound changes in the elementary school course of study. Arithmetic was reorganized on the basis of object teaching so that pupils passed gradually from the observation of sensible objects to an understanding and manipulation of abstract numbers. Mental arithmetic assumed a prominent place in school work. Object teaching likewise led to oral instruction with heavy emphasis upon oral language training. Geographies of a "dictionary-encyclopedia" type were replaced by home geography; and natural science as an out-

---

[7] Quoted by Parker, S. C., *The History of Modern Elementary Education*, Ginn and Co., 1912, p. 54.

growth both of object teaching and oral language received recognition.

When we turn, however, to the methods of teaching into which the Pestalozzian system crystallized we discover a dismal formalism. It is said that a French-Swiss officer once remarked to Pestalozzi, when the latter was explaining his methods, "I see, you want to mechanize instruction." Whether or not Pestalozzi believed his psychological procedure was identical with mechanical routine, there is no doubt of the fact that his followers at least succeeded in mechanizing instruction. And they mechanized it in the direction of formal group work which in the hands of the average teacher became deadly routine. Parker states of oral instruction that a proper method of questioning became the sole requisite and a teacher's knowledge unimportant. Frequently a teacher "simply questioned the children about their experience and told them nothing."[8] No better indication of the dangers resident in this method can be found than in the following "model" lesson printed in Elizabeth Mayo's *A Manual of Elementary Instruction for Infant, School and Private Tuition.*

A PIECE OF BARK

"What is this? A piece of bark. All look at it. Where do we find bark? On trees. On what part of trees? Look and see. (The teacher brings in a piece of the stem of a tree on which the bark still remains.) On the outside. Repeat together—'Bark is the outer part of the stems of trees.'

"Look at the bark; what do you perceive? It is brown. Repeat—'Bark is *brown.*' Look again; is it like glass? No, we cannot see through it. What can you say of it then? We cannot see through bark. Compare it with glass. It does not shine. When anything does not shine at all, it is said to be dull. What is the bark? It is dull. Repeat—'The bark is *dull.*' Show me some things in the room that are dull. Now feel the bark. It is *rough.* And what more? It is *dry.* Now look: (The teacher separates the fiber.) It has strings or hairs. These strings or hairs are called fibers, and we say the bark is fibrous. Repeat—'The bark is *fibrous.*' Some plants have very fibrous stems, and are very useful to us on this account; here are some of the fibers of hemp; and here are some of flax, which supplies much of our clothing. I think you can find out something more if you feel the bark again. Yes; it is *hard.*

"Now repeat all you have said. 'Bark is the *outside covering of the stems* of trees: it is *brown:* we cannot *see through it: it is rough, dull, dry, hard,* and *fibrous.*' "[9]

[8] Parker, S. C., *op. cit.,* p. 329.
[9] Quoted by Lois Coffey Mossman in *Changing Conceptions Relative to the Planning of Lessons,* Teachers College Contributions to Education, No. 147, 1924, p. 4.

The characteristic tendencies in Pestalozzian teaching in this country are very well summed up by Dr. Mossman in her monograph on *Changing Conceptions Relative to the Planning of Lessons.* She writes:[10]

"Examination of books, magazines, and reports of educational meetings published in the three decades following the introduction of object teaching at Oswego, shows its wide acceptance as a definite method and form of instruction. It was based upon a psychology which stressed prominently the significance of perception in learning. It was based upon a theory of pupil acceptance of subject matter handed to him. It made very slight provision for teacher initiative and no provision for pupil initiative. It assumed teacher dictation of every step in the learning process."

Herbart's influence on classroom work has likewise tended in practice to strengthen rather than to weaken group methods of instruction and thus to perpetuate the recitation system. He too has added new materials to the school curriculum. The prominence, for example, of the social sciences in the present curriculum and the emphasis of these subjects upon training for citizenship are logical developments, modified to be sure by present needs, of Herbart's emphasis upon moral development as the supreme aim of education and the use of historical materials for the realization of these ends.

"Virtue" was for Herbart the final aim of education. As a means for realizing this end he stressed the significance of interest and apperception. Had pedagogues taken these doctrines seriously and applied them to the learning of individual children, they would have been impressed with the significance of individual differences in pupils' backgrounds and interests and the consequent necessity for modifying traditional group instruction. The outstanding effects of the Herbartian movement upon teaching method have been until recently, however, to accentuate the importance of the teacher's activity and to mold the performances of children according to stereotyped patterns. Thus they have taken Herbart's description of the way the mind works in organizing a subject as a whole and converted it into a method of instruction which requires that children, in the acquisition of new knowledge, move in lock-step fashion through five steps in learning.

Even so original and independent a disciple as Professor W. C. Bagley lends encouragement to this tendency when discussing the Inductive Lesson in his *Educative Process.* Thus he states that the "dominant method" in *Preparation* should be the question and answer procedure, and the time devoted to preparation should not involve "more than one-fifth of the time allotted to the entire lesson." In the course of *Presentation,* the second step, pupils secure their facts directly and

[10] *Op. cit.,* p. 5.

indirectly, from "lecture, textbook, or some other medium of instruction," and consequently the time element varies, perhaps extending over half of the period. The third step, *Comparison and Abstraction,* again calls for the question and answer method with the time varying accordingly as one derives one or more generalizations from the accumulated data. Professor Bagley pauses, however, to urge that if possible all five steps be completed in one day. Consequently, the conscientious teacher will hurry on to the fourth step, *Generalization,* which consists in summing up in a class definition the results of previous labors. "At no time," writes Professor Bagley, "should the step cover more than three or four minutes." The last step, *Application,* like *Presentation,* may be either direct or indirect and consequently is somewhat elastic in method and consumption of time.

This brief outline of the steps of instruction clearly indicates how Herbartian teaching concentrates the activity and initiative of the classroom in the person of the teacher. Pupils are assumed to think in unison and, in less skillful hands than those of Professor Bagley, all spontaneity is in danger of disappearing.

By and large, this is precisely what has happened. Beginning roughly in 1890 the Herbartian influence tended to dominate theory and practice in normal schools and teacher training institutions. Detailed and careful attention to lesson planning is one of the outcomes of this situation and young teachers have been carefully drilled in methods of teaching in accordance with Herbartian precepts. While the original Herbartian procedure has undergone progressive modification, emphasis upon the teacher's technique and detailed lesson planning for group teaching of a formal and stereotyped character has not been relaxed. These plans include pivotal questions, devices for securing and holding group attention, advanced assignments, etc. It is not uncommon for public schools under well-organized supervision to require teachers to write out in detail their recitation plans several days or a week in advance, from which the teacher is expected rarely to deviate. Courses of study indicate the ground to be covered by all pupils within a specified period of time, and the good teacher exercises his "technique" so that his pupils will arrive at the goal in a body neither before nor after the appointed time.

And thus it is that the developments since Lancaster have led to little more than the pouring of new wine into old bottles. We teach different subjects and we have altered the contents of old subjects. We have originated more economical devices for learning and we have profited from careful studies in the technique of acquiring skill and information. We classify and grade our pupils more skillfully. But withal we have not fundamentally reconstructed the recitation system which Lancaster devised a little more than a century ago.

No one acquainted with American education can seriously question the valuable contributions of the recitation method of instruction. Except for it, as we have seen, we should probably not have universal public education in this country. Consequently we should give all honor to the educational leaders who perfected it as a method of teaching and incorporated it as an integral part of their school organizations. They solved effectively the chief educational problems of their day and laid the basis for future progress.

But when we have granted all this, we have still to face the problems peculiar to our day. We must ask the question, "Is the recitation method best adapted for present needs?" What is invaluable at one stage of development is frequently injurious at another. It is always worth while to raise the question of the suitability of an old tool for the realization of new purposes. It is for this reason that we wish to inquire whether the traditional lock-step method of teaching, with its daily assignments of like tasks for all pupils, is adequately designed to realize present-day educational aims and ideals.

12. *A Criticism of the Formal Steps*
JOHN DEWEY

Before following up this comparison in more detail, we may raise the question whether the recitation should, in any case, follow a uniform prescribed series of steps—even if it be admitted that this series expresses the normal logical order. In reply, it may be said that just because the order is logical, it represents the survey of subject-matter made by one who already understands it, not the path of progress followed by a mind that is learning. The former may describe a uniform straightway course, the latter must be a series of tacks, of zigzag movements back and forth. In short, the formal steps indicate the points that should be covered by the teacher in preparing to conduct a recitation, but should not prescribe the actual course of teaching.

From John Dewey, "The Recitation and the Training of Thought," chap. XV, *How We Think* (Boston: D. C. Heath and Company, 1910), pp. 204–207. Internationally acknowledged as this century's leading philosopher and educator, Dewey's influence on educational thought and practice continues to be worldwide. This reading and the one that follows are included in books published during his years as Professor of Philosophy at Columbia University, a tenure which lasted from 1904 to 1930. Reprinted by permission of D. C. Heath and Company.

Lack of any preparation on the part of a teacher leads, of course, to a random, haphazard recitation, its success depending on the inspiration of the moment, which may or may not come. Preparation in simply the subject-matter conduces to a rigid order, the teacher examining pupils on their exact knowledge of their text. But the teacher's problem—as a teacher—does not reside in mastering a subject-matter, but in adjusting a subject-matter to the nurture of thought. Now the formal steps indicate excellently well the questions a teacher should ask in working out the problem of teaching a topic. What preparation have my pupils for attacking this subject? What familiar experiences of theirs are available? What have they already learned that will come to their assistance? How shall I present the matter so as to fit economically and effectively into their present equipment? What pictures shall I show? To what objects shall I call their attention? What incidents shall I relate? What comparisons shall I lead them to draw, what similarities to recognize? What is the general principle toward which the whole discussion should point as its conclusion? By what applications shall I try to fix, to clear up, and to make real their grasp of this general principle? What activities of their own may bring it home to them as a genuinely significant principle?

No teacher can fail to teach better if he has considered such questions somewhat systematically. But the more the teacher has reflected upon pupils' probable intellectual response to a topic from the various standpoints indicated by the five formal steps, the more he will be prepared to conduct the recitation in a flexible and free way, and yet not let the subject go to pieces and the pupils' attention drift in all directions; the less necessary will he find it, in order to preserve a semblance of intellectual order, to follow some one uniform scheme. He will be ready to take advantage of any sign of vital response that shows itself from any direction. One pupil may already have some inkling—probably erroneous—of a general principle. Application may then come at the very beginning in order to show that the principle will not work, and thereby induce search for new facts and a new generalization. Or the abrupt presentation of some fact or object may so stimulate the minds of pupils as to render quite superfluous any preliminary preparation. If pupils' minds are at work at all, it is quite impossible that they should wait until the teacher has conscientiously taken them through the steps of preparation, presentation, and comparison before they form at least a working hypothesis or generalization. Moreover, unless comparison of the familiar and the unfamiliar is introduced at the beginning, both preparation and presentation will be aimless and without logical motive, isolated, and in so far meaningless. The student's mind cannot be prepared at large, but only for something in particular, and presentation is usually the best way of evoking associations. The emphasis may fall now on the familiar concept that will help grasp the new, now on the new facts that frame the problem; but in either case it is comparison and contrast with the other term of the pair which gives either its force. In short, to transfer the logical steps from the points that the teacher needs to consider to uniform successive steps in the conduct of a recitation, is to impose the logical review of a mind that already understands the subject, upon the mind that is struggling to comprehend it, and thereby to obstruct the logic of the student's own mind.

Bearing in mind that the formal steps represent intertwined factors of a student's progress and not mileposts on a beaten highway, we may consider each by itself. In so doing, it will be convenient to follow the example of many of the Herbartians and reduce the steps to three: first, the apprehension of specific or particular facts; second, rational generalization; third, application and verification.

13. The Unity of Subject Matter and Method

JOHN DEWEY

The trinity of school topics is subject matter, methods, and administration or government. We have been concerned with the two former in recent chapters. It remains to disentangle them from the context in which they have been referred to, and discuss explicitly their nature. We shall begin with the topic of method, since that lies closest to the considerations of the last chapter. Before taking it up, it may be well, however, to call express attention to one implication of our theory; the connection of subject matter and method with each other. The idea that mind and the world of things and persons are two separate and independent realms—a theory which philosophically is known as dualism—carries with it the conclusion that method and subject matter of instruction are separate affairs. Subject matter then becomes a ready-made systematized classification of the facts and principles of the world

From John Dewey, "The Unity of Subject Matter and Method," in chap. XIII, *Democracy and Education* (New York: The Macmillan Company, 1916), pp. 193–200. Reprinted with permission of the publisher from *Democracy and Education* by John Dewey. Copyright 1916 by The Macmillan Company. Renewed 1944 by John Dewey.

of nature and man. Method then has for its province a consideration of the ways in which this antecedent subject matter may be best presented to and impressed upon the mind; or, a consideration of the ways in which the mind may be externally brought to bear upon the matter so as to facilitate its acquisition and possession. In theory, at least, one might deduce from a science of the mind as something existing by itself a complete theory of methods of learning, with no knowledge of the subjects to which the methods are to be applied. Since many who are actually most proficient in various branches of subject matter are wholly innocent of these methods, this state of affairs gives opportunity for the retort that pedagogy, as an alleged science of methods of the mind in learning, is futile;—a mere screen for concealing the necessity a teacher is under of profound and accurate acquaintance with the subject in hand.

But since thinking is a directed movement of subject matter to a completing issue, and since mind is the deliberate and intentional phase of the process, the notion of any such split is radically false. The fact that the material of a science is organized is evidence that it has already been subjected to intelligence; it has been methodized, so to say. Zoölogy as a systematic branch of knowledge represents crude, scattered facts of our ordinary acquaintance with animals after they have been subjected to careful examination, to deliberate supplementation, and to arrangement to bring out connections which assist observation, memory, and further inquiry. Instead of furnishing a starting point for learning, they mark out a consummation. Method means that arrangement *of* subject matter which makes it most effective in use. Never is method something outside of the material.

How about method from the standpoint of an individual who is dealing with subject matter? Again, it is not something external. It is simply an effective treatment *of* material—efficiency meaning such treatment as utilizes the material (puts it to a purpose) with a minimum of waste of time and energy. We can distinguish a *way* of acting, and discuss it by itself; but the way *exists* only as a way-of-dealing-with-material. Method is not antithetical to subject matter; it is the effective direction of subject matter to desired results. It is antithetical to random and ill-considered action,—ill-considered signifying ill-adapted.

The statement that method means directed movement of subject matter towards ends is formal. An illustration may give it content. Every artist must have a method, a technique, in doing his work. Piano playing is not hitting the keys at random. It is an orderly way of using them, and the order is not something which exists ready-made in the musician's hands or brain prior to an activity dealing with the piano.

Order is found in the disposition of acts which use the piano and the hands and brain so as to achieve the result intended. It is the action of the piano directed to accomplish the purpose of the piano as a musical instrument. It is the same with 'pedagogical' method. The only difference is that the piano is a mechanism constructed in advance for a single end; while the material of study is capable of indefinite uses. But even in this regard the illustration may apply if we consider the infinite variety of kinds of music which a piano may produce, and the variations in technique required in the different musical results secured. Method in any case is but an effective way of employing some material for some end.

These considerations may be generalized by going back to the conception of experience. Experience as the perception of the connection between something tried and something undergone in consequence is a process. Apart from effort to control the course which the process takes, there is no distinction of subject matter and method. There is simply an activity which includes both what an individual does and what the environment does. A piano player who had perfect mastery of his instrument would have no occasion to distinguish between his contribution and that of the piano. In well-formed, smooth-running functions of any sort,—skating, conversing, hearing music, enjoying a landscape, —there is no consciousness of separation of the method of the person and of the subject matter. In whole-hearted play and work there is the same phenomenon.

When we reflect upon an experience instead of just having it, we inevitably distinguish between our own attitude and the objects toward which we sustain the attitude. When a man is eating, he is eating *food*. He does not divide his act into eating *and* food. But if he makes a scientific investigation of the act, such a discrimination is the first thing he would effect. He would examine on the one hand the properties of the nutritive material, and on the other hand the acts of the organism in appropriating and digesting. Such reflection upon experience gives rise to a distinction of *what* we experience (the experienc*ed*) and the experienc*ing*—the *how*. When we give names to this distinction we have subject matter and method as our terms. There is the thing seen, heard, loved, hated, imagined, and there is the act of seeing, hearing, loving, hating, imagining, etc.

This distinction is so natural and so important for certain purposes, that we are only too apt to regard it as a separation in existence and not as a distinction in thought. Then we make a division between a self and the environment or world. This separation is the root of the dualism of method and subject matter. That is, we assume that knowing, feeling, willing, etc., are things which belong to the self or mind in its isolation, and which then may be brought to bear upon an independent subject matter. We assume that the things which belong in isolation to the self or mind have their own laws of operation irrespective of the modes of active energy of the object. These laws are supposed to furnish method. It would be no less absurd to suppose that men can eat without eating something, or that the structure and movements of the jaws, throat muscles, the digestive activities of stomach, etc., are not what they are *because* of the material with which their activity is engaged. Just as the organs of the organism are a continuous part of the very world in which food materials exist, so the capacities of seeing, hearing, loving, imagining are intrinsically connected with the subject matter of the world. They are more truly ways in which the environment enters into experience and functions there than they are independent acts brought to bear upon things. Experience, in short, is not a combination of mind and world, subject and object, method and subject matter, but is a single continuous interaction of a great diversity (literally countless in number) of energies.

For the purpose of *controlling* the course or direction which the moving unity of experience takes we draw a mental distinction between the how and the what. While there is no *way* of walking or of eating or of learning over and above the actual walking, eating, and studying, there are certain elements in the act which give the key to its more effective control. Special attention to these elements makes them more obvious to perception (letting other factors recede for the time being from conspicuous recognition). Getting an idea of *how* the experience proceeds indicates to us what factors must be secured or modified in order that it may go on more successfully. This is only a somewhat elaborate way of saying that if a man watches carefully the growth of several plants, some of which do well and some of which amount to little or nothing, he may be able to detect the special conditions upon which the prosperous development of a plant depends. These conditions, stated in an orderly sequence, would constitute the method or way or manner of its growth. There is no difference between the growth of a plant and the prosperous development of an experience. It is not easy, in either case, to seize upon just the factors which make for its best movement. But study of cases of success and failure and minute and extensive comparison, helps to seize upon causes. When we have arranged these causes in order, we have a method of procedure or a technique.

A consideration of some evils in education that flow from the isolation of method from subject matter will make the point more definite. (*i*) In the first place, there is the neglect (of which we have spoken) of concrete situations of experience. There can be no discovery of a method without cases to be studied. The method is derived from observation of what actually happens, with a view to seeing that it happen better next time. But in instruction and discipline, there is rarely sufficient opportunity for children and youth to have the direct normal experiences from which educators might derive an idea of method or order of best development. Experiences are had under conditions of such constraint that they throw little or no light upon the normal course of an experience to its fruition. "Methods" have then to be authoritatively recommended to teachers, instead of being an expression of their own intelligent observations. Under such circumstances, they have a mechanical uniformity, assumed to be alike for all minds. Where flexible personal experiences are promoted by providing an environment which calls out directed occupations in work and play, the methods ascertained will vary with individuals—for it is certain that each individual has something characteristic in his way of going at things.

(*ii*) In the second place, the notion of methods isolated from subject matter is responsible for the false conceptions of discipline and interest already noted. When the effective way of managing material is treated as something ready-made apart from material, there are just three possible ways in which to establish a relationship lacking by assumption. One is to utilize excitement, shock of pleasure, tickling the palate. Another is to make the consequences of not attending painful; we may use the menace of harm to motivate concern with the alien subject matter. Or a direct appeal may be made to the person to put forth effort without any reason. We may rely upon immediate strain of "will." In practice, however, the latter method is effectual only when instigated by fear of unpleasant results.

(*iii*) In the third place, the act of learning is made a direct and conscious end in itself. Under normal conditions, learning is a product and reward of occupation with subject matter. Children do not set out, consciously, to learn walking or talking. One sets out to give his impulses for communication and for fuller intercourse with others a show. He learns in consequence of his direct activities. The better methods of teaching a child, say, to read, follow the same road. They do not fix his attention upon the fact that he has to learn something and so make his attitude self-conscious and constrained. They engage his activities, and in the process of engagement he learns: the same is true of the more successful methods in dealing with number or whatever. But when the subject matter is not used in carrying forward impulses and habits to significant results, it is just something to be learned. The pupil's attitude to it is just that of having to learn it. Conditions more unfavorable to an alert and concentrated response would be hard to devise. Frontal attacks are even more wasteful in learning than in war. This does not mean, however, that students are to be seduced unaware into preoccupation with lessons. It means that they shall be occupied with them for real reasons or ends, and not just as something to be learned. This is accomplished whenever the pupil perceives the place occupied by the subject matter in the fulfilling of some experience.

(*iv*) In the fourth place, under the influence of the conception of the separation of mind and material, method tends to be reduced to a cut and dried routine, to following mechanically prescribed steps. No one can tell in how many schoolrooms children reciting in arithmetic or grammar are compelled to go through, under the alleged sanction of method, certain preordained verbal formulæ. Instead of being encouraged to attack their topics directly, experimenting with methods that seem promising and learning to discriminate by the consequences that accrue, it is assumed that there is one fixed method to be followed. It is also naïvely assumed that if the pupils make their statements and explanations in a certain form of "analysis," their mental habits will in time conform. Nothing has brought pedagogical theory into greater disrepute than the belief that it is identified with handing out to teachers recipes and models to be followed in teaching. Flexibility and initiative in dealing with problems are characteristic of any conception to which method is a way of managing material to develop a conclusion. Mechanical rigid woodenness is an inevitable corollary of any theory which separates mind from activity motivated by a purpose.

14. The "Project" as a Teaching Unit
DAVID SNEDDEN

For purposes of school-room administration, the subject-matter used to realize any particular purpose in education must be broken up into subdivisions so as to form serviceable "teaching units." Broadly speaking, a subject itself is such a unit—e.g., history, American history, ge-

From David Snedden, "The 'Project' as a Teaching Unit," *School and Society*, IV (September 16, 1916), 419–423. David Snedden was Professor of Education at Teachers College, Columbia University, from 1916 until 1935. He was the author of numerous books on secondary education, educational sociology, and vocational education. State Commissioner of Education in Massachusetts from 1909 to 1916, and President of the National Society for Vocational Education from 1918 to 1920, Snedden was uniquely qualified to discuss the origins of project teaching. Reprinted by permission of *School and Society*, The Society for the Advancement of Education, Inc., New York.

ography, French. An amount of one of these subjects suitable or convenient for a year's work (or other long period) gives us the "course" —another type of unit. We speak of a course in First-year French, Advanced Mathematics, etc. Also, for purposes of convenience, we divide courses into subdivisions of various sorts—e.g., the book, part, chapter (at least in the text-book), section, topic, lesson, etc. For pedagogical rather than administrative reasons, these divisions are also often broken up into sections, such as definitions, exercises, explanations, assigned readings, references, rules, questions, vocabularies, conspectuses, tables, etc.

Now the primary purpose of making all these divisions and subdivisions is, of course, some form of efficiency—efficiency of organization, of accessibility, of mastery. Usually, as in all other forms of activity we prefer to have the dividing lines or boundaries in educational subject-matter fall where nature itself or the work of man has created channels, cleavages or natural classifications. But if this can not be done, we create purely arbitrary divisions. To use comparable situations in other fields, we find that a grain of wheat, a natural subdivision of "wheat," is too small for practicable handling, but a "field" of wheat too large. Hence we arbitrarily subdivide into bushels, centals, or "sacks" where "manhandling" is necessary. But in rendering a beef portable we first naturally "quarter" it, and these we again subdivide, partly along natural lines. For ease of ascent we break a steep slope up into "steps" and we also often create large divisions by landings.

Sometimes we find we have pushed the subdividing process too far or in wrong directions. We are trying now to blend elementary algebra and geometry, botany and zoology, etc. Or we subdivide what before was merged—e.g., physical geography and commercial geography, English language and English literature, etc. We have given up the old catechetical unit—the question and answer; and in such subjects as geography and history, the lesson (which was usually based on one day's working energy of the child in a stated subject, and hence could rarely be a "natural" unit) has largely disappeared. It can still be retained in reading and "language lessons" because these consist largely of exercises which can be cut off at any point suggested by the limitations of energy on the part of the learner.

The importance of having good teaching units in education is no less than is the importance of having good working subdivisions of time, matter, force, distance, difficulty, etc., in practical activities elsewhere.

In packing goods we devise packages adapted to, or controlled by, the conditions to be met. A box or small crate of cantaloups may be very light for a man to carry, but a larger box would result in damage to the melons. But these small boxes can be crated for handling by trucks. Wheat is sacked in bags adapted to a strong man who must "use no hooks"; while fabrics can be boxed in packages that no man can lift because truck handling with hooks is practicable. The size of a newspaper, the weight of a volume, the length of a sermon, the duration of a call, the size of a "portion" of food, the height of a table, the width of cotton fabrics, the speed of a car, the size of a farm, the length of a day's work, the height of a room—all these units or divisions are the resultants of certain natural conditions working in greater or less opposition to man's forces and necessities. They all represent compromises, gravitating towards optimum standards.

But in the organization of the "means" of education—the studies, lectures, "tellings," discussions, experiments, exercises, assigned readings, memorizings, reports, activities, problems, trials, tests, examinations, etc., through which we achieve our desired ends—we have given, as yet, insufficient attention to the organization of effective teaching units of the smaller kind—those that would be especially significant to the learner. The "question and answer" unit—as seen at its best in the catechism—was the smallest unit ever devised. It was in part definitely pedagogical and in part definitely logical. It was eminently suited to an age in which authority was the source of all knowledge for the learner, and verbal memorization the chief means of fixing in the minds of each new generation the dogmas and other authoritative teachings of the older generation. This unit had also the peculiar advantage of being most easily handled by unskilled and uninformed teachers.

The "lesson" unit was in part a pedagogical unit—that is, based upon the powers and weaknesses of learners—rather than a logical unit—that is, based upon the inherent characteristics of subject-matter. It was, of course, not a true pedagogical unit—that is, taking account of all of the characteristics to be found in the child as active learner; it might be called a unit based roughly upon the capacity of the learner to give attention, to endure application, or to give working time. It was, in other words, a convenient task, a sort of day's work, so far as a particular kind of activity was concerned. It was often an arbitrarily sliced-off portion of subject-matter, and represented frequently no logical division of that subject-matter at all—resembling, therefore, as a unit, a stated length of board or cloth or a slice of bread rather than a tree trunk, a garment or a biscuit.

The "topic" which in many studies succeeded the lesson as the teaching unit of chief importance was especially characterized by its logical relation to some larger unit or "whole" of subject-matter, while at the same time it was endeavored in it to take account of the possible focusing of interests and the intellectual "spanning powers" of young learners. In many respects it was therefore an advance upon units previously developed. It lent itself especially well to teaching in which some reasoning, inference and comparison on the part of the learner was sought in lieu of the verbal memorizing which had formerly prevailed.

A few years ago some of us began using the word "project" to describe a unit of educative work in which the most prominent feature was some form of positive and concrete achievement. The baking of a loaf of bread, the making of a shirtwaist, the raising of a bushel of corn, the making of a table, the installation of an electric bell outfit—all these, when undertaken by learners, and when so handled as to result in a large acquisition of knowledge and experience, were called projects. Projects of this kind might be individual or joint (cooperative). They might be executed in an ordinary lesson period or they might claim the efforts of the learner for one or more hours per day for several weeks.

The following were the primary characteristics of projects as thus conceived: (a) the undertaking always possessed a certain unity; (b) the learner himself clearly conceived the practical end or outcome to be attained, and it was always expected that this outcome was full of interest to him, luring him on, as to a definite goal to be won; (c) the standards of achievement were clearly objective—so much so that the learner and his fellows could, in large part, render valuable decisions as to the worth—in an amateur or in a commercial sense—of the product; and (d) the undertaking was of such a nature that the learner, in achieving his desired ends, would necessarily have to apply much of his previous knowledge and experience—perhaps heretofore not consciously held as usable in this way (e.g., art, science, mathematics, special tool skill)—and probably would have to acquire also some new knowledges and skills.

As in many other forms of learning, the objectives held in view by learner and teacher were often unlike. What the learner imagined as an end the teacher conceived often as a means to some remoter end.

In the early stages of the development of certain forms of agricultural and industrial vocational education, a number of educators favored the project as the chief pedagogic unit of organization. In a sense any concrete job undertaken in a vocational school where the realization of valuable results in product constitutes an important end, might be called a "project"; but to be an "educational project" such a job (e.g., turning a spindle, wiring a room, growing a half acre of potatoes, taking commercial charge of three cows for a year, cooking family breakfasts for a month, making ten saleable shirtwaists, cooperatively building and selling a cottage, etc.) must be of such a nature as to offer large opportunity, not only for the acquisition of new skill and experience in practical manipulation, but also for application of old, and learning of new, "related knowledge"—art, science, mathematics, administration, hygiene, social science, etc.

The alternatives of the project as a teaching unit in vocational education are several, nearly all of which are exemplified in any commercial school. They include: (a) the "practical exercise," the processes of which resemble in many respects the actual processes of the practical world (e.g., typewriting, stenographic drill, bookkeeping exercises), but which give no marketable or otherwise usable product; (b) technical subjects, organized topically, but commonly not definitely related to practical exercises then being considered—e.g., commercial arithmetic, business English; (c) joint enterprises of practical but nonproductive character—e.g., commercial school banks, or offices; and (d) jobs on a "gang" basis, largely for the commercially profitable ends of the institutions (not found in commercial schools, but often characteristic of the "practical" agricultural school with a large farm, and of institutions, as seen in chair caning, tailoring, gardening, dish-washing, etc.).

In industrial schools the alternatives to the project chiefly found are: (a) the practical job contributing towards building equipment or resulting in gifts to the learner; (b) the exercise; and (c) the series of technical lessons. But these are seldom related, whereas in the "project" it is expected to integrate them all.

About the same time that the word "project" came into popular use in discussions of vocational education, it was also becoming popular in writing on manual training. The system of sloyd* had long used the word "model" as descriptive of a single unified achievement in working wood, metal or clay. The older manual training, as distinguished from sloyd, had taught "processes" largely, using "exercises" for this purpose. In each case any given item of practical work was conceived of as belonging to a very definite and logical series cumulative towards some general form of organized knowledge or skill. The model was, apparently, more "integral" than the exercise as a stage in a "process";

---

* Editor's Note: Snedden assumed that his readers would understand this reference to the system of sloyd. However, a brief note may be of value to contemporary readers, especially for those not acquainted with the industrial arts. "Sloyd" was a system of manual training introduced in 1858 as a part of elementary instruction in Finland. It involved bench and metal work, wood carving, and basket weaving. The object of sloyd instruction was to prepare boys and young men for educational tool work rather than for a vocation. It emphasized the value of working toward useful goals and cited useful goals to justify its curriculum rather than for reasons of faculty psychology as was common at the time. Sloyd instruction spread rapidly to Sweden and other countries including the United States. A sloyd school had been established in Boston by 1888.

but it did not meet all the pedagogic needs later expressed in the practical arts "project."

In practical arts (as distinguished from vocational education) the project was expected to give an integrated outcome and one which appealed to the child's sense of the "worth-while." Hence the logical sequence of a series of projects might be hard to find, whereas, presumably, their pedagogic appeal to interests was manifest. By 1912 the project as a pedagogic unit of organization in practical arts and in vocational education had found a place, if not always a welcome.

Then arose interest in the more effective teaching of science. In science teaching the "experiment" (which was in reality more often simply a directed exercise) corresponded to the "model" and "exercise" in the practical side of manual training. Logical considerations inherent in the subject-matter of science gave rise to the so-called "logical order" (another name for the organization which seems most economical and effective to the specially informed and mature adult) which had always dominated in the selection and serial disposition of exercises and abstract studies of school science. Pedagogical organization (another term for the selection of matter and arrangement of steps making the subject most accessible to uninformed and youthful learners, with their childish motives, powers and frailties) had been largely ignored. But when a new start was attempted under the flag of "general science" it was found that a few units of the proposed rearrangement of the materials of science could be described properly as projects.

For example, if a group of pupils set out to make some photographs with school or borrowed equipment (clearly a project) it is possible to seize the interest and opportunity thus created to give a considerable amount of new knowledge (facts, interpretations), regarding the formation of the image, the use of the lens in adding to the light making the image, the chemistry of light action on certain compounds, the chemical significance of developing, etc. Similarly if a group of pupils sets out to grow some plants under controlled conditions in the schoolroom, it is readily to be seen that this project gives varied opportunities to extend their comprehension of scientific facts and principles. Other projects of a similarly useful and informing nature are now seen to be practicable: to exterminate flies in the schoolhouse; to purify the water supply; to correct smoky lamps; to improve the time-keeping qualities of a pendulum clock; to arrange soil conditions for tree planting on the grounds; to improve a school-bell system; to cleanse spotted clothing; to ascertain the wholesomeness of the home milk supply; to prevent breeding of mosquitoes; to set up a home call-bell system; to keep the teeth clean; to improve the home processes of making biscuits; and a thousand others of similar nature.

We find, however, that the term "project" is hardly elastic enough to cover all the types of units of instruction which might well be organized under the head of general science. We might want our pupils to obtain some information as to comets; can we devise what can legitimately be called a project for this purpose? Of course we can call an enterprise destined to give the pupil more knowledge of comets (using books, pictures, and, perhaps, if circumstances favor, some naked-eye observations and a peek through a telescope) a project in learning; but this simply stretches our useful term to unmanageable and unserviceable dimensions. I do not forget that Webster defines project as: "that which is projected or designed; something intended or devised; a scheme, design, or plan."

Nevertheless I had hoped that we could give to the educational project a limited and definite meaning which would make it the designation of a useful type of teaching (or learning) unit, distinct from the lesson, the exercise, the topic, the experiment, the reading assignment, the inquiry, the investigation, etc.

Perhaps it would be well to introduce modifiers to designate different grades or classes of projects. Recently, when cooperating with a committee preparing a manual on household arts, wherein it was desired to set forth as much of the work as possible on a project basis, it early became clear that in the divisions relating to the preparation and serving of food, and the making and repair of clothing, it was easy to find many projects suited to the ages and conditions of the pupils (girls 12–16) planned for. But in the divisions relating to the care of children (nursing) and the choice and equipment of the home (housing) it was difficult, if not impossible, to find suitable projects as these are ordinarily conceived. To meet the difficulty we planned a new type of project, called an "Observation and Report Project," to apply in nursing and housing. For example, a girl would undertake to survey a given house and study its location, yard, drainage, water supply, exposure to light, cold, etc., and make a report, with drawings, etc., thereon. Similar possible projects as to nursing were described.

We therefore divided all our projects into the following classes: Execution projects (school); execution projects (home and school); and observation and report projects. In addition, we described other learning units involving chiefly book study, telling by teacher, exercises and school experimentation (calling them all topics), and of these topics we distinguished several kinds.

The foregoing is submitted as a small contribution to a discussion which should receive careful attention in the near future, namely, the establishment for the various subjects of suitable teaching units. Just at present this need is acutely felt in the new secondary-school subjects, social science and general science.

15. The Concept of Purpose in Project Teaching
WILLIAM H. KILPATRICK

The word "project" is perhaps the latest arrival to knock for admittance at the door of educational terminology. Shall we admit the stranger? Not wisely until two preliminary questions have first been answered in the affirmative: First, is there behind the proposed term and waiting even now to be christened a valid notion or concept which promises to render appreciable service in educational thinking? Second, if we grant the foregoing, does the term "project" fitly designate the waiting concept? Because the question as to the concept and its worth is so much more significant than any matter of mere names, this discussion will deal almost exclusively with the first of the two inquiries. It is indeed entirely possible that some other term, as "purposeful act," for example, would call attention to a more important element in the concept, and, if so, might prove superior as a term to the word "project." At the outset it is probably wise to caution the reader against expecting any great amount of novelty in the idea here presented. The metaphor of christening is not to be taken too seriously; the concept to be considered is not in fact newly born. Not a few readers will be disappointed that after all so little new is presented.

A little of the personal may perhaps serve to introduce the more formal discussion. In attacking with successive classes in educational theory the problem of method, I had felt increasingly the need of unifying more completely a number of important related aspects of the educative process. I began to hope for some one concept which might serve this end. Such a concept, if found, must, so I thought, emphasize the factor of action, preferably wholehearted vigorous activity. It must at the same time provide a place for the adequate utilization of the

. From William H. Kilpatrick, "The Project Method," *Teachers College Record,* XIX (September, 1918), 319–335. William H. Kilpatrick was Professor of Philosophy of Education at Teachers College, Columbia University, from 1918 until 1938. He continued active teaching at numerous colleges and universities into the 1950's. His many publications in educational philosophy, curriculum, and the school and society established Kilpatrick as a renowned proponent of project teaching and of progressive education generally. This excerpt is from one of his earliest writings on the subject of project teaching. Reprinted by permission of the author and the *Teachers College Record.*

laws of learning, and no less for the essential elements of the ethical quality of conduct. The last named looks of course to the social situation as well as to the individual attitude. Along with these should go, as it seemed, the important generalization that education is life—so easy to say and so hard to delimit. Could now all of these be contemplated under one workable notion? If yes, a great gain. In proportion as such a unifying concept could be found in like proportion would the work of presenting educational theory be facilitated; in like proportion should be the rapid spread of a better practice.

But could this unifying idea be found? Here was in fact the age-old problem of effective logical organization. My whole philosophic outlook had made me suspicious of so-called "fundamental principles." Was there yet another way of attaining unity? I do not mean to say that I asked these questions, either in these words or in this order. Rather is this a retrospective ordering of the more important outcomes. As the desired unification lay specifically in the field of method, might not some typical unit of concrete procedure supply the need—some unit of conduct that should be, as it were, a sample of life, a fair sample of the worthy life and consequently of education? As these questionings rose more definitely to mind, there came increasingly a belief— corroborated on many sides—that the unifying idea I sought was to be found in the conception of wholehearted purposeful activity proceeding in a social environment, or more briefly, in the unit element of such activity, the hearty purposeful act.

It is to this purposeful act with the emphasis on the word purpose that I myself apply the term "project." I did not invent the term nor did I start it on its educational career. Indeed, I do not know how long it has already been in use. I did, however, consciously appropriate the word to designate the typical unit of the worthy life described above. Others who were using the term seemed to me either to use it in a mechanical and partial sense or to be intending in a general way what I tried to define more exactly. The purpose of this article is to attempt to clarify the concept underlying the term as much as it is to defend the claim of the concept to a place in our educational thinking. The actual terminology with which to designate the concept is, as was said before, to my mind a matter of relatively small moment. If, however, we think of a project as a pro-ject, something pro-jected, the reason for its adoption may better appear.

Postponing yet a little further the more systematic presentation of the matter, let us from some typical instances see more concretely what is contemplated under the term project or hearty purposeful act? Suppose a girl makes a dress. If she did in hearty fashion purpose to make the dress, if she planned it, if she made it herself, then I should say the instance is that of a typical project. We have a wholehearted purposeful act carried on amid social surroundings. That the dressmaking was purposeful is clear; the purpose once formed dominated each succeeding step in the process and gave unity to the whole. That the girl was wholehearted in the work was assured in the illustration. That the activity proceeded in a social environment is clear; other girls at least are to see the dress. As another instance, suppose a boy undertakes to get out a school newspaper. If he is in earnest about it, we again have the effective purpose being the essence of the project. So we may instance a pupil writing a letter (if the hearty purpose is present), a child listening absorbedly to a story, Newton explaining the motion of the moon on the principles of terrestrial dynamics, Demosthenes trying to arouse the Greeks against Philip, Da Vinci painting the *Last Supper*, my writing this article, a boy solving with felt purpose an "original" in geometry. All of the foregoing have been acts of individual purposing, but this is not to rule out group projects: a class presents a play, a group of boys organize a base-ball nine, three pupils prepare to read a story to their comrades. It is clear then that projects may present every variety that purposes present in life. It is also clear that a mere description of outwardly observable facts might not disclose the essential factor, namely the presence of a dominating purpose. It is equally true that there can be every degree of approximation to full projects according as the animating purpose varies in clearness and strength. If we conceive activities as ranging on a scale from those performed under dire compulsion up to those into which one puts his "whole heart," the argument herein made restricts the term "project" or purposeful act to the upper portions of the scale. An exact dividing line is hard to draw, and yields indeed in importance to the notion that psychological value increases with the degree of approximation to "wholeheartedness." As to the social environment element, some may feel that, however important this is to the fullest educative experience, it is still not essential to the conception of the purposeful act as here presented. These might therefore wish to leave this element out of the defining discussion. To this I should not object if it were clearly understood that the resulting concept—now essentially psychological in character—generally speaking, demands the social situation both for its practical working and for the comparative valuation of proffered projects.

With this general introduction, we may, in the first place, say that the purposeful act is the typical unit of the worthy life. Not that all purposes are good, but that the worthy life consists of purposive activity and not mere drifting. We scorn the man who passively accepts what fate or some other chance brings to him. We admire the man who is master of his fate, who with deliberate regard for a total situation forms clear and far-reaching purposes, who plans and executes with nice care the purposes so formed. A man who habitually so regulates his life with reference to worthy social aims meets at once the demands for practical efficiency and of moral responsibility. Such a one presents the ideal of democratic citizenship. It is equally true that the purposeful act is not the unit of life for the serf or the slave. These poor unfortunates must in the interest of the overmastering system be habituated to act with a minimum of their own purposing and with a maximum of servile acceptance of others' purposes. In important matters they merely follow plans handed down to them from above, and execute these according to prescribed directions. For them another carries responsibility and upon the results of their labor another passes judgment. No such plan as that here advocated would produce the kind of docility required for their hopeless fate. But it is a democracy which we contemplate and with which we are here concerned.

As the purposeful act is thus the typical unit of the worthy life in a democratic society, so also should it be made the typical unit of school procedure. We of America have for years increasingly desired that education be considered as life itself and not as a mere preparation for later living. The conception before us promises a definite step toward the attainment of this end. If the purposeful act be in reality the typical unit of the worthy life, then it follows that to base education on purposeful acts is exactly to identify the process of education with worthy living itself. The two become then the same. All the arguments for placing education on a life basis seem, to me at any rate, to concur in support of this thesis. On this basis education has become life. And if the purposeful act thus makes of education life itself, could we reasoning in advance expect to find a better preparation for later life than practice in living now? We have heard of old that "we learn to do by doing," and much wisdom resides in the saying. If the worthy life of the coming day is to consist of well-chosen purposeful acts, what preparation for that time could promise more than practice now, under discriminating guidance, in forming and executing worthy purposes? To this end must the child have within rather large limits the opportunity to purpose. For the issues of his act he must—in like limits—be held accountable. That the child may properly progress, the total situation—all the factors of life, including comrades—speaking, if need be through the teacher, must make clear its selective judgment upon what he does, approving the better, rejecting the worse. In a true sense the whole remaining discussion is but to support the contention here argued in advance that education based on the purposeful act prepares best for life while at the same time it constitutes the present worthy life itself.

16. The Dalton Plan in Practice

HELEN PARKHURST

I come now to a consideration of the Dalton Laboratory Plan in its practical application to the problem of education. Perhaps in order to clear the ground it is well to begin by indicating what it is not.

The Dalton Laboratory Plan is not a system or a method, which through ages of use has petrified into a monotonous and uniform shape, to be branded on to succeeding generations of pupils as sheep are branded on going into a fold. It is not a curriculum, which, all too often, is simply the machine by means of which the brand is stamped upon the individuals caught in the meshes of the system. Practically speaking, it is a scheme of educational reorganization which reconciles the twin activities of teaching and learning. When intelligently applied it creates conditions which enable the teacher to teach and the learner to learn.

In order to apply the scheme it is not necessary or even desirable to abolish classes or forms as units of organization in the school, nor the curriculum as such. The Dalton Laboratory Plan preserves both. Each pupil is classified as a member of a form, and for each form a maximum and a minimum curriculum is drawn up. But at its inception it lays the whole work proposition before the pupils in the shape of a contract-job. The curriculum is divided up into jobs and the pupil accepts the work assigned for his class as a contract. Though dispensed with above middle school, the younger children may sign a definite contract which is returned to each individual as soon as his job is completed.

From Helen Parkhurst, "The Plan in Practice," chap. III, *Education on the Dalton Plan* (New York: E. P. Dutton and Company, Inc., 1922). Helen Parkhurst originated a laboratory plan for individualized teaching in the schools of Tacoma, Washington, in 1910 which later became internationally known as the Dalton Plan. She established the Children's University School in New York City in 1916 to demonstrate the laboratory plan and served as Principal until her retirement in 1942. Modifications of the Dalton Plan and similar plans are today generally accepted as part of good teaching, especially in the elementary schools. Long recognized as one of the leading educators of the twentieth century, Miss Parkhurst has lectured throughout the world and has been honored and decorated by many foreign governments for her contributions to education and psychology. Her latest book, *Undertow*, was published by Farrar, Straus and Company, New York, in 1963. A simultaneous edition of *Undertow* was published in Canada by Ambassador Books, Ltd., Toronto. This selection from one of her earliest writings is reprinted by permission of E. P. Dutton and Company, Inc. Copyright 1922 by E. P. Dutton and Company, Inc. Renewed 1950 by Helen Parkhurst.

"I———, pupil of ——— standard form, contract to do the ——— assignment.

                                        Date and signature ———."

As every month of the year has its own assigned work, a contract-job for any one form comprises a whole month's work. For convenience we arrange the different parts of the curriculum under the heading of major and minor subjects:

Major Subjects.	*Minor Subjects.*
Mathematics	Music
History	Art
Science	Handiwork
English	Domestic Science
Geography	Manual Training
Foreign Languages, etc.	Gymnastics, etc.

The first category of subjects is not more important than the other, but they are classified as "major" because they are used as the basis of promotion in most schools, and college entrance examinations thus necessitate that more time should be given to them. The value of the minor subjects lies in their expansive influence upon the student. The study of them creates a response to beauty and also an increased power of expression. But if in the lower school, which includes children ranging from eight to twelve years, foreign languages are not required as a basis for promotion, they should be classified as minor subjects for lower-school pupils.

For the purpose of simplifying the initial application of the Dalton Laboratory Plan, I recommend that it should be applied firstly to major subjects alone. As the new scheme becomes familiar it can gradually be extended to the minor subjects. Take, for example, a school wherein the major subjects for Form II are Mathematics, Science, History, Geography, English, and French. The first contract-job for a pupil belonging to that form would be a block of the year's curriculum comprising a month's work in each of these major subjects. In the United States we reckon a school month as twenty days. The contract would therefore cover the ground divided as below:

Twenty Days

FORM II CONTRACT JOB

1 month of French	1 month of English	1 month of Science	1 month of Mathematics	1 month of Geography	1 month of History

This diagram represents a required standard of work for the performance of which each pupil in Form II would contract. Though the standard is the same, the pupils are not. As their mental legs must be of
different lengths, their rate of speed in study must vary also. Some
may not even need the twenty days for their contracted work; others
may not be able to get it done in that time. It is of the essence of the
Dalton Laboratory Plan that pupils should progress each at his own
rate, for only so can the work be assimilated thoroughly. Thus each
pupil must be allowed to organize his method of working as he thinks
best. Unfortunately at the outset we cannot assume that these pupils
know how to work, though as the new plan is put into operation they
will gradually learn to organize both their time and work to better and
better advantage. But efficiency means speed, and speed will only be
attained when good habits of work are established. It takes time to coun-
teract the habit of dependence bred in the pupil by constantly telling
him what to do, when and how to do it. This system made him a servant, occasionally an efficient servant, but always dependent on orders.
And though the reorganization of school machinery is quickly effected
the response of the pupil to the changed conditions is not always as
rapid. It is the business of the teacher to see that the adjustment proceeds, however, slowly. The process can be helped by making the
divided curriculum clear, and by seeing that the pupil grasps the whole
scope and nature of the work he contracts to accomplish. Unless he understands what is required of him his organization of his time will
be defective.

By giving his task in the form of a contract for whose execution he
feels himself responsible, we give the work dignity and him the consciousness of a definite purpose. This feeling is increased if we make him
aware of our confidence in his desire and in his power to execute it. A
pupil must not, however, be permitted to continue the study of any
major subject beyond the limits of the month's assignment unless he
has completed his contract in every subject. He must not be allowed
to work up to a higher standard than his form average in one or two subjects and fall below it in the rest of them. This would merely give him
an opportunity of evading progress in those studies in which he is weak
and lose to him the value of correlated and vitalized subjects. Uniformity of standard insures that he will so organize his time that most of it
will be devoted to overcome his individual weaknesses and difficulties. The plan teaches him to *budget his time* so that it is sufficient
to his needs and to have him go slowly and thoroughly. In this way
he will be well prepared for each succeeding step. His subject diet will
be well balanced and his culture will be well rounded.

The amount of any monthly assignment is a part and a very vital part of the teacher's problem. A good curriculum should be so balanced and co-related that neither too much nor too little is included in the contract-job. In the lower school not more should be required than the pupils can easily accomplish by a wise division of their time. That a ten-year-old child should learn all that a normal child of his age can learn is the ideal to set before us. A study of child psychology is necessary if we are to reorganize the machinery of education so that it corresponds to his powers and satisfies his needs at every age.

Turning from the pupil to the school building, it is evident that the Dalton Laboratory Plan exacts the establishment of laboratories, one for each subject in the curriculum, though with a small teaching staff two subjects may be studied in a single laboratory. A specialist in that particular subject, or subjects, should be in charge of each laboratory whose relation to the scheme I will deal with later on. For the moment I want to emphasize the point that these laboratories are the places where the children experiment—where they are free to work on their jobs, not places where they are experimented upon.

The text-book library of the school must be distributed among these laboratories according to subject. It is of course essential that the necessary books should be always accessible to every student—a supply of scientific books in the science laboratory, history books in the history laboratory, and so on. With regard to these books, it is well to have a few standard text-books and to increase as far as possible the number of reference books. Do not be afraid of including in the school library books that are designed for adult readers, the kind of books which have hitherto been found rather on home, than on school, bookshelves. Remember that no book can be too well written to interest a child. The dry terseness of the ordinary school manual, devoid of any literary quality, is responsible for half the distaste of learning so characteristic of the average school boy or girl. It is at school that our future men and women should become acquainted with those literary treasures which are the common heritage of humanity. And regarded merely as a mine of information, nothing could be more valuable in the development of the pupil's intelligence than the opportunity thus given him of comparing the different views of different authors on the subject he is studying.

Among the impediments to true education which is ruthlessly abolished by the Dalton Laboratory Plan is the time-table. Even to the teacher the time-table is a bugbear. How often have I heard head masters and mistresses complain of the difficulty of dividing time so that no member of the teaching staff should feel his special subjects slighted! As a result the time-table is usually compiled rather in the interest of the instructors than of the pupils. To the latter the time-table is nothing less than a curse. Its banishment is in fact the first step towards his liberation.

Let us assume that in a given school laboratory time for all classes or forms extends from 9 to 12 o'clock every morning. Under the Dalton Plan this three-hour period is devoted to the study of the major subjects—Geography, History, Mathematics, Science, English, and French. Before setting out to organize their time themselves each pupil consults his teacher, who, under the new plan, has become a subject specialist, or adviser. Together they go over the pupil's contract work, classifying his subjects as strong and weak. Those subjects which a child loves and enjoys studying will usually be found among his strong subjects. The subjects he is weak in are almost invariably those which he finds difficult to understand and assimilate, chiefly because he has not hitherto been able to give enough time to them.

For the sake of clarity I will take a concrete example. Mary Smith is a member of Form II. When, with the aid of her adviser, she has sorted out her subjects, we will suppose that they fall into the two following categories:

Weak Subjects.	*Strong Subjects.*
Mathematics	English
French	History
	Geography
	Science

In relation to the three hours' laboratory time at her disposal we may express her individual needs by the following equation:

Three Hours' Laboratory Time

Mathematics + French = English + History + Geography + Science
(Weak Subjects)   (Strong Subjects)

Having accepted her contract-job she must keep the whole job in mind, and being weak in French and Mathematics she needs to devote as much time to them as to her four strong subjects. But if the time-table were in force, Mary, despite her difficulties, would only be allowed as long for her Mathematics and French as the other pupils in Form II, many of whom might be strong in them. Can a more complete condemnation of the time-table be found than this simple demonstration of its working?

Emancipated from its tyranny, Mary's equation will change as she eliminates antipathy to, or weakness in, those subjects. But as long as her problem can be expressed in the terms of the above equation, she should devote half of her three available hours every day to Mathematics and French, and only the remaining half to the other four subjects. If she is stronger in French than in Mathematics then the one-and-one-half hours should be divided accordingly.

Mary, will, however, be free to choose which subject she will take up first, and she will go into the laboratory consecrated to that subject. Having chosen it at the moment when her interest in it is keen, she will do better work and do it more quickly too. Once in the laboratory Mary proceeds to study as an individual, but if she finds other members from Form II there she works with them. This is the rule of the laboratory under the Dalton Plan. It subdivides and reduces the large class group and it creates a small group of pupils doing intensive work, which stimulates discussion and exercises social influence. The educative value of such small groups is immense in giving an atmosphere to the laboratory, in providing occasions for social adjustment and experience. It provides invaluable play of mind upon mind. As Mary has entered that laboratory voluntarily, and can leave it for another when she feels inclined, no problems of discipline arise. Her mind comes in with her and goes out with her, disciplined by interest in the subject, harnessed—the whole of it—to her job. No time is wasted, for though the general time-table has gone Mary has, in consultation with her adviser, made a time-table for herself. This is very important, especially in the case of the younger children, in order to inculcate the value of time. To spend it in supplying our mental and moral needs is to put it to the wisest use.

It is also essential to Mary that she should realize exactly what progress she is making in the subject of her choice. For this purpose I invented the graph device before alluded to. As it merits a chapter to itself I will only now refer to it casually as a part of the laboratory equipment and procedure. There are three sets of graphs. The first provides each special teacher and adviser with the means of following the individual progress of each pupil, and of comparing it with that of the other members of the class. It also enables the pupil himself to compare his progress with that of his classmates. But Mary has also her own contract-job graph, on which she records her daily progress. The third graph pictures the progress of the class or form as a whole, as well as the individual progress.

So that the pupil should never lose sight of the job in its entirety, progress is measured in weeks of work accomplished. Mary has six major subjects with four weeks of work on each of them. Her contract thus entails twenty-four weeks of work. On the weekly graph she is therefore marked, not in each separate subject, but in the number of weeks' work done out of the total required, week by week.

In this manner a pupil advances steadily, job by job, through the curriculum of his class. If in a school year of nine or ten months he only finishes eight jobs on account of absence or illness, he begins the ninth job in the following year. The clever child may, on the contrary, accomplish in one year the work mapped out to cover eighteen months. Often the slow, apparently less intelligent, child gains in rapidity, and in any case he builds well and soundly at his own natural rate.

17. Let's Give Winnetka Another Chance

M. L. STORY

On March 16, 1926 Dr. Robert H. Goddard successfully fired, for the first time in history, a liquid-fueled rocket into the air. Acknowledged today as an event of incalculable significance, Dr. Goddard's experiment was scarcely noted beyond the limits of the Massachusetts meadows where it was conducted. Few people could sense its future importance because of then-existing limitations, not in the theory, but in its practical implementation. Efficient fuels and large-thrust motors were not to come for several decades.

With a sense of excitement, even urgency, one may establish a strikingly exact kind of educational parallel by recalling such a momentous educational experiment as the Winnetka Plan, also developed in the '20's. This experiment too was beautifully flawless in theory. It was, in fact, infinitely more acceptable to a thinking public than Goddard's epochal fireworks because it struck decisively at obvious and well recognized flaws in education—its antiquated horizontal organization characterized by the absurd lockstep pattern, its failure to allow an individual to progress at his own best speed, its lack of a specific program which emphasized the pupil's social development, its failure to provide adequate creative and recreative activities, and its woeful lack of individual and group guidance.

From M. L. Story, "Let's Give Winnetka Another Chance," *The Educational Forum*, XXVII, No. 1 (November, 1962), 99–102. M. L. Story is Assistant Chief, Educational Services Branch, National Aeronautics and Space Administration, Washington, D.C. Reprinted by permission of *The Educational Forum* and Kappa Delta Pi.

Locked away in the old patent files of educational history are secrets of astounding import for modern times. Why? Because we are suddenly in a position today to *make them work successfully*. The necessary new fuels and thrust—programmed learning, standardized testing, television, techniques of guidance, and a veritable host of new teaching aids and audio-visual techniques—furnish the vital new ingredients, none of which was available when Dr. Carleton Washburne and his staff boldly outlined a truly rational program of education. Calmly and methodically, these educational pioneers accomplished all the major steps toward the goal by doing one thing thoroughly. *They raised all the right questions.* Today the sequel remains simply to be enacted. The answers, as in the case of rocket technology, have at last become available.

One might, of course, cite with equal logic the Dalton Plan, the Contract Method, or a dozen other experimental patterns which originated in the dynamic '20's and '30's. None was actually a failure. Their effects remain as lasting evidence of the prophetic soundness of their educational diagnoses.

What is the Winnetka Plan? To quote a brief excerpt from the *Dictionary of Education*, edited by Carter V. Good,

the curriculum is divided into two parts, namely, common essentials and social and creative activities; pupils work individually at their own rates on the first part, largely by means of workbooks, progressing only as rapidly as their abilities permit; in the social and creative activities, measurement of achievement is not attempted, and much group work is done.

Embodied in this all too brief and unpretentious statement is a simple theory, an idea about education. Yet it undoubtedly has greater potential significance for humankind than the combined discoveries of Newton, Einstein, and Goddard. While physicists protest in laughing astonishment, let us actually consider its implications in the full light of such a bold claim.

If such a theory is completely accurate, there can be little doubt of its superiority to any theory which simply involves control or manipulation of the material universe. Isn't it fairly obvious that a real breakthrough in the education of the human potentiality would completely overshadow and transcend any and all kinds of advancements in the mere use of machines? After all, these are the mere products of working intelligence and can never conceivably have comparable status with it.

The extraordinary merits of the Winnetka Plan and other similar innovations have long been recognized, but the means to make them work with unqualified success have seemed almost inaccessible. What these plans developed in common, however, is precisely the ingredient for which our modern schools are frantically groping. They began, boldly and unabashedly, with the acceptance of *individual rates of learning* and tried, in a revolutionary way, to actually do something about it *for every student*. They recognized with equal logic and directness the psychological and social importance of peer groups and meticulously provided for socialization patterns far superior to those in most modern schools. In short, they recognized the blunt distinction between tool-subject mastery, which must be individualized (even in the lonely isolation of machine booths), and that learning which must (in a democracy) be socialized to be effective. In most cases the school day was about equally divided between these two categories.

What they lacked were the clear cut means to develop and administer effective individual programs of learning. They were forced to rely upon unprogrammed workbook exercises, or upon units or "contracts" which were largely unvalidated in terms of specific learning objectives. Typically, a student was handed his learning materials and allowed to proceed as rapidly as he was able toward the mastery of them. Proper guidance, supervision, and evaluation were the crucial factors. Most important of all, however, were the difficult intangibles involved in the basic *media* of instruction in the individualized, "common essentials" program. It is in this area, as well as those of guidance, supervision and evaluation, that modern educational advancements can furnish a new assurance of success.

Today's statistical techniques and computer speeds make possible and feasible almost any type of standardization study in the skill and content areas. Above all, they permit test standardization which can literally guarantee an accurate evaluation of results. Not only can basic tool-subject mastery be accurately evaluated, but inventories in a variety of other areas such as attitudes, interests, and personality permit a comprehensiveness of evaluation undreamed of in the early experiments. Evaluation was undoubtedly a crucial factor in all such early experiments simply because such systems, in order to survive and spread, had to prove beyond all doubt that they were superior to conventional and traditional school patterns. This was simply not possible three or four decades ago. It has become easily possible today for any superior system of education to prove this fact conclusively simply because modern techniques of appraisal have not only become exceedingly effective but have also achieved public acceptance.

The important factor is that, once such a program is under way, its unmistakable right direction will give steady impetus to the solution of problems which may still exist. Rapid progress in education has never been possible because its philosophy and accustomed pattern have been almost completely static since the days of Socrates. A dynamic pattern, which provided a great number of open-ended avenues of improvement and refinement of process, would immediately challenge our best minds and resources to the task and also provide for a freedom of direction which would inevitably lead to prodigious advancement. Something like the Winnetka plan is undoubtedly the right point of departure. Its general adoption, even for a decade, would lead to amazing advancement in American education.

Such a proposal is anything but radical. The seed has long since germinated in the rich soil of America. It has the highest compatability with the modern search for superior and gifted pupils. It offers a much more logical approach than most patterns of acceleration and enrichment, and, most important of all, it applies the same logic to every pupil, including the "dull normal."

Also, it is especially significant that two decades of public anguish about education should just about make the time ripe for real innovation. We are at last in a position to circumvent the well known cultural lag, which, of course, has always been the knottiest problem of all. If the American public is still inertia-bound, we can at least extend its scientific benefits to some of the underprivileged nations which we are currently helping as they formulate new education systems. Let us begin to be bold and actually practice these fundamental laws of education which cry for general acceptance:

1. An efficient system of education must allow for upward progress through the system at the individual pupil's own best rate of speed.
2. Wholesome social and psychological development of pupils must be systematically accomplished.
3. Our best understanding of the democratic process must govern every facet of the school program at all times.

To attempt, as we have awkwardly done for many years, to apply these principles within a rigid grade-system whose unconsidered rational is the strange one of culling, sorting and classifying pupils within the weird strait jacket called a grade in school—and all this merely because they are chronologically the same age, is some sort of insanity. We have reached universal agreement that holding a youngster back or pushing him forward too rapidly is an injustice. Why not use the new developments now available to us to take down the horizontal bars which have held students rigidly within grade compartments and throw them away forever. Let us put up instead a vertical ladder of great height for each student and encourage him to climb it as rapidly as he can.

18. *The Shift Toward Unit Teaching*

HARRY LLOYD MILLER

The negative approach to our problem is easily stated. Now that the field is cleared for a new adventure, a single sentence is enough to raise the issue. *The daily "lesson" must go.* It fits nobody. All the paraphernalia of pedagogy fabricated to negotiate the "lesson" must go. The practice of setting up an undifferentiated object, called the average mind, in front of which the customary motions of teaching are performed, however systematically, must go. A clean sweep will have to be made. A working group will be substituted for the conventional class organization. *Units of learning, comprehensive in their nature, will be substituted for "lessons."* The shift of emphasis is perfectly definite.

If a broken line is drawn and above it is written the word *Process* and then the line is continued with a heavy bar separating the two parts, and the other side labelled *Product,* we shall get from the picture a start in the new direction by way of antithesis. Different lines are pursued in the processes of arriving at a similar product. The three broken lines are supposed to represent the paths three different pupils might trace in arriving at a given result. No two pupils will travel identical roads. The roads are built in the process.

Process *Product*

From Harry Lloyd Miller, "Building Creative Units of Learning," chap. I, *Creative Learning and Teaching* (New York: Charles Scribner's Sons, 1927), pp. 10–12. Harry Lloyd Miller was Professor of Education and Principal of the Wisconsin High School at the University of Wisconsin when this pioneering book was published. Glenn Frank, then President of the University of Wisconsin, recognized Miller's shift of emphasis in a perceptive introduction to the book which concluded with the following words.

"The Miller approach to the educational process promises to give us schools in which there will be more learning and less teaching. He is showing us both by what he is doing and by what he is saying that the teacher's first duty is to keep out of the student's way and that his highest function is to serve as stimulator and guide in the learning process. Under Mr. Miller's leadership the teacher ceases to be a mere clerk in the storeroom of accumulated knowledge."

We have been delivering the product to our students in the forms of ready-made conclusions, printed pages, formulated truth, lectures, lessons, "moving" pictures, slides, laws, and the like. A vast *structure* of learning has been developed and stereotyped. The student is now to be started in the processes by which these products are achieved and by modes of participation enter into a creative significance. Diagnosis of processes will supersede criticism of finished products. *Directing study* will take the place of hearing lessons recited and any form of supervised study which the lesson-hearing school has found palliative. In technique the teacher will be concerned mainly with the pupils' habits of study, and he will seek to make productive the activity of boys and girls in a class hour characterized by the work-spirit. More and more the pupil will be guided in the appraisal of his own product. Self-criticism will be far more significant than teacher-criticism. An error the pupil is stimulated to discover in his own work will be valued far above a hundred canonized mistakes listed by the teacher under the *rain* and the *reign* of red ink. No longer will teachers be found examining the *finished* product of their students and rejoicing over student failure. Criticising and scolding will give way to refreshing forms of guidance in the pursuit of central ideas. The spectacle of the recitation in which a half-dozen pupils hold up hands apparently eager to recite and in the same class a half-dozen or more not engaging in that form of physical exercise will also pass. The shift of emphasis calls for a new technique. Failures and mistakes will not be used to confirm bad habits. Guidance in the *creative* will take the place of testing the *accretive*. It is the chance to make one's own appraisal that furnishes the basis of growth in intelligence. *Pupil power* will have the right of way over *teacher talk*. To guide mental life and to stimulate curiosity are vital in any true education.

19. *Society And Education*

BOYD H. BODE

A characteristic trait of the American people is its faith in education. Our public school system is the embodiment of the belief that
the individual is entitled to enter upon his social heritage and that the
cultivation of a body of common interests is essential to the life and
security of the nation. On the whole the tendency of our educational
system has been in the direction of the democratic ideal and away from
the ideal of caste or class. Yet it must be admitted that the democratic ideal is not always clearly and steadily envisaged, and that
our educational achievements do not always conform to the spirit of
real democracy. As a nation we have not been remarkably successful in
understanding the psychology of other people, and as individuals we
easily become absorbed in material pursuits, to the neglect of other values. For this result our educational system cannot wholly disclaim responsibility. If national history becomes a matter of self-glorification,
or if earning power becomes our chief measure of success, the result of
education becomes, to that extent, a source of division and not of coöperation and mutual understanding. Again, if education is mainly a
matter of rote and drill, if it touches no vital enthusiasms, and arouses
no deep-seated sympathies, there is no enrichment of life, except incidentally, and no development of that humane, tolerant, broadly sympathetic temper of mind which we call the democratic attitude. The
results achieved by our educational system have been, to a considerable
extent, random and incidental, and fall short of what we might reasonably expect if our educational activities were pervaded and directed
by a conscious ideal.

It is worth while to remind ourselves that there is no inherent magic

From Boyd H. Bode, "Education and Democracy," chap. III, *Fundamentals of
Education* (New York: The Macmillan Company, 1921), pp. 58–62. Boyd H. Bode
was Professor of Education at The Ohio State University when *Fundamentals of Education* was published. He authored or co-authored more than a dozen major works
in education, psychology, and philosophy during a career of professional leadership
that spanned more than forty years. Although influenced by John Dewey, Bode was
a recognized giant of the progressive education movement in his own right. Reprinted by permission of Eleanor B. Browne.

in education by virtue of which it automatically promotes the ends of democracy. Education is a tool that can be made, and has been made, to serve many masters. It can deepen lines of cleavage and can consolidate one class as against other classes or one interest as against other interests. Education was never more widespread or more effectively conducted than in recent times, yet it did not prevent the World War; it made this war more terrible than any that preceded it. There is no good reason to think that more education will, in itself, safeguard democracy or safeguard us from other catastrophic wars. To bring about this result we must have a different quality of education, which means education conducted in a different spirit and with different standards of value.

It appears, then, that society and education stand in a relation of reciprocal cause and effect. The character of a given society determines the character of its educational system, and the character of this system, in turn, determines the character of the society. At first sight this looks like a hopeless circle. If a society were not subject to changes arising from other than educational sources, this would presumably be the case. But in this world of change new conditions are constantly arising, which call for corresponding changes on the side of education. The development of commerce and industry, for example, brought with it a new social and political consciousness on the part of the various groups or classes. With such changes there comes a demand for vocational training, and also a demand for a type of training that has a more direct bearing on social and economic conditions than the older forms of education, which were the expression of the needs and the organization of an earlier social order. There is always some change taking place, so that the social order never becomes entirely petrified, but always retains a certain degree of flexibility. Education, consequently, tends to be somewhat broader than it would ordinarily be if classes or occupations were fixed and unchanging. And this is precisely where education finds its unique obligation and opportunity. Its proper function is not merely to preserve the achievements of the past, but to prepare the way for further changes. In other words, education must cultivate the knowledge and the temper of mind by means of which progress can be made to depend less upon conflict and haphazard adjustment and more upon intelligent coöperation on the basis of mutual understanding or sympathetic insight. This does not mean that the schools are to be used as a means of propaganda, but as a means of cultivating an interest in the things that pertain to our common life and an appreciation of the fact that we are "members one of another." If we make the social criterion our measure of educational values, we shall be employing the most effective method for making education an agency both for preserving the achievements of the past and for promoting social progress and reform.

What counts, in short, is not only the materials that are taught, but the spirit in which they are taught, the spirit that is made to pervade our educational system. A system is not democratic simply because it is made available to everybody or because it is administered without distinction of persons. In a Spartan scheme of education all are included and all are treated equally, but it is not democratic because the individual is subordinated, is made a means to an end; and that end, the State. To be truly democratic, education must treat the individual himself as the end and set itself the task of preparing him for that intellectual and emotional sharing in the life and affairs of men which embodies the spirit of the Golden Rule. In proportion as common interests are permitted to outweigh special interests, the individual is becoming humanized and the successive adjustments of life will be made in the direction of democracy and in accordance with the needs of an expanding life.

20. The Nature of Subject Matter and Two Methods of Organizing It

ROY O. BILLETT

Relation of Subject Matter to Racial Experience. A few educationists have regarded subject matter as a sort of fifth wheel in secondary education. Whether they are right or wrong should be apparent from a consideration of the nature of subject matter.

A first effort at definition of subject matter is likely to stop with the statement that subject matter is English, social studies, mathematics, science, foreign language, practical arts, business studies, physical and health education, music, and art. This definition seems all right as far as it goes. But such a statement leaves unexpressed a number of important facts about subject matter.

From Roy O. Billett, "The Nature of Subject Matter and Two Methods of Organizing It," chap. VII, *Fundamentals of Secondary-School Teaching* (Boston: Houghton Mifflin Company, 1940), pp. 161–167. Roy O. Billett was Professor of Education at Boston University when this comprehensive volume on unit organization and teaching was published. Emeritus Professor since 1957, he has continued to publish major works and to teach at universities in Florida. Reprinted by permission of the Houghton Mifflin Company.

In the first place, it should be recognized that the several subject-matter fields are collectively broad enough to encompass the whole of human learning. Subject matter began when some individual first represented in words or other symbols the meanings, insights, concepts, skills, and resultant ideals, attitudes, and appreciations which he had derived from interaction with his environment. Today, collectively, the subject-matter fields represent all the vital and meaningful experiences of the race.

Second, each of the subject-matter fields is elementary enough to extend down to the nursery school, and complex enough to include the farthest upward and outward reaches explored by professional workers, by university workers at the research level, and by all other creative workers.

Third, no natural boundaries separate the several subject-matter fields one from another. They are parts of a whole cloth woven on the loom of human experience.

Fourth, no subject-matter field is static. It is as dynamic as human life. It may seem at times to have been locally mummified in outmoded texts and courses of study never revised. But subject matter itself changes, now slowly, now kaleidoscopically, from year to year and from day to day as the race acquires new capacities for and tendencies toward behavior.

Fifth, because of its changing and cumulative nature, subject matter has undergone countless organizations and reorganizations. Similar reorganizations will continue to be necessary as long as civilized man endures. In the past, the organization and reorganization of subject matter has been dominated by a logical purpose, by the intent to facilitate the acquisition of new subject matter and to test out the old.

Certainly, for the specialist in a given subject-matter field the logical[1] type of organization will always be desirable and necessary, but whether logical organization suits the purposes of the elementary- or secondary-school teacher is another question. In fact, it is conceivable that the valid objection to the past use of subject matter for educative purposes at the elementary- or secondary-school level is to be found in the way subject matter has been selected and organized and not in the intrinsic nature of subject matter. To try to think of secondary education without any reference to subject matter is to conjure up teacher and pupil activities distressingly akin to the blind interplay of primitive cosmic forces. The relation of subject matter to racial experience would seem to make the former indispensable in systematic efforts to guide and direct the educative growth of individual human beings.

---

[1] The differentiae of logical and psychological organization are brought out in subsequent paragraphs.

The outcry against subject matter indicates that something is wrong somewhere, and the assertion is ventured that it is the selection and organization of subject matter and not the subject matter itself. At least, the discussion proceeds on that hypothesis. Two or three questions seem in order. What is the objection, if any, to the use of logically organized subject matter in elementary and secondary education? Is any other systematic type of organization possible? If so, how does it differ from logical organization?

Logical and Psychological Organization of Subject Matter. Answers to these questions can be suggested by stating the salient general differences between *logical* organization of subject matter and a second distinctly different type of organization, which for the time being can be referred to as *psychological*. These major differences seem to be about as follows:

First, logical organization is determined by the present level of racial development in the area represented by the subject; psychological organization is determined by the present level of development of the individual pupil in the same area.

Second, logical organization is relatively constant; psychological organization varies for different pupils at the same time and for the same pupil at different times.

Third, logical organization is comprehensive, including all the outcomes of human experience to date in the sector covered by the subject, and implies the placement of these outcomes in their proper cause and effect, or sequential, relationship from the point of view of the expert in the field;[2] psychological organization is selective, making important omissions of materials without being a mere process of omitting.

Fourth, used for educative purposes below the university level, logical organization encourages learning processes characterized by rote memory and teaching processes characterized by indoctrination; psychological organization encourages learning processes characterized by logical memory and problem-solving, and teaching characterized by guidance and direction of the pupils' experiences.

Fifth, logical organization presumes the same ratio of direct and vicarious experience for all ages and for all types of pupils; psychological organization seeks a constant proper balance between direct and vicarious experience.

In a word, subject matter can be psychologically organized only with reference to the experiential levels and rates of educative growth of the pupils for whom it is prepared. It is a practical recognition of the fact that learning is not absorption but the result of experi-

[2] Hence, logical organization does not proceed "from the simple to the complex," as is so often said.

ence; that, proverbs notwithstanding, experience keeps the only school, and fools and geniuses and normal people learn in it, if they learn at all. Psychological organization in no way prevents the teacher from capitalizing on the possibilities of vicarious experience, which, after all, is one kind of experience and must play an important rôle in education. In reality, vicarious experience is the interaction of one individual with the results of the first-hand experiences of others. It is essential if the individual is to learn some things and survive. Psychological organization does not require that pupils fall off cliffs, be struck by express trains, or contract contagious or infectious disease in order to know the disastrous or unhappy results of such first-hand experiences or to know how to avoid them. On the contrary, psychological organization attempts a constantly modified and proper balance between direct and vicarious experience for each pupil. This is essential because the amount and kind of first-hand and vicarious experience which leads to optimal educative growth varies with individual pupils at a given age level, and varies with the individual pupil at different age levels. At any age level the greater the general mental ability of the pupil, the greater the possible rôle of vicarious experience; and for any given individual pupil the rôle of vicarious experience can be increased as the child grows older. Logical organization of subject matter in its very nature, not only overemphasizes vicarious experience at the elementary- and secondary-school levels, but also presents the same ratio of direct and vicarious experience to all pupils, regardless of age, aptitude, ability, interest, aim, or need.

Schematic Diagram Relating the Logical and the Psychological. The point of view being set forth here is that psychological organization is a variable which in the case of each individual pupil over a period of years tends to approach logical organization as a limit. Unlike certain mathematical variables, psychological organization ultimately reaches and temporarily coincides with its limit (Figure 21). For those individuals who arrive at this limit, the logical and the psychological are one and the same thing. But the logical level does not remain stationary. It moves to ever higher levels through the continued experience of the race, and particularly through the experiences of the comparatively small number of individuals who have arrived at the present logical level.

These statements can be illustrated by a diagram. Let point A (Figure 21) and its projection, the line AB, represent the logical level of organization of a given subject-matter field at a given time. Let lines A^1B^1 and A^2B^2 suggest the constant rising of this logical level as the race acquires new insights, meanings, concepts, skills, and hence new ideals, attitudes, and appreciations in the area represented by the sub-

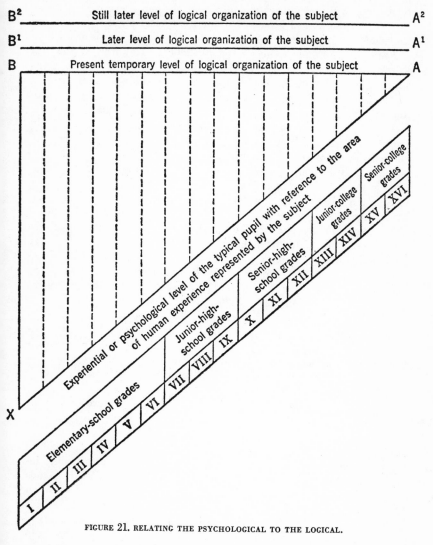

FIGURE 21. RELATING THE PSYCHOLOGICAL TO THE LOGICAL.

ject. For any given pupil at any given time, the difference between logical and psychological organization of materials varies directly with the difference between the experiential level of an expert in the field and the experiential level of the pupil in the area represented by the subject. Let the line *AX* suggest this fact. As the pupil moves from the first year of the elementary school through the successive grades to the end of the secondary-school period, the gap between the psychological and the logical lessens, but for the typical pupil it is real and impassable, even at the end of the junior-college years. This is as it is.

The Subject-Matter Criterion of Education. However, if the fact worries the teacher he can reflect profitably on the strenuous years which elapsed before he could deal with one subject-matter field at the logical level. He can try to recall how the same area appeared to him at 6 years of age, at 12, and at 18. He can study the experiential level and outlook of as many secondary-school pupils as possible in the area represented by his subject. Moreover, it would help if he considered the countless gaps in his own knowledge from the standpoint of completely logical organization, outside his own special field. These gaps in the knowledge of any adult, highly educated or not, are so numerous that the questions of fools and children have been found disconcerting to a proverbial degree. Consider the following items taken at random: (1) *a cappella;* (2) ablative; (3) binomial theorem; (4) Compromise of 1850; (5) band-saw; (6) Beowulf; (7) Mendel; (8) synecdoche and metonymy; (9) T-square; (10) *le* and *la;* (11) Gresham; (12) mortise and tenon; (13) Rosetta stone; (14) Avogadro; (15) parabola; (16) $s = \frac{1}{2}gt^2$; (17) *die, der, das;* (18) quadratic; (19) law of regression; (20) *Il Penseroso.* These items have not been selected for their relative obscurity, as the appropriate subject-matter specialist will testify. Yet it is a rare teacher who even recognizes offhand the source of all twenty, and who can employ ten or more in effective extemporaneous thought; or who can place a half dozen in complete logical relationship to the body of subject matter from which they have been abstracted. The moral is obvious.

People have always met the problems of daily life more or less effectively in total ignorance of tens of thousands of items superordinate, coordinate, or subordinate (in the logical organization of some subject-matter field) to the twenty listed above. Under the most ideal conditions of elementary, secondary, and higher education imaginable, individuals must continue to remain totally ignorant of tens of thousands of such items. Secondary-school teachers have done their duty when they have insured that within the limits of the pupil's time and of his biological heredity the items which compose the subject matter actually used in secondary-school courses have been selected because they contribute to the development of concepts, skills, ideals, attitudes, and appreciations most likely to help the individual to understand, to appreciate, and to participate in an intelligent and socially desirable way in the social and physical environment of which he is a part. This is no trivial duty, as the length of the sentence suggests.

It is folly to expect most pupils appropriately enrolled in the secondary school to achieve the logical level in any subject-matter field. With the vast increase in human capacities in all fields, particularly within the past fifty years, the phenomenal prodigy will fall far short of achieving the logical level in any field during his secondary-school career. Even in the sixteenth century that exceptional genius Francis Bacon, who proclaimed in a moment of enthusiasm, "I have taken all knowledge to be my province," expected to give his life to the realization of his ambition.

Logical organization is the indispensable tool of specialists. It is not a formula for the educative growth of all pupils at the secondary-school level.

The upshot of these considerations seems to be that the command of logically organized subject matter can no longer be the sole and direct criterion of education at the secondary level. Here it seems desirable to stop long enough to say that this is just as true of certain limited areas of traditional subject matter as it is of subject matter logically organized in toto. In the name of an outworn concept of what constitutes culture, secondary education has consisted in the past of exposure to certain bodies of subject matter distinguished chiefly by their relative antiquity and lack of application to everyday life, save through the hocus-pocus of formal discipline. These cultural materials once constituted a badge of membership in a privileged class. They were the curricular materials of a selective secondary school. They set off the educated from the untouchables; and worse yet they set off a degenerate present from a past that was only glorious. They left the unfortunate impression with many a secondary-school pupil that the world's thinking had all been done. All who could think had thought, expressed themselves in more or less (so it seemed to the pupil) incomprehensible ways, and died, long, long ago.

Some knowledge of the past and due respect for its real contributions are essential parts of a modern secondary education. But there is a time for everything under the sun, and much that baffled secondary-school pupils in the past generation never should have been encountered by them until college and university years, if at all. Moreover, it should be self-evident that worship of one's own or anybody else's ancestors is not the goal of education at any level in a democracy. The childhood of the race should not be overemphasized, nor clothed deceptively. The past should be seen as a stage out of which society has evolved and not a stage to which it should return, even if it could. So far as the writer can see, all connotations of culture incompatible with an education that functions in the best interests of the social order that maintains it, and functions according to the accepted principles of human learning, are specious and subversive of modern efforts at sound curricular reorganization. Is not culture in the modern sense a matter of degree? Is not one cultured to the extent to which he understands, appreciates, and is able to participate intelligently and in socially desirable ways in the social and physical environment of which he is now a part? Is such a concept of culture less tenable because it makes a unit dealing with the gas engine or advertising potentially more cultural for secondary-school pupils than a unit dealing with Sanskrit roots?

Present Predominance of Logical Organization and of Traditional Materials in Secondary-School Courses.   The psychological organization of secondary-school courses begins with the selection of materials on the basis of criteria which neither the subject itself nor tradition can supply. In Sections 4 and 5 of this chapter these criteria and their application will be considered in greater detail. Enough has been said so far to indicate that the psychological organization of a seconday-school course is likely to prove uphill work in its initial stages. The course which is patterned after either tradition or logical organization is still common the country over because it comes to the teacher's hand ready-made. Texts determined more by considerations derived from the logical organization of the subject or by tradition than by any other criteria are available in abundance. Fortunately the trend in textbook construction for secondary schools is toward psychological organization. Texts which reflect this trend are characterized (1) by careful attention to vocabulary burden, (2) by the use of materials in general adapted to the age level of the pupils for whom the book is intended, and (3) by an organization of those materials so far as possible in harmony with psychological principles; but, even when the textbook writer has done all that is scientifically and artistically possible, much remains to be done by the teacher and the supervisor. The textbook writer cannot know all the pupils in all the classes likely to use the book. Neither can he know all the specific learning situations of which the volume is to become a part. If he did, he could not meet all the demands of all occasions in one book. Teachers and supervisors must take up the organization of secondary-school courses where even the most able and enlightened of textbook writers necessarily leave off. The first practical step to be made by teachers and supervisors should be made in the adoption of texts which have moved as far as possible toward psychological organization at the level where the texts are to be used. As a result more books will be used than ever before; and the total number of books will be distributed among a number of titles rather than given over to a single title.

However, in the truly psychologically organized course the text is not the starting point. Instead, the books and all other materials used will be determined by accurate estimates of the levels and rates of growth of the individual pupils, in the experiential areas with which the course is primarily concerned, and by the specific phases of educative growth which the course exists primarily to promote. The course should determine the texts, not the text the course.

21. Change with Implications for Education

MAURICE P. MOFFATT

Change is rapid in our mobile, scientific and technological society, a fact which presents many challenges. As we look ahead, the implications for education at all levels are many and challenging. Keeping pace holds both sociological and economic consequences. We seem to be living in an era of astounding accomplishment in many fields of endeavor. The accumulation of knowledge is rapid, and we must think of education for today and tomorrow. In the path of this acceleration the complexity of change becomes a potent reckoning force. Any estimation of the future needs of society demands deep consideration and sound evaluation. The population of the nation and that of our schools and colleges is elevating noticeably. This factor alone is of major importance and should have a high priority in American educational thinking.

Considerable literature is appearing that depicts change and suggests some possible directives. An excellent volume is *Educational Administration in a Changing Community*.[1] In it the trends and issues in public education are discussed. Some insights into today's community are provided and suggestions are projected for gathering information and studying the community. Another interesting brochure is *Images of the Future*.[2] It deals with a new approach to the secondary school. This material is most interesting and should provoke con-

From Maurice P. Moffatt, "Change with Implications for Education," *The Journal of Educational Sociology*, XXXIII (April, 1960), 339–341. Maurice P. Moffatt is Chairman of the Department of Social Studies, Montclair State College, Montclair, New Jersey, and Chairman of the Board of Trustees, the Payne Educational Sociology Foundation. Reprinted from *The Journal of Educational Sociology* by permission.

[1] American Association of School Administrators, Department of the National Education Association. *Educational Administration in a Changing Community*. Thirty-Seventh Yearbook (Washington, D.C.: The Association, 1959).

[2] J. L. Trump, director, *Images of the Future*, Commission on the Experimental Study of the Utilization of the Staff in the Secondary School (Urbana, Illinois, 1959).

siderable thought in projecting plans for tomorrow's secondary educational structure. It touches such topics as curriculum, instructional staff, community relations, educational facilities, and administration.

The needs of society at all age levels have changed in recent decades. This necessitates the constant evaluation of education at all grades of instruction including adult education. The surge of technology and scientific development moves unabated on an unprecedented scale. The fields of transportation and communication as they play a role in the necessities of daily living are typical of current advances. Even our changing living and social habits are reflected in the creation of new types of industry. Furthermore, the increased amount of leisure provides a possibility of greater recreational time for the individual. Changes in family life are noted in various areas. The size of the American family is steadily growing larger.

Thus education in today's constant change becomes a vehicle by which the individual is provided an opportunity to continue his growth. In this process new knowledge and a variety of skills can be acquired to meet emerging demands for charting a career.

Architectural design reveals typical change in school plant construction. The ultra-modern one-story elementary school with its various features is unique in purpose. The new sprawling junior or senior high school with its distinct units and wings is a streamlined structure. It has adequate acreage for athletic fields and an area for all-weather play. At the college level the architecture may reflect the past, present, and seemingly point toward the future with their new buildings. Accordingly, the business sections of some communities are being streamlined and show the trends of the modern age in recent projects.

Confronted with a rapidly growing school population, some communities are forming a jointure with surrounding administrative units or townships at the secondary level. Furthermore, the secondary school has and is facing the problem of a split or dual session to accommodate the increased number of pupils and at the same time carry through a program. Usually a planned building expansion solves the problem at least temporarily. Colleges are being confronted with the challenge of operating the physical plant throughout the year. This type of scheduling plan would permit accelerating in the program for the undergraduate student. It would permit students to finish the regular four years of college preparation in possibly three years. Each particular institution will no doubt carefully study the advantages and complications of such a plan before coming to a decision. Some colleges across the country are expanding plant facilities with a look toward the future and increased enrollments.

Some colleges will experiment with specific programs and methods of instruction to meet the mushrooming enrollments. The lecture, independent study including reading and research, and audio-visual materials may be utilized to a greater advantage. Modern learning tools and teaching devices will be employed when deemed effective and applicable. Research in these areas will reveal new knowledge that may prove productive. No doubt class size will be a major consideration in selecting fruitful procedures.

Looking ahead to curriculum offerings and areas for study, science and mathematics will receive considerable attention. However, the social sciences, humanities and business administration will become avenues of importance. These offerings will assist the individual in better living as well as working in society. The quality of learning in a particular curricula will be in line with the demands of industry, business, professions and society. There is little doubt that well-trained graduates will be in demand as prospective leaders in various fields in the space age.

At the secondary level we are noting specific courses or enrichment programs for seniors. An advanced placement program offers college level work in specific courses that will challenge the more capable students. Colleges have instituted small group seminars with direct guidance to assure satisfactory achievement and honors programs for superior students. There is a strong probability that some colleges may make changes in the matriculation requirements as well as tighten their standards for scholastic achievement. This will tend to make undergraduates work harder and get more out of their education. Furthermore, it will alert high school pupils to consider preparation for college more seriously.

The future gives promise of obtaining increased funds from foundations and corporations to finance research in education. A growing supply of fellowships, scholarships and travel grants from various sources will be available for individuals. American institutions of higher learning will expand their summer study program abroad for students and teachers. All such projects should provide rich opportunities to enlarge one's knowledge through first-hand observation with the opportunity for study and delving into research materials.

In conclusion, the necessary leadership, financing, planning, research, experimentation and constant evaluation of programs will be most essential for education in the era ahead. Our nation's growth and expansion will present new problems and challenges for education. Small colleges have much to contribute and should play a major role with the coming bulging enrollments. At both the secondary and college levels course enrichment will receive considerable attention to meet the demands of life and the processes of society. More library materials will be needed to furnish sources for a vast increase in new knowledge.

Change, automation implications, new trends, and advanced project areas of research all will challenge education as progress, in its relentless drive, moves ahead.

22. *The Assessment of the Teacher's Personality*

A. S. BARR

Many educators believe that the teacher's personality is important in teacher effectiveness, and research seems to support the belief. Personality may be considered a factor in teacher effectiveness in somewhat the same way as scholastic proficiency, understanding of children, or verbal fluency. Whether one considers personality as a factor in teacher effectiveness depends on how one conceives of personality and its relation to the means, goals, and processes of education. In any case, the problem of personality assessment as it relates to teachers' effectiveness merits thoughtful consideration.

There are many theories of personality. As the word *personality* itself suggests, most of these theories relate to characteristics of the person; thus we speak of *personality traits*. Another way of looking at the subject, however, is to consider not qualities of the person but characteristics of performance or behavior. Whichever approach is used, there is trouble ahead, since almost any approach has limitations and advantages. For this discussion we have chosen to make a behavioristic approach.

In pursuing such an approach, we must recognize that we remove from consideration such aspects of personality as height, weight, age, complexion, bodily proportion, and physique. These are static aspects of personality, unless they can be translated into behavioral equivalents. Even though these aspects of personality may present difficul-

From A. S. Barr, "The Assessment of the Teacher's Personality," *The School Review*, LXVIII (Winter, 1960), 400–408. A. S. Barr was Professor of Education at the University of Wisconsin from 1929 until his death in 1962. He was President of the National Society of College Teachers of Education in 1949–1950, Editor of the *Journal of Educational Research* since 1928, and Editor of the *Journal of Experimental Education* since 1932. Professor Barr was widely known for his many writings and his extensive research on the personal characteristics of teachers and the measurement and prediction of teaching efficiency. Reprinted from *The School Review* by permission of The University of Chicago Press. Copyright 1960 by The University of Chicago.

ties to those who would interpret personality in behavioral terms, a behavioristic approach still has advantages, particularly since the behavioral approach makes it possible to integrate the concept of personality with that of methods of teaching. In a sense method, broadly conceived, encompasses all teacher behavior and thus personality. If we approach the problem in this way our concern expressed as a question becomes: Can descriptions of behavior provided by such terms as *considerateness, co-operativeness, expressiveness, objectivity, ethicality,* provide helpful ways of considering teacher effectiveness? Possibly, though perhaps the whole approach is too remote to have any great practical value. Perhaps some other approach would be better.

Psychology has defined the conditions for effective learning in terms of certain principles of learning. This suggests the question: Are the techniques of teaching that are presumed to grow out of learning theory encompassed by the behavioral aspects of personality, or are the behaviors found in the techniques of teaching something different? Possibly techniques of teaching grow out of another constellation of values that one needs to keep in mind. Possibly there is some unique constellation of human relationships that behavioristically constitute the essence of personality and another constellation of teacher activities that constitute technical competency.

If we attempt to characterize behavior in such broad terms as those suggested here, we must give some attention to choosing and defining the aspects of behavior that appear to be pertinent to teacher effectiveness. Many words in a standard collegiate dictionary purport to describe behavior. How does one choose from these? The literature gives the impression that the choice of vocabulary has rested pretty much on personal preference.

Some years ago the writer served on a professional jury that was attempting to prepare a short list of descriptive terms to be used in teacher evaluation. More recently the author compiled a list of terms used to describe teaching effectiveness in studies on the measurement and the prediction of teacher efficiency.[1] The project made it clear that we need a commonly accepted list of the aspects of behavior to be considered. Once a list is agreed on, each term in the list must be defined.

Before turning to problems of definition, there are several questions one might ask about the list. How long should it be? How much overlap can one expect or tolerate? Are qualities of behavior to be looked on as supplementary or complementary, or may they be conflicting? Are there hierarchies, patterns, or sequences of behaviors or aspects of behavior

[1] A. S. Barr, "The Measurement and Prediction of Teaching Efficiency, A Summary of Investigations," *Journal of Experimental Education,* XVI (June, 1948), 202–83.

that we should consider? Can some aspects of behavior be thought of as superficial, unimportant, or trivial and others as basic, highly potent, and primary? Should the terms used to describe teacher behavior reflect some particular philosophy of education, theory of learning, or concept of desirable teacher-pupil relationship?

To provide acceptable working definitions of the descriptive terms to be used in such an adventure is extremely difficult. Presumably, in keeping with a behavioristic approach all definitions need to be operational definitions. What does a reliable, emotionally stable, and resourceful teacher do? If judgments about teachers are to be based on observations of teachers' behaviors, how do we know what to look for? What to ignore? Over and above the counting of behaviors, there is, thus, the matter of pertinency. Whether a behavior, or aspect to behavior, is pertinent depends on how the behavior or the aspect is defined. If the list of terms is highly condensed, many subtle shades of meanings will probably need to be considered.

Having listed and defined the terms to be used, we may then turn to the collection of the data. Aside from pertinency, other questions must be considered: By what means may observers reach sound judgments about whether the teacher behavior observed is to be considered as evidence of the presence or the absence of some particular characteristic? Are there extenuating circumstances to be considered in passing judgment on the behavior under observation? Can behavior be considered out of context? What aspects of the context whould one consider? Is the noting of the presence and absence of behaviors sufficient? What dimensions of behavior should one consider? Is counting enough, or should the behaviors be evaluated according to some scale of values? As skilled observers know, teachers do not all have the same qualities. How does one summarize the data? Should we consider isolated behaviors or patterns of behaviors? Is the importance of items of behavior as contrasted with the mere presence or the absence of behavior a matter to be considered? Degree of pertinency? Extent? Duration? Intensity? How will the score, if there is a score, be expressed?

When one attempts to reach some over-all judgment about teacher effectiveness from judgments about the separate aspects of behavior, one is confronted with a troublesome necessity. It is common practice to calculate some sort of average, but can we safely assume that the data can be added? Is an average an adequate representation of the data? Do some aspects of behavior have special potencies in and of themselves? Are there upper and lower cutoff points? May a teacher's over-all efficiency rest on the presence or absence of some particular quality of behavior? Do various combinations of behaviors or qualities have particular significance?

If one may judge from the literature or from the vocabulary of people who talk about the effectiveness of teachers or from letters recommending teachers for positions, it would appear that there is some basis for talking about teachers in terms of personality traits or the quality aspects of behavior, but much needs to be done with the word *personality* before this approach can be useful. One might correctly say that, notwithstanding the tremendous amount of time, money, and energy expended on this approach, the adventure has not been particularly successful. Possibly, however, with more care in choosing, defining, scaling, and summarizing values the adventure may be more successful; or possibly some other concept will have to be substituted for it.

For a new look at personality testing the writer recently used an approach somewhat different from those commonly used to secure information on teachers' self-perception and the perception of others concerning certain qualities thought to be associated with teacher effectiveness. The instrument, which calls for forced judgment, was drawn on a plan somewhat different from the paired-comparison scale. The instrument is not presented as a completed one. Actually, it may create more problems than it solves, but it does illustrate certain difficulties associated with personality assessment. The approach is behavioristic, and there is some attempt to define terms. While the scale is an instrument for self-evaluation designed to be used by teachers, the approach can be used to assess supervisors, principals, and superintendents. By comparing scores and related data one may reach a judgment about the professional compatibility of teachers and administrators. Responses may be based on past experience with various types of educational personnel, or responses may be based on current behavior in situations where purposes, conditions, and achievements can be more precisely defined.

In Part A of the instrument, the participant is asked to rank himself on fifteen qualities thought to be associated with teacher effectiveness. He is also asked to rate the administrators with whom he has worked and his fellow teachers on both their value systems and their observed behavior. In Part B of the instrument the participant is asked whether he thinks he possesses "more" or "less" of each of fifteen qualities than other teachers, administrators, and members of another profession, such as law. In Part C, he is asked whether he thinks that school administrators and other teachers and finally whether he himself has "little" or "much" of each of the fifteen qualities.

To fill in the scale is tedious, but personality is complex and most attempts to evaluate it are oversimplifications. The ranking of fifteen items is difficult. Few people think of themselves as the scale asks them to. Certainly few people think of themselves as precisely as the scale asks them to. The experience of performing such a task raises all sorts of questions. We may even ask whether the personality approach to the study of teacher behavior is worth the effort devoted to it. The answer to this question should not be sought in personal preference but in further research.

The scores on Part A of the scale are coefficients of correlation calculated by any one of the several methods. The author has used the rank difference method of calculating these coefficients. Some of the correlations are related to self-perception and some to the perception of others. If one attempts further interpretation, some of the scores might be interpreted as self-sufficiency scores; and others, as measures of realistic self-perception, should this be a matter of concern. In Parts B and C scores are obtained by counting responses. These scores may be compared with those of Part A as part of a study of consistency. If the scale is used again later on, further information can be had on consistency. As one examines the information secured through such an instrument, it seems reasonable to ask: Is it possible to secure in this manner predictions about the behavior of teachers that will be more accurate than predictions arrived at by other approaches—predictions that will be useful in employing teachers or in engaging in school improvement? The question calls for further research.

The qualities used in the scale were condensed from many lists of descriptive terms used to characterize the behavior of teachers. The descriptive terms are referred to as *qualities,* but the term *quality* is used to describe behavior, not to designate the constituents of persons or traits. It is thought that the behavior of individuals will exhibit these qualities with varying degrees of consistency. It is expected that some qualities will be exhibited with high levels of consistency almost without exception, and others with less consistency. An attempt was made to distinguish between surface traits and source traits. These descriptive terms as a group are assumed to encompass the basic prerequisites to teacher effectiveness when expressed as qualities of behavior.

Because the words used in the scale may mean different things to different people, it seemed best to start with some consideration of the many meanings attached to each word. Important characteristics of behavior can be designated verbally in a variety of ways. Some of the synonyms thought to be associated with each of the fifteen qualities are listed below:

1. *Buoyancy*—Optimism, enthusiasm, cheerfulness, gregariousness, fluency, talkativeness, sense of humor, pleasantness, carefreeness, vivaciousness, alertness, animation, idealism, articulation, wittiness.

2. *Considerateness*—Concern for the feelings and well-being of others, sympathy, understanding, unselfishness, patience, helpfulness.
3. *Co-operativeness*—Friendliness, easygoingness, geniality, generousness, adaptability, flexibility, responsiveness, warmheartedness, unselfishness, charitableness.
4. *Emotional stability*—Realism in facing life's problems, freedom from emotional upsets, constancy, poise, self-control.
5. *Ethicalness*—Good taste, modesty, morality, conventionality, cultural polish, refinement.
6. *Expressiveness*—Skill in expression, verbal fluency, vivaciousness, communicativeness, literateness.
7. *Forcefulness*—Dominance, independence, self-sufficiency, determinedness, purposefulness, persuasiveness.
8. *Intelligence*—Mental alertness, academic aptitude, capacity for abstract thinking, power to comprehend relationships.
9. *Judgment*—Wisdom in the selection of appropriate courses of action, discretion in dealing with others, foresight, prudence, common sense, clearheadedness.
10. *Objectivity*—Fairness, impartiality, open-mindedness, freedom from prejudice, sense of evidence.
11. *Personal magnetism*—Dress, physique, absence of defects, personal magnetism, neatness, cleanliness, posture, personal charm, appearance.
12. *Physical energy*—Readiness for effective action, force, vigor, energy, eagerness to succeed, ambition, motivation, vitality, endurance.
13. *Reliability*—Accuracy, dependability, honesty, punctuality, responsibility, conscientiousness, painstakingness, trustworthiness, sincerity.
14. *Resourcefulness*—Capacity for approaching things in a novel manner, initiativeness, originality, creativeness, enterprisingness.
15. *Scholastic proficiency*—High scholastic aptitude, high scholastic grade point average, thorough knowledge of subject matter, well informed on many subjects, high verbal aptitude, widely read.

Many characteristics are associated with teaching success, and the words used to indicate these characteristics have many meanings, as the many synonyms listed indicate. To further orient the respondent, he was given a word-meaning test on the fifteen qualities. In this test he was asked to underline three words or groups of words that best expressed his understanding of the term under consideration:

I. *Buoyancy*

(1) Enthusiasm (2) Optimism (3) Vivaciousness (4) Cheerfulness (5) Bouncing (6) Wittiness

II. *Considerateness*

(1) Sympathy (2) Easygoingness (3) Unselfishness (4) Understanding (5) Patience (6) Helpfulness

III. *Co-operativeness*

   (1) Friendliness (2) Positiveness (3) Flexibility (4) Unselfishness (5) Adaptableness (6) Easygoingness

IV. *Emotional stability*

   (1) Self-control (2) Constancy (3) Punctuality (4) Dependability (5) Unemotionality (6) Unsympatheticness

V. *Ethicalness*

   (1) Modesty (2) Morality (3) Conventionality (4) Prudishness (5) Refinement (6) Respectability

VI. *Expressiveness*

   (1) Talkativeness (2) Vivaciousness (3) Communicativeness (4) Verbal fluency (5) Literateness (6) Intelligibility

VII. *Forcefulness*

   (1) Determinedness (2) Persuasiveness (3) Courageousness (4) Purposefulness (5) Dominance (6) Proneness to action

VIII. *Intelligence*

   (1) Mental alertness (2) Academic aptitude (3) Capacity for abstract thinking (4) Sagaciousness (5) Power of comprehending relationships (6) Practical insightedness

IX. *Judgment*

   (1) Common sense (2) Discretion (3) Foresight (4) Wisdom (5) Capacity for unbiasness (6) Clear thinking

X. *Objectivity*

   (1) Impartiality (2) Unemotionality (3) Factuality (4) Open-mindedness (5) Unprejudicality (6) Faithfulness

XI. *Personal magnetism*

   (1) Cleanliness (2) Seduciveness (3) Neatness (4) Sociability (5) Physical attractiveness (6) Comeliness

XII. *Physical energy, drive*

   (1) Persistence (2) Vitality (3) Ambition (4) Endurance (5) Vigor (6) Restlessness

XIII. *Reliability*

   (1) Honesty (2) Accuracy (3) Punctuality (4) Dependability (5) Responsibility (6) Trustworthiness

XIV. *Resourcefulness*

   (1) Self-sufficiency (2) Originality (3) Uninhibitedness (4) Creativeness (5) Enterprisingness (6) Initiativeness

XV. *Scholastic proficiency*

> (1) Good school grades (2) Love of books (3) Love of the abstract (4) Learnedness (5) Wisdom (6) Rationality

In the search for patterns of response, the ranking of the fifteen items was carried out in a prescribed manner. In filling in the scale the participant was asked first to consider the items in groups of three:

The three qualities most characteristic of the respondent's behavior

The three qualities least characteristic of the respondent's behavior

The three that appear to be average

The three above average

The three below average

This exercise was followed by the ranking of the fifteen qualities. In formulating the directions care was taken to keep the respondent's mind on behavior, as contrasted with traits.

Preliminary use of the scale seems to indicate that the scale can be scored with some degree of objectivity; that the scale is discriminating in that it presents a wide range of scores and marked individual differences among teachers; that there also appear to be definite patterns of response.

Whether the scores have any practical value remains to be determined by further research.

23. *Open* v. *Closed Classrooms*

MARIO D. FANTINI

We hear a great deal these days about the open *v.* the closed society. In the one camp we have the totalitarian social order, referred to as a "closed" society, wherein individuals are actually subservient to the state. In the other camp we have those societies which value the individual over the state and are referred to as "open" societies. It is said further that in one society the individual is "free"; in the other, that he is not.

The seriousness of the conflict between open and closed societies

From Mario D. Fantini, "Open *v.* Closed Classrooms," *The Clearing House*, XXXVII (October, 1962), 67–71. Mario D. Fantini is Director of the Madison Area Project (Youth Development Department), Syracuse Public Schools, Syracuse, New York. Reprinted by permission of *The Clearing House*.

cannot be slighted because both societies are willing to preserve their prized values even at the expense of an all-out war. Consequently, we are talking about very important concepts. Moreover, there is a parallel between societies and the classrooms in which teachers find themselves. There are also open and closed classrooms, which, in a sense, are miniatures of open and closed societies.

If you were to view the schools in this light, you might examine a classroom and see the teacher in the front of the room talking to the class. The class might be listening and taking notes; if an assignment were being made, the students might be writing down the assignment, after which perhaps certain students might ask questions. Soon the class is over and a new class comes in. The teacher again asks for the homework assignments from the previous day, goes on to some new work, dictates some important facts, asks a few questions on the work which should have been prepared for the day, makes an assignment for the following day, and answers some last-minute questions. Then a new group comes in and this pattern is repeated.

You might then examine another room where the teacher is, at first, hard to find. She is in the background, but the students are moving around freely. Various projects are being undertaken by small groups of students, while other students are working alone. In this classroom, there does not seem to be a routinized approach.

In a sense, you could say that these were observations of open and closed classrooms. In the foregoing descriptions, the first exemplified a closed classroom, while the second one approached the open classroom.

It is my assumption that both classrooms are miniature social systems, in which certain values are being developed (whether the teacher realizes it or not) because of the kind of conditions which the teacher has set up. It is my further assumption that the values sponsored by these miniature social systems parallel many of the values which underline the open and closed societies. It is my belief, also, that there are in operation more of the closed classroom systems than the open classroom systems. If these assumptions are valid, then a possible conclusion is that our schools are actually developing more closed society values than open. This means that American schools are preparing individuals for a closed society, when it is obvious that the schools should be doing just the opposite.

Why do we seem to have more closed than open classrooms? For one reason, the closed system seems to be much more systematic. It appears to be more logical. Since we seem to have inherited this pattern, this seems to be the "way to do it"; so this structure is perpetuated. Since in the closed classroom system the teacher is the center of attraction, this becomes a teachercentric type of arrangement. The individuals, the learners, take their signals largely from the teacher. You can compare this with the closed society, in which the individual takes his signals from the state. Thus, the model projected here is one based on the assign-recite-test sequence. This is the normal methodology. Conformity is being fostered because of the teacher-ascribed standards, which are supposedly sanctioned as being objective. The individual here is in competition with others. The climate fostered here is one in which the prize is on convergent values. The individual must conform or he does not succeed. These convergent values breed conformity, so that ultimately you have a miniature conforming classroom society.

In a closed classroom, such student questions as these are typical: "How long do you want this assignment?" "May we use other textbooks?" "Do you want a bibliography?" The emphasis on these questions is to get permission from the teacher in order to proceed. The teacher is the source of "truth." As long as one goes along with the values and standards that the teacher has imposed, he will gain status and recognition and thereby succeed. The ironic aspect here is that we are making conformists of bright students, those very students who may be called upon to give us the creative leadership we need on a national level. Some students do rebel against the system. These become "outsiders" and usually fail. Most learners conform to the system and, in the process of conforming, internalize these convergent values which, in turn, become an excellent orientation for participation in a closed society.

Moreover, in the closed system the important thing is to *acquire knowledge*—that is, you must know *about* subject matter. The knowing about subject matter is what will be tested, and if the recall is good, the learner will be rewarded. The entire approach in the closed classroom is deductive; the *answers* are more important than the *process* for achieving answers. In all probability, facts will be emphasized at the expense of the conceptual structure. The school administration seems to be satisfied with this operation because it creates little organizational conflict. Parents do not object since this is the same pattern to which they themselves were exposed.

The open classroom, on the other hand, is a replica of an open society and, hopefully, can develop those values needed to support and advance an open society—that is, freedom with self-direction. In the open classroom the teacher is largely in the background and the situation is one in which the pupils are the center of attraction. This is the pupilcentric structure. The important value which is developed here is creative self-expression. Just as the center of the open society is the individual and not the state, the center of the open classroom is the student and not the teacher. The climate being fostered is one which permits the development of the creative person and the inner-directed person (to use Riesman's term), since the individual takes his signals from within himself. He is competing with himself, and not with others, so that standards are actually relative to the individual. Critical thinking is being fostered because the process here is *inductive*. It is a search. It is the process of exploration. The answer is not given first; rather, the learner must attempt to discover new ideas and new concepts which will give meaning to further performance.

In the open classroom, the process is valued as much as the product. Further, the open classroom is more prone to be action oriented than is the closed system, where the learner is passive and the teacher is the dominant force. The open classroom swings the emphasis from teaching to learning, to those conditions which surround learning for each student.

If you were able to move through the school systems in our country, you would not find it difficult to determine whether the emphasis is more on the open or closed classroom systems. Certainly, there are values to both, but this is not the major point that is being discussed here. What is being suggested is that an important relationship exists between the classroom and society. Ultimately, what is being learned in the classroom should prepare individuals for competent societal roles. The values of freedom, creativity, and self-direction, so basic to our society, do not just happen. They are developed, and the classroom is one of the important laboratories in the process. Not being cognizant of the values being developed in the classroom is to damage the foundations of a free society. The emphasis today in a free society is on the development of creative individuals. Everyone has the potential for creativity and everyone has a potential for excellence in some area of human endeavor. Each person is born with a particular set of abilities which can be developed to the fullest if the school would provide favorable conditions which foster this development. The emphasis on the creative individual, it seems to me, is founded on an important philosophical position which states that in our type of civilization, the dignity and worth of the individual are supreme. Under this concept, the individual, because of his uniqueness, has the ability to express himself in a unique way. The fruits of his uniqueness can lead to creative expression, whether it be in music, in dance, or in play-acting. This development, it seems to me, is more likely to find expression in the open classroom environment.

If you stand apart to view the educational process as it takes place in the schools, you can see a kind of continuum from the open to the closed system. It is surprising how we begin our education with an open system and gradually proceed to a more closed type of classroom system. For example, the kindergarten is an excellent model of the open classroom, but as we move through the grades the situation changes. What we are doing actually, instead of nurturing creativity, is creating conditions that stymie creative growth.

However, the open system is not a panacea and there are certain important arguments against the open classroom systems. The first is that it is difficult for a teacher to control an open system—that it lacks discipline—that there is a lack of teacher control. The argument continues that in the absence of someone in charge in the room, utter chaos would follow. For example, it is often cited that the teacher who is weak and does not have authority is subjected to behavior abuses because of lack of control.

My answer to this argument would be that in an open society, the highest form of discipline is not imposed discipline but self-discipline; i.e., the internalization of a certain set of values which give meaning and purpose to behavior. This is the sought-for kind of ideal. If this is not true, then the argument is really in favor of a nation of followers. One of the most severe criticisms of our times is that we have become a nation of conformists. If you were to look back in time, a counter argument could be raised, based on the school years; i.e., retracing the causes of conformity could lead logically to the classroom and to the lack of sufficient opportunities to exercise and to internalize types of behavior patterns which would develop self-direction. Consequently, since the development of self-discipline is inherent in the open system, its practice should be encouraged. Conversely, the closed system is more likely to sponsor the other-directed orientation.

Another argument that is often cited is that the open system is one that is more apt not to cover the subject matter that needs to be covered. The knowledge which we should be giving to the students would not be taught under an open system. The argument continues that it is important to outline the course work in a logical fashion and to cover a certain amount of work each day so that, over a period of time, the essentials are covered.

However, if you examine knowledge today, you realize that it is expanding at a geometric rate. It is impossible to expect one person to know all. Moreover, the nature of knowledge is changing. The orientation of many teachers took place at a time when knowledge was not expanding at a geometric rate, and there is no guarantee that the teacher has kept up with changing perspectives in his own discipline. Consequently, it is not knowledge that is important, but the ideas and concepts which underly the change in the framework of knowledge. This is the very thing that an open classroom seeks—to give the person, through the process of inquiry, the method for discovering the big ideas which have given meaning to change. In addition, those who would argue that knowledge would be neglected under an open system, at the same time underestimate value development. The open classroom system stimulates the process for development of such values as freedom, critical thinking, self-direction, creativity, and cooperation—those very values which give meaning and direction to democratic functioning. Students in this open system are experiencing patterns of behavior which are more like the ideals of the open and free society in which they will eventually become members.

An argument often cited against closed systems is that the closed system is more prone to developing a passive individual. Since the teacher is the center of dominance in the closed system, the student's role is primarily passive. The student is the recipient of a flow of communication from the teacher. By contrast, the learner in the open system is quite active because he must go through the process of exploring and discovering. Moreover, this active process, encouraged by the open system, serves also to fortify the learner with a particular method for discovering answers to problems, which is based on a major tool of science—the scientific method. The breakthroughs which we have in the field of science are largely attributable to increased sophistication in the implementation of this method. Actually, an open classroom is fortifying the learner with tools for problem solving in an age when it is necessary for a person to be able to think through the complexities of modern life to the degree, at least, of gaining insights which would enable him to recognize the significant from the insignificant. These are all attributes which are possible of development in a classroom which takes on the characteristics more of an open than of a closed system.

The question arises, "Why are there not more open than closed classroom systems?" This is, again, a complex problem. One answer is that this would necessitate a new orientation for most teachers. It is actually a much more difficult challenge to create the learning environment of an open classroom. For example, as a new teacher moves into the school situation, he becomes a member of a social system. He usually is not in a position to initiate change, and must go along with the norms of the system. The process of shifting a classroom situation from a closed to an open one is often fraught with hazards for the beginner. It may be that over a period of time the beginner succumbs to the pressures of the system. More likely, however, the closed system is found to be the easier way out. The closed system seems to be more definite. The teacher sees the logic of the approach more readily. He feels more satisfaction in having covered a given body of subject matter and in testing the student to see what he has learned. He seems to get more reward out of knowing his place in teaching.

The open system, on the other hand, is difficult to assess in terms of the teacher's role. The teacher in the open system is more of a climate setter, one who, while remaining in the background, is actually the agent who brings into the classroom environment all of the resources which implement learning.

Whether we realize it or not, education is playing a vital role in terms of national purpose. We are getting an awakening of the importance of education in the total process of developing an ideal type of society. Sooner or later we must come to the conclusion that schools have specific and major functions in society, and that this function concerns itself mainly with socializing all the citizens to perform effectively and maturely in the society in which they will function. That is, the school should attempt to develop the individual to the fullest, because, as a self-realizing individual, he will best make a contribution to the development of a free and open civilization.

Certainly, we are hopeful that the schools will develop the kind of individual who has social responsibility, one who feels deeply for humanity. In order to develop the kind of individual called for in this type of free order, the schools have a vital role to perform.

As we examine the educational process closely, it becomes apparent that serious consideration should be given to the nature of the teaching front, to that environmental situation in which teaching and learning take place. Hopefully, that direction will be more toward the model of the open classroom system.

24. *Learning Theory and Teaching Practice*

HENRY CLAY LINDGREN

The educational picture today is full of paradoxes and inconsistencies. The same people who use pragmatic grounds for criticizing the schools—that is, who find fault because graduates are not able to function adequately as employees—are often the same ones who urge

From Henry Clay Lindgren, "Learning Theory and Teaching Practice," *Educational Leadership*, XVI (March, 1959), 333–336. Henry Clay Lindgren is Professor of Psychology at San Francisco State College, California. Reprinted by permission of the author and of *Educational Leadership*.

that the curriculum be "beefed up" with subject matter that has little "transfer value," as far as employment skills are concerned. Teachers, too, sometimes display inconsistencies in their behavior, stressing one point of view when talking to colleagues but displaying classroom behavior that is obviously at variance with the philosophy of education they are in the habit of expounding. An example of such "compartmentalized thinking" is the elementary teacher who claimed that she ran her classroom strictly according to democratic principles—each year she wrote the rules for classroom conduct on the board, and the children voted to observe them.

Underlying our complex and sometimes confusing patterns of behavior are some rather basic beliefs or theories about learning. Each of us has such beliefs or theories. The comments and criticisms that the layman makes regarding education are based on theories of learning that he considers to be soundly supported by common sense, while the teacher's behavior regarding educational matters, both within and outside the classroom, is based on theories that he considers to be equally valid.

The term "theories of learning" has a formidable sound to it. It may connote research with mice and monkeys, complex mathematical formulae, and esoteric research papers. Unfortunately, our ability to relegate learning theories to the laboratory and thereby to divorce them from the everyday give and take of the classroom has enabled us to dissociate ourselves from any awareness of the part played by theory in our own educational practices. If the question as to the kind of learning theory we are using ever comes up, most of us are inclined to beg the question and direct the discussion to the "more practical" aspects of the teaching situation. Some people in education are even concerned lest anyone think of them as in any way "theoretical." It appears that our emphasis on the practical in America has led us to create an unnatural dichotomy between "theory" and "practice."

THEORY AND PRACTICE

The plain fact of the matter is that all practice—in education, as well as in other fields—is based on theory. Usually the theory is not consciously stated in so many words. Rather, it is what Lee J. Cronbach terms an "implicit theory"—a theory that may be inferred from behavior. Some of the confusion and contradiction I described in my opening paragraph is the result of our unwillingness or inability to identify the theories underlying our statement regarding learning or our classroom behavior. If we *were* able and willing to probe into the concepts basic to our behavior, perhaps we would become more aware of the inconsistencies.

There are three main sources from which we draw or develop the learning theories that form the basis of our attitudes and behavior regarding education: tradition, personal experience, and research. Most of us, laymen and teachers alike, depend most heavily on the first two sources. This may be true even of the researcher in the field of teaching methods. All of us have had the experience of taking courses in educational practices from instructors whose own methods violated every one of the principles they were expounding. Timothy Leary tells of a psychology professor who was advising his class of the importance of getting students to solve their own problems. "Don't let them get dependent on you," he said, "make them think for themselves." After the lecture, a graduate student came up to ask a question. He said that in the section of undergraduate students he was supervising as a teaching assistant, he was continually plagued by requests for answers to problems that could and should be solved by the students themselves. "What should I do?" he asked. The professor cleared his throat and said that students were always trying to trap instructors into solving their problems for them—problems that they themselves should work out. "Now what I would do, if I were you," he went on, "is to ——."[1]

The aim here is not to point with scorn to the inconsistency of psychology professors, but rather to show how difficult it is to break away from beliefs and attitudes that have, so to speak, become second nature.

Most of us are strongly influenced by the first of the three sources mentioned in the above paragraph—tradition. Our culture tells us, in effect, how people learn. In our culture, one of the main theories of learning is what might be called the "reward-and-punishment" theory —the theory, that is, that people learn because they are appropriately rewarded or punished. There are other traditional theories—the theory of practice, the theory that learning is a process of assimilation; but the reward-and-punishment theory is one of the most basic, and it is this theory that I shall refer to as symbolizing the traditional point of view on learning.

There is, of course, a great deal of truth in this theory. For example, any one of us can think of instances in which the behavior of a child was changed because of the desire to please a teacher (and this in itself is a kind of reward) or because of the fear of being marked as a failure (one of many forms of punishment). Many teachers carry this theory to an ultimate and unwarranted conclusion—namely, that if children were not rewarded or punished by the teacher, they would not learn. This is, essentially, the traditional and autocratic or authoritarian approach to teaching.

The uniqueness of our experience and personality means that each

[1] Timothy Leary. *Interpersonal Diagnosis of Personality.* New York: Ronald Press Company, 1957.

of us will develop a somewhat different arrangement or pattern of learning theory to serve as a basis for our behavior as educators. Some of us will be eclectic, attempting to combine traditional theory with theory based on research. Some will depend more directly on personal experience, fortified with a liberal dosage of reward-and-punishment theory. As each of us becomes involved in the teaching-learning process, he learns that certain approaches are more effective for him than others. Or perhaps certain practices are particularly expressive of his personality and attitudes toward life in general.

One person may thus come to believe that learning is fostered best when the teacher is cool, crisp, detached, and objective in his relations with students. Another may believe that students are more likely to learn when the teacher shows a personal interest in the lives of his students, even to the point of involving them in counseling relationships with him. These are but two of the many kinds of theories that teachers may develop with respect to the way in which learning is influenced by their behavior.

EFFECTS OF RESEARCH

Although most of us in the education profession are inclined to believe that research has had a marked effect on our theories regarding learning, an examination of our actual behavior in the classroom would probably show a considerable disparity between the research-oriented theories we publicly avow and the implicit theories that may be deduced from our behavior. One of the reasons for this disparity lies in the nature of the theories that derive from research.

Let us examine two theories that have important implications for the learning process. One, that derives from research in the field of social psychology, holds that individual behavior can be more readily modified by group decisions than by recommendations emanating from authority figures. Another, deriving largely from clinical research, holds that emotional factors in the life of an individual play an important part in directing his behavior. The teacher who accepts the first theory would be inclined to develop classroom situations in which students have an opportunity to learn through making their own decisions. The second theory leads to an instructional approach based on an understanding of and a concern for the feelings of students.

Note that both these theories are democratic in their implications. They place the student at the focal center of the teaching-learning process, in contra-distinction to traditional theories, which are adult-centered and teacher-centered—authoritarian and autocratic. And therein lies a major source of the disparity between the theories we preach and the theories that are implicit in our own behavior.

RESEARCH ORIENTATION

Rudolf Dreikurs points out, in an insightful essay, that we are to-day in a period of change from an autocratic to a democratic way of life.[2] This is a development that has been in progress for hundreds of years. We have now reached a point where many, if not most, of us have accepted democratic modes of conduct as just and proper. At the same time, we have not been able to develop modes of behavior that are always consistent with our democratic ideals and instead must continually fall back on traditional and more autocratic approaches. The latter are, after all, a part of our cultural heritage that goes back to our most primitive beginnings.

When we are confronted by a difficult and frustrating situation in our classrooms, the tendency is for us to want to exert our authority rather than to examine the situation critically in the light of our democratic ideals or research-oriented learning theory. It calls for a great deal of maturity and self-control to respond to frustration in ways that are likely to improve classroom learning, because our personal needs to take out our frustrations on our students struggle for expression. Further-more, as Dreikurs points out, we are not even sure how to resolve dif-ficult situations in ways that are consistent with our democratic ideals. This is true not only of difficult and frustrating situations, but of everyday classroom teaching as well.

We still have a great distance to go in finding ways to translate the findings of clinical and social psychology into classroom practice. Hence there are many individuals, the present writer included, who continually find themselves falling back on the traditional and teacher-centered educational methods of lecture, assignment, examination, etc. What we obviously need is a great deal more classroom experimenta-tion in approaches that attempt to translate research-oriented theory into classroom practices that are consistent with its democratic implica-tions. I refer here to the efforts of individual teachers to find ways to improve learning in their classrooms, as well as to the more rigorous ex-periments of the educational or social psychologist.

It will not be easy to conduct such experimentation. Laymen and colleagues alike whose learning theories are essentially traditional will object to any approach that to them seems inconsistent with com-mon sense. And the recent attacks on education have not created a cli-mate that encourages much experimentation, informal or otherwise. Such attacks increase anxiety, defensiveness, and insecurity, which in turn foster a resurgence of traditionalism. But it is easy to place the blame

[2] *Character Education and Spiritual Values in an Anxious Age.* Boston: Beacon Press, 1952.

on others. When the opportunity for experimentation presents itself, our chief problem will be ourselves.

Our first task will be that of becoming aware of the ways in which our practice is at odds with our democratic ideals, as well as the principles that have evolved from research findings. This is a task that takes considerable insight and self-understanding, but it is a task that must be resolved if we are to develop learning theories and teaching practices that are more effective. If we are able to face our own deficiencies, then we will be able to move on to the creative thinking and improvisation that constitute the preliminary phases of experimentation with new methods.

25. A Walk on the Altered Side
JAMES D. FINN

> *One thing that is new is the prevalence of newness, the changing scale and scope of change itself, so that the world alters as we walk in it, so that the years of man's life measure not some small growth or rearrangement or moderation of what he learned in childhood, but a great upheaval.*
>
> —J. Robert Oppenheimer

As I write these lines, I am travelling 35,000 feet above the Grand Canyon of the Colorado River at a speed in excess of 600 miles per hour. A voice comes on the intercom—a mild technical miracle in itself. It is the voice of the pilot relaying, in a matter of fact way, one of the greatest stories of this generation. For above me—a hundred and fifty miles or so—a Marine colonel by the name of John Glenn is traveling in a space capsule at a speed of 17,000 miles per hour. While I have been reaching Arizona from Los Angeles, he has come half-way around the globe. Glenn has been twice around the world since his flight began; the decision has just been made to try for the third orbit.

Below me the Arizona desert—dimly seen through a covering of white clouds—sits ancient and quiet. Memories are buried here—of

From James D. Finn, "A Walk on the Altered Side," *Phi Delta Kappan*, XLIV (October, 1962), 29–34. James D. Finn is Professor of Education at the University of Southern California. Reprinted by permission of the *Phi Delta Kappan*. This article was delivered as a paper before a meeting of the John Dewey Society at Las Vegas, Nevada, March 3, 1962.

the conquistadores who explored it, of the Indians and, before them, of geologic time. A contrast, heightened by the middle ground, the limbo, the partial ascent to the stars symbolized by the magnificent aircraft in which I ride—a contrast greater than man has ever known—exists in this relationship of ancient desert and the capsule called Friendship 7. Between them rides the jet, symbol of our generation. For we, truly, must be the midwives of the new era.

The conquistadores were inevitable after Columbus and Magellan. John Glenn was inevitable only after Newton, Einstein, Planck, Helmholtz, and generations of other scientists and unknown but dedicated engineers, technicians, and inventors. The distance between the caveman and Magellan is as nothing compared to the distance between Magellan and Glenn. Most of us do not live in the world of John Glenn; many of us cannot or will not; many of us do not take kindly to the role of midwifery in this birth of newness. Returning to the Oppenheimer metaphor, the world does, indeed, alter as we walk in it; the world of John Glenn, not our transitory world, is the world of our children. Their side is the altered side, where, as gap-bridgers, as educators, we must learn to walk.

It is in this context that I should like to remark upon a relatively new relationship in the world of education. A new world, symbolized at least to a modest degree by the flight into space, seems to be forming within the educational society. This world is technological in nature. Men are seeking to solve some of the problems of education by technological means. Technology is not, as many of the technically illiterate seem to think, a collection of gadgets, of hardware, of instrumentation. It is, instead, best described as a way of thinking about certain classes of problems and their solutions.

This view of technology when applied to education becomes a legitimate object of concern for the educational philosopher. We are met here in the name of John Dewey, in the name of educational philosophy. I would like, in the short time at my disposal, to outline some of these philosophic concerns as I see them from the point of view of a student of instructional technology.

THE REVOLUTION'S POTENTIAL

Perhaps it would be useful to indicate briefly some of the dimensions of this *potential* technological revolution in education. I emphasize potential because it has not yet happened; it may never happen; education may remain the only natural (primitive) sector of our culture, but I strongly doubt it.

Since about 1930 we have had a slow development of a group of tools for communication and teaching, and a program of research into their use. These instruments and materials include what today we call conventional audio-visual devices—the sound motion picture, various forms of projected still pictures, recordings, etc. Since 1950, this arsenal has expanded to include television, electronic learning laboratories, teaching machines of various kinds, and, recently, computers. Accompanying these devices and materials, again, has been a vigorous program of research into the nature of learning and communication, supported by a rapidly growing body of theory derived from experimental and social psychology and related disciplines such as linguistics, criticism, and engineering.

In other sectors of the educational enterprise, other technological innovations are being tested. The work of Lloyd Trump and his associates in school organization, the various attempts at team teaching, and experimentation with new school environments are examples. I shall confine my remarks principally to the main line of instructional technology—audio-visual materials and the so-called newer media and their intellectual bases.

I mentioned a slow development of these approaches to instruction. More important, this development was also almost discontinuous with any main lines of growth of American education during the past thirty years. It was so little connected with progressive education, for example, that I found the word "films" only in a footnote relating to Alice Keliher in Lawrence Cremin's book.[1] It has not notably influenced the theory of school administration or the education of superintendents. In preparing this paper, I had occasion to examine a number of recent books on educational philosophy. With one or two exceptions, they are so little concerned with these developments that, using the philosophers as a source, one must conclude that a technology of instruction does not exist. The Association for Supervision and Curriculum Development, until very recently, also turned a blind (and horrified) eye in the direction of instructional technology.

Within the last five years this discontinuity has ended and the possibilities of a technology of instruction have suddenly thrust themselves into the educational mainstream. The philosophers have begun to cluck, if not in books, then in speeches, articles, and conversation; the curriculum specialists have been seen running about throwing up barricades to protect the child from the machine monster; and educational statesmen have managed to raise the adrenalin of their constituents with speeches that sound as if they were ghostwritten by Ned Ludd or Jean Jacques Rousseau. We are urged to destroy the weaving machines and return to nature—all in the same breath.

[1] Lawrence A. Cremin, *The Transformation of the Schools: Progressivism in American Education,* 1876–1957. New York: Knopf, 1961.

I am not concerned here either with educational statesmen or curriculum specialists. I would like to concentrate on the philosophers. For I come not to defend instructional technology, as I am sure our chairman would like me to do, but instead, I come to indict. I feel that many educational philosophers have lost the way and that they have committed an even worse crime—they have failed to understand.

FROM APATHY THROUGH ANTAGONISM

First, there is a generalized, non-specific attitude that holds that instructional technology is both trivial and, at the same time, dangerous. This position is well stated in Van Til's excellent paper[2] in which, on the one hand, he dismisses technology as mere tinkering when compared to the real concerns of education and, on the other, sees it as a threat for mind control of Orwellian proportions. In fact, I get the impression that in some philosophical and curriculum circles the attitude toward instructional technology runs all the way from apathy through antipathy to antagonism.

This negative approach is not surprising. The intellectual has, for the most part, always hated the city which makes his intellectuality possible. And a technological civilization is an urban civilization. Thoreau, of course, was the great prototype of the intellectual who hates the city. He refused to stay in the city and once said, "The only room in Boston which I visit with alacrity is the gentlemen's room at the Fitchburg depot, where I wait for cars, sometimes for two hours, in order to get out of town." There is something comically ironic— perhaps Freudian—about this. For it has always seemed to me that plumbing—and I assume they had plumbing in the gentlemen's room of the Fitchburg depot even in those days—is a rather appropriate symbol of a technological society.

OPPOSITION TO SCIENTISM

Morton and Lucia White remind us that John Dewey himself, between 1899 and 1927, developed the same attitude toward the city and its industrialization. They said, "Instead of taking the city as the model *for* the progressive school, he almost speaks as though the urban community should be modeled *on* the progressive school. . . . At the end of his life Dewey seemed to conclude every speech with the words, 'Divide the cities into settlement houses.' "[3] And, a bit later, White

[2] Presented by William Van Til, president of the ASCD, at the March convention of this group at Las Vegas, N.M. See also Van Til's article in the Feb. 17, 1962, *Saturday Review*.

[3] Quoted in Morton and Lucia White, "The American Intellectual versus the American City," *Daedalus*, XC (Winter, 1961), p. 168.

and White summarize, "For functionalism, like pragmatism, is one of a complex of American ideals that could not exist in a non-urban society, and yet its greatest spokesmen seem to hate the American city."[4] I suggest that educational philosophy has reached the stage when, in order to remedy what is a special case of the same general syndrome, it should cease hating the city.

Second, to this day there is in educational philosophy a distrust and a strong antagonism to what in the Thirties was called "scientism" in education. Charters, Judd, and Bobbitt all felt the hot-tipped shafts of Dewey, Kilpatrick, Bode, and Childs. Kilpatrick was even spanked for too much attachment to Thorndike's connectionism, although, for the life of me, I could never see it in his project method.

Scientism in those days was Charters and educational engineering and activity analysis; scientism today is B. F. Skinner and pigeons and programed learning. Charters was demolished for inventing a system of curriculum-making designed—so it was charged—to preserve the social status quo, and the measurement movement was subject to blast after blast. Today philosophers and curriculum specialists make jokes about pigeons not being people—neglecting, by the way, many other forms of learning research and programing theory.

For those of you who follow Dewey, Bode, and Kilpatrick, whose god was the method of science, this is, indeed, a strange attitude. It was strange when they had it; it is stranger now.

Take only one facet of this scientism—Charters' theories of analysis. The philosophy group at Ohio State University ridiculed them. Yet, today, those theories are being used for identical problems by psychologists who never heard of Charters or of his contemporary in the industrial field, Allen. For analysis is neeeded in all sorts of programing, in the statement of objectives and throughout the developing technology of instruction.

Analysis, in the sense that Charters used it and as it is being used today in a hundred ways, is, in part at least, the discrimination of details. As Gerard Piel points out, Bronowski, the mathematician, in commenting on the contributions of Leonardo Da Vinci, said, "[He] gave science what it most needed, the artist's sense that the detail of nature is significant. Until science had this sense, no one could care— or could think that it mattered—how fast two unequal masses fell or whether the orbits of planets are accurately circles or ellipses."[5] I suggest that, because of a social bias characteristic of the Thirties, the great exponents of the scientific method in education successfully

---

[4] *Ibid.*, p. 176.

[5] Quoted in Gerard Piel. *Science and the Cause of Man.* New York: Knopf, 1961, p. 208.

struck down one of the great educational scientists of that generation and prevented a generalized scientific technique from becoming more effective in education. I suggest that the educational philosophers of this generation ought to avoid such a mistake. I can tell them this: Even if they do not, their strictures will not have the same effect.

THE QUESTION OF MEANS AND ENDS

A third point on which I should like to offer advice is in the other direction. I think current educational philosophy should pay more instead of less attention to Dewey on the questions of means and ends in education. Mr. Van Til continually restates the point that until the question of aim is settled by philosophic reflection, it does absolutely no good to consider the means necessary to achieve those ends. The means in this case, of course, are the devices, materials, and approaches of a technology of instruction. Bode made the same point somewhat more succinctly when he said many years ago, "Unless we know where we are going there is not much comfort in being assured that we are on the way and traveling fast."[6]

There has probably been more confusion on ends and means, method and subject matter, than on any other point in educational theory these last thirty years. We need, first of all, clarification once again of this question; and clarification, I take it, is one of the jobs of the philosopher.

The confusion began with Dewey, who has to be read very critically in order to determine when he is talking about the method of science as such and educational method as such. Kilpatrick tossed in the notion of concomitant learnings, which introduced so many variables into the learning process that method, subject matter, student, and the school flagpole got mixed into a great ball of fuzz. When the curriculum specialists got through with it, curriculum was defined as no less than life, in which there was really no method except, perhaps, the pursuit of happiness. While all of these views had much to recommend them, and all had laid hold of a piece of the truth, the usefulness of these generalizations for intelligent action had been reduced, not only to zero, but into the negative.

On the other hand, a much more naive view about method also still prevails, fostered in such intellectual circles as the Council for Basic Education and the California State Legislature. This view holds that method is a mere manipulation of a few variables such as good enunciation on the part of the teacher—skills that can be learned in less time than it takes to learn to drive a car.

[6] Boyd H. Bode, *Fundamentals of Education*. New York: Macmillan, 1921, pp. 241-2.

WE STILL NEED DIRECTION

The ultimate result of the development of the Dewey position through Kilpatrick to the ASCD was that method, on the one hand, reduced itself to a worship of group dynamics while pacifying the god of child individuality; on the other hand, it was completely subordinated to something called aim, which was the result of a process of navel contemplation, either on the part of educational philosophers or curriculum committees. In either case, we have received little help in doing our job from these statements of aim, most of which degenerate into generalized propositions from which no action may be deduced. The ultimate result of the other concept—that method is nothing but the manipulation of a few tricks—is, first of all, ignorance; and, secondly, a perilous bypassing of both individuals and values.

The suggested direction for clarification of this long-suffered problem is to return to Dewey and work from there. Because he believed in a unified, nondualistic universe, Dewey maintained that method could not, *when in use,* be separated from subject matter; that eating and food were inseparable, for example. However, for purposes of study and control, he was equally firm on the point that method had to be teased out of this universe, examined, analyzed, and put to work in the most intelligent way possible.

Now, add to this idea the fact that, as early as the time of writing *School and Society*, Dewey suggested that we live in a technological, industrial culture and that technology was, in fact, the main determinant of its direction. The school, he felt, should reflect this. Such a view could be considered a special case of the general law of pragmatism—that ends and means are inseparable, that ends become means to further ends.

If you now consider technology from two perspectives—the entirety of technology that has transformed our society in about two hundred years and the special application of technology to the instructional process—it is possible to indicate the direction the educational philosopher must go to clarify the problem of method in relation to aim.

First, as the perceptive students of general technology continually insist, technology in society is an organic process. This concept is central to Hannah Arendt's *The Human Condition*. In it she said, "As matters stand today, it has become as senseless to describe this world of machines in terms of means and ends as it has always been senseless to ask nature if she produced the seed to produce a tree or the tree to produce the seed."[7] Slightly later, she quotes Werner Heisenberg to the effect that general technology is no longer " 'the product of a con-

[7] Hannah Arendt, *The Human Condition*. Garden City, N.Y.: Doubleday Anchor Books, 1959, p. 133.

scious human effort to enlarge material power, but rather like a biological development of mankind in which the innate structures of the human organism are transplanted in an ever-increasing measure into the environment of man.' "[8]

The first obligation of the philosopher is to understand these concepts—a task that is not easy because the views they represent, as Kurt Marek has pointed out, are qualitatively and psychosomatically different from any ever held before. They do not fit into the tight, abstract, three-dimensional world of Euclid and the present educational philosopher. They would, strangely enough, fit into Dewey's world—a world of organic unity, although, as I indicated before, if his later work is a clue, he would probably not have been happy with the consequences of his own thought.

Taking technological development as the central organic process of our society, the implications, as this process invades education, are interesting indeed. The process does not destroy aim and its role, but it binds aim inevitably to technology. For technology is an aim-generator as much as purpose or philosophy is a technical direction-giver. Each conditions the other and is not, as Mr. Van Til maintains, arranged in a hierarchy with aim on top and method at the bottom.

An example might serve to throw some light on this relationship. In any number of technological approaches to instruction—programed learning, the use of massed films, or in the developing instructional systems, for example—there is one unvarying requirement. That requirement is an absolutely clear statement of objectives. The general statements of the philosopher and the curriculum specialist are not good enough. Objectives must be developed from general aim statements as experiments and hypotheses are developed from general scientific laws. There is no guarantee in either case that the specific will correspond completely with the general. The specifics are conditioned by the instructional reality—a condition that philosophers abhor but that scientists, in the case of scientific laws, do not worry about.

At any rate, objectives can only be developed in this sense by a thorough analysis heretofore rarely applied in education. This is where a technology gets its direction. It is hard work to create such objectives and, if the philosophers resent everything else, they should see that such a procedure, in fact, brings philosophic thinking into practice more than a hundred generations of philosophers have been able to do.

Further, I should like to remind you of my introductory point that technology is, fundamentally, a way of thinking. As such, it inevitably will play some role in the development of educational aims. Once a

[8] Quoted in Arendt, *loc. cit.*

technology exists, certain aims dreamed of in philosophy may disappear. As Marek has said of technology in general,

> In our technological age, man can conceive of nothing that he might not invent. A magic carpet is no longer a scientific problem, but only a problem in construction. All the pipe dreams of the old high cultures can today be made to come true, but some of them are so primitive (like the magic carpet, for example) that it is no longer worth the trouble. The pipe dreams of the men of the old high cultures appear to have been consummated in the same historical period as the old high cultures themselves.[9]

Take care lest the educational philosophy you are preaching does not meet the same fate.

In discussing the hatred of the city, the attack on scientism, and the problem of ends and means, we have only scratched the surface of the great job of readjustment needed in educational philosophy as technology, reflecting the increasing technical complexity of our culture, invades the instructional process. In the space left, all that can be done is to list some other tasks which, I suggest, should occupy the attention of educational philosophers.

These include a thorough study of the process of technology in our culture as a whole. Outside of some indication in Phenix's new book[10] and in Thelen,[11] I find little evidence that this is going on. What has gone on, incidentally, is inadequate; philosophers have presumed too much. They have presumed that they can study technology in a vacuum without, for example, the cooperation of engineers and without the mastery of certain languages and concepts. In order to look properly at the altered side, such multi-disciplined study is necessary. To give the philosophers something to think about, why is it that recently the greatest visions (in, it is true, a somewhat restricted sense) of what might be possible in education have come from Simon Ramo, a technologist?[12]

WHAT ARE THE MYTHS ABOUT THE MACHINE?

Educational philosophers should spend some time in examining current myths and destroying them. Many educators have demonized

[9] Kurt W. Marek, *Yestermorrow*, trans. by Ralph Manheim. New York: Knopf, 1961, p. 43.

[10] Philip Phenix, *Education and the Common Good: A Moral Philosophy of the Curriculum.* New York: Harper and Brothers, 1961.

[11] Herbert Thelen, *Education and the Human Quest*, New York: Harper and Brothers, 1960.

[12] See, for example, Simon Ramo, "A New Technique of Education," in *Teaching Machines and Programmed Learning*, A. A. Lumsdaine and Robert Glaser, editors. Washington, D.C.: Dept. of Audio-Visual Instruction, NEA, 1960, pp. 367–81.

the machine in the manner of witch doctors. Concerning this practice generally, Marek said somewhat bitterly, "The machine is demonized only by those who feel helpless in its presence. Where such demonization occurs today, its authors are neither scientists, nor engineers, nor managers, nor workers, but only outdistanced philosophers and writers sulking in their historical corner." Shades of C. P. Snow! And there are other myths of our age of midwifery that must disappear under the hand of the philosopher.

Another challenging area opened up by the organic processes of technology includes both technical and practical problems. For examample, who among you will follow Bode's great example and, continuing his work which stopped in 1940, relate concepts of mind in their newer sense to educational theory? To do this today you would have to consort with cyberneticians, electrical engineers, and neurologists. Related to this is the general problem of knowledge—its nature, its size, its structure, if any. At the level of so-called practical problems, I *urge* you to face the economic and productivity problems inherent in an attempt to educate all Americans. These things have never concerned you centrally. They must now.

Finally, you must face the consequences of the generation in which you have been born and the world in which you live. You cannot deny technology on arbitrary, literary, uninformed grounds. If you deny the teaching machine, the computer, television, and the motion picture, if you deny new ways of teaching and learning, you cannot stop until you deny yourselves fire, the wheel, and even the very language which you speak. For, as Karl Jaspers so well put it, "A denial of technology's last step is equivalent to a denial of the first."[13]

And, as Max Lerner reminds us, we Americans have not sold our souls to the devil of technology in a Faustian bargain. It is as true of education as of society as a whole that "truer than the Faustian bargain . . . is the image of Prometheus stealing fire from the gods in order to light a path of progress for men. The path is not yet clear, nor the meaning of progress, nor where it is leading: but the bold intent, the irreverence, and the secular daring have all become part of the American experience."[14] Does this not imply that, as midwives to the new era, as conductors to the altered side, the vista of educational philosophy is more exciting than ever? I think John Dewey would have liked that.

[13] Karl Jaspers, *The Future of Mankind*, trans. by E. B. Ashton. Chicago: University of Chicago Press, 1961, p. 192.

[14] Max Lerner, *America as a Civilization*, Vol. I: *The Basic Frame*. New York: Simon and Schuster, 1957, p. 263.

26. Is Progressive Education Obsolete?

WILLIAM VAN TIL

Is progressive education outmoded? One's first impulse is to say "yes." Who today, among the voices being heard on education, is talking about the concerns which characterized many leaders of education during the first half of the twentieth century? Specifically, who today is talking about the ideas which occupied John Dewey, George Counts, Boyd H. Bode, and William Heard Kilpatrick, those symbols of the intellectual leadership of the "new education," symbols of the varied versions of the progressive movement in education? Practically nobody, at least nobody who is being heard widely.

Instead, American education in the early 1960's is engrossed with the application of technology to education, with competing new proposals for organization of the school program, and with stress on reconstruction of academic disciplines. The mass media foster the interest in technology, organization, and disciplines. If an educator tries to be heard on more fundamental aspects, he often encounters the silent treatment.

The Industrial Revolution has finally reached education. As a result, matters of technology have virtually become table talk in education today. In professional discussions and in the mass media reporting we hear constantly about educational television, language laboratories, courses on film, and programmed learning through teaching machines.

A second stress in today's education emphasizes organization of the school program. Proposals are varied and often conflicting. They include such organizational proposals as team teaching, the dual progress plan, the nongraded school, and increasing the course requirements within the existing Carnegie unit structure.

Currently, a third stress is the new interest in the academic disci-

From William Van Til, "Is Progressive Education Obsolete?" *Saturday Review*, XLV (February 17, 1962), 56–57, 82–84. Reprinted by permission of the author and *Saturday Review*. William Van Til is Professor of Education and Chairman of the Department of Secondary Education at New York University. This article is based on a talk delivered at a meeting sponsored by the School of Education of New York University and by the John Dewey Society.

plines. In part, the emphasis is upon updating knowledge through efforts by specialists in the disciplines. The work of such groups as the Physical Science Study Committee and the varied mathematics programs at Yale, Maryland, and Illinois are watched intently. Science, mathematics, and foreign languages ride high as the favored fields of the national government, which has become a significant curriculum maker on the elementary and high school levels. The fields of English and physical education make frantic and failing attempts to latch onto the benefits of the National Defense Education Act; leadership in reconstruction of the curriculum in these fields has been assumed by the College Entrance Examination Board and by a football coach, respectively. There are indications that Commissioner McMurrin intends to attempt to do for the arts as well as for English what post-Sputnik apprehension did for the sciences. Rumors, alarms, and confusions surround the status of the social studies. The phrase "structures of the disciplines" is being bandied about, with none too clear a definition emerging as yet.

Technology, organization, and the disciplines seem a far cry from the philosophical, social, and psychological ideas that engaged the leaders of the progressive movement in education in the first half of the twentieth century. There appears to have been a change in "fashions in ideas," to use the chilling and accurate phrase Irwin Edman coined for a phenomenon of our times. Consequently, progressive education seems outmoded. Lawrence A. Cremin even consigned it to history in his "The Transformation of the School: Progressivism in American Education, 1876–1957." He began his preface as follows: "The death of the Progressive Education Association in 1955 and the passing of its journal, *Progressive Education,* two years later marked the end of an era in American pedagogy. Yet one would scarcely have known it from the pitifully small group of mourners at both funerals." Martin Mayer recapitulated the Cremin position in his widely read book, "The Schools."

One might readily conclude that progressive education is outmoded save for a stubborn fact. The fact is that the questions raised by the progressive movement in education are not obsolete. They will not die. They cannot be killed. They cannot be exorcised by any voodooism yet known to technology, organizaton, or the reconstruction of disciplines which remains aloof from these questions.

The basic questions which men like John Dewey, William Heard Kilpatrick, George Counts, and Boyd H. Bode raised are inescapable questions: What are the aims of education? Upon what foundations should the school program be built? Given such aims and foundations, what should the schools teach? To these probing and fundamental questions, matters of organization and technique, while important, are necessarily subordinate.

The progressive education movement of the first half of the twentieth century, symbolized by Dewey, Kilpatrick, Counts, and Bode, was essentially a quest for workable answers for our times to questions such as these. No one claims that the Holy Grail was found; no one claims that the questioners came up with final, definitive, eternal answers. The "new educators" did not completely agree among themselves on workable answers for our times. But at least the "new educators" asked the right questions.

One wing of the progressive movement sought the answers primarily in the potential of the individual learner. A pioneer in this respect was the man whose ninetieth birthday was celebrated on November 20, 1961—William Heard Kilpatrick. Many of today's schoolmen will remember Kilpatrick's classes in the Horace Mann Auditorium of Teachers College, Columbia University. Hundreds attended each session, yet the quiet man with the mane of white hair used committees and reports so skillfully that each student found opportunities to speak out and battle over ideas.

The heart of Kilpatrick's first major contribution to education, "The Project Method," was founded on his faith in the potential of the individual learner. In back of the recurrent Kilpatrickian phrases which valued "purposeful activity," "intrinsic motivation," "planning," in back of his opposition to "extrinsic subject matter" which disregarded individuals, in back of his opposition to meaningless rote learning, lay Kilpatrick's belief that clues to significant content can be found within the learner and can be developed fully in collaboration with a mature adult who fosters self-direction and independent thought. The later Kilpatrick increased his stress on the importance of social orientation and the urgency of meeting social problems. But the mark Kilpatrick lastingly left on the progressive movement still derives largely from his faith in the potentiality of the learner when that potentiality is cultivated by skillful and sensitive teachers. To many educators, probably to most, insight into the relationship between the individual and his education was the major contribution of the progressive education which Kilpatrick espoused, though he was concerned for philosophical and social, as well as psychological, foundations. And—mistake it not —the insight derived from Kilpatrick made a massive contribution to education in an era that had lost sight of the importance of the learner and his purposes and potential.

A second wing of the progressive movement set forth answers to the perennial questions of aims, foundations, and content largely in terms of the society which surrounded the schools. George Counts, a battler for socially oriented schools in a democracy, serves as a symbol of this emphasis. To George Counts, for instance, the times cried out for an education realistically geared to the new social order which was emerging. He threw his eloquent challenge to the Progressive Education Association assembled in convention in 1932. He amplified his ideas in the pamphlet "Dare the Schools Build A New Social Order?" and for years educators found themselves forced to face the issues Counts raised. Whether one condemned aspects of his viewpoint as indoctrination and a potential abuse of the method of intelligence, thus classifying it as a new liberal's version of authoritarianism, or whether one hailed it as a realistic recognition of the overpowering importance of social problems, as an indication that the social sciences had come of age, an educator who heard Counts had to take into account stress on society. The role of education with respect to social change and to reform was an imperative and recurrent theme with Counts and his fellow social reconstructionists. The pivotal place of social realities in education could not be forgotten after Counts was heard, even though indoctrination might be repudiated.

George Counts lived his faith. He helped turn back Communist infiltration of teachers' unions. He was a tower of strength in the Liberal Party; he was a candidate for public office and in the vanguard of social movements of his time. He is still active in his retirement.

To others equally immersed in the progressive movement, democratic values were central to all considerations. For instance, to Boyd H. Bode, the Lincoln-like man from Illinois who made his major contribution through Ohio State University, the crucial need was for the clarification of differences between the democratic way of life and the way of its authoritarian competitors. As he saw it, the road out of value confusion led through a remorseless and unremitting use of the method of intelligence in human affairs. To Bode, progressive education was at the crossroads and a child-centered view would never suffice. Nor was indoctrination the road to a better world. He conducted his classes in philosophy of education through the Socratic method and he fostered thought with every heckling, humorous, or trenchant exchange of ideas into day-by-day learning experiences.

I venture for your consideration the bold hypothesis that each of these men touched on part of the whole, that each perceived and particularly stressed an aspect of education which we neglect at our peril, that each succeeded nobly, and, where he failed, failed gallantly in building the "new education." Each asked the right questions; each responded with relevant contributions toward workable answers for our times.

The thinker who came closest to the reconciliation of the individual, society, and philosophical foundations—was the extraordinary John Dewey, whose centennial was celebrated by the John Dewey Society three years ago through meetings in scores of universities across the nation. The word "extraordinary" is used advisedly. During his long lifetime, this incredible man lived a full life as a person, participated in social and civic action, conducted the most famous laboratory school in history, became the father figure of the progressive education movement (and, to shift the analogy, sometimes served as mother hen by reconciling conflicts and even smoothing ruffled feathers in the flock), became a towering figure in philosophy, and, in the process, managed to leave for posterity a legacy of 5,000 pages of articles and 18,000 pages in book form.

Yet even Dewey, prodigious though his endeavors were, never achieved extensive translation of his ideas into a new curriculum. Underbrush in philosophy needed to be cleared. After his Laboratory School experimentation, and after setting forth his pedagogical creed in such books as "The School and Society" and "Democracy and Education," Dewey gave himself to this Herculean labor as he built his philosophy of experimentalism. He constantly reacted to trends and tendencies in progressive education, as he did in his critique "Experience and Education." He made only occasional critical forays into program building. He would be the first to admit, were he alive, that much remained to be done to implement his ideas on what he preferred to term simply "education," rather than "progressive education."

So we turn back to the thinking of representative intellectual leaders of the progressive movement in education, not in any spirit of ancestor worship, but for the inescapable questions they raised and for the insights they contributed toward workable solutions for our times. Cremin says it well in his final paragraphs: "There remained a timelessness about many of the problems the progressives raised and the solutions they proposed. . . . And for all the talk about pedagogical breakthroughs and crash programs, the authentic progressive vision remained strangely pertinent to the problems of mid-century America. Perhaps it only awaited the reformulation and resuscitation that would ultimately derive from a larger research and reform in American life and thought." With these words Cremin partially redeems the strange inconsistency of pointing out brilliantly in early chapters that social currents created progressive education well before the official establishment of a Progressive Educational Association, yet conveying the impression in his final chapter that the demise of an organization and a magazine meant the death of progressive education. The fact that ideas live beyond organizations apparently escaped the overanxious gravediggers who gleefully greeted Cremin's book as the definitive obituary for progressive education as a force in American ideas.

The questions raised and many of the tentative answers ventured by the early leaders of progressive education are not dead nor will they die. In time, the sponsors of new educational technology, the advocates of varied forms of educational organization, the proponents of study of the structure of separate disciplines, must face the inescapable questions and consider the possible solutions proposed.

The problem for sponsors and users of programmed learning through teaching machines does not lie in the capacity of the machine to produce positive reinforcement, whether it takes the form of a kind word, a pat on the head, or, indeed, a bottle of Coca-Cola. Given technical ingenuity, a reinforcing reward will be forthcoming. The harder problem for sponsors and users of the teaching machine is whether positive reinforcement will be used to bring nearer George Orwell's "1984" and Aldous Huxley's "Brave New World," or whether programmed learning, using positive reinforcement selectively and with discrimination, will reduce the skill-drudgery of education and free teachers and students for more humane aspects of learning and human development, such as creativity, the use of reflective thought, and experiences in freedom. Consider, for instance, this quotation from "Walden Two," a Utopia envisioned by the pioneer of teaching machines, B. F. Skinner of Harvard, a Utopia which appears to some of us an authoritarian nightmare world of behavioristic conditioning. T. E. Frazier, spokesman for "Walden Two," says approvingly, "Now that we *know* how positive reinforcement works and why negative doesn't . . . we can be more deliberate, and hence more successful, in our cultural design. We can achieve a sort of control under which the controlled, even though they are following a code much more scrupulously than was ever the case under the old system, nevertheless *feel free*. They are doing what they want to do, not what they are forced to do. That's the source of the tremendous power of positive reinforcement—there's no restraint and no revolt. By a careful cultural design, we control not the final behavior, but the *inclination* to behave—the motives, the desires, the wishes.

"The curious thing is that in that case *the question of freedom never arises.*"

In the light of this quotation we can understand why Aldous Huxley recently reminded us in "Brave New World Revisited" that it may be later than we think. He wrote as his conclusion, "The older dictators fell because they never could supply their subjects with enough bread, enough circuses, enough miracles and mysteries. Nor did they possess a really effective system of mind-manipulation. . . . Under a scientific dictator, education will really work—with the result that most men and women will grow up to love their servitude and will never dream of revolution. There seems to be no good reason why a thoroughly scientific dictatorship should ever be overthrown."

The problem before the sponsors of educational television is not how wide a circle over six states, or indeed a nation, can be reached by a plane flying for Midwest Airborne Television. Nor is it bouncing beams off satellites for global television. Technology will solve those problems. The real problem is whether the device will realize the gloomy prophecy of an old Vanderbilt University professor who once said at a meeting of the American Association of University Professors, "Gentlemen, the time is coming when one Harvard University professor will determine through his history course on television what history is taught in the United States—and even if it's Arthur Schlesinger, Jr., I say the hell with it!"—or whether imaginative educational TV will provide learners with a magic carpet to a wider world of experience made at once more expansive and more closely detailed.

The problem before the sponsors and users of team teaching is not precisely how many students to instruct at any given time in any given space. It is not whether a new magical number combination, proposed for better staff utilization, or some flexible magic of numbers out of Lexington, Massachusetts, will take the place of the former magic number—25 or 30 in each classroom. Experience and, we hope, genuine controlled experimentation, will supply the answer here. The real problem is whether team teaching actually will improve learning, whether it will evolve toward emphasis on the *interrelationships* of subject matter, whether it can provide sufficient personalized contacts with teachers and sufficient firsthand experiences by students to enable young people to deal with significant problems.

The problem before the sponsors and users of the dual progress plan is not the technical difficulty of introducing specialized science, mathematics, and arts teachers into elementary school organization through the demonstrations at Ossining and Long Beach in New York. The real problem for the sponsors and users of the dual progress plan is recognized by the originator of the plan as whether the dual progress plan will or will not better answer some of Dewey's persistent queries; George Stoddard poses the issue in his new book, "The Dual Progress Plan," which should be read along with the Association for Supervision and Curriculum Development pamphlet, "The Self-Contained Classroom," for differing organizational approaches to possibly compatible goals.

The problem before the liberal arts professors currently reconstructing and updating knowledge in such disciplines as physics, biology, and mathematics is not whether they can cram all of man's new knowledge into separate watertight compartments, which will then be siphoned off during the elementary and high school years. They can't. Even if they could, they would endlessly face true obsolescence, for knowledge swiftly dates and, like fish, won't keep. The real problem, of which some of the reconstructors of disciplines are aware and of which others appear quite unaware, is whether the scholars can identify concepts in their new knowledge which can be made meaningful to children and youth, appropriate to both the general and specialized education needed for living in today's society, crucial in the process of critical thinking and problem solving—or whether their reconstructed and amplified knowledge, however new, will prove to be inert subject matter in Alfred North Whitehead's sense.

The problem for those who are studying the structures of the disciplines may be first to make clear what they mean. Granted that they can and do, the question will face them as to whether their studies of structures of disciplines are to be achieved as culminations built upon the experience of learners, as Dewey recommended. Or will their studies of structures of disciplines be evasions of problems central to general education, formal orientations to content which bear little relationship to how young people live and learn?

One can derive little encouragement for the future of study of the structure of the disciplines from the views of Charles R. Keller, director of the John Hay Fellows Program, who believes "too many social studies teachers have emphasized the creation of good citizens rather than the content and discipline of their subjects." He says, "Attitudes cannot be taught in formal classroom situations. We weaken education—and schools—when we try to do so. What students should do in school is to study subjects and become acquainted with facts and ideas. Subjects as such have disciplines that will help to develop students' minds." Is this the conception of educational aims and psychology of learning which is to characterize the new advocacy of studying the structure of disciplines? Surely this was not the conception of Arthur W. Foshay when, in his presidential address to the Association for Supervision and Curriculum Development in 1961, he advised "that we educators take directly into account the nature of the organized bodies of knowledge, in addition to the nature of the growing child and the nature of our society, as we try to make curriculum decisions."

If their work is to have meaning, rather than to be innovation for unclear purposes, the sponsors and users of the new technology, organization, and approaches to disciplines must come to terms with the questions that engaged the intellectual leadership of the progressive movement in education. Questions of "why" and "what" have necessary precedence over questions of "how" and "when." The inescapable questions relate to the aims of education, the foundations of the program, and what the schools should teach as appropriate content based on such aims and foundations.

Is, then, the progressive movement in education obsolete? I think not. The questions raised by the "new education" are remorseless, inevitable, demanding. The answers provided by the intellectual leaders of the progressive movement were promising beginnings, useful leads, valid foreshadowings.

When considerations of "why" are dodged, we get prescriptions which simply cannot be appraised. One cannot truly evaluate the proposals made in widely read books which are characterized by indifference to aims and purposes in the early chapters and which then constantly smuggle in unanalyzed value assumptions through the remainder of the pages. Two knights entered in the educational jousting show this tendency: both the great and good James B. Conant and the provocative and prancing Martin Mayer.

Conant, for instance, does not set forth aims for education in "The American High School Today." Yet he steadily makes assumptions as to what knowledge is of most worth.

In "Slums and Suburbs," Conant says, "It is after visits to schools like these that I grow impatient with both critics and defenders of public education who ignore the realities of school situations to engage in fruitless debate about educational philosophy, purposes, and the like. These situations call for action, not hair-splitting arguments." Yet "Slums and Suburbs" is permeated with proposals for action which must be based on philosophic assumptions.

In "The Schools," Martin Mayer colorfully rejects all possible formulations of aims. He says, "It is well to rid oneself immediately of this business of 'the aims of education.' Discussions on this subject are among the dullest and most fruitless of human pursuits. Whatever the ideal general 'aims of education' may be, they certainly cannot be accomplished in schools." He then proceeds to lace through his book individualistic approbations and denunciations based on his acceptance of undefined aims.

One of the myths of our times is that the several tendencies which characterized what is broadly termed progressive education prevailed, were fully achieved, and are now being repudiated. This sedulously cultivated myth is incomprehensible. The reality is that progressive education has never been tried on any significant scale.

As the inescapable queries reassert themselves and the tentative proposals of the varied interpretations of progressive education are reconsidered, educators will find it necessary to utilize the insights of Dewey, Bode, Counts, and Kilpatrick. An education which takes into account the individual, his society, and his values—an education which builds upon the soundest possible scholarship derivative from psychological, social, and philosophical foundations—is imperative in developing a curriculum appropriate for twentieth-century man.

The central questions posed and the relevant contributions toward workable answers for our times made by such interpreters of the progressive movement in education are not obsolete. They must and will persist. In time, they will be embodied in the form of new proposals for modern education, new syntheses which build upon our predecessors, as is common in the world of ideas. The overanxious gravediggers, and those who currently give them comfort, will discover as this twentieth century moves along that what they have mistaken for a corpse is indeed very much alive.

27. Methods in Teaching

STANLEY S. STAHL, JR.

It is widely recognized today that teacher education occupies an ever-increasing role of importance in our society. We have accepted as a mandate the necessity of planning educational programs which will meet the needs of all American youth. Obviously, this dictate of quantity must also be tempered with quality if the challenges to American leadership are to be met. This desire for quality has led us to a searching look at the teacher education concepts developed in the past and to give increasing attention to those elements unique to the profession.

From Stanley S. Stahl, Jr., "Methods in Teaching," *The Journal of Teacher Education*, XII (December, 1961), 397–400. Stanley S. Stahl, Jr. is Associate Professor of Education and Assistant Dean, School of Education, University of Virginia, Charlottesville, Virginia. Reprinted by permission of *The Journal of Teacher Education*.

A study of the programs of typical institutions quickly reveals that all professions expect certain degrees of competency in that loosely defined area described as general education and further depth in the content of the field under study. Equally well understood is the specialized or professional course work in education, the nucleus of which has traditionally been the methods of teaching courses. Concern has been expressed for many years about the role and relative importance of these methods courses in the preparation of teachers. This concern has ranged from loud criticism, on the one hand, to an equally vociferous defense, on the other, with each position being defended by both classroom teachers and those who are administratively concerned with teacher education programs. Both positions, even though seemingly opposed, are assumed to be taken in an effort to improve the calibre of personnel entering the teaching profession and to strengthen the ability to make a contribution to the learning process. The following summation represents an attempt to bring together various points of view and to arrive at some suggestions upon which intended improvement might be based.

ISSUES

The first major issue that emerges would seem to be the place of methods courses in the teacher education curriculum. A study of typical curricula reveals that these methods courses may be divided into two major types, the specific and the general. The older or traditional type represents the approach of teaching the prospective teacher the techniques appropriate to a particular field, such as a course on teaching arithmetic in the elementary school. This approach can, and often has, resulted in a proliferation of "teaching of" courses. In some colleges, not only is there one for each of the usual content areas but also courses on related topics such as mental hygiene and the use of audio-visual materials. Such a pattern has led to much criticism of the curricula, particularly in elementary education, charges of duplication and lack of practicality being the most common.

A more recent development in the professional course work has been the general approach of merging or combining the methods work into a single course. This course is concerned with the general, overall principles of teaching that should apply to the teaching act, regardless of the subject or content. Although this has eliminated some criticism of duplication and overlapping, critics point out that the basic assumption may be false. Various content areas do necessitate the utilization of specific, often unique techniques, many of which could not be spelled out in a general approach. A compromise can be discerned in some programs in which a sequence has been set up, beginning with a basic general information course applicable to all subjects, followed by a selection of special methods for the intended field. This would appear to be more practical at the secondary education level, although some programs do call for a degree of specialization at the elementary education level also.

Another fundamental consideration involves more than the teacher education program. Preparation of teachers must be based upon the underlying philosophy and objectives of the school system in general and must be adaptable to the needs of a changing society. It is not necessary to list the pressures under which schools operate, but it must be kept in mind that emphases and concepts are undergoing constant revision. The emphasis for some time has been upon a fused and integrated program, particularly at the elementary school and junior high school teaching levels. Recently, however, even at the elementary levels, certain pressures are mounting for a higher degree of proficiency in specific content fields. Although advocates of the core or broad fields curriculum and the self-contained classroom have generally opposed any extension of specific methodology, the general approach would appear to be less and less acceptable if present trends continue.

FEATURES OF EDUCATIONAL METHOD

Successful teaching is teaching that brings about effective learning. It is not defined in terms of methods or procedures, i.e., whether the teaching is typed as old-fashioned or modern, time-tested or experimental, conventional or progressive. The ultimate criterion for success in teaching is the result: the degree to which the objective has been reached. This is what society wants, and this must be kept in mind whenever a particular method is upheld as "the method." These desired results do not indicate any particular plan or procedure or methodology. This is not to imply, however, that a prospective teacher should be told, "this is the content; teach it in whatever way you can, but get results." There are basic principles and procedures behind all successful endeavors. Helping learners achieve authentic results calls for skill, insight, and resourcefulness on the part of the teacher. Method, then, must give the teacher these strengths.

Featherstone,[1] emphasizes that the formulation of basic principles of a technical nature is not sufficient to insure the hoped-for results. There must be a valid situation in relation to which learning is to take place. "Valid situation," as used here, means a situation that is of obvious demonstrable or felt concern to the learner and one in which he is already actively involved to some degree, or one in which he can pre-

---

[1] See William B. Featherstone, *A Functional Curriculum for Youth* (New York: American Book Company, 1950) p. 276.

sumably become more intimately involved and more competent to manage.

TOWARD A BETTER METHODOLOGY

Any discussion of the role that methods play in teacher preparation must also be concerned with the multiplicity of approaches (or methods) to the teaching act. The search for a better methodology has been going on for many years and will, of course, continue. The teacher in preparation should know of this search and have some understanding of the relationships of the changing philosophies to the emerging society. Change, regardless of how radical, is based upon past experience and the achievements and errors of earlier attempts.

Mursell[2] highlights some of the major attempts to improve teaching and points out that, although the search has not been co-ordinated, it has evolved in a rather definite direction. The traditional, and undoubtedly typical, method of teaching is usually referred to as the textbook-assignment-recitation procedure. Basically, this calls for an organizing of the content into some unitized form incorporated into a textbook, the assigning of certain portions or lessons, a reciting or daily check in lesson coverage, and finally an examining of the student on his degree of mastery. Although utilized universally and defended by many who have known no variation, teachers today are becoming increasingly aware that the pattern is hardly compatible with the desired emphasis upon individual needs and interests. Even at the turn of the century, scholars were reporting efforts to work out a better and more effective method of presentation. In 1900, McMurry and McMurry[3] described the inductive-development lesson, originated by Johann Friedrich Herbart. Herbart's formal steps of instruction, even though rather formalized, were widely acclaimed in this country and were instrumental in originating a valuable movement to improve educational practice. Basically, his approach was an attempt to lead the child's mind in a sequential movement from concrete experience and concrete data to the understanding of a general concept. The formal steps included preparation, statement of aim, presentation of new material, comparison and abstraction, and finally generalization and application. Later contributors to pedagogy, notably John Dewey, devised or rejected many of the original principles.

Bagley[4] describes another deviation from the traditional approach

[2] James L. Mursell, *Successful Teaching* (New York: McGraw-Hill Book Company, Inc., 1954) Chapter 2.
[3] Charles A. McMurry and Frank M. McMurry, *The Method of the Recitation* (New York: The Macmillan Company, 1900).
[4] William C. Bagley, *The Educative Process* (New York: The Macmillan Company, 1917).

as the deductive-development lesson, which differed mainly from Herbart's theories in that general principles were applied to the data, rather than drawing the principles from the data. A set of steps was again applied: presentation of data, assimiliation, inference, and, finally, verification. This same text describes other variations, each of which attempted to improve the methods used in varying learning situations.

The neophyte in teaching, after an initial period of frustration, begins to draw certain conclusions about methods. He sees that any one approach, even with its advantages and disadvantages, will still have inherent defects of either standardization, superficiality, or both. If the method is too rigidly followed, flexibility is not apparent and the various classroom situations soon return to the basic recitation. Research results, surprisingly enough, seem to reveal that it makes little difference what method or approach is followed, but the many variants in a learning situation have great effect. It soon becomes evident that the chances for improving instruction by any standardized methodology, or even an array of clever devices, are relatively small and that an over-all understanding of the learning process offers more merit. As Mursell[5] states:

> Learning must be organized in terms of understandings that seem real and compelling and valuable to the learner, that engage his active purpose, that confront him with significant challenges, that lead to deeper and wider insights, more discriminating attitudes and more adequate skills.

CURRENT TRENDS IN METHODS TEACHING

Any attempt to summarize what is happening or could happen in the teaching of methods courses becomes rather general in nature because of the countless individual patterns which are being followed. One seldom encounters a professor who is teaching methods to beginning teachers who is not actively experimenting and changing his patterns in an attempt to bring about greater understanding and efficiency in teaching. To say what is new tends to negate the contributions referred to above or to suggest some startlingly novel approach. It is apparent, however, that there are several definite trends that can be cited:

1. Methods courses in teacher education are becoming more functional, with the professor himself attempting to teach as the students will teach, drawing constantly upon basic principles of learning. This approach includes the utilization of laboratory experiences, audio-visual materials of all types, the relatively recent teaching-machine programming, unit organization, recognition of individual differences, and other desired classroom practices. It is also noteworthy that attempts

[5] *Op. cit.*, p. 32.

have been made to make a fundamental change in the relationship between teacher and pupil. Methods courses are borrowing heavily from
the supervised-study movement, as advanced by Brownell, and the
project method advocated by Kilpatrick. Since in these approaches we
see a shifting of the teacher's role from merely teaching to active participation with the learner, the future may see many changes in the
traditional role played by teachers.

2. Many critics of teacher education programs lament that there is
too much time consumed in learning the "how" and not enough in
learning the "what." Such statements, although possibly true in past
years, can hardly be justified today. The ratio of professional education
to general or liberal education in teacher preparation has gradually become less, giving the prospective teacher much more "content." Methods courses also reveal the effect of this pattern, with efforts being made
to give more substance and more content. The Thirty-Seventh Yearbook of the Association for Student Teaching[6] describes a number of
reported attempts to have students develop a more complete understanding of basic concepts as presented in the classroom.

3. The team approach to methods, utilized in many of the block
semester plans, is a related trend. Here we find the methods courses
combined in a block, often representing the equivalent of a semester
of credit, co-ordinated by one person, but drawing upon the specific
skills and special preparation of the entire staff. In addition to the educational specialists, other resource persons are drawn from the liberal
arts fields, presenting basic reviews of content, and from other areas,
with implications for education.

[6] *Improving Instruction in Professional Education* (Lock Haven, Pennsylvania:
State Teachers College, 1958) Chapter IV.

PART
TWO

CLASSROOM PROCEDURES: WIDELY-USED
ACTIVITIES FOR TEACHING AND LEARNING

Introduction

Guides to better learning and teaching are furnished by the principles of teaching. Educational practice rests upon a foundation of beliefs about learning as well as upon factual knowledge about how humans learn. But beliefs about teaching and learning, even factual knowledge about educational practice, are only guides to actual classroom teaching. The techniques of guiding and directing the work of pupils are skills which must be studied and practiced in order to be learned. The teacher's framework for teaching, that is, the general pattern which he accepts as a sound basis for approaching his work, constitutes his philosophy of education. But the means of carrying out that philosophy are shown by the classroom methods which he employs.

For example, a teacher may believe sincerely in the principle that learning is an active and not a passive process. This is probably a sound principle that most teachers have been taught to verbalize and probably is one that most teachers accept. However, the teacher might run into all sorts of difficulties in his attempt to use class methods and to devise learning activities that are consistent with the principle. He might become confused about the meanings of the words "active" and "passive" when applied to the work of pupils and decide that the definition of "active" implies physical movement. Consequently, his pupils go on field trips, build objects, form into committees, engage in numerous discussions, paint posters, prepare exhibits, conduct polls, and perform other tasks that the teacher decides are "active." However, they do little reading, seldom listen, and only infrequently watch what the others are doing or look at that which has been done because these activities are not physical, hence are believed by this teacher to be passive processes. Of course, the teacher has taken a very narrow view of what constitutes an active versus a passive process of learning. Intellectual activity in school work is the key to learning, and reading, listening, and watching are at least as intellectual as any other school activities that have been devised. The process of learning becomes active, not so much because of what the pupil actually does in order to learn as because of the interest and motivation with which he attacks his problems. Reluctantly tagging along at the end of the line during a field trip can be a very passive process of learning. Serious study of a well-organized chapter in a textbook with the goal of understanding its content can be a highly active process. The principle that learning is an active, not a passive, process is sound but it refers not so much to what the pupils do as to how they go about doing whatever they do.

Similar comments might be made about any other principle of teaching that could be stated. To illustrate, one might accept the idea that teaching through democratic procedures is a more effective way to teach good citizenship than to talk to pupils about good citizenship or to lecture about democracy. But one would still face the problem of defining democracy and deciding exactly how the acceptable definition applied to teaching and learning. Do democratic procedures decide the answers to questions in academic areas? Do the votes of children decide what they will learn and how they will learn it? Are democratic procedures always best? Is good citizenship such an overriding goal that all the means of education must be devoted to this end? Does the principle apply to the teaching of algebra to the same degree that it does to the teaching of civics?

It is not necessary to list pages of educational principles and questions about them to make the point that principles, in themselves, do not describe for the teacher that which he and his pupils will do. Principles help establish the general route for ushering the teacher into the classroom. He still must decide what to do after he arrives.

And here is where the teacher, especially the beginning teacher, confronts a bewildering problem because the variety of choice in teaching methods appears almost endless. Just about the time that he has prepared a good outline for lecture and discussion on a particular topic the teacher discovers an excellent filmstrip with an accompanying talk on the same topic. Before long he finds that the topic is treated even more adequately in a motion picture. And eventually he may discover that the topic may be discussed on television, described in the encyclopedia, treated in a current article in a nationally distributed magazine, or even that the father of one of his pupils is an expert on the topic and is willing to come to school to address the class. The problem of choice is complicated further when it is discovered, as it is discovered by all teachers, that the methods which lead some pupils to learn do not always have the same result with others. Variety in the methods of the classroom may not be an end in itself, but reasonable variety may be the crucial factor that allows some pupils the opportunity to learn.

Every teacher finds his favorite classroom procedures. Some methods become favorites because of the personal strengths and weaknesses of the teacher. Obviously, a teacher with a slight speech defect, not serious enough to bar him from the profession but noticeable in ordinary conversation, would be unlikely to place himself in a position where he had to act as chairman for a series of panel discussions. Some methods become favorites because they are particularly appropriate to the grade level or to the subject. Discussion may not be the best way to solve a problem in chemistry, but it may be an appropriate way to present all positions of a highly controversial topic in the social studies. The availability of equipment may explain a seeming partiality for some methods. If a recorder is not available, one can hardly expect the teacher to use it.

Despite the fact that most teachers in service do utilize some classroom methods which they favor over others, professional teachers are always alert to the possibility of new approaches and new ideas in the classroom. Educators diligently continue to warn against the dangers of overdone academic routine. Professional journals carry numerous articles listing the do's and don't's of specific learning activities. Teachers constantly report their experiences with especially successful techniques, and both articles in magazines and talks at conferences are likely to be centered on successful practices in specific schools. Textbooks on teaching ordinarily contain chapters devoted to the most generally used learning activities. Textbooks have appeared in special areas such as audio-visual education; in fact, textbooks may be found which treat only a single activity such as discussion or television. New methods and techniques are being promoted continually, and old practices endure. From them all the alert teacher selects those that appear to be most appropriate.

The selections that follow constitute a sampling of writings on some of the most widely-used learning activities recommended for general classroom use. This group of readings should provide a start, but only a start, along the road toward mastery of each. They are presented as beginning readings for the future teacher and perhaps have value as reference readings for the experienced teacher. But, as they are read, a number of questions should be kept in mind. If the article is one of opinion, does the author endorse the practice and point out its uses, or does he criticize and suggest its limitations? Can other articles be located which take different viewpoints? If the reading reports a practice in a particular school or in a specific subject, does its content apply to other schools and to other subjects? If more than a few years old, is the reading still appropriate? If new, does it appear that it will last in school practice? If the item is a research report, does the evidence appear to justify the conclusions or recommendations, and if not, why not? Can other research be located which either supports or contradicts these findings? Does the article list specific uses for an activity or suggest certain steps for directing the activity? If so, are the suggested uses practical and do the steps given appear logical and necessary? Finally, what can the reader find in each that is worth remembering or that appears to have particular applicability for his own work in the classroom?

28. *What To Look For in Choosing a Textbook*
MALCOLM E. MELLOTT

Thirty years ago the selection of textbooks was almost invariably made by the superintendent or the schoolboard. Today, things have changed; most teachers have a chance to select, or to help select, their own textbooks.

The textbook should be thoroughly examined and understood so that it can easily, speedily, and adequately serve its intended use.

Teachers have had to pick up on a rather hit-or-miss basis their knowledge of the books to be used. Little attention has been paid to the professional instruction of teachers in the matter of selecting books. Often an hour or two during a curriculum-materials course has served as the only time given to discussion of this vital instructional tool. Tho there are definite signs of improvement, inservice education programs have been doing only a little better.

When considering a new textbook, these factors must be studied: organization, content, method, illustrations, and general appearance.

From Malcolm E. Mellott, "What To Look For in Choosing a Textbook," *NEA Journal*, XLIV (March, 1955), 158–159. Malcolm E. Mellott is Vice President and Editor-in-Chief, Educational Book Division, Prentice-Hall, Inc., Englewood Cliffs, New Jersey. Reprinted by permission of the *Journal* of the National Education Association.

LOOK AT THE ORGANIZATION

What are the objectives for your particular course? What areas do you want to cover? What areas *must* be covered? How well does the textbook you are considering cover these areas? Does it offer additional areas which will help in the work of your course? Or will the additional material be distracting?

Some textbooks are organized into parts; others, according to units, chapters, or similar devices in order to facilitate block examination and study.

Remember, the author and publisher had to select from a wealth of available material the particular things which they thought cogent. Even with general agreement provided by a course of study, there would still be a selection factor to reckon with.

Prior to the actual publishing of a textbook, authors and publishers spend time and effort in finding out how educators all over the country are organizing courses. The resultant organization of the book reflects their findings.

As an evaluator, you will determine whether or not you are in substantial agreement with the author's choice of topics. Your judgments will depend on how well the author's selection fits your course of study, whether or not the selection is based on pupil interest, and whether the material is useful.

INVESTIGATE THE CONTENT

If you are in substantial agreement with the over-all organization of the textbook, then examine the content, with your particular students in mind. Are the concepts clearly stated? Are these concepts really developed or merely mentioned? Are too many concepts jammed together? Will the vocabulary be understood by your pupils?

Next, see if there is a sensible sequence in the development of the content. Does the text build up concepts in an order acceptable to you? If not, then decide whether the book will still be effective if the order is altered.

Examine the book carefully to see whether it assumes too little or too much prior knowledge for your particular group of children. Finally, decide whether the book provides a basis on which to build the succeeding class subjects required in your curriculum.

EXAMINE THE METHOD

The modern textbook has built-in methods which you may wish to adapt to suit your own objectives, your students, and yourself. Publishing companies attempt to find authors who are abreast of the times and who are themselves expert teachers. Often a combination of authors with a variety of skills produces the best results.

The method should suit your purpose and, of course, should be in line with modern educational theory. Generally speaking, the good text provides for pupil planning and participation in the development of the concepts, and the material in the text is correlated in various practical ways with other subject fields.

A text also should suggest ways of utilizing and relating ideas from other sources. No textbook should be expected to be the lone source of authority, but should provide for the use of other material.

The mere recital of fact is not enough. The good textbook consistently provides for visualization, evaluation, generalization, summation, and application. Opportunity should be provided for the handling of social problems of childhood in an enlargement of the pupil's horizon.

Examine the suggested activities. Are they stimulating, interesting, meaningful learning activities that are within the realm of possibility for your pupils in your school and community?

Some activities should be simple enough so that each pupil can make a contribution, while others should be of sufficient complexity to challenge the more rapid learner. It is not necessary, however, to have page after page of suggested activities.

EVALUATE THE ILLUSTRATIONS

Don't let the pictures fool you; illustrations do not always contribute to the content of a book. If they are merely decorative, they don't do the job that textbook illustrations should do. Make sure that the illustrations are suitable for your pupils, that they are good teaching devices, and that there are enough so that you are not constantly plagued with the need for supplementary material.

Don't be disappointed if the book doesn't have certain specific pictures, for it is impossible to put a full page of illustration and a full page of type on the same page! For every picture another might have been chosen, but only one could be used.

Ordinarily, illustrations should be next to or as close as possible to the idea discussed in type. And good picture captions are interesting, stimulating, and useful.

Good maps and charts are easily understandable. Single-purpose maps and charts are superior to those that are cluttered and multipurpose.

CONSIDER THE GENERAL APPEARANCE

Textbooks ought to be attractive and reasonably durable, but neither of these factors should have as much weight as the aforementioned items. The durability is reasonably controlled by uniform state specifications as to weight of paper, binding, and the like.

Attractiveness is frequently a matter of taste. The amount and kind of color illustration bear more relationship to reducing sales resistance than to teachability.

I think it has never been proved that a child learns more or better because illustrations are in color. However, color may give a child greater interest in one book than in another.

The size, style, and distribution of type on the page is also a matter of taste, but it is vital that the type face and size chosen be legible and not burdened with fancy formations. Teachers insist on large type for first-graders but accept progressively smaller type up thru the grades. Actually, studies show that the best type size for the beginning reader is about the same as that which is best for the accomplished older reader.

As far as I know, there are no studies on the relationship of general appearance or format to learning. What we know is experiential rather than experimental. From the standpoint of appearance it is unfortunate that adults rather than children choose the books, because all too frequently the choice is made in terms of adult rather than child standards.

SELECT A GOOD ASSISTANT

It is doubtful that you will ever find the book that does all the things you want. You will have to select the best available textbook for the specific needs of your subject, your pupils, and your community.

Too often the textbook is blamed for faulty teaching in a school when the trouble actually lies in the paucity of classroom reference books, library facilities, and visual aids. Deficiencies on the part of the teacher may also enter into the picture.

Textbooks have been criticized and defended, lampooned and supported. But their careful selection is one of the top responsibilities of an educator. For the textbook is an assistant teacher in print.

29. Using Textbooks Wisely

ARTHUR W. FOSHAY

Teaching is a highly personal affair. You have to teach in a way that fits you, not someone else. If you try to teach someone else's way, your teaching becomes spurious. A teacher is the main person in a classroom, in the sense that what goes on in the class depends mainly on what the teacher does.

The teacher's work is artful, imaginative, and good for the children only if the teacher makes it that way. The art of teaching consists in applying what one knows about the subject matter to be learned, the learning process, and the development of children to a particular group of children and to one's self. If it all fits well, then the teaching works out well. If it doesn't fit, the teaching works out badly. Anything less than this conscious fitting of the science and art of education to a particular group of children isn't teaching at all. It's mere taskmastering.

Obvious? There are lots of people who don't know these things, or who have forgotten them. These include some laymen, some college professors, and some teachers. When it comes to textbooks, these teachers let the textbooks use them, instead of their using the textbooks.

Here are two things to do and two things to avoid, if one wishes to use textbooks wisely.

TWO THINGS TO DO

1. Read the textbook and the manual thoroughly and thoughtfully before putting the text in the hands of children.

You have to understand that the writers of textbooks and the accompanying teachers' manuals are attempting the impossible task of suiting everybody. Typically, they do this by being extremely concrete, keeping the text exceedingly simple, and offering a highly definite

From Arthur W. Foshay, "Using Textbooks Wisely," *The Instructor*, LXVIII, No. 7 (March, 1959), 76–78. Arthur W. Foshay is Professor of Education, Executive Officer of the Horace Mann-Lincoln Institute of School Experimentation, and Director of Research and Field Service of Teachers College, Columbia University. Copyright 1959 by the F. A. Owen Publishing Company. Reprinted from *The Instructor* by permission.

series of things to do. Someone who does not know a thing about teaching could take a modern textbook and simply do what it says to do, and the children would learn somewhat. But this would not be teaching.

If you are going to use the textbook to suit your children and your teaching style, then you must first of all know thoroughly what the text contains, and what the manual says about the author's intent. This is the only way you can be free to depart from the highly specific sequence of the text, yet make use of the many good ideas usually offered. Comb the text and manual thoroughly for good ideas. Opportunistic "hopping around" in a textbook is an unwise use of the book.

But you are not bound to use the author's sequence. You may violate it freely to make the book fit your plan, provided you know what you are doing and what the author is trying to do. Remember, you don't owe the author anything. His job is to serve your purposes; it is not your job to serve his.

2. Have the children use the text critically; teach them how to be intelligently critical of the book.

There are two main reasons for this. First, any professional teacher knows that one must involve children in their own learning, if the learning is to have real meaning. The goal of the child's efforts should be to learn the material to be grasped, not merely to "mind the book." One way to keep the child from being misled into merely following the book is to make the object of his learning so clear to him that he can judge how well the textbook helps him achieve it. If your children have suggestions for the improvement of a textbook, have them write their suggestions to the author and the publisher. You can be sure that these suggestions will be taken seriously. One reason some textbooks don't improve as they should is that the users are silent about their faults. The publishers want to give teachers what they will use, but they have a hard time finding out what you really want if you are silent. Instead, they publish what will sell—but that's not the same.

A second reason for teaching children to be critical of the textbook is that you want them to feel free to break with authority. If there's one important lesson everyone should learn these days, it is that what is in print is not necessarily true; that putting words between hard covers does not endow them with any virtue. The school textbook is an excellent place to begin this lesson. By its very nature, the text seems authoritative and final. Here, if any place, the distilled truth of mankind seems to be offered. What a wonderful place, therefore, to begin teaching the children how to be intellectually free—how to avoid a totalitarianism of the mind! The most subtle intellectual lesson of all has to do with the proper use of authority. One man's opinion is not as good as another's; it depends on whether the opinion is informed. But even a well informed opinion is only an opinion. It is not a law. It is not to remain unchallenged, simply because it is based on information. On the other hand, we do not want to drift into the cheap arrogance some people show, who challenge all opinions simply because they are offered.

TWO THINGS TO AVOID

1. Don't have the children do everything in the book.

Most texts—possibly with the exception of some readers—try to give enough practical material so that there will be enough for the child who needs the largest amount. This means that if you have all the children do all the exercises in an arithmetic, for example, a good many will be over-drilled and bored. Set up standards of speed and accuracy with the children, and when the standards have been achieved, move on. There is no more reason for having all children do the same arithmetic than there is to have them all do the same reading. To do so is to hold back the fast ones and discourage the slow ones. Have the children (and the parents, too, if possible) help to make up practice material. This is another way to involve the children in their learning, and it is good because it gets beyond the book.

2. Don't take the content of the textbook as the "core" to be "mastered."

The core of any subject matter is the logic of the subject itself. The core of history is not the facts, but the way the facts can be put together to be interpreted. The core of reading is not vocabulary, but getting meaning from a page. The core of arithmetic is not the processes, but problem solving. Most textbooks are not written in such a way as to present these "cores"—perhaps they cannot be. This kind of "core" material has to be developed with a class in a great variety of ways. To take the text as the core is to abdicate; the children learn the facts, but not the history; the processes, but not the arithmetic; the vocabulary, but not the reading. The text is an aid, and no more.

Here's how the American Textbook Publishers Institute puts it in *Textbooks in Education,* p. xi: "Every salesman, like every author, editor, and teacher, is personally and professionally concerned with the advancement of education as a whole. The oar which we in the publishing business pull is labeled *textbook.* We are proud of the contribution that we have made with that oar; we are willing to experiment with new techniques of rowing, but we don't—ever—mistake ourselves for the boat." To allow the textbook to become the core is to misuse it —"mistake it for the boat."

Remember that any textbook is the culmination of the most conscientious efforts of some very good people, who are trying to do something for everyone. The book was not written for your class, or for you. It was written for the "average teacher," who, like the "average child" or the "average man," is nothing but a group of lifeless statistics. The book is the end product of a lengthy cooperative effort. Here's how the American Textbook Publishers Institute describes it in *Textbooks in Education*, p. ix.

". . . . Just write what you believe that an editor will believe that a salesman will believe that a superintendent will believe that a supervisor will believe that a teacher will believe that a child will read with understanding, with pleasure, and with profit.

"No, I'm not joking. A textbook is a house-that-Jack-built kind of product. There are a lot of people between author and child . . . . Between the author and the child there are always dozens, sometimes hundreds, of people involved in the making and selection of that book for that child."

What it comes down to is this: A textbook is used wisely when the teacher knows what he is up to, and uses the text to fit his purposes. Texts are used unwisely when they are used literally, page by page, or when teachers "hop around" without knowing the text thoroughly. The opportunity exists for texts to be used in such a way as to aid learning in depth, but only when teachers make the educational purposes of school so clear to children that the children can know what to make use of and what to ignore in a textbook.

The great educational aim of the schools is to make pupils into students—that is, to teach children to be self-teachers. The textbooks can be of great aid in this process, provided the child knows what he is trying to learn. It is under these circumstances that teachers have used texts wisely ever since there were texts. Only when the teacher and the child both know what they are trying to accomplish can the textbook assume its proper role as "the assistant teacher in print."

30. Workbooks

RICHARD MADDEN

"Why are teachers so eager for workbooks? I have to fight against their use all the time." These words of a school administrator point up a controversy of concern to educators thruout the country today. Why

From Richard Madden, "Workbooks! Tool or Crutch?" *NEA Journal*, XLV (February, 1956), 94–95. Richard Madden is Professor of Education at Sonoma State College, Rohnert Park, California. Reprinted by permission of the *Journal* of the National Education Association.

do so many elementary-school teachers demand workbooks, and why do so many administrators and supervisors reject the requests?

What are the arguments for and against workbooks? Are these arguments more valid in some situations than in others? How may an elementary-school teacher use workbooks in the most profitable manner? A simple resolution of the controversy is not likely to emerge immediately.

Opponents of the workbook list these objections:

The teacher comes to rely upon the workbook and ceases to do developmental teaching.

The workbook often becomes the textbook in fact, even tho it may not be so designed.

School becomes monotonous and uninspiring. Pupils do the exercises with very little reflective thinking. Independence is lost.

All pupils do the same things, regardless of individual needs.

Workbook activity is piecemeal and seldom reaches the high level of creative thinking.

Workbook children are weak in writing complete sentences and are often poor in written expression in general.

In a market flooded with workbooks, teachers find it difficult to select wisely.

Teachers and school programs lack time for workbook activities to be tailored to pupils' needs.

Advocates of the workbook deny that the aforesaid evils need result, or that their occurrence is unique to the usage of workbooks. They list these reflections upon the use of workbooks:

Workbooks are but tools; misuse need not occur. Teachers who cannot use workbooks properly usually do other things no better.

Workbook exercises are usually prepared by writers much more skilled than the teacher who duplicates his own materials.

The time needed to write and duplicate materials is prohibitive.

In early school years, when pupils are beginning to write, their versatility is so limited that workbook activities help greatly. Various pencil-and-paper activities are needed to aid in the transition from concrete experiences to abstractions.

A workbook accompanying a textbook complements the learning and adds variety. Pages may be used to give parents an idea of pupil achievement.

Instruction in overcrowded classes is not going to be completely efficient; no instructional material will be completely adapted to individual needs.

Readily available materials aid class control.

Inappropriate drill leads to distaste and eventually to dislike for a subject. Copying problems is a waste of students' time.

Workbooks contain good diagnostic tests. They also provide concrete evidence of an individual's performance and needs.

Good work habits are established.

Workbooks encourage independence by setting a task, a plan, and a time to do the task.

Altho the arguments for and against workbooks are confusing, an examination of the issues may aid one's judgment regarding the use of workbooks in specific situations.

Four principles of learning should be kept in mind as one makes choices as to what pupils should or should not be doing:

1. Basic to all learning is personal mental activity on the part of the learner.

2. Activity operates best when it is purposeful for the learner.

3. Learning is best when the understanding of the learner is high.

4. The teacher's primary task is to provide experiences that continously evolve understandings at each pupil's level of development.

With these principles in mind, let us examine questions that one should answer as he decides for or against workbooks, or as he may choose a specific workbook or type of workbook.

What would pupils be doing if they were not using workbooks?

Some pupils might be reading in the rich heritage of children's literature. Some might be engaged in a construction activity in order to have a wholesome experience in planning, in cooperation, in reading for information, and in the development of manual skills. Some might be doing an experiment in science. Others might be expressing ideas in writing or in art media.

Skilful and creative teachers may duplicate arithmetic exercises that are especially needed or reading exercises about pupils' activities. Countless teachers in our classrooms prove that good teaching can be done without workbooks.

Another teacher who is equally creative in his teaching may be doing these same things, but, with judicious use of a workbook, may be conserving some time. Excellent as he is, he may feel a special need for the support of a well-organized aid in arithmetic or he may not yet have mastered the finer points of word analysis.

The third teacher, representing a type considerably more numerous than the first two, is less creative or has had less experience working with children. Possibly he does not understand well the sequences of learning in arithmetic or the broader objectives of teaching reading. This teacher's control in a free activity period may result in pupil experiences which are not productive of good learning. Workbooks may bring orderliness to certain areas of instruction and save time.

One infers from the principles of learning stated above that personally organized activity, with adult help, is most productive of growth in learning. But there are enabling knowledges and skills which need to keep pace with a pupil's growth in thinking and in the expression of his thoughts. The role of the workbook must lie primarily not in the mainstream of mental growth but in the coves where the pupil develops these enabling abilities.

Is the workbook activity worthwhile, or is it busy work?

Some teachers will maintain that any device which will bring stability into a classroom of 35 pupils is worthwhile. Values must be judged relatively. In the growth of a pupil's higher mental processes, certain knowledges and skills must be pinned down. Once achieved, these are better maintained in lifelike activities than thru the practice exercise.

Workbooks least likely to be "busy work" are those designed to supplement the textbook used in the class. Their activity has meaning in reference to another portion of the work of the day. If well-developed, they provide a variety of goals and of objectives. They are usually quite superior to a teacher's hurriedly duplicated efforts. Pupils accept them more naturally than they accept unrelated exercises.

What are the problems of a consumable text?

One must first ask whether the consumable text is sufficiently complete in itself, or is merely supplementary.

Is it an exercise book or is it one that develops understanding?

Spelling books are the most widely used self-contained consumable textbooks. In many ways they are similar to nonconsumable spelling texts. They contain the same word lists, similar suggestions for developing insights into word structure, and a similar program for teaching the spelling of sounds and the use of the dictionary. Differences may appear, however, as one answers these questions:

Does one stimulate pupil writing more than the other?

All things considered, which is cheaper?

Will pupils keep useful notebooks with both?

How motivating is the pride of ownership of a consumable?

How helpful is the consumable's provision for identifying one's own misspelled words for systematic review?

Will the teacher permit blank-filling to supplant word study, or will he use the exercises to promote related abilities and insights?

Is the clothbound text more likely to become merely a word list?

How can teachers who are using workbooks be guided into more effective use of them?

The abuse of workbooks has led some educators to conclude that workbooks should not be used at all. Others meet the issue by limiting the number that may be used. But some teachers do use them, and education will be advanced if they learn to make wiser use of them.

These guidelines are offered to teachers who are using workbooks:

1. What kind of workbook will meet your pupils' needs? Do you want a workbook that continues the learning of the text? Do you want a practice or drill book that ignores understanding? Do you want a self-contained consumable text?

2. Do the pupils of your class need workbooks of different levels of difficulty or development?

3. Are pupils aimlessly filling in blanks, or have you taught or retaught the learnings involved, so that practice always follows understanding?

4. Do you analyze pupils' work and reteach where necessary?

5. Do you use the diagnostic provisions of a workbook, or determine by your own analysis which portions are profitable to a pupil and which he should omit?

6. Are you continuing to search for alternative procedures of greater value? Pupils need to develop initiative in their own learning activities. Do you provide a library corner, interest tables, and opportunities for reference work and the writing of reports?

7. Do you avoid having pupils spend too much of their time with workbooks? Use of several workbooks is likely to interfere with pupils' growth in organizing their own expression.

The workbook is a tool in education which may be used well or may be used badly. A highly competent teacher may have greater need of it with a class of 40 than with a class of 25. An inexperienced teacher may have more need for its use than he will have after he gains experience. A teacher well-prepared in most curriculum areas may profit by use of a workbook in his weaker areas, but he must prevent it from becoming a crutch.

31. *Magazines in the Classroom*
NEA RESEARCH DIVISION

To meet the challenge of offering increasingly high-quality education to generally overcrowded classes, America's classroom teachers use a large variety of aids to increase their effectiveness. One of the most widely used is the magazine of general circulation. Intended chiefly for adult readers and not designed primarily for school use, these periodicals are here called "lay magazines."

Replies to a questionnaire survey on the extent of magazine use brought to light many original techniques for using periodical materials successfully in the classroom, in addition to a number of noteworthy facts.

- Magazines are one of the few sources of information in areas of current or constantly changing knowledge.

- Use of magazines offers specific benefits for slow-learning, average, and rapid-learning students.

- Some of the most imaginative classroom projects are sparked by materials appearing in lay magazines.

- The comparative study of magazines provides training in independent, critical, and evaluative thinking.

- Obstacles to wider use include limitations of time, funds, physical facilities, and adaptability.

- The real key to effective use of magazines is the ingenuity and resourcefulness of the teacher.

WHAT ARE THE BROAD FINDINGS?

Both elementary- and secondary-school teachers responded to the questionnaire, and in some respects their replies were closely similar.

From "Teachers in All Fields Use Magazines in the Classroom," *NEA Research Bulletin*, XXXVIII, No. 1 (February, 1960), 27–31. Reprinted by permission of the NEA Research Division.

For instance, one of the most common uses mentioned by both groups of teachers was in developing bulletin board displays or in providing materials for student scrapbooks.

Other ways in which teachers at all levels use magazines include the maintenance of a file of useful reference information, the provision of materials for free reading and for enrichment, the use of illustrations by means of an opaque projector, and the stimulation of student writing by the use of magazine writing as a model.

While a great many magazines were named by the teachers as being used with some regularity in their classes, those mentioned most frequently were *Life, National Geographic, Newsweek, Time, Reader's Digest, Look, Saturday Evening Post, U. S. News and World Report,* and *Holiday.* These are in addition to publications aimed directly at the schools, which were not within the scope of this study.

Because of the nature of magazine materials and their levels of interest, however, certain fundamental differences in the use of magazines do exist among the grade levels. Many of the most useful techniques in the upper grades would be unfeasible in the elementary grades.

ELEMENTARY SCHOOL

In the earliest grades, because of the limited abilities of the pupils, magazine use remains quite restricted. Most respondents reported drawing from them rather heavily for displays, for which the pictorial materials are invaluable. All parts of the magazines serve for this purpose, including illustrations and advertising. For slightly older children, an entire article related to a subject under study may be included in a display.

In addition, even the youngest pupils enjoy games centering on magazines. These usually involve searching the publication for pictures, cutting them out, and using them to spur the creation of the pupils' own ideas.

In many units of work, the children prepare scrapbooks, using, at least in part, materials gleaned from lay magazines. Scrapbooks are commonly made on subjects having to do with health, science, art, religion, and history.

Even in the early grades, where the pupils are unable to use the textual material themselves, magazine articles can make a contribution to classroom work. Many teachers either read interesting articles to the class or summarize them in understandable language. One of the major contributions is often in broadening the background of the teacher and in enriching his own preparation for a specific unit of work.

Many teachers expressed enthusiasm for the way in which magazines motivate independent reading. Occasionally pupils are allowed to take school copies home, where they may use them and share them with their families. In this way the children gain practice in reading skills and also are introduced to new areas of possible interest.

In addition to employing the factual material, teachers frequently use magazine articles as the basis for training in other skills such as outlining, punctuating, creative writing, and bibliographical recording.

For current events study, teachers at all levels are obliged to rely heavily upon periodical materials. In addition, many features dealing with historical subjects have been used in the classroom for a background against which current events are viewed and understood. The recent visit of Khrushchev was followed by elementary classes throughout the land, and many of them undertook a study of Russia which gave added meaning to the history they were witnessing. Various magazine features on Russia were utilized for this purpose.

In general, magazine materials dealing with subjects included in a textbook have an added realism which appeals to pupils. Geography teachers find this especially useful, since an article can draw the material under study out of the realm of the academic and into the world of real places and things.

In science courses, too, periodical publications provide up-to-the-minute news of scientific advances and principles. Seeing a magazine article on a subject under study in class has a double advantage for the pupils: First, written for popular tastes, and often accompanied by striking illustrations, the magazine material usually is readily understandable. Textbooks, with large bodies of content to present, cannot emphasize and illuminate a single major point as can an article. Second, information featured in magazines is clearly of current interest to a wide segment of readers. Pupils thus acquire a feeling for the importance and meaning of what they are studying, and also gain the benefit of up-to-date findings to supplement their text and reference books. Once again, magazines help bring abstract learning into the realm of the concrete.

Most teachers reported a fairly high degree of pupil enthusiasm for work with magazines. In general, even at the elementary level, magazines arouse interest in a wide variety of subjects, offer encouragement to read (especially for slow readers), teach pupils to locate information and to value current publications as a source of information, and develop recreational reading habits.

WHAT OBSTACLES EXIST IN EARLY GRADES?

Many teachers indicated that they would make even greater use of magazine materials but for a number of obstacles. Chief among them were lack of time and money. A crowded teaching schedule too often means that the teachers themselves do not have time to search for usable materials or to adapt them to the level of the class or to a particular subject under study. In addition, a crowded course of study or curriculum, through the pressure it exerts to cover a specified amount of text material, often deters the teacher from introducing anything extra into the classroom work. Many teachers stated that all they can do is cover the material required.

To teachers this is an important obstacle, since it is so frequently mentioned. Yet many teachers have solved the problem by using magazine materials as extra-credit references, or for displays, or with an opaque projector to enrich the class work without an undue investment of precious time.

Almost all teachers indicated that lack of sufficient funds stands in the way of acquiring enough magazines. Some regret that a greater variety of magazines is not available for pupil use, while others would like more copies so that more than one pupil could use the material at the same time.

Many teachers have taken at least some steps toward solving this problem by collecting used magazines from friends and neighbors.

Other obstacles to greater magazine use include inadequate physical facilities for magazine storage, the presence of objectionable materials in the magazines, the general difficulty of adaptation, and in some cases, at least, a small degree of parental opposition. The fact that magazine use is so widespread indicates that these obstacles can be overcome with ingenuity and determination.

SECONDARY SCHOOL

In junior and senior high schools, the most common uses parallel closely those encountered in the elementary grades, including displays, scrapbooks, reference materials for panel discussions, and models for creative writing.

Certain more advanced techniques, however, are particularly adapted to the subject matter of the secondary schools. English classes, for instance, frequently include a unit on magazines, in which attention is focused on style, makeup, viewpoint, and authors. This gives the students an over-all view of what is available and teaches discrimination in the use of periodicals.

A number of teachers reported that they encourage students to compare articles in different magazines in order to identify editorial bias and arrive at an objective view. Development of a critical approach is also fostered by analyzing the background of the authors, their qualifications to write on the subject concerned, their purpose and bias, and their success or failure in dealing with the subject.

The better literary magazines serve in many English classrooms as a secondary text for contemporary literature; many teachers report great student enthusiasm for the articles and stories they contain. English classes also make wide use of articles containing historical or literary background for enriching literature courses. Foreign-language classes also find these useful; in addition, they welcome articles of a geographical and cultural nature.

As in elementary school, a major use of magazines in social studies is in the field of current events and contemporary history. In the secondary school, current information of this sort is frequently used for more than its merely factual value; it is likely to serve as a basis for panel discussions, analyses of major historical trends, the study of basic human problems, and an understanding of causes underlying the ultimate facts.

Homemaking teachers expressed general enthusiasm for the various magazines providing material on fashions, fabrics, appliances, styles, foods, and other facets of homemaking.

One aspect of the value of magazines in the total school framework which might not have been suspected upon casual consideration is in the guidance program. Useful information is available on occupations, education, personal hygiene, and similar topics. Some schools maintain bulletin board displays devoted to professional or vocational opportunities, college information, local job opportunities for students, and other useful information of a guidance nature.

Some teachers use magazines in particularly original ways. For example, articles and magazines have been the basis for class dramatizations, mock radio programs, and class publications. Using information from periodicals, one class studied the stock market and available securities, each student planning an individual portfolio. A study in wise purchasing has been based on reports contained in a consumers' magazine. As the replies to the questionnaire revealed, there is almost no limit to the types of classroom activities that either use magazines or find their original inspiration in them.

OBSTACLES AT THE SECONDARY LEVEL

As in elementary school, a shortage of time and money stands in the way of greater magazine use. A few objections, however, were voiced only by secondary-school teachers. Some, for example, find editorial bias a deterrent to greater use. At the same time, others have turned this potential disadvantage to good use by drawing students' attention to bias and training them to recognize it and develop a well-rounded, accurate picture from a variety of sources which may cancel out each other's individual slants.

Several teachers advanced suggestions for increasing the usefulness of magazines in the classroom. One urged the presentation of information on current economic trends. Another cited the need for the *Abridged Reader's Guide* in all school libraries, so as to multiply the effectiveness of whatever magazines are locally available. Several others indicated that one of the major problems is in timing, since often useful articles do not appear when they would best fit into the program. Though this is inevitable, it was believed that if teachers could be provided with advance notice of scheduled articles in at least some of the major magazine features, they could plan their teaching schedule so as to exploit them to the fullest.

In this connection, many teachers appreciated the reprint service offered by some publishers, which makes it possible to supply a whole class with copies of important articles. Teachers believe that the expansion of this service would be extremely helpful.

Even teachers who suffer from the greatest obstacles to effective magazine use, however, have devised ways to overcome them. If the school budget cannot stretch far enough to provide magazines in adequate numbers, teachers arouse the interest of private citizens in their problem, and old issues of magazines donated to the school are made available to the students. When there is inadequate space to store large numbers of issues, file systems are devised to keep articles of potential interest. An added dividend of this technique is the bibliographical experience in keeping the file up to date and indexing its contents. Teachers who lack the time to glance through enough magazines for useful material assign students to do the sifting and bring in articles of interest to the class. Where there is imagination and a will, there seems to be a way.

One of the chief advantages of magazines to the teacher faced with an outsized class covering a wide range of abilities is that their use seems to appeal to all types of students. For the slow learner they offer encouragement to read in areas of special interest. For the average student, they offer enrichment of the regular course work and the heightening of interest that goes with new and current material. And for the superior student, they offer the challenge of adult materials, a broad range of topics, and in many cases a depth which the regular classroom material does not approach.

This survey has revealed that magazines have entered the classroom as a welcome and valued teaching aid. Given a creative teacher, their uses are legion, and their contributions to the total teaching program impressive indeed.

32. Term Papers

EVELYN CORNISH

Have you assigned any term papers lately? If you can't recall, your public or school librarian probably can—and vividly! Under pressures toward "higher standards," "intellectualizing the curriculum," and "getting them ready for college," teachers in high schools, junior highs, and even the upper elementary grades are now requiring long, formally written, documented papers on anything from the life history of the salmon to the control of alcoholism, the social reforms of eighteenth century England, or the marriage customs of the ancient Egyptians. And of course, as they should do, these students go from the classroom to the nearest library to begin their quest.

Many young people, by the time they leave high school, have learned to handle this type of assignment with considerable skill. Many others, alas, have learned only to copy pages of dimly comprehended words from the nearest encyclopedia, blithely willing to break off in the midst of an exposition, a paragraph, nay, even a sentence, when the minimum number of words acceptable to the teacher has been reached. A few fortunate and well-beloved youths have persuaded a doting mother or current girl friend to "do" their papers at the public library, while they themselves attend basketball practice or eat hamburgers with their cronies at Joe's Drive-in. The beautifully organized, neatly typed masterpieces produced in this way are a revelation to the teacher accustomed only to the grubby, semiliterate efforts made by these same students in class.

If we librarians view this type of assignment with some alarm, it is not because we are unwilling to work at finding materials for students, or are reluctant to have too many of them invade our quiet quarters. What disturbs us is not the volume of work. Rather it is the unnecessary frustration of students unprepared for their task, and the shoddy, superficial, muddled quality of much that is done under the name "term pa-

From Evelyn Cornish, "So They're Writing Term Papers," *The Clearing House,* XXXV (January, 1961), 287–290. Evelyn Cornish is Director of Elementary Libraries, Bellingham Public Schools, Bellingham, Washington. Reprinted from *The Clearing House* by permission.

per." According to librarians, some teachers assign obscure topics to large classes, giving little thought to guiding the work in progress except to stress that the paper must be of a certain length and contain so many bibliographic entries. Apparently these teachers are willing to accept whatever plagiarized material the student hands in, without question. If this be raising educational standards, perhaps they should be lowered again to a realistic level!

One reason for the ineffectiveness of many term-paper assignments is that teachers, on the whole, have not been prepared to direct students in this particular activity. Their expectations are usually based on what they themselves were able to do, as college students, using well-stocked college libraries. Without thinking much about it, the teacher expects to find the same plentiful source materials at hand in the small school or public library. He forgets that organizing and presenting information in term-paper form is a complex task, particularly for students accustomed to writing only the briefest examples of informal personal essays, or "themes." While librarians can help the student find what he needs, only the teacher can make an effective assignment and supervise its completion as he would any daily assignment or shop project.

When you assign your next term paper, presumably it will be for one or more of these reasons: (1) You believe it will add to the students' knowledge of your subject; (2) you feel it will strengthen their ability to locate information for themselves; and (3) you believe it will further develop their ability to organize and communicate that information in written form. If your students have little understanding of your subject, are completely unacquainted with reference techniques, or have poor writing ability, you would do well to plan a simpler assignment. Requiring a lengthy and formal term paper will force such students to do poor and probably dishonest work.

If you decide to go ahead with the term paper, you will need to do some advance work. Who would think of starting merrily off on a field trip of even an hour's duration without some advance teaching, and without making arrangements with the personnel of the industry to be visited? Yet the greatest complaint of librarians in this area is that teachers rarely consult or notify them of term-paper assignments, and still more rarely visit the library before the die is cast.

Do a little scouting in your school library before you talk with your librarian. Take time to look up a few of your projected topics in the card catalogue, and move from there to the indicated sections of shelving. Check the reference section to find what general sources, such as encyclopedias, are available, and what special books there are in your subject field. What magazines does your library keep on file, and for how many years? Is there an index available?

Now you are ready to talk to your librarian about your plans. What does she think of the subjects you have in mind? Will there be enough material for the number of students concerned? She can also tell you how much instruction in the use of the encyclopedia, card catalogue, and indexes your students have had. Can your whole class be scheduled to the library for a period or two, or will students need passes from study hall? Will the librarian be able to review library skills with them? Can certain materials be taken to your classroom or placed on reserve? Does your assignment conflict with that of another teacher planning to use the same materials?

Even though your school library may be small, it is good practice to send your students there first. Once they have mastered the basic reference skills, they can begin work in any library without initial help. It is more economical to teach them these skills at school, in a group, than to expect the public library staff to do this for each individual student as he comes to the library.

Do not fail, however, to make contact with your public library. Ask your school librarian how to do this; many school and public libraries have set up systems of working together on such requests. The large public library may have a staff member assigned to work with schools. Unless you are a regular patron of the public library and familiar with its holdings, plan to make a preliminary visit there, too. Take along a brief fact sheet giving your name, the assigned topics, number of students and grade level, and date when the assignment is due. This will assure your students the best possible help.

Remember that even though your own library is small, it can usually obtain additional material for your work from larger libraries through interlibrary loan. You may find you are eligible for such service from a large county library unit or from your state library. Requests should be made at least three weeks ahead for best results. Needless to say, you should educate students to take good care of such specially loaned materials and to return them on time.

When you make your assignment, allow students considerable choice of topics, and guide their choices, considering the ability of the student as well as the material available. The best student in a biology class might work on studies of mutations due to radiation, while his slower neighbor prepares a simple life story of some animal. An average student in a U.S. history group might be writing about the early life of George Washington, while a more capable student is investigating methods used to finance the Revolutionary armies. A good practice is to ask each class member to submit two or three possible topics, and then to make a preliminary survey of materials before telling you his final choice.

Before students begin work in the library, make some suggestions about note taking. This is the time to discuss bibliographies and the problem of acknowledging sources of quotations. Make sure each student understands he is merely to take notes and to write an *original* paper using his notes to prove his points.

If your whole class can be accommodated in the library at once, this is a good way to get everyone to begin promptly. But don't take this time to leave your students with the librarian and go to the cafeteria for that extra cup of coffee! By watching them tackle this new task, you can learn a good deal about work habits and the sort of help needed.

If your public library is accessible to a large number of your students, why not set aside an hour or two one evening when you will be there to help them? This will be an educational experience for you, too, if you have never observed one or two reference assistants struggling to give help to from ten to fifty high-school students and the few hardy adult patrons willing to compete with youth's demands.

You will want to set not one, but two, deadlines. The first, and probably most important, is the date on which students will hand in their notes and rough drafts for a quick checking. Be very definite about one thing: *No finished paper will be accepted unless you have first checked a rough draft several days in advance.* Notes will not be neat, the trial copy will be patched and scribbled, but it will be each student's own work. You need not read every word, but make a check for general progress, give suggestions on organization, and mark composition errors you detect.

Now you are ready to talk about form requirements for the finished paper. If possible, prepare a mimeographed sheet with examples and explanations. The primary aim should be a clearly written, interesting paper, which sums up what the student has learned from his reading. Form should be secondary, but whatever requirements you do establish should be followed *exactly*.

If you want honest work, do not set rigid requirements on the length of papers or the number of reference sources to be used. Every librarian has heard remarks like these:

"I've already written my paper but I have to have three more sources."

"This material looks good, but I don't think it's 3,000 words, and that's what I have to have."

"Can you help me find a short magazine article? I need fifty more words."

Remember that some topics require longer treatments; that some writers have a terse style while others ramble and elaborate. There is little value in fake bibliography entries, made to satisfy a numerical requirement. To prod the lazy or timid, you can make some general requirement, such as the use of some sources outside the encyclopedia, or one or more magazine articles. Point out that a good source list strengthens a paper, but that it should contain only material that actually was useful to the writer.

If younger students have previously done a great deal of paste-and-scissors work on notebooks, emphasize the fact that a term paper does not have illustrations, except possibly diagrams drawn by the author to explain intricate processes. Such embellishments, along with the fancy cover beloved by many, simply mean the student has not spent his time on the contents.

Your own grading policies will determine the value you place on the papers submitted. Many teachers feel it is wise to use two grades, one for content and a less important one for form and documentation. Remember that term papers, properly done, represent hours of student time and should be carefully graded. When you return the papers, take time to discuss with students the work they have done, what they gained from it, what they found especially difficult. Be sure that good papers are displayed in the classroom, the library, or the school showcase. One teacher I know took time and postage to send several excellent papers to parents with a note of commendation. One of these went to parents who had received a poor work slip in the same way during a previous grading period.

As you complete the term-paper project, take time to make a repeat visit to your librarian. This is an excellent time to offer suggestions about new materials to be added to the library, and to pass on constructive comments from students. In turn, get her ideas on how to improve the unit when it is taught again. If you have used reserve materials, or students have used interlibrary loan materials, make certain that these have all been returned. Librarians need the backing of teachers in teaching respect for materials and the rights of future borrowers.

Your term-paper assignment can be considered successful if your students have learned something about independent reference work, the resources of the library, and the organization and presentation of materials. And you will have discovered that your librarian, in school or public library, can actually help you teach. Her knowledge of materials and her efforts to help students will reinforce and complement your own—but only if you let her know what you are doing.

33. *Improving Speech Activities*

MAGDALENE KRAMER

In the process of communication, speech is an instrument with which a person reveals much of his personality, his power of thought, his emotional state. It is the principal tool by which we adjust to other people, gain the cooperation of others.

The psychological effect of speech on individuals cannot be over-emphasized. The choice of words, the pronunciation, the voice quality, the intonation, the rhythm, the tempo, and the volume are particularly significant in determining an individual's personal relations and status within a group.

If we honestly believe that every individual has a right to develop to the fullest his potentialities, time and attention should be given within the classroom to speaking, to listening, and to analysis.

In order to make such provision within the curriculum, it will be necessary to ask every classroom teacher to assume certain additional responsibilities. The speech specialist is needed to teach the children with serious speech problems and to advise and cooperate with the classroom teacher, but the classroom teacher will be in charge of teaching speech to all the children.

What responsibilities can the teacher assume?

1. *Development of good voice and speech.* The good teacher tries, first of all, to help the pupils develop speech that is audible, intelligible, and pleasant to hear. In the United States we exhibit little pride in speaking our language acceptably. We tend to drop or to slight final consonants, to omit syllables, and to mispronounce certain letters and whole words. Too many voices are high-pitched, loud, and strident in quality.

In striving for improvement in ourselves and in our pupils, we can

From Magdalene Kramer, "Everybody Talks, but How?" *NEA Journal*, XLV (December, 1956), 561–563. Magdalene Kramer is Professor Emeritus and former Chairman of the Department of Speech and Theatre, Teachers College, Columbia University. She is now Visiting Professor, College of the City of New York. Reprinted by permission of the *Journal* of the National Education Association.

try to develop the most pleasant voice quality possible, by eliminating nasality, throatiness, harshness, flatness, thinness, high pitch, and huskiness. We can also aim for clear-cut articulation and correct pronunciation. The dictionary and the current pronunciation used by the educated people of the community may serve as guides in determining correct pronunciation.

The teacher's own voice and speech serve as models and are important teaching aids, especially in the primary grades, for children learn speech essentially thru imitation. When the teacher attempts to develop vocabulary in relation to objects or experiences, he should stress the correct pronunciation the first time the child hears and uses the new word.

It is advisable to teach largely thru imitation until the child has built a positive attitude toward speech. This approach can be made thru story-telling, sharing of poems, choral speaking, and rhythms.

Individual correction can come only after the child feels secure in speaking.

In the intermediate and upper grades as well as in the high school, direct attention needs to be given to speech improvement; and the purpose for doing so, clearly understood by the pupils.

Improvement may be assured by having all the members of the class (a) participate in a speaking experience, such as making oral reports or explaining a process of some type; (b) analyze with the teacher the speech needs of the group, which may be greater audibility, projection, or more clear-cut articulation; (c) select from the stated needs the one which should receive immediate attention; (d) practice to attain the needed skill; (e) try out the improved skill in another speaking situation.

Pupils should always understand that practice on a particular skill is for the purpose of using that skill more effectively in speaking.

2. *Communication of ideas and feelings.* Speech is a tool for the sharing of thoughts and feelings. The close relationship between speech and thinking must always be remembered, and teachers in the primary grades particularly need to be aware that speech and thinking can be developed side by side.

If a teacher understands the developmental process of each, he can direct the learning so that speech will grow as thinking grows. For example, when a child is ready in his thinking to formulate compound and complex sentences, the teacher can be ready to show him how an involved thought can be well expressed orally.

It is essential that everyone be taught to express his ideas clearly and concisely. A teacher can help pupils to cultivate effective communication by emphasizing the value of choosing the exactly right word to convey a certain meaning.

A teacher can be of further assistance by stressing the fact that oral expression should differ from written expression in sentence structure, logical organization of ideas, and psychological appeal.

If communication is to be complete, considerable stress must also be given to helping the listener analyze ideas. Our future citizens must be prepared to recognize false assumptions, incorrect analogies, illogical reasoning; to distinguish between fact and opinion, reasoning and emotional appeal.

Students can listen to speeches given over the radio, on television, and from the platform, always with the purpose of understanding and evaluating.

In a group discussion, students can seek to discover why the ideas of one student are more readily accepted than those of another student, altho the ideas are of equal worth. What speech characteristics of the one student cause his ideas to be received favorably? What speech characteristics cause the students to hesitate to recognize the other student's contribution?

3. *Development of technics for speaking situations.* To be successful in a speaking situation one must have some knowledge of the rules of the game and a command of basic technics.

Speaking experiences, already an integral part of the classroom work, may be similar from the kindergarten thru the high school, but each year the pupil ought to show progress in acquiring more knowledge and more skill in speaking to an audience, large or small; speaking in a give-and-take situation; reading aloud; creating a role in a play.

On the lower elementary level, speaking to an audience may involve sharing an experience with the class, explaining a procedure, or describing a toy or a trip.

In the intermediate grades and junior and senior high school, the speaking experiences may well include, in addition to those already mentioned, presiding at assembly, introducing speakers, giving specific directions, presenting evidence to support a point of view, appealing for action on a certain proposition or situation, giving an after-dinner speech, presenting or accepting an award.

In order to cultivate facility in a give-and-take speaking situation, attention ought to be given, at all school levels, to conversation, discussion, argumentation, interviewing, and parliamentary procedure.

In addition to the special technics required, the good teacher also emphasizes the following: the importance of having something worthwhile to say and of being a good listener; the difference between discussing all sides of a controversial issue and merely arguing the rightness of one side of a proposition; and the need for knowledge about a subject as a basis for discussion or debate.

Everyone should learn to read aloud effectively, not only because of the practical value of this ability in reading minutes of a meeting, committee reports, and the like, but also because of its esthetic value in reading stories, poems, essays, or dramas. The full import of many literary selections, especially poems, can be expressed only thru reading them aloud.

Group reading or choral speaking is an activity greatly enjoyed by pupils at all levels; all types of children may take part and so may improve their speaking and their appreciation of literature.

Storytelling is also valuable in arousing the imagination and cultivating a love of literature. Pupils on the upper levels may profit from the experience of telling stories to younger children.

All children may well have opportunities to participate in dramatic play, creative dramatics, and formalized dramatics. What fun a child has in just pretending to be someone else! What fun it is to build a play from a story, an event, or a classroom celebration! How the imagination may be stirred and speech improved when a pupil creates a character in a play!

4. *Provision of special help for children with speech problems.*

It is hoped that each community will have at least one speech specialist who will (a) make a survey to locate the children with serious speech problems, such as stuttering, lisping, delayed speech, cleft-palate speech, speech of the hard of hearing, speech accompanying cerebral palsy; (b) plan and carry out a remedial speech program for these children; (c) cooperate with the classroom teacher in formulating a speech program for all children; (d) advise the classroom teacher and demonstrate speech procedures whenever necessary.

Finally, if inservice courses in speech for classroom teachers seem desirable, these should be provided.

The classroom teacher, on the other hand, needs to cooperate closely with the speech specialist. He should follow the plans, mutually formulated, for the child with the serious speech problem. He is responsible for the speech improvement of children with minor problems, such as high pitch, inadequate volume, substitutions and omissions of sounds, and poor voice quality. He needs to know how to utilize activities within the classroom in order to bring about speech improvement.

Speech plays so vital a part in the life of every individual that it is essential that the subject become part of the daily classroom work both on the elementary and high-school levels.

The activities necessary to teach speech are already included in the

school program. The great need is for classroom teachers who are prepared to teach speech. Teacher-preparing institutions and school administrators should meet this need so that every child can develop
his powers of oral communication to their fullest potential.

34. Four Dangers in Class Discussions

ROBERT C. McKEAN

Class discussion techniques are key tools in the successful teacher's
equipment. These techniques, while most often aiming at subject matter mastery, have important values in promoting equally vital, concomitant outcomes such as the development of skill in critical thinking. However, too often class discussions tend to smother independent
student thinking rather than to produce situations wherein this skill
may be practiced and improved.

Inexperienced teachers find it especially difficult to plan and guide
intelligent and rewarding discussion activities. Experience with student
teachers and first-year teachers has pointed up four problems which
seem to be most prevalent. High-school principals, as they work with
these people through supervision and inservice training, might find
it profitable to use these four dangers as a starting point.

1. The beginning teacher, fresh from college classes, may *phrase the
questions in adult terms*. It may be very logical and possibly quite
clear to adults, but often is simply not communicated or only partially
communicated to the students because of the wording. The question
or topic is not fully understood by the students and good discussion is
impeded at the outset. Symptomatic of this situation is the sight of
students stumbling and fumbling verbally around the general area of
the discussion subject in general terms until, through chance or trial
and error, the question is clarified. There follows a surge of effort when
the students finally gain understanding of what the teacher wants them
to discuss.

2. The teacher may *structure the discussion in terms of the logic of
the subject matter* as she sees it. Thus, it may be very abstract and

From Robert C. McKean, "Four Dangers in Class Discussions," the *Bulletin* of
the National Association of Secondary-School Principals, XLII, No. 240 (October,
1958), 82–83. Robert C. McKean is Professor of Education at the University of
Colorado, Boulder, Colorado. Reprinted by permission from the *Bulletin* of the
National Association of Secondary-School Principals, Washington, D.C. Copyright
October, 1958.

there may be few if any ties with the lives of the pupils. The discussion becomes an exercise in the manipulation of verbal symbols. If the students, themselves, are encouraged to formulate the discussion topics and questions in their own words, the very statement of the problem is likely to bring the whole discussion in line with student problems, interests, and backgrounds of experience. In this way discussions are more likely to be vital and stimulating to the class.

3. *Over-emotionality* in the classroom is another condition inimical to critical, independent thinking. Often the beginning teacher is tense, striving for control and her self-concept of teacher role may impell her to pit herself against the class. Teachers should strive to promote relatively minimal conditions of emotionality in the interests of objective, logical thought. The classroom activity should be discussion rather than argument. Emotion may be desirable when you have a bear chasing you. The effects of the emotional state—amounts of sugar are released into the blood for quick energy, the heart steps up its beat making more blood available, the circulation is said to be changed sending more blood to the heavy muscles, the digestive process is stopped or reduced, *etc.*—tend to contribute to physical retreat from a dangerous or threatening situation. However, the individual's ability to reason, to think clearly, in other than habitual patterns is reduced. Thus over-emotionality is not desirable as an accompaniment to mental problem solving in the classroom.

4. The teacher may actually and directly inhibit creative thinking by *over-planning*, by pre-thinking through the anticipated discussion topics or questions and carefully formulating "logical" answers or solutions. This pre-thinking should be done in general terms, of course; but, if these answers or conclusions are too rigidly adhered to, the teacher may find herself saying, "No, that is not it. That is not quite what I had in mind."

Students quickly sense what is happening (they have experienced it before), and it becomes a guessing game rather than real problem-solving activity. They watch very carefully for facial expressions, gestures, attend to subliminal cues, *etc.* for the game is to try to read the teacher's mind for *the answer* hidden there. The effect is more likely to produce students gifted in mental telepathy than in creative problem-solving skills.

As a process, classroom discussion should begin with questions which have some relevance to the lives of students and proceed to conclusions based on logic and the prizing of the authority of evidence. If inexperienced teachers are assisted in avoiding the above four dangers, they will be well on their way toward developing a vital method of teaching which fosters critical, independent thinking in our students.

35. Decision by Debate: A Re-examination

DOUGLAS EHNINGER

Readers of this journal, I assume, are familiar with the criticisms commonly leveled against debate as a method for settling differences and arriving at shared beliefs and decisions. Prominent among them are these: (1) Debate, unlike other available modes of deliberation, does not result in a reflective or critical judgment because it does not employ a critical method. (2) Debate, instead of being a technique of investigation—a means for discovering and testing ideas, is a technique of persuasion, suitable only for propagating ideas and impressing them on others. (3) Debate, instead of implementing the desirable attitudes and processes of co-operation, emphasizes the undesirable attitudes and processes of conflict.[1]

Admittedly, these charges strike at the heart of the debate process. Insofar as they are justified debate is not only undesirable but dangerous, and must, therefore, be rejected as a method for making collective choices and formulating collective judgments.

But are these criticisms valid? In my view, each of them arises out of a misconception of the nature and purpose of debate. I believe that if we will examine its rationale afresh, and without predisposition or prejudice, we will see (1) that the end and method of debate are critical, (2) that debate is of the genre of investigation rather than persuasion, and (3) that debate is a co-operative rather than a competitive enterprise.

2.

First, then, on what ground may the method of debate be called critical?

From Douglas Ehninger, "Decision by Debate: A Re-examination," *The Quarterly Journal of Speech*, XLV (October, 1959), 282–287. Douglas Ehninger is Professor of Speech at the University of Iowa, Iowa City. Reprinted by permission of the author and of the Speech Association of America.

[1] Much of the philosophical groundwork for these charges was furnished more than three decades ago by John Dewey. See, for example, *The Public and Its Problems* (New York, 1927), especially Chapter VI, "The Problem of Method," Cf. Harrison S. Elliott, *The Process of Group Thinking* (New York, 1928), pp. 1–8; James H. McBurney and Kenneth G. Hance, *Discussion in Human Affairs* (New York, 1950), pp. 3–14.

The distinguishing marks of a critical instrument, I take to be these: (1) The end aimed at by that instrument is a reasoned or reflective judgment, rather than a judgment made impulsively through the dictates of desire, prejudice, or authority. (2) The method employed in arriving at judgment is equipped with such internal checks and controls as render it essentially self-regulative.[2] Debate, I submit, meets both these requirements.

In order to insure that judgment will be critical rather than impulsive, in the courtroom and legislative chamber debate is surrounded with an elaborate code of rules. These determine the types of evidence and appeal that are admissible and the points in the argument at which they may be introduced, and sometimes even dictate the inference that is to be drawn from a given set of facts. But in addition to these imposed regulations, any form of debate worthy of the name —whether it occurs in the smoking car, on the street corner, or at the business conference—has embedded in the essentials of its procedure important controls which help guarantee that judgment will be reflective. (1) Each party has an equal opportunity to develop his view. (2) Each calls upon the other to set forth for public examination the facts and reasoning upon which that view is based. (3) Judgment is suspended until both sides have been fully heard. (4) The decision that finally emerges is made not by the contending parties themselves, but by an impartial individual or body playing the responsible role of arbitrator.[3]

These controls, of course, may deliberately be circumvented, or debate may be so ineptly practiced that much of their effectiveness is lost. This, however, is human failure. As Mortimer Adler reminds us, we must not confuse the self-regulative character of a method with "the disciplinary measures necessary to make human nature capable of the manner of discourse so regulated."[4] The important point is that the process of debate provides the necessary internal checks and balances. These will operate in proportion as we can discipline our appetites and develop our skills so as to give them effective play.

If built-in controls were not so inescapably a part of the structure of debate, debate would not invariably be avoided by those speakers or writers whose purpose is to "short-circuit" the reflective process. Nor, on the other hand, would it be so eagerly sought out and practiced by

[2] Morris R. Cohen and Ernest Nagel, *An Introduction to Logic and Scientific Method* (New York, 1934), p. 191ff.

[3] This characteristic alone is sufficient to establish the critical nature of the debate process. The debater does not appeal for "acceptance," but for "arbitration." The judging or adjudicating agency is not a passive and inert "sink"; it is a thinking, reflecting, considering force that uses the evidence and arguments presented to *come* in its own mind to the decision they appear to warrant.

[4] Mortimer Adler, *Dialectic* (New York, 1927), p. 185.

those who regard the public welfare as paramount. To the earnest debater, the inherent controls of his method are not obstacles, but aids
to informed and critical judgment. Unlike the unscrupulous persuader
who seeks to evade them, the debater believes that a reflective judgment produced by the aid of these controls is the only sort worth the
winning. Valuable in its own right, it will also, he is convinced, prove
best for the group or society concerned.

So much, then, for the end or aim of debate. Let us now consider its
method.

Whereas the judgment invited by debate is critical because it is reflective, the method employed by debate in pursuing that judgment is
critical because it is self-regulative.

In addition to presenting his own view of the matter under discussion, each debater also has the obligation of probing and criticizing
the view of his opponent. This is so commonplace a feature of debate
that its significance is easily overlooked. Yet it is the most important of
all the built-in controls. As a method, debate not only allows but *requires* that an informed partisan systematically probe in public a view
of a matter which if adopted will result in the rejection of an alternative
view in which he sincerely believes.

William James termed this "the test of enlightened self-interest."[5]
In areas where the empirical methods of the laboratory are inapplic-
able it is, perhaps, the most searching test of an idea that can be devised. If under such probing, false claims are not exposed and debate
is not critical, the fault, again, lies exclusively in application. The
method itself provides each party ample opportunity to police the
views of his opponent.

In short, debate, when properly and competently practiced, is a
critical instrument not only because it aims at a reflective judgment,
but also because it does this by employing a method that is persistently self-regulative.

3.

Why, let us next inquire, should debate be regarded as a mode of investigation rather than of persuasion?[6]

It is a mode of investigation for the very reason that its end and
method are critical.

As distinguished from the general run of public persuaders—the prop-

[5] William James, "The Will to Believe," *The Will to Believe and Other Essays
in Popular Philosophy* (London, 1909), p. 21.

[6] In this and the following section I have drawn at several points upon the excellent essay by Professor Wayne N. Thompson, "Discussion and Debate: A Re-
examination," *The Quarterly Journal of Speech*, XXX (October, 1944), 288–299.

agandist, the ad writer, the pitchman, the "public relations expert,"
the "psychic huckster"—the debater does not seek conviction regardless of the terms. To him it is more important that his method be
sound and that decision be reflective than that any particular result be
obtained by his appeals. If this were not the case he could easily find
quicker and surer ways to win acceptance for his view—ways that involve far fewer risks to the success of the cause he espouses. These
are available in legion. They range downward from the blatant devices of censorship and open threat to the subtlest modes of suggestion and indirect persuasion. Most professional public persuaders re-
sort to such methods daily. Instead of turning to any of these, however, by the very act of selecting debate as his method, the debater
openly renounces them. Fully aware of what he is doing, he foregoes
the convenience and easy sureness of "short-circuit" persuasives,
shouldering the labors and accepting the risks implicit in the critical approach. In the debater's code, investigation not only must precede decision, but is an integral part of the decision-making process. Persuasion
must run the gamut of the silent criticism of the judge and the open
attack of an opponent. In all phases of the process of debate labors and
dangers abound for him who chooses it.

To understand the full significance of the choice the debater makes,
one may perform five mental experiments. (1) Inquire, "Do fanatics
and rigid sectarians appeal for arbitration or for unqualified belief and
unthinking acceptance?" (2) Contrast the patient examination of evidence in a court of law with the impulsive, emotionally charged decision of a mob fired by its leader. (3) Recall how frequently a certain
cut of candidate for political office refuses to meet his opponent in
public debate. (4) Answer this question: Does the advertiser contract
for equal time or space for his closest competitor, and ask that buyers
delay their decision until both sides have been fully heard? (5) Most
revealing of all, perhaps, listen to an hour of earnest debating in a courtroom or legislative assembly—or, for that matter, even in a school debate tournament. Then compare it with an hour's run of radio or television commercials.

These experiments should help to clarify the difference between the
debater and most professional public persuaders, and should help us
understand why he, unlike them, is essentially an investigator. They
should emphasize the difference between the way of the truth-seeker
and the way of the speaker or writer whose concern is conviction, no
matter what the price.

In deciding whether a man is essentially an investigator or essentially a persuader the crucial test is this: Does he prefer truth at the
expense of victory, or does he prefer victory at the expense of truth?

When faced with this alternative, the man who chooses "truth" has by that very choice rightfully earned the name of investigator. The man who chooses victory can only be regarded as a persuader.

By drawing this dichotomy, I do not mean to imply that truth and victory are incompatible. Not only may they coincide; it may even be, as Aristotle argued, that they have a natural affinity for each other.[7] Such speculation is, however, irrelevant to our present purpose. For this it is enough to know whether a man prefers truth to victory or victory to truth. And it is inconceivable that anyone who makes victory paramount would grant an opponent the opportunities and advantages he enjoys in free debate between equals.

Because debate is a critical instrument, it is, then, by virtue of this fact, also an instrument of investigation rather than of persuasion.

4.

What, now, of the third and last of the propositions advanced at the outset? On what ground may we argue that debate is fundamentally a co-operative enterprise?

It is, of course, altogether understandable why debate should so frequently be regarded as a species of conflict—as a pitched battle in which two fixed and unalterable judgments engage in a life-and-death struggle for supremacy. The debater attacks an opponent's view for the purpose of defeating it and thus making his own prevail. Moreover, by the logic of debate method, these competing views are mutually exclusive. When one is accepted the other is automatically rejected and cast aside.

At the same time, however, we must not lose sight of two important facts. The first is this: In debate ideas come into conflict within the broader framework of a distinctly co-operative endeavor—one that is co-operative because it is governed by the four basic terms and agreements outlined above. Each party has an equal opportunity to be heard; each grants the other the right of examining and criticizing his arguments; each is willing that judgment be suspended until the facts are in; and each agrees to abide by the decision of a neutral arbitrating agency.

Let us contrast these stipulations and agreements with the characteristic attitudes and procedures of conflict. Here, whether the conflict occurs in the realm of words and persuasion or in the realm of physical combat and war, the picture is markedly different. In conflict, instead of freely granting an opponent an equal opportunity, every effort is made to curb his freedom of statement and action; instead of willingly opening one's resources to his inspection, every effort is

[7] *Rhetoric*, 1355a.

made to conceal or disguise them; instead of asking that a decision be suspended, all efforts are directed toward curtailing or terminating the contest; and instead of openly seeking an awarded or arbitrated decision, this sort of resolution is accepted reluctantly, and only when all hope for victory through force has been lost. These, I suggest, are the characteristic attitudes and procedures of conflict, and they are a far cry from the attitudes and procedures that characterize the debate process.

The second, and equally important, fact to keep in mind in this connection is that in debate the elements of conflict which are present operate on the level of "means," and not of "ends." Ideas are put into competition not for their own sake, but in order to determine which of two formulations will better implement a common value or which of two paths will more surely lead to a common goal.

It is as if a party of mountain climbers, concerned for their mutual safety, were to test two ropes in every conceivable way, and then to select for their common use the one that proved stronger. In debate, two parties, concerned for their mutual well-being and the well-being of society as a whole, assume that the view which better withstands exhaustive criticism will more often than not prove to be the "truth" or to "work out" in practice. And just as the principal test used on the ropes is to determine how much strain each will bear, so in debate the principal test of an idea is to see how well it will stand up under attack. In order to claim a place among those instruments which seek to formulate social choices and decisions co-operatively, a mode of argumentative deliberation need not exhibit harmony on the level of "means" as well as on that of "ends." The test applicable to means is not to ask whether they implement an atmosphere of deference, but whether they adhere to those basic attitudes of fact-centered objectivity that earn for them the name of critical. In this sense, as even its most enthusiastic devotees admit, the rational conflict of ideas lies at the heart of creative group discussion, just as it lies at the heart of debate.

While the procedure employed in debate is to try the mettle of ideas by entering them into competition, the debate process as a whole is, then, not an intellectual combat, but a co-operative testing device. Men, as Aristotle long ago pointed out, deliberate "not about the ends to be attained, but about the means of attaining them."[8] Every debate that ever has occurred or ever will occur must be dominated by a basic harmony of aim, growing out of a set of values common to both of the contending parties. Unless the opposing debaters have the same end in view—peace, prosperity, social welfare, national security, or

[8] *Ibid.*, 1362a.

whatever it may be—no debate is possible. There is no ground upon which they may come together in argument; no area where the thrusts of proof and the counterthrusts of refutation may meet and interact. The absence of such a ground is what made it impossible for the Democracies to debate with Hitler in 1936 and 1938, and what makes it difficult for us to debate with the representatives of the Soviet Union today. Where values and ends are disparate, ideas don't get across; proofs fail to clash; facts are meaningless.[9]

Because the purpose of debate is to test alternative means of achieving a common end, the proposition advanced in a debate is not, as some suppose, a fixed and unalterable conclusion or "outcome of thought." Instead, it is a close relative of the scientist's "hypothesis." The debate itself is not a process of intentional analysis and reasoning aimed at the confirmation of a prior premise. It is a "rational elaboration" of the hypothesis that is offered—a careful tracing out of its implications as a means of estimating its validity or worth.

Without some conflict of ideas in the sense of examining or testing, no intellectual life would be possible. The very notion of "truth," embodying, as it does, the correlative notion of "falseness," implies selection and rejection, choice and avoidance, the acceptance of one alternative and the consequent discarding of another. Even the most self-evident of propositions—the wetness of water, the greenness of grass, the inevitability of death and taxes—imply the rejection of their contraries. To this extent at least they are the end products of conflict, with its inevitable elements of victory and defeat.

The important question about conflict in any intellectual process is not its presence or absence. Present it must be if any constructive thought or deliberation is to occur. What we must always ask is this: On what level does the conflict take place? What end does it serve? In what spirit is it conducted?

So far as debate is concerned, our answers are these: Conflict occurs on the level of means, and in the service of ends. It is used for constructive, not destructive purposes. And it is conducted in a critical fashion because it is articulated by a self-regulative method. While conflict is present in debate, as it must be in all intellectual activity, it constitutes only a sub-movement within the broader framework of a co-operative enterprise. As a result of conflict the preferred decision emerges at once chastened and strengthened by the measure of truth that resides in its rejected opposite, for in debate that measure of truth is presented in a way that compels full attention to its claim. "He that wrestles with us," said Edmund Burke, "strengthens our nerves and

---

[9] See A. Craig Baird, "Responsibilities of Free Communication," *Vital Speeches*, September 1, 1952, pp. 699–701.

sharpens our skill. Our antagonist is our helper." To call debate a species of conflict is, in short, to confuse the part with the whole—to mistake the role of the participant for the method itself. Debate, considered as a generic mode of deliberation, is, we must conclude, a co-operative endeavor.

5.

Lest I be misunderstood, by way of conclusion let me emphasize the fact that it has not here been my purpose to undertake to write a clean bill of health for debate as practiced—to argue that as it is carried on in the schoolroom, the courthouse, the legislative assembly, the political campaign, or the business conference debate is uniformly pure and unabused. Aberrations have been, are today, and undoubtedly always will be committed in its name. Nor, for that matter, would I even contend that debate as a method of collective decision-making is without limitations. Applicable only when problem situations have been reduced to alternatives, it tends to disregard the view of the minority, is rigid and formal, and is an extremely difficult form of deliberation for the average person to practice effectively. But no method—even the one we call "scientific"—is as flexible and responsive, or as widely applicable or easily mastered as we might like it to be.

Excesses in practice or limitations in scope do not warrant the making of unjust charges against the process itself. Properly practiced, debate as a method is not uncritical, is not *a priori*, and does not emphasize unduly the attitudes and procedures of conflict. On the contrary, as I have undertaken to demonstrate: (1) because it pursues a reflective end by employing a self-regulative method, debate may legitimately be regarded as a critical instrument; (2) because it is critical, it may further be regarded as investigatory; and (3) because in debate conflict takes place within a framework of commonly accepted terms and stipulations, and on the level of "means" rather than of "ends," it may be called a co-operative rather than a competitive enterprise.

36. What Is a Question?

JEAN WELLINGTON
AND
C. BURLEIGH WELLINGTON

Where is the capital of Georgia? Who was Descartes? What did Cae-
sar do in France? Why does New York have tall buildings? How do you
make an S? Up and down the corridors of the nation's schools ring questions. Always questions. Who? What? When? Where? How? Why?
Of course we all know what a question is, those of us in teaching at
any rate. We utter them hour after hour, day after day, until they reverberate in the old school walls where the same questions were asked these
youngsters' parents, and perhaps grandparents.

A colleague of ours recently asked a young student teacher "When
are you going to stop asking questions and start teaching?" This was
a question, too, but not one to which the student teacher possessed
the ready answer which she was expecting from her social studies pupils when she asked them, "Who was Stonewall Jackson and what did
he do?" The student teacher had not yet learned that the definition
of the word *teaching* is not "to ask questions."

Sometimes we wonder what students really think when a teacher
poses: What is Mars? Who was Socrates? Where is Stratford-on-Avon?
Are they saying to themselves, "So who cares?" or perhaps, "I hope
I remember this until after the test tomorrow and then I can forget it"?
As our friend implied, asking and answering questions do not neces-
sarily involve any learning whatever.

Then why do teachers persist in so many questions that their ghosts
stalk the corridors of school buildings from grade 1 through graduate
school? Sometimes, being facetious, we wonder if the teacher does not
know where Stratford-on-Avon is and, therefore, he asks the student so
he may find out. Every teacher we have asked, however, insists that

From Jean Wellington and C. Burleigh Wellington, "What Is a Question?" *The
Clearing House*, XXXVI (April, 1962), 471–472. Jean Wellington is Assistant
Professor of Education, Tufts University, Medford, Massachusetts. C. Burleigh
Wellington is Associate Professor of Education and Director of Student Teaching
and Teacher Placement, also at Tufts University. Reprinted by permission of *The
Clearing House*.

such a situation is absurd; they assure us they do not seek information, for they always know the answer themselves. Then perhaps he is trying to find out if the student knows what he knows. The teacher knows that Socrates was a Greek philosopher who lived around 400 B.C. So he asks the students who Socrates was in order to discover if they know what the teacher does. But this seems absurd too, and who can blame the student for his reaction—so who cares?

Robert Frost once said, "Long ago I gave up the idea of asking my students to tell me what I knew that I might discover if they knew as much as I did. Now in classes I ask questions in the correct sense of the word, for I want them to tell me something new, something I do not know."[1] Here is a man who asks a question for a reason which is not absurd. But if we are to follow his procedure, most of the questions now asked in schools will not stand the test. If we seek to learn something new from students, we cannot ask them to tell us anything which we already know.

Let's imagine for a moment that a school board passes an edict: No more questions allowed in the classroom, even on tests, unless a teacher finds out something new. An unfortunately large group of teachers might find that they had absolutely nothing to say in class as a result. A goodly number would find that half or more of a class hour was unused.

The edict might force them to revise their questions and to begin instead to seek knowledge and understanding. Why do you think we talk about men from Mars? Why do you feel Socrates is passé? Why would you want to visit Stratford-on-Avon? Obviously just prefacing a question with "why" is not enough. It is a matter of not having a preconceived answer in mind, not asking the student to guess what we already know, but of seeking his thinking and reasoning and beliefs.

Or perhaps we should introduce a Pavlov's gong every time teachers asked questions without good reason. This might help them to turn to themselves to ask a question in the true definition of the word. Something like "Is this question necessary?" should serve admirably. For the dictionaries give such meanings as these for *question:* "debate," "investigation," "problem," "matter to be inquired into." In no dictionary does it state that a question is defined by the term "teaching," or by the idea of asking someone to play a guessing game for the answer the teacher has thought of.

Of course we do not seriously ask edicts or other Big Brother tactics. But we should like to question teachers about their questions. Do your questions teach? Are they a crutch to check up on students? Or if you were absolutely honest, are questions asked to fill up some of the time? Are questions the easy technic requiring neither planning

[1] Elizabeth S. Sergeant, *Robert Frost* (New York: Holt, Rinehart and Winston, 1960), p. 249.

nor creativity? Do you use mostly "give it back" questions, and if so, have they any learning value? Could you teach without one single question which did not honestly ask for something new from students? Does a question promote your desired aim better than another approach?

To be consistent with ourselves we cannot ask questions unless we seek something new. The questions we would ask here or in the classroom are designed to create anxiety for learning and to put in motion the process of critical thinking.[2] They would develop first the individual's ability to define his own questions, and then his ability to discover answers which he can use to make his own conclusions and judgments in the light of known facts and research. This is the definition of the questions which we believe should reverberate through the corridors of our schools and through the minds of our youth.

We aren't quite sure—what did *you* say a question is?

[2] C. Burleigh Wellington and Jean Wellington, *Teaching for Critical Thinking* (New York: McGraw-Hill Book Co., Inc., 1960).

37. *Teaching Children To Listen*
MAURICE S. LEWIS

Never in the history of our country have we had a greater need for listening skill than we have today. We desperately need citizens who can comprehend the vast amount of oral discourse which emanates daily from our radio and TV sets; citizens who withhold judgment until the facts are known; citizens who are not easily moved by emotion-laden words woven skillfully into political speeches, news reports, and commercial advertising; citizens who do not panic easily at startling emotional outbursts by those whose responsibility it is to lead us.

We have long emphasized the importance of speaking ability, and silver-tongued orators are among our list of heroes. The ability to influence listeners is cherished by all who possess it. Our schools have done a good job of teaching oral language, but they have done little to help those who are on the receiving end of communication, the listeners.

Until recently, the instructional program in listening amounted to

From Maurice S. Lewis, "Teaching Children To Listen," *Education*, LXXX (April, 1960), 455–459. Maurice S. Lewis is Professor of Education, Arizona State University, Tempe, Arizona. Reprinted by permission from the April, 1960 issue of *Education*. Copyright 1960 by The Bobbs-Merrill Co., Inc., Indianapolis, Indiana.

no more than admonishing children to listen in most classrooms. Good listening was identified with sitting quietly with folded hands, good posture, and attentive eyes.

RESEARCH IN LISTENING

Listening, in the past, was assumed to be like reading. While thousands have studied the reading process, few have paid attention to this comparable assimilative skill. In recent years, however, researchers have awakened an interest in listening, and we have begun to give it its rightful place in the school curriculum.

Studies by Rankin (9) and Wilt (11) have helped us to realize the importance of listening as a communication skill in daily life and as a tool for learning in the classroom. Nichols (6) analyzed the factors in listening and set up a successful instructional program for teaching college freshmen. Brown's (1) study resulted in the first published test of listening comprehension. Lewis (3, 4) studied the effect of listening upon reading and constructed tests to measure the listening ability of intermediate-grade children. Pratt (8) and Marsden (5) evaluated the effectiveness of instructions in listening. These and other studies have opened the door for further development of methods and techniques for teaching listening.

Listening is the process of attaching meaning to the spoken word. It is a complex process involving much more than the physical act of hearing or the external attitude of paying attention. Like reading, it is an assimilative communication skill which includes the understanding and interpreting of symbols and requires the development of certain skills and attitudes. It is unlike reading in that the listener has but one opportunity to comprehend, whereas, in reading, he may reread that which he does not understand.

The development of listening skill begins in the cradle as the newborn child uses his most highly developed organs, his ears, to attach meaning to the many sounds in his environment. In the process of learning to communicate, much energy is expended in imitating those sounds.

It is through this interaction with his environment that the preschool child acquires his listening and speaking vocabularies. Early studies estimated the size of these vocabularies to be relatively small. However, a more recent study by Smith (10) found that first-grade children had an average listening vocabulary of 23,700 words (16,900 basic words and 6,800 derived words) with a range from 6,000 to 48,000 words. From these and other facts, we must assume that children enter school with considerable listening skill.

Research has shown that children continued to show improvement in listening until about the end of the sixth grade. Then, as they achieve a fair degree of proficiency in reading, they cease to improve in listening.

A comparison of reading and listening leads one to conclude that, with a few exceptions, the actual skills involved are identical. Both are dependent upon the same experience background of the child; both require thinking; both have an inherent developmental sequence. It would seem, then, that listening skills, because of the vocabulary advantage, should always precede comparable reading skills. Proficiency in a specific listening skill, in effect, should constitute readiness for learning the same skill in reading.

Research has shown that listening can be improved by providing definite instruction in listening. It has shown also that reading improves when children are given training in listening. On the other hand, it has been found that listening does not improve when only reading is taught.

It is the purpose of this paper to suggest: some goals for listening; some aspects of a desirable listening environment; and some principles of learning to be observed in teaching listening—all of which may be helpful in planning a program of instruction.

GOALS FOR LISTENING

Before we can make curricular revisions to include an adequate program of instruction in listening, we first must ascertain what skills, attitudes, and understandings our elementary children need to learn. This can be done best by describing some of the aspects of the behavior of a good listener and by suggesting different levels of maturity which children may attain.

A good listener does more than sit quietly and look attentive while someone is speaking.

1. *He is aware of the importance of listening in the learning process.* Through discussion in the classroom, the good listener becomes aware of the many sounds in his environment and what they mean. He becomes aware of the fact that he learns many things by listening. He learns that the concepts he has are a product of many types of learning, and that many concepts have been learned by listening. He uses listening as one of his most important tools for learning.

2. *He understands the roles of the speaker and the listener in the communication process.* The good listener plays these roles in small groups; he may act as speaker in one group and as listener in another group. As a more mature listener, he understands the responsibility that is shared by the speaker and the listener. He participates in evaluative activities to determine the effectiveness of communication in reports, storytelling, and oral reading.

3. *He listens through to the end of a discourse before he attempts to draw conclusions.* The good listener listens through to the end of a story read by the teacher in order to participate actively in a discussion of the ending. He withholds judgment until all the facts have been presented. He is aware of certain emotion-laden words which affect his listening. He can summarize discussions and help his group reach decisions based upon facts.

4. *He can follow directions given orally.* The good listener remembers the first step and, with the teacher's guidance, can complete the task. He listens to remember the first time the direction is given. He learns to keep a sequence of steps in mind.

5. *He adjusts his listening to the purpose at hand.* At first, all listening seems to be very general. Later, the good listener learns that one listens for several different purposes: to follow directions, to remember details, to get the general idea, to draw conclusions, and to enjoy.

6. *He enjoys listening.* The good listener enjoys listening to stories and music. His tastes mature as he matures. He likes to listen to increasingly difficult discourse, because it challenges his listening ability. He enjoys listening to classical music.

7. *He is a critical listener.* The good listener learns to discriminate between fact and fiction. He learns to question the validity of statements and to check the competence of the authority before making a final decision. He learns to check his own understandings and to modify them in light of new evidence. He learns the art of skillful questioning to make certain that he understands the speaker's viewpoint and the facts upon which the speaker bases that viewpoint.

LISTENING ENVIRONMENT

Children have the best opportunity to improve their ability to listen in a classroom environment which is conducive to good listening. It will be most helpful if:

1. *The classroom environment stimulates speaking and listening.* Children communicate about those things which they find in their classroom environment. The vocabulary they use and the richness of their experiences will depend upon what they and the teacher create within the four walls of that room. The room may be quite empty, with only bare walls and basic textbooks, resulting in a minimum of interaction, or it may be alive with materials and activities which stimulate communication, not only in the classroom, but in the cafeteria, on the playground, and in the home. It is this meaningful speaking and listening which affects both the quantity and quality of learning.

2. *The classroom arrangement is flexible.* Children learn to communicate best when they have opportunities to practice in small groups first, and, later, in increasingly larger groups. Furniture which allows free-

dom of movement from one type of organization to another is desirable. However, a creative teacher can find ways to group children in the most traditionally equipped classroom.

3. *There are opportunities for reaction.* Communication is a two-way process. It involves the transmission of ideas between individuals through speaking and listening. When the listener is active in the process, his level of personal involvement reaches its highest peak, and the quality of the experience is best. Children need opportunities to react to the ideas expressed by their peers, their teachers, and others.

The amount of reaction possible is dependent upon the group structure. A minimum of reaction is possible in a discussion involving the total class with the teacher asking the questions and the children providing the answers. A maximum amount of reaction occurs when children work in pairs in problem solving, oral reading, and other activities. We should provide opportunities for children to practice communicating in many sizes of groups and for many different purposes.

4. *There is a permissive atmosphere.* Children who are permitted to interact with their environment and to communicate about the things they are trying to learn will probably learn to listen better. They must learn, of course, to recognize and live within the limitations imposed by the teacher or those democratically constituted under the skillful guidance of the teacher.

Children should learn to adjust the type and amount of communication to the situation at hand. It may be loud or soft, much or little, depending on the activity. The maximum noise level is reached when children work in pairs.

PRINCIPLES OF LEARNING

There are several basic principles of learning which seem to apply to the teaching of listening in the elementary school.

1. *Children learn what they practice.* Unless positive steps are taken to teach listening, it is fair to assume that the learning may be negative.

2. *Children need to understand what it is that they are trying to learn.* Talking about listening will help them to understand that it is like reading in some ways, but unlike it in other ways.

3. *Children need to become aware of their ability to listen.* Listening has been taken for granted for so long that it is best to begin any program of instruction by administering a standardized test (2), or a teacher-made test, as a means of motivating children to set up individual and group goals for the improvement of listening.

4. *Children need opportunities to discover that they can improve their listening ability.* It is difficult to tell children exactly what they must do to improve their listening ability. However, if they are given

an adequate number of opportunities to listen for various purposes and to evaluate the results of their efforts, they will discover those things which make a real difference in their comprehension.

5. *Oral reading should be taught so that it fosters good listening.* When children read new material in a well-prepared manner to their classmates, they are providing good listening experiences. When these experiences are followed by discussions and other activities, they provide the listener with an opportunity to react.

6. *Oral language is taught with an emphasis upon communication.* Young children should have many opportunities to express ideas orally to their classmates and to be judged by what they communicate, not by how they speak. When the emphasis is upon communication of ideas, children will become concerned with what they say and whether it is understood by their listeners. As the communication process becomes understood, there will be a need to teach children to use better posture, a more pleasing voice, and accurate grammar.

7. *Children have opportunities to listen to difficult material read to them by the teacher.* Elementary-school children usually can comprehend materials read to them, which are one or more years above their reading level. Content materials read by the teacher, or by a child who is a good oral reader, will provide excellent listening experiences.

8. *Individual differences in listening should be recognized.* It is common practice for teachers to repeat directions and instructions so that the slowest child in the room will comprehend. This teaches brighter children not to listen the first time but to adjust to the pattern followed by the teacher. Children will become better listeners if instructional talking is done at a higher-than-average level to challenge all children. If a few children comprehend less well, they should be helped to improve their listening in a separate grouping.

CONCLUSION

We need more experimental research which will provide us with further data about the listening process. We need more action research in the classroom to develop methods and techniques for teaching and evaluating listening skill. We need more creative teachers of listening. Will you meet the challenge?

REFERENCES

1. Brown, James I. "The Construction of a Diagnostic Test of Listening Comprehension," *Journal of Educational Research,* Vol. 43 (April, 1950), pp. 626–636.
2. *Cooperative Sequential Tests of Educational Progress* (Princeton, N.J.: Cooperative Test Division, Educational Testing Service, 1957).

3. Lewis, Maurice S. "The Effect of Training in Listening upon Reading," *Journal of Communication* (November, 1953), pp. 115–119.

4. Lewis, Maurice S. "The Construction of a Diagnostic Test of Listening Comprehension for Grades Four, Five, and Six" (Unpublished doctor's field study, Colorado State College of Education, 1954).

5. Marsden, Ware W. "A Study to Determine the Effect of Training to Listen upon Ability to Listen" (Unpublished doctor's field study, Colorado State College of Education, 1952).

6. Nichols, Ralph G. "Factors in Listening Comprehension," *Speech Monographs*, Vol. 15, No. 2 (1948), pp. 154–163.

7. Nichols, Ralph G. and Stevens, L. A. *Are You Listening?* (New York: McGraw-Hill Book Co. Inc., 1957).

8. Pratt, Edward. "Experimental Evaluation of a Program for the Improvement of Listening," *The Elementary School Journal* (March, 1956), pp. 315–320.

9. Rankin, Paul T. "The Importance of Listening Ability," *English Journal* (college ed.), Vol. 17 (October, 1928), pp. 623–630.

10. Smith, Mary K. "Measurement of the Size of General Vocabulary through the Elementary Schools and High Schools," *Genetic Psychology Monographs*, Vol. 24, second half (1941), pp. 311–345.

11. Wilt, M. E. "Study of Teacher Awareness as a Factor in Elementary Education," *Journal of Educational Research*, Vol. 43 (April, 1950), pp. 626–636.

38. *Dramatic Experiences*

JOHN H. HUNT

Returning to her alma mater for Alumni Reunion, a young teacher took advantage of the opportunity to discuss a problem encountered during her first year of teaching. In her student teaching experience, she had helped to plan and guide dramatic play activities. Convinced of the many values which children may realize through creative experiences in dramatic play, she had been much disturbed to find that in her community some people took a dim view of her efforts to provide such experiences for children. "The time and effort should be devoted to teaching the 3 R's," they said.

Now that assembly programs were optional, some teachers felt that

From John H. Hunt, "Dramatic Experiences: Fads and Frills?" *New York State Education*, XLIX, No. 7 (April, 1962), 36–37. John H. Hunt is Associate Professor of Education, State University College, Plattsburgh, New York. Reprinted by permission of New York State Teachers Association.

dramatic play might be ignored, especially in the middle grades. A few looked upon dramatics as a waste of time, a show-off or downright exploitation of children. A course taken at a nearby college had merely added to the young teacher's confusion. The professor had managed to give the impression that dramatic play belonged in the "fads and frills" category.

It would be comforting to assume that this young teacher's problem was an isolated one. However, in view of the pummeling which schools are enduring from critics within and outside the profession, one might well wonder if this problem indicates a trend in the wrong direction. The threat of "crash" programs and demands for a return to the "fundamentals" are very real indeed. It behooves all teachers to re-examine their philosophies of education and reaffirm their faith in those educational procedures which have withstood the test of time. Silence may be golden, but it can also be deadly.

When used properly, dramatic play undoubtedly has many educational values. However, it has probably been twisted completely out of shape and has become an almost meaningless ritual in some schools. It may be about time for us to view the problem objectively. Perhaps the first step in gaining objectivity is to place dramatic play in its proper perspective.

Even a brief visit in the primary school reveals that dramatic play is probably the most natural activity of children. There one is likely to find children playing house, school, storekeepers, drivers of vehicles, firemen, pilots and other games portraying activities of the society in which the children live. The teacher capitalizes on these natural reactions in helping children to understand and appreciate their environment, find means of self-expression, develop their imaginations, learn how to work and play with others, acquire self-confidence in speaking, add to their vocabularies and release pent-up feelings.

Thus, dramatic play emerges from the natural and spontaneous activities of young children. As youngsters progress through the middle and upper grades, their interest and pleasure in dramatics continue. Ideas and motivation for dramatic experiences may occur in reading stories, summarizing units, celebrating special days, visualizing historical events, studying about people of other times and places, listening to plays on the radio and observing plays on the screen or stage.

The children's own dramatic experiences may be in the form of simple dramatizations of stories, original plays, pantomimes, marionettes and simulated or actual broadcasts. Original plays tend to provide more opportunities for creativeness, self-expression and spontaneous action than do printed plays. If done in the right way, however, producing a good published play can be a valuable, satisfying experience for children. The language of competent writers helps youngsters to broaden their vocabularies, develop style and appreciate artistic writing. If children are encouraged to interpret the lines and actions of the printed play, they can realize some of the values obtained in producing an original play.

Older children, no longer satisfied with earlier "babyish" performances, will strive to make their dramatic play as authentic and realistic as possible. They delve into reading, writing and research. Preparing dialogues, invitations, programs, simple costumes, scenery or stage properties entails the use of other basic skills and imagination. The wise teacher meets the need for more help and guidance without stifling enthusiasm, originality and spontaneity.

When placed in its proper perspective, dramatic play can be seen as valuable educational experiences rather than exhibitions "put on" by the teacher and having little meaning or purpose for children. The following brief description of a fourth grade's Open House suggests how dramatic experiences may grow out of and extend regular classroom activities.

Toward the end of the school year, the children were asked how they might help their parents better to understand what had been accomplished. It was pointed out that room meetings, conferences and report cards are helpful but need to be supplemented. During the discussion someone suggested that parents might be invited to school and see for themselves. Exhibits, displays and the pupils' individual folders could be used. Further discussion indicated that the exhibits and displays should be explained. Moreover, the children became aware of the fact that they themselves were vague about some of the things they had "learned."

It was decided that the class should spend some time reviewing before attempting to tell parents about their school work. This was done. Eventually committees on social studies, science and health, language arts, arithmetic, art and music were set up. Each committee assumed responsibility for deciding how the work in its particular area might be presented in an interesting manner. Materials for exhibits and displays were taken from the class file and individual folders.

Although the social studies committee was quite busy preparing a panel discussion and bulletin board pertaining to "Our Friends Around the World," the group suggested that the class might present a play based on units completed during the year. The suggestion was warmly received but required further review, reading, planning, sharing of ideas and working out the play content and form. Problems concerning costumes, scenery, music, invitations, taking care of guests, etc., had to be solved. Obviously, everybody's help was needed if Open House was to be a success. And a success it was!

39. Homework

LLOYD McCLEARY

Reflection upon the subject of homework seems to open a Pandora's box for the educator. Pupils, parents, teachers and administrators hold a wide range of beliefs and opinions relative to homework. Beliefs and opinions not only differ within and between each of these groups, but they also vary as attention moves along the line from the practical concerns to the deeper philosophical questions which arise whenever problems of homework require attention.

As if this were not enough, opinions are likely to be affected by "side" concerns, for administrators *are* concerned about public relations; teachers *are* concerned about how "respectable" they appear to their colleagues; and parents *are* concerned about their child's readiness for College Boards. Since standard prescriptions of policy and practice are not likely to end the intense concern over this subject, perhaps an attempt in this article to indicate some of the major problems and some of the operating principles revealed by research and by current best practice may be of value to the reader.

THE "WHAT" AND THE "WHY"

In an analysis of the topic of homework, we first face a semantic problem. To the uninitiated, perhaps it would appear that homework should mean work assigned by a teacher to be completed at home. This definition of homework is of little help in understanding what a given teacher is likely to mean by the term.

Because of the protests of some pupils, the author questioned an English teacher about the amount of homework she had assigned. The teacher in question denied vigorously that the required reading of a novel within a period of one week in addition to a strong dose of writ-

From Lloyd McCleary, "Homework," *Educational Leadership*, XVII (January, 1960), 217–220, 225. Lloyd McCleary is Professor of Education and Chairman of the Department of Educational Administration, College of Education, University of Illinois, Urbana, Illinois. Reprinted by permission of the author and of *Educational Leadership*.

ten work was unreasonable because the reading of a novel (although required) was not homework! Likewise, a Latin teacher became incensed with the author because he objected to the fact that she kept students after school each night to do the work she had assigned in class that day. She held many of her pupils until five o'clock almost daily because she didn't believe in having them do work at home! These are extreme but actual examples of the practices of teachers.

In the literature of the 1930's the term homework apparently had a very clear meaning. The assign, study, recite, test methods in common use gave rise to this parent reaction reported by Butler[1] in 1939. A parent wrote to a superintendent:

> I have four little girls attending your schools. I am up at five o'clock in the morning to get them off to school and to get myself off to work. It is six o'clock in the evening when I reach home again, pretty well worn out, and after we have had dinner and have tidied up the house a bit, it is eight o'clock. Then, tired as I am, I sit down and teach the little girls the lessons your teachers will hear them say over on the following day. Now, if it is all the same to you, it would be a great help and a favor to me if you will have your teachers teach the lessons during the day, and then all I would have to do at night would be to hear them say them over.

Unfortunately, as late as 1950, Burton[2] reported an investigation which showed that four-fifths of the assignment procedures in the social studies classes studied were nothing more than page assignments of a single textbook.

Curriculum workers find the need to distinguish between formal or traditional practices and modern practices relative to teaching methods and techniques including homework. Very largely the distinction is based upon the degree to which practice is related to the findings of modern research dealing with individual differences in ability, in interests, and in rates of learning. The few statistical studies which have been made show that home study of the formal sort even when accompanied by questions, study guides and the like have little effect upon achievement. As teaching methods and homework shift from the expository-memory type of activity to the problem solving-independent study type there will be many activities to be carried on outside of the scheduled class time. However, these homework activities do not resemble the "assigned textbook pages" kind of homework.

[1] Frank A. Butler, *The Improvement of Teaching in Secondary Schools*. Chicago, Illinois: The University of Chicago Press, 1939, p. 208.

[2] *Learning and Instruction*. The forty-ninth Yearbook of the National Society for the Study of Education, Part I. Chicago, Illinois: The University of Chicago Press, 1950, p. 227.

THE "HOW"

The newer approach equates study with learning. The emphasis as far as homework is concerned becomes that of teaching pupils how to learn and how to become self directing in their study. Continuity between classroom and out-of-classroom study is sought. Teachers know very well that the demands of the classroom will largely condition the approaches the pupil will use in independent study. If factual tests are a major element of the teaching method, memory will be the habit of study employed by the pupil. The habit of memorizing is likely to be employed as the means of study even in situations in which memorizing is completely inappropriate. Thus, classroom activities should require a variety of individual and group learning experiences which are completed outside the classroom. Examples of these activities are identifying and defining problems; analyzing problems through library, laboratory or action research type of activity, interviews, visits, experiment and the like.

Needless to say, this kind of homework emphasis does not reduce the range of opinion or the number of issues relative to homework. Rather the shifting emphasis to problem-solving and independent study type of outside of classroom learning has introduced new problems and issues. The efforts to develop independent study have largely centered upon (a) the lengthened period with time devoted to the teaching of appropriate study techniques, (b) the development of separate how-to-study courses, (c) the use of special or remedial teachers such as a reading teacher to develop certain skills, and (d) the provision of supervisory help for the teacher in teaching study habits through regular class procedures. Within any given staff one will almost certainly find advocates of these various approaches. Obviously the direction of curriculum development being taken in a given school, administrative procedures, preparation of staff and the like will determine which, if any, steps are taken to alter the quality of homework and to prepare pupils to profit fully from it.

Regardless of the teaching methods employed, teachers need to understand and to recognize good study procedures and be able to diagnose cases of inefficiency in or ignorance of study procedures. Aids to the teacher in the form of books and monographs on effective study procedures, diagnostic tests, remedial materials, guides, inventories and the like are plentiful and are of excellent quality. In addition, the teacher can detect evidence of poor study habits through observation, examination of pupils' work, conferences, and self constructed questionnaires.

Unfortunately, many schools attempt to initiate curricular changes without the proper preparation of the staff. The incidents of comic if not pathetic attempts are legend. In one school known to the author, the principal abolished all study halls and lengthened the class periods accordingly with the expectation that teachers would immediately begin teaching independent study techniques appropriate to their subject but with no preparation other than the announcement in a faculty meeting that this would be done.

During the 1940's a large number of controlled studies were conducted. The author was, however, unable to find a study which actually compared various techniques rather than various administrative schemes for facilitating study. A Project for the Improvement of Thinking, now being conducted by Professors Henderson and Smith of the College of Education of the University of Illinois, is an excellent example of a project which developed and tried out materials for improving pupil learning within the classroom. This study and others like it, however, have not directly investigated the aspect of independent study or the transfer of these learnings to use beyond the classroom. Soundly conceived experimental studies are badly needed in this area.

Although the nature of instruction and the development of sound habits of independent study are important to worthwhile out-of-class study, the assignment is a crucial element in productive homework. Regardless of the nature of the homework assignment, the pupil should clearly understand what he is to do and have definite leads to begin his work. There is ample research data to support the belief that pupil failure relative to study is as much caused by factors indicative of a poor assignment (frustration, lack of interest, failure to understand the relationship of the assignment to the classwork, etc.) than to poor study habits.

THE "WHEN" AND THE "HOW MUCH"

Definite answers to the "when" and the "how much" questions are offered from many quarters. Generally these answers are not derived from the nature of a particular unit of school work or from the needs of particular pupils. Unfortunately, the professional journals contain just as many such answers as do the newspapers and popular magazines. In a 15 minute scanning of professional journals the author found seven separate (and each surprisingly similar) statements of the amount and timing of homework. Generally these statements were policies adopted and in force in some school system and apparently their publication implied their recommendation to the profession to be used as a standard for adoption in other schools. One such statement recommends: "In kindergarten to grade four: no homework; in grades five and six: one-half hour; in grades seven and eight: one hour; (and so on). It is suggested that no homework be given over weekends or holidays." Another article with the same time requirements is headed by the words "homework may harm the child's health and the school's public relations"!

These kinds of statements are not likely to be of much help to parents or to teachers. If such policies are taken seriously they may be a source of frustration to the teacher and a cause of irritation to parents that could defeat the public relations purpose which the statement professes to serve. Louis Brumer, the father of a pupil in a New York City high school, wrote his reaction to homework policy in the June 1956 issue of *High Points:*

Do responsible members of the high school teaching corps recommend 30–50 minutes (of homework) daily in each prepared subject?

Do they believe students should be encouraged to give services to the school?

Do they believe youth should be encouraged to attend school club meetings, and/or community religious group club activities after school?

Do they believe school children at the high school level should continue with music lessons, dancing lessons, or art lessons ... ?

Should children develop responsibility toward the home and family by performing special duties ... ?

Should families be encouraged to dine together nightly for an hour to review the day's events ... ?

Should there be an occasional free afternoon ... ?

Should at least one morning a week be assigned to formal religious devotions?

Should time be set aside for shopping for a suit or dress, other wardrobe essentials, or an occasional birthday gift ... ?

Should any unscheduled time be left for an adolescent to read a *book of his own choice* ... ?

How many hours of sleep should a growing young man or lady require?

Some school-wide policies relative to homework seem to be required but it is doubtful that rather fixed time limits are either effective or meaningful. The most fruitful approach seems to lie in the direction of the study of the curriculum and the teaching procedures out of which the homework evolves. A knowledge of home conditions and the out-of-school experiences of pupils should help teachers to devise learning activities which develop into stimulating out-of-class study and which can be tailored to individual needs.

Another avenue to independent study that is important to those concerned about homework is the use of the extended school day. Shops, libraries, science and language laboratories, work space and equipment for the use of tapes, television kinescopes and the like under the care of a para-professional teacher or a laboratory assistant are already available in some schools during out-of-class study time. Such facilities with proper provision for their use create excellent study conditions and do not involve the taxation of teacher time. This kind of activity meets many of the objections to homework held by parents and teachers. These activities could be incorporated with leisure time pursuits, relieve the home of the burden of providing materials and equipment, enrich and extend classroom experiences and promote the development of independent study.

In an opinion poll of school administrators conducted by *The Nation's Schools,* 96 percent of the administrators polled favored scheduled study during the school day; 95 percent favored homework assignments for junior and senior high school pupils; 79 percent favored homework at the upper elementary school level; and 31 percent favored homework for pupils in the lower elementary grades. According to reports from the administrators involved in this poll, the average time spent doing homework was about three hours per week for elementary pupils and from four to six hours per week for high school pupils. If these reactions represent homework conditions generally, there is wide acceptance of the practice of assigning homework; and at least at the high school level, the average time spent doing assigned homework is the equivalent of one school day each week. If this time is to be employed effectively and if it can be invested to produce independent, self directing students, the effort by teachers to improve the quality of homework becomes one of education's most compelling tasks.

40. *What Is a Good School Contest?*

NORMA R. MILLER

At an advertising and public relations conference of a corporation not long ago, executives were winding up plans for a new promotion.

"Our program is shaping up, George. I think we're about ready to fly it, but it does leave one audience area completely uncovered. That's the school children."

From Norma R. Miller, "What is a Good School Contest?" NASSP *Bulletin,* XLIII, No. 248 (September, 1959), 28–31. Norma R. Miller is an independent public relations consultant in Washington, D.C. Reprinted by permission of the *Bulletin* of the National Association of Secondary-School Principals, Washington, D.C. Copyright September, 1959.

"I've been thinking the same thing, Bill. And here's an idea right off the top of my head. How about an essay contest? We could offer a $1,000 cash prize. That'd get a lot of youngsters into the act."

Judging from the number of ill-conceived contests offered to schools each year, this scene must be repeated hundreds of times in offices across the country.

How do teachers and administrators react to sponsored contests? A classroom teacher recently wrote in the *N.E.A. Journal*, "Some of these contests are carefully planned efforts to reward talent. With these, teachers are happy to cooperate. Others, principally in the write-an-essay group, are poorly conceived, selfishly planned, and disliked by teachers." Because the growing number of sponsored contests tends to increase pressure on the teachers' time, many districts have passed flat no-contest rules. And yet, contests have a long tradition in schools.

The old fashioned spelling bee, with a book for a prize, is one of the earliest examples. The problem is not that there *are* contests, but that there are *so few good* contests from the school's point of view. Educators have always recognized that contests can provide incentive for student effort. For this reason, few educators turn their backs on contests altogether. Instead, they continue to face the almost daily decision-making needed to sort out the few educationally sound contests and discard the many poor ones.

What are the criteria for a good school contest? What is and is not acceptable? First of all, a contest for schools must serve school needs. It must help teachers to achieve some of their educational objectives. In determining whether any given contest does this, several questions are crucial.

WHAT IS THE CONTEST'S OBJECTIVE?

The objective of a contest is educational if participation in it contributes to the intellectual development and understanding of students or contributes to the creative and artistic development of students. For example, the objective may be to get as many home economics students as possible to create original recipes or bake excellent pies. It may be to gain wide interest and participation in taking better photographs, painting posters, or devising scientific experiments. Contests with objectives such as these can serve the broader educational aims of stimulating the students' intellectual or creative development. Contests designed to select the most beautiful girl or the strongest or most popular boy are not likely to make any contribution to education.

WHAT DOES THE CONTESTANT HAVE TO DO?

What the contestant does to prepare the contest entry should contribute to his or her education. Contests which require research or the exercise of creative imagination or special talents meet this challenge. The required activity must be within the capabilities of the students of the age and grade level to which the contest is directed, and it must appeal to student interest. An important, but often overlooked, factor is that the process or activity required should be one which the student *can* do entirely himself, and one which it is difficult to get someone else to do for him. One objection to essay contests is that they may tempt some students to be dishonest. It is relatively easy to get an older person to write the essay, or at least to "correct and revise" it to a point where it is not actually written by the contestant. The contestant's research also often leads him to discover many tempting examples in books and newspapers of just exactly the right way to say what he wants to say.

WHAT ABOUT THE RULES AND REGULATIONS?

The mechanics of a contest include rules for eligibility, participation, and the means by which the contest is administered and judged. No unfair limitations should be placed on eligibility. It goes without saying that a contest for public schools should not rule out any group because of race, color, or creed. Nor should the entrants be required to purchase any product, include box tops, or other commercial gimmicks. This limits eligibility to users of certain products or those who can afford to buy. Although some bright youngsters may be able to make good showings, in most cases it is unfair to place children in competition with adults who have had more education and experience. A contest will be most successful from the school's as well as the sponsor's point of view when the rules are simple, clear, fair, and free from confusing exceptions, and when no demands are made on teachers' time for judging or other services.

HOW IS THE CONTEST JUDGED AND BY WHOM?

Good contest announcements always explain the criteria for judging, the methods to be used, and the names and qualifications of the judges. Both objective and subjective judgments have their uses in judging contests, but the tendency generally is to lean too heavily on the latter. It depends somewhat on how the contest is set up and the subject matter it deals with, but, where possible, it is a good idea to set up entry blanks to include questions based on validated or psychometric forms, which can be machine scored, as well as open-end questions which must be evaluated subjectively by the judges.

Judges should be selected for their knowledge and judgment in the professional field involved, and for their familiarity with educational methods. Some contests weaken their value here by selecting famous people for judges, regardless of their professional qualifications. A newspaper editor, schooled in the William Jennings Bryan tradition, may not be the most competent judge for student speakers being trained for to-day's more informal speaking techniques. If the sponsor himself is the judge, he may unknowingly favor his own viewpoints and ideas. This is a pitfall particularly for the judges of essay contests.

Some contests which measure up in other respects fall down because they call for activities which are virtually unjudgable. For example, a contest to pick the boy or girl with the best posture. Such a contest may have the worth-while objective of encouraging better posture and better health among students. Few, if any, judges could separate out factors such as general appearance and body build to judge purely on posture. Even then, the margin of difference between the winner and others would be so minute that fair judgment would hardly be possible.

Other unjudgable contests from a school's viewpoint center around areas which depend primarily on personal taste. For example, in a con-test for girls, the prize was to go to the girl who had selected the most attractive place setting from a variety of flatwear, china, linen, and glass.

WHAT PRIZES ARE OFFERED?

Prizes, as well as the contests themselves, should further the con-testant's education. A trust or scholarship is preferable to cash awards. An educational trip is preferable to an expensive medal.

WHAT DOES THE SPONSOR GET OUT OF IT?

Contests are usually a part of a company's public relations program, and may involve thousands of dollars' expense for time and materials. In general, all the sponsor expects to receive is favorable attention for the company name and products. Sponsors feel that school contests, like sponsored teaching aids, help to create among future customers and employees the kind of general good will that is necessary if the company is to grow and prosper. Teachers understand and accept this purpose. They object when sponsors try to spread biased ideas or attempt to discredit competitive companies and products.

A good contest is not a simple matter, either for the sponsoring or-ganization or for the schools who must pass judgment on it. Here are two examples which sum up the do's and don't's for good school con-tests. First—a sponsor offers schools an essay contest. The required ac-tivity is to write 500 words on a subject defined by the sponsor. The purpose, as the sponsor sees it, is to stimulate thinking and research on this important subject. To insure that teachers also think about it, he suggests that the teachers screen the essays and forward only the top three for final judging. This kind of contest has advantages from a spon-sor's standpoint. It is inexpensive. It can be run by one man who sends out the announcements and reads and judges the final entries. But it fails the schools on several points. If the essay is written at home, it may tempt some students to be dishonest. Screening entries demands much teacher time. The subject matter is seldom closely integrated with the curriculum. Final judging is by a person who may be an authority on the subject matter, but who is not necessarily an authority on English style, and who may consciously or unconsciously impose his own bias on the judgment.

A second example is a contest offered by a food manufacturer to home economics teachers and students. Its objective is to stimulate interest in creative cookery. The activity required is the development and preparation of an original recipe. Dishonesty is discouraged by permitting mothers or sisters to help in the first preparation of the dish which is carried out at home. The dishes are then brought to school for judging. The second preparation is carried out in school, thus assuring that the contestant can prepare the dish independently. Judges for the preliminary rounds are appointed by the teacher. Prizes for school winners are certificates of honor. School winners' recipes are entered into state contests where they are judged by a competent judging organization, and where state and national winners are selected. Prizes are scholarships, grants, or savings bonds. The entire program is supervised by a committee of home economics educators and it is integrated into the curriculum.

This contest assists teachers in achieving several of their teaching objectives; namely, developing interest and experience in creativity, shared family experiences, food preparation, money management, and balanced meals. It does this by providing an interesting activity which appeals to teachers, students, and parents, and by providing suitable rewards for excellence.

Many excellent contests such as this one are given class time. The announcements of many others which involve participants in educational activities are posted on school bulletin boards. Teachers may or may not call attention to these or offer assistance, but students are free to enter on their own initiative. Unfortunately, by far the largest number of contest announcements end up, after study by educators, in school wastebaskets. The reason is because they were not carefully and imaginatively planned with a full understanding of the school's needs in mind, as well as those of the sponsor.

What is a good school contest? It is that rare successor to the old fashioned spelling bee that succeeds by today's educational methods in making a real contribution to the education of students.

41. Mass Media

JAY W. STEIN

Educational philosophies and methods in today's schools have grown out of a world in which mass media were dominated by the printed word. For generations education had been regarded as essentially an interpersonal procedure centered in the classroom, with the book its highly respected teaching tool. But for centuries neither book nor classroom reached more than a small fraction of the people.

Today the role of communicating to almost unlimited millions of the people, to audiences which might conceivably approach the total population, is shared among books, magazines, newspapers, recordings, movies, radio and television. Although still reaching only a part of the population, classrooms, too, have multiplied in number, developed in quality and received some impact from the technical aspects of modern communications media. But by and large the professional educator lags far behind in understanding the mass media, especially outside the classroom, and in realizing their potential for educational benefit or harm. A comprehensive view of the challenge, much greater than the sampling below, is long overdue.

Most dramatically, perhaps, the mass media boast the quality of transmitting relatively direct "life" scenes, although directness of sensory appeal varies from reading to televiewing. In reading, one sees the words on the page and one indirectly "sees" the images and "hears" the sounds they represent. One hears the sounds and voices of recordings and radio; one sees and hears the programs of television and films. Aware of the impact of strong sensory appeal, producers in all media vie with each other for vividness, drama and dynamism of presentation. In reality or imagination, it is held, "man is predominantly eye-minded,"[1] and "the eye is the most important gateway to the mind."[2]

From Jay W. Stein, "Mass Media: An Educational Challenge," *Peabody Journal of Education*, XXXVIII (November, 1960), 161–166. Professor of Education at Drake University, Des Moines, Iowa when this article appeared, Jay W. Stein is now Assistant to the President of Drake University. Reprinted by permission of the *Peabody Journal of Education*.
[1] Brockway McMillan and others, *Current Trends in Information Theory*, Pittsburgh, University of Pittsburgh Press, 1953, p. 93.

The visual emphasis of television and movies and the rivalry to appeal to the senses of the most individuals of the greatest audience has had a "picturizing" effect on all media. With technical device and dramatic appeal, even the audial media of radio and recordings try to "picture" their messages. Photography has provided the foundation for new kinds of pictorial and "trick" realism. Comics and cartoons are said to speak for a thousand words. Picture books and pictorial magazines which, of course, are not new to education, abound in ever richer variety; arguments in their favor include the facts that more people can see than can read and that for many people reading is an intermediary hindrance to perception and appreciation. It is fitting to speak of the "picture generations" of a "picture age."

Pictorial emphasis, unlimited audiences and mass appeal are among the confusing factors often identifying communications content with the vulgar, the sensational, the crass and the sordid. Called an ideological malignancy and a half-truth, this culture promises quick relief, fine results and rich rewards.[3] It appeals strongly to poverty, dissatisfaction, unrest, ignorance, irresponsibility, insecurity and fear. The sensate ideologies flourish via the informal education of television and the other mass media, and from there they penetrate the formal education of elementary and secondary schools and institutions of higher learning.

After completion of formal schooling, an average child and youth is supposed to be prepared to weigh the good and the evil in his community, to sift for the best among its passions and prejudices, friendships and hostilities, loyalties and follies. But now an overwhelming, pre-selected measure of conformities is thrust upon an untutored child, a gullible youth and an unthinking adult via the mass media during pre-school years and in out-of-school moments day in and day out. Surely, fear many observers, youth and adult are doomed to passivity and superficiality. There is dishearteningly small indication "that the great mass of the public senses its ability to influence what it is asked to see and hear. It accepts what it is given and does little to force change or improvement." Mass media are "growing faster and developing and spreading more rapidly than the apparent skills of the general public in living with them, handling them, and mastering them."[4]

Most of the denunciations and fears of mass media relate to a conflict in tastes among the viewing, listening and reading audiences. A small audience of people who claim to have "high culture" pits itself

[2] W. L. Sumner, *Visual Methods in Education*, New York, Philosophical Library, 1956, 2d ed., p. 1.

[3] Pitrim A. Sorokin, *The Crisis of Our Age*, New York, Dutton, 1942.

[4] Maurice B. Mitchell, "A Forward Look at Communications," *Britannica Book of the Year, 1958*, Chicago, Encyclopaedia Britannica, 1958, pp. 63–64.

against a vast majority of other Americans whose culture "runs to different things: to ball games rather than art museums, to popular songs rather than symphonies, to swiftly-told action drama rather than subtle studies of character."[5] One recalls James Boswell's report of an eighteenth century gentleman maintaining that the art of printing had hurt real learning by disseminating idle writing and that a general diffusion of knowledge among a people was a disadvantage for it made the vulgar rise above their humble sphere. Today a gentleman will note that if a mass medium ceases to reflect the diverse interests of the society it serves, and aims to please only a high level of taste, it is no longer one of the vital mass links of modern society. No less emphatically, he may assert that educators have an obligation constantly to raise the popular level of tastes.

If the peculiar characteristics of any one medium, such as television, are so dominant as repeatedly to attract brazen, sensation-seeking or self-centered charlatans and to repel meek, modest and altruistic personalities; if it persistently attracts the demon and repels the angel in man, there may be justification for some reproach. At the same time, suspicion or censure of television, radio, film, tape, disc or print is misplaced if one overlooks the fact that each is a medium of a certain neutrality and nothing more. A medium can transmit the bad as readily as the good, the mediocre as readily as the superior. Its good or bad, its use, misuse or abuse is neither to its credit or discredit. The responsibilities lie with people. The potential of a mass medium for magnifying the best thus merits and demands the superior in professional influence and leadership, in creative and imaginative talent, from such groups as devoted educators and their students and associates.

Mass media qualities and dimensions of size, speed, flexibility and vividness combine to revolutionize educational potential. The school provides services only to citizens of those communities where the distance for each participant is convenient or reasonable. Its methods center around the classroom. Mass media, in contrast, may reach almost everyone wherever he is, either simultaneously or ultimately. They can offer much variety and adaptability in the communication of vital informational, inspirational and educational messages to almost all citizens.

The variety of communications channels extends even beyond those already noted. The noisier television, movies and radio, the subtler recordings and books are direct and deliberate, that is, their main purpose is to communicate. In contrast, some are indirect, that is, their communicating function is secondary to a commercial, governmental or institutional purpose. Mass communications becomes a secondary func-

[5] Frank Stanton, *Television and People*, New York, Columbia Broadcasting System, 1949, p. 19.

tion or value of many packaged goods, manufactured articles and consumer services. Consider the breakfast food carton with its educational projects and puzzles of cut-out and pasting for boys and girls, or a verse or proverb on a pencil. Consider the postage stamp, particularly the commemorative, as it recalls and honors anniversary events in all branches of knowledge and achievement, or the postmarks: "Great Books are Great Teachers" and "Continue Your Education."

Thus, against the most stubborn will, an educator's effort to isolate or segregate his educational product or service, is futile. Educational influences are abundant. A flood of radio and television programs, filmed productions, recordings, and printed matter inundates the life of almost every child, youth and adult. They may re-inforce the learning of the classroom. They may also carry ideas and values very different from and in conflict with those that the schools attempt to inculcate. Playing a competitively powerful role with face-to-face relationships of home, church and school in formulating thought and behavior of child, youth and adult, the mass media of communications have had an indisputably strong impact on education and present a revolutionary challenge unlike any yet known in its history.

Mass media have revolutionized education in a three-phase manner. On the one hand, classrooms are increasingly equipped with a wide array of "audio-visual" devices and gadgets as an integral part of the instructional process. In all of their variety, more and more institutions accept them as auxiliary methods of transmitting the content and achieving the objectives of the curriculum for enrollees in elementary, secondary or higher education. For topics in many subjects, the mass media give faculty and students a vivid and effective advantage over class lecture or discussion. They bring to students educational experiences which are more realistic and better planned. By greatly extending the reach of the nation's best teachers, they allow many more students to obtain the prescribed course content for academic credit and eventual graduation with a degree.

Secondly, the mass media extend the wares of professional education to a heterogeneous, multiple audience little interested in course credit. It includes recipients interested in education itself as well as those with little or no understanding of education and its values. It is little apt to include individuals with utter distaste for any content that has the flavor of learning. To this out-of-school audience, larger than that in the classrooms, educators send forth school publications and productions via media installations under educational sponsorship or ownership.

Besides classroom registrants and community audiences of educational institutions a third very large grouping receives education by mass media. This is the greatest audience of ultimately all the population, persons who enjoy or suffer exposure to the mass media, those who seek to cultivate learning and taste and those who do not. To them an essentially commercial sponsorship provides content with maximum appeal but not without educational value. Over this good or bad content educators refrain from exercising much influence. Often the effect of "commercialism," they fear, is such as to counter their efforts in planning a proper school curriculum. The educator's choice becomes one of laissez-faire indifference or of aggressive cooperation based on searching understanding of mass media as a whole.

In brief, the educational potentials of the mass media of television, radio, film, recording and press range from those of classroom course instruction for more students, and community citizens reached by institutional ventures, to the audiences of unlimited size and variety sought by commercial endeavors. For the educator, the multiple scope of mass communications means the possibility of effectively serving more millions of Americans in their vital role of sustaining a cultured citizenry and an alert democracy. This is a challenge greater than any he has yet known.

42. The Vertical File

GUY WAGNER

Everywhere we look there is evidence of man's effort to enrich his life: from goose grease to penicillin; from the raspy cylinder phonograph records of Thomas A. Edison to high fidelity; from the drafty, dirt-floor log cabin to the modern ranch-type house with its push button conveniences; from Dobbin plodding along at five miles per hour to his machine counterpart powered by 250 horses purring quietly underneath the hood. And most of us today will not buy a loaf of bread unless it is enriched with vitamin B_1 and a host of other health-building ingredients.

Education, too, is pursuing this concept of enrichment. Schools everywhere are becoming increasingly aware of new ways and new ma-

From Guy Wagner, "Don't Overlook the Classroom Vertical File," *Education,* LXXVIII (September, 1957), 3–8. Guy Wagner is Professor of Education and Director of the Curriculum Laboratory, State College of Iowa, Cedar Falls, Iowa. Reprinted by permission from the September, 1957 issue of *Education.* Copyright 1957 by The Bobbs-Merrill Co., Inc., Indianapolis, Indiana.

terials for improving learning. Because education in the past was based largely on textbook teaching, we may identify this trend as enrichment *beyond* the textbook.

Much of this enrichment calls upon the taxpayer to open up his pocketbook. And rightfully so! Children are our greatest natural resource and it would be poor business judgment as well as adult selfishness to provide them with an inferior education.

Most of our schools are meeting this challenge to a reasonable degree although there is a wide variation in both local attitudes and local potentials in this respect. However, in an increasing number of schools, we find a wide range of science apparatus, numerous and often expensive items for the physical education program, up-to-date maps and globes, classroom encyclopedias and dictionaries, facilities for working in a number of art media, well-equipped industrial art shops, and expensive musical instruments often furnished by the schools. School libraries, too, have improved vastly in facilities, services, and reading matter.

SPOTLIGHTING VERTICAL FILE MATERIALS

But this article is designed primarily to spotlight vertical file materials as a somewhat neglected as well as potentially profitable source of enrichment. First of all, it should be recognized that vertical file materials, like many of the best things in life, are free or at least easily accessible. Their acceptance and use is often only a matter of teacher interest and initiative.

We know that the beautiful colors of autumn are overlooked by many to whom they are most accessible. The intriguing sounds of nature are seldom identified and listened to with appreciation. The art treasures of our museums are not even thought of, let alone studied and enjoyed by the overwhelming majority of people. Even stimulating conversation with friends is often forsaken in favor of the more passive and expensive types of pleasure. In like fashion, there is a wealth of valuable instructional materials easily accessible to teachers, often at little or no cost. The puzzling thing is that such materials often are permitted to lie dormant when they would, properly used, heighten pupil interest and give greater depth of meaning to the subjects being studied.

What is the reason for this lack of use? Possibly many teachers are unfamiliar with these materials and their sources. Furthermore, it may be that time does not *seem* to be available for searching out and obtaining these materials. The main reason, however, probably lies in the lack of any systematic plan to classify and house the many items that teachers either already have or know about. If this is the case, the solution to the problem lies in the development of the classroom vertical file.

WHAT IS A VERTICAL FILE?

A vertical file is simply what its name indicates. It is a system for filing pamphlets, booklets, etc., vertically—on edge. It is a system for housing certain learning materials which normally are stacked in cupboards or on shelves, item upon item, thus making accessibility to desired materials difficult and time consuming. It is a system of classifying pamphlets, folded posters, bulletins, paper covered booklets, tearsheets, flat pictures, and clippings so that they may be quickly found according to designated labels. In other words, it is a *filing* system rather than a *piling* system.

Metal cabinets, with four drawers running on sliding rollers, are recommended for housing vertical-file materials. Many schools and offices are now using folders which can be suspended from a metal frame in the file drawer thus keeping the tabs on the folders at a horizontal level. It is also relatively efficient to use stiff cardboard dividers or manila folders with projecting tabs for labels. The weakness in this latter system, however, is that the tabs are likely to be at varying levels, thus making quick finding of the file headings more difficult.

If money is not available to purchase this commercial type of filing system, the teacher and children may prepare appropriately such containers as egg crates or orange cases. Some teachers have had children finish this "free" type of filing cabinet by sanding and painting it with a selected color. For dividers they used manila folders or some form of heavy cardboard that would stand upright in the filing box.

DEVELOPING THE VERTICAL FILE

It seems essential that some form of a vertical file system be developed and that the materials be classified according to subject headings most favorable for classroom use. Within the limits of their maturity and ability, children should be called upon to obtain the materials, evaluate these materials, determine key terms for classification, write key terms on the materials (or use typed labels), and then place the materials correctly in the filing cabinet.

It should be recognized that most vertical file materials are likely to have been produced recently and thus are up to date. Probably the major type of material is that which may be called "sponsored." Such materials come from business, industry, government, and civic organizations. The values inherent in such materials, as well as cautions to be observed in their selection, will be discussed later on.

In addition to sponsored materials, however, it is evident that the vertical file will house many other materials available to the pupils in their homes and the classroom. For instance, some teachers have found it advisable to staple or bind tearsheets from discarded textbooks.[1] To illustrate, a story in a reader dealing with the subject of insects may be torn out and prepared for inclusion in the vertical file. Other commonly available materials include pictures from calendars, magazines, and newspapers. Frequently clippings from magazines and newspapers contain graphic aids and reading that might well be used time and again. The vertical file can house them as long as they are useful. Such items as the common road map, and especially the state highway maps can be housed in a vertical file and certainly no one would criticize their use in the classroom. Then, too, children often own informational booklets that no longer hold personal interest for them. These booklets, rather than being discarded, might find a useful place at some grade level in the school system.

One seldom-thought-of-value of vertical file materials lies in the dynamics which accompany something which is new and fresh in the daily routine of study. Oftentimes children will write thoughtful businesslike letters requesting materials which fit the units or topics being studied. A visit from the mailman is as curiosity-developing to children as it is to adults. "What's in the package? Where did it come from?" The materials thus received are pretty likely to challenge the youngsters to fairly detailed study. This sort of enrichment beyond the textbook helps give purpose and meaning to learning.

SCREENING VERTICAL FILE MATERIALS

It is obvious that free and inexpensive materials from industry and other organizations should not be used to promote the interests of private concerns, nor should they ever be permitted to foster causes which are not in the public interest. Teachers need to consider carefully the effect, good or bad, that the materials may have upon the pupils who use them. This means that some sort of screening plan should be devised so that all donated material (as well as that which is purchased) is admitted to schoolroom use only after its merits have been carefully judged.

It can be noted, however, that most sponsored materials today, prepared for classroom use, have little or no advertising or propaganda. Most of this material is in good taste, is authentic, gives more detail than can be found in the textbook, is up-to-date, and is written in an engaging style. Donors seem to be increasingly sensitive to the kind of materials desirable for young people to study, thus they carefully

[1] An excellent device for giving tearsheets a simple, inexpensive binding is the U-File-M binders, obtainable from the U-File-M Binder Manufacturing Company, Inc., Syracuse, New York.

avoid introducing content or illustrations that could be justifiably criticized. They apparently recognize that an excessive amount of advertising or the promotion of an unacceptable cause will likely pre-
clude the use of their publications in the classrooms. A comparison of
such materials with the advertising in current magazines will usually
show quite a divergence in the "come on" approach.

A CRITICAL APPRAISAL

Teachers should recognize that pupils in our schools are constantly
confronted with many kinds of persuasive influences. Some of these influences come via radio and TV. Magazines and newspapers carry
many articles and advertisements designed to influence the reader to
think a certain way or to buy a specific product. If our children are to
live thoughtfully and successfully in a world of persuasion, then it is up
to society to help them make good judgments regarding what they hear
and read, whether it be mildly slanted or strongly biased. Perhaps wise
classroom guidance in the use of learning materials produced by industry and other organizations will help our young people make sounder
judgments as to what is false, what is only half-truth, and what is true.

On the other hand, schools must be aware of, and understand, the
arguments commonly offered against the use of sponsored materials
in the classroom. A thoughtful appraisal of these arguments will not
necessarily close the door to sponsored materials, but it should make
teachers intelligent appraisers and users.

Perhaps the four most significant arguments are: (1) schools have
no right to use any material which might help to promote a specific
product, (2) schools must be "foolproofed" against the possibility of
promoting ideas that may not be in the best interest of our society, (3)
in some instances, the material is misleading, chiefly by presenting
false claims, half-truths, and incomplete information, and (4) the
overuse of sponsored materials may steal time from other important aspects of the curriculum.

In all fairness, it should be recognized that there may be a case against
certain sponsored materials. It seems, however, that an increasing number of schools feel that the value inherent in much of this material
outweighs the possible hazards and disadvantages. Such schools avoid
a closed-door policy, but at the same time set up effective guards to the
admission of undesirable materials. Among the more important criteria
by means of which these schools evaluate sponsored materials are: (1)
all vertical file material should make a constructive contribution to the
educational program of the school, (2) there should be no direct sales
promotion or boastful, exaggerated claims, (3) the materials do not
mislead by presenting false claims, half-truths and incomplete infor-

mation. (However, some misleading material might have a place in a high school class where students are given guidance in critical analysis. Teachers should help young people to detect "phony" information in what they read and hear.), (4) the material is true to life and authentic, (5) in case of controversial issues, each side of the case is presented without bias, (6) the material is geared to the maturity and interest levels of the pupils, (7) the content is presented in readable style, having the marks of literary craftsmanship, (8) the illustrations are pertinent to the content; not merely eye-catchers that have little or no relationship to the subject, and (9) the material must not promote a product—even a good one—out of proportion to its merit. Here teachers should help young people to become sensitive to "exaggerations."

THE VERTICAL FILE IN ACTION

In a sense, the vertical file contributes to learning in two different yet closely related ways. In the first place, the very act of searching out, obtaining, evaluating, classifying and filing is often an important series of learning experiences. As pupils pursue the study of a topic, it makes sense that their research points toward the discovery of learning materials not already available in the school. Thus, they look for pertinent magazine articles, pamphlets, and the like which may later deserve inclusion in the classroom vertical file.

Under the guidance of a teacher, these pupils will learn to critically evaluate what they discover. If the materials are of high merit, steps will be taken to decide on key classification terms; subsequently placing the materials appropriately in the vertical file. Thus it appears that in obtaining and servicing these materials there will be valuable concomitant learnings in such fields as interviews, business correspondence, geography, critical reading, alphabetizing, word choice, classification, and filing. Here it is the *process* of developing the file that is the contributor to learning.

The more commonly-thought-of-value of the vertical file, however, is in its use as a resource containing a wide range of information. For instance, a pamphlet *The Story of Rubber* may give much more elaboration to the subject than would be possible in a geography textbook. Furthermore, the information may be more up-to-date and more fully illustrated.

The vertical file has resource value also in providing bulletin board materials such as pictures, charts, and diagrams. Many of these will not be found in textbooks, and if they were, the textbook illustrations would likely be on a much smaller scale.

Vertical file materials are useful, too, in meeting the needs and interests of individual pupils; they provide reading materials at varying difficulty levels and cover a wide range of interest. And when their needs and interests are met, children will "dig in," attacking their studies with sincerity and zeal.

It would be enlightening to visit a thousand classrooms, chosen at random, throughout the nation. Most of these classrooms would probably reveal a modest use of vertical file materials, but there would be found little attempt to obtain, classify, file, and use these materials in a systematic way. There would be a few sparkling classrooms, however, where the dynamics of current materials, as developed in the vertical file, would be infusing both teacher and pupils with purpose and an increasing desire to learn. Educators may well ask the question, "To what extent is a top-notch classroom vertical file a 'barometer' of good teaching and pupil achievement?"

REFERENCES

1. American Association of School Administrators. *Choosing Free Materials for Use in the Schools.* Washington 6, D.C.: the Association, a department of the National Education Association, 1955.
2. American Library Association. *The Booklist and Subscription Books Bulletin.* 50 E. Huron Street, Chicago 11: The Association (frequently carries a selected list of free and inexpensive publications—published bi-monthly, $6.00 a year).
3. Association for Supervision and Curriculum Development. *Using Free Materials in the Classroom.* Washington 6, D.C.: the Association, a department of the National Education Association, 1953.
4. Consumer Education Study of the National Association of Secondary-School Principals. *Commercial Supplementary Materials.* Washington, D.C.: National Education Association, 1954.
5. *Elementary Teachers Guide to Free Curriculum Materials.* Thirteenth Annual Edition. Randolph, Wisconsin: Educators Progress Service, 1956. ($5.50)
6. Field Enterprises, Inc., Educational Division. *Sources of Free and Inexpensive Educational Materials.* Merchandise Mart Plaza, Chicago 54: Field Enterprises, Inc., 1955. ($5.00)
7. *Free and Inexpensive Learning Materials.* Bulletin of George Peabody College for Teachers, Nashville, Tennessee: George Peabody College for Teachers, Division of Surveys and Field Studies, 1956. ($1.00)
8. Grant, Martin L. "How the Teacher's Literature File Can Serve Students in Laboratory and Classroom Work." *American Biology Teacher,* Bryan City Schools, Bryan, Ohio. Vol. 14, No. 4, April, 1952. pp. 83-90.
9. Harap, Henry. "The Use of Free and Inexpensive Learning Materials in the Classroom." *The School Review,* Chicago: The University of Chicago Press, October, 1955.
10. Kinney, Lucien and Dresden, Katharine, Editors. *Better Learning Through Current Materials.* Stanford, California: Stanford University Press, 1949.

11. Miller, Bruce. *Sources of Free and Inexpensive Aids.* Ontario, California: Box 369, 1956. (50 cents)
12. *Pamphleteer Monthly, The.* 313 West 35th Street, New York 1, N.Y.: The William-Frederick Press. (Subscription $2.00 a year.)
13. Sinclair, Thomas J. *A Report About Business-Sponsored Materials.* Dansville, N.Y.: F. A. Owen Publishing Company, 1949.
14. United States Superintendent of Documents. Washington, D.C. (Price lists describing available pamphlets on such topics as Forestry, Plants, Occupations, Territories and Weather.)
15. *Vertical File Index.* 950 University Ave., New York 52: The H. W. Wilson Company. Issued monthly except in August, and cumulated annually. (Annual subscription, $5.00.)
16. Wagner, Guy. "Developing a Classroom Vertical File." *Midland Schools,* Iowa State Education Association, Des Moines, November, 1950.

43. *Drill, Practice, Review, and Memorization*

FRANK L. STEEVES

A favorite straw man for educators is the claim that past educational patterns were characterized by drill and memory activities. Some contemporary educators characterize the recitation as a method of drill and memory. But, as noted earlier in this volume, the leading recitation theorists claimed to be Socratic and described the method as one of inductive-deductive reasoning. They stressed the ability to generalize and to apply knowledge. Recitation writers themselves maintained that *their* immediate past was one of drill and memory from which the principles of the recitation would free the teacher. But, if 1900 is accepted as the zenith of the recitation theory and if a generation prior to that date falls about 1860–1870, Pestallozian theorists are noted in the forefront of educational thought. They, too, at least in theory were against blind drill and unmotivated repetition.

Actually it is necessary to return to the early 1800's and the briefly-popular Monitorial system to find any massive, general stress on drill and memory as part of teaching routine. Even there, the shortcomings of the teaching were so obvious that the system was soon abandoned for one employing trained teachers.

From Frank L. Steeves, "Drill, Practice, Review, and Memorization," chap. VII, *Fundamentals of Teaching in Secondary Schools* (New York: The Odyssey Press, 1962), pages 168–170. Frank L. Steeves is Professor of Education at the University of Vermont.

It is unlikely that the recommended teaching for any age was solely one of drill and memory. Two facts appear certain. (1) Reason, through discussion, questioning, and debate has been defended amply from the time of Socrates to the present. Unthinking memory drills may have been practiced through all ages, but they were not set forth as the best general method of acquiring education. (2) Some facts, skills, and understandings do have to be practiced or memorized or education will stop where it is. If one is asked, "What is the product of five times five?" he replies, "twenty-five," and no figuring is necessary. This is because "five times five" has been practiced, drilled, and used so many times that the answer has been memorized. It would be ridiculous to have to figure out the answer for this kind of question. If we are in doubt about the exact meaning of "protagonist," we consult a dictionary. But we could leaf through the dictionary for a long time without finding "protagonist" if we had not memorized the alphabet. A concert pianist practices until he no longer has to read each note. The football team drills until the plays are automatic. These various practices and repetitions are necessary if further learning is to take place.

Practice, repetition, drill, and memorization cannot and should not be eliminated from school work. However, this type of activity should not characterize the work of the school day, and certain cautions should be noted.

1. *The word "drill" implies unmotivated, unquestioning repetition whereas "practice" suggests meaningful, motivated repetition.* Practice suggests a variety of repetitions centered around a central problem. Drill indicates the same repetition over and over. Neither drill nor practice is an end in itself. Both are means toward the ends of critical thinking and problem solving.

2. *"Review" suggests a later look at something previously studied.* Methods of reviewing are not strictly set for the pupil but probably require the skills of summarizing, outlining, and taking notes.

3. *The purposes of practice, drill, and review should be understood by the pupil.* The goal is not the practice itself but some larger problem to be solved, some greater skill or concept to be attained. The team cannot function as a team if each individual player does not drill and practice regularly. The song cannot be played if the practice exercises are not mastered. The letter cannot be typed until the keyboard is learned. The story cannot be written until sentences and paragraphs can be written. Pupils will practice and learn more readily if they perceive the larger goals. They will lag, object, and waste time if the practices are not meaningful.

4. *Practice sessions should consist of short periods separated by the opportunity to engage in other activities.* Long, concentrated periods of practice are not as rewarding. The typical eighth-grade pupil will learn

more in two thirty-minute sessions than he will in one hour-long practice session. Naturally, the older the pupil and the more motivated he is the longer he can practice without fatigue or loss of interest.

5. *It is the teacher's responsibility to know what skills are basic to his field of study.* If practice and drill are important in the attainment of those skills, he should not apologize for requiring practice sessions. But practices should not be inserted into a course merely to make the work seem respectable or hard. The practice should be an inherent requirement for attaining the course objective.

6. *Memorization for the sake of memorizing should be avoided.* However, if the future demands of the subject require thorough learning to the point of memorization, the teacher should expect memorization. Note that such demands usually are few and that memorized material is quickly forgotten unless used regularly. In memorizing, it should be noted that the material to be learned should be perceived and learned in meaningful divisions. A short poem should be treated as one whole poem. A long poem should be learned by stanzas. Memorizing is quicker and easier if meaningful relationships are perceived.

44. *Audiovisual Aids*

ESTELLE W. HODES

Among the goals of education are the developing of the pupil's ability to deal with environmental factors and forces, and promoting his growth in an appreciation of his cultural heritage. Others we could include are the fostering of an intelligent allegiance to American ideals and active participation in democratic practices, and guiding the student in gaining an understanding and appreciation of the contributions made to human welfare by individuals and by the various national, religious and racial groups.

The teacher who makes intelligent, effective use of the wealth of audiovisual materials available to him can make subject matter vividly interesting and exciting, and can offer an enriched and much broader program of study. These teaching aids can help the student acquire better understandings, provide him with vicarious experiences and mo-

From Estelle W. Hodes, "How Audiovisual Aids Make Teaching and Learning Easier," *Educational Screen and Audiovisual Guide*, XXXIX (December, 1960), 644–645. Estelle W. Hodes is Administrative Secretary of the Board of Education, Newark, New Jersey. Reprinted by permission from *Educational Screen and Audiovisual Guide*.

tivate him in the learning process. They provide the student with many learning opportunities through which he can see, examine, hear and participate in classroom activities. Thus audiovisual aids play an important part in teaching, particularly since verbal descriptions do not always make clear the thing described, and often a lack of background experiences of the student prevents full comprehension.

For example, filmstrips are easily projected and studied in the classroom and are extremely valuable in teaching, among other things, understandings of word symbols, vocabulary building, symbols involved in maps and in arithmetic. The many and varied education filmstrips make possible group instruction in learning skills, developing aesthetic appreciations or providing in visualized form reproduced factual information which might otherwise not be directly observed. A single frame may be repeated and discussed, and when the teacher wishes to emphasize a particular point, he can control the timing and vary the speed to meet the needs of the students or adjust the commentary to the level of the students. Filmstrips and equipment are small, compact, not too expensive and easy to operate. The filmstrip projector may easily be operated by students and therefore an excellent opportunity is afforded for participation by students in this class activity. A filmstrip used during the first part of a period may be best utilized if discussion takes place at the end of the period, after the viewing experience has been thoroughly explored. Since filmstrips do not need to be shown in total darkness, students may be encouraged to take notes in preparation for further discussion or follow-up research.

Another good teaching aid is the slide projector, which utilizes 2 by 2 inch slides. Though slides are somewhat more difficult to handle than filmstrips, they are extremely flexible in that the teacher may determine the sequence according to the special needs of a particular class. Slide sets may be easily revised and kept up to date simply by replacing outdated pictures with newer materials, or adding individual slides made by the teacher or student. The teacher should, of course, preview the slides and prepare a preliminary plan of the slides to be used for a given lesson.

Other projection materials adaptable for classroom use are $3\frac{1}{4}$ by 4 inch lantern slides, stereo reels and microfilms. The lantern slides have a larger area of transparency image, with more detail and screen brilliance and are particularly good for use in reading instruction with a tachistoscopic attachment on an overhead slide projector. The stereoscopic 3D slide reel may be used either in a hand viewer or a special projector, and it helps to create an illusion of reality. The low cost and ease of handling by individual students make stereo reels a desirable medium for special enrichment studies.

The imaginative teacher tries to make use of the many types of still pictures obtained readily and inexpensively from magazines, newspapers, books and other sources all around us. The opaque projector provides the teacher with the means for enlarging pictures for viewing and extended study and to develop a common learning experience through sequence collection. Pictures can be easily understood, have great value as a medium of communication, and can serve as an international language for the social studies program.

The teacher who can avail himself of the great variety of educational motion picture films and necessary viewing equipment is in the forefront of educational-technological development; he virtually is in the position of bringing the world to the classroom. Through dramatized films, the teacher is able to help recreate the past in teaching ancient, recent or contemporary history. He can present geography in a vivid way through travelogs and can span time and space through use of time-lapse photomicrography in teaching science. The alert teacher keeps informed of sources for obtaining these films and encourages school administrators and interested parent groups to make them available to the school.

Radio and recordings also play an important part in helping the teacher achieve many worthwhile educational goals, and through them, the teacher is able to bring to his classroom the full range of the "world of sound." Through discs and tape recordings, the teacher can relate the student to his present day world as he weaves a continuous story of the political, economic and social development of our country—how our social institutions and democratic principles came into being; how customs of other nations helped to build our own; and how the citadel of democracy, the United Nations, became a reality. Appreciation of other cultures and desirable attitudes toward ethnic groups may be fostered through recordings of music of other lands, and at the same time "how to listen to music" may be another desirable outcome.

Good citizenship can be taught and emotional responses to the American ideal evoked through the vitalizing recordings about the lives of famous men in history. The history lessons may be effectively dramatized and students made to feel that "they were there" as the illusion of reality is created through use of recordings of history-making speeches. The voices of famous news analysts; the oratory of Winston Churchill; the dramatic voice of Franklin Delano Roosevelt as he spoke to his people and the people of the world through the difficult war years, and then the recording of his funeral procession; the booming, dictatorial voice of Adolph Hitler, the sound of the Nazi storm troopers marching; the epoch-making occasion of the acceptance by Douglas MacArthur of the Japanese surrender; and the voice of the then secretary of state,

Edward Stettinius, as the San Francisco conference of the United Nations is opened—all of these and many more, including musical recordings, are at the disposal of the teacher.

These vital events, which are permanently "alive" through recordings, plus the beautiful music of our land and of other cultures, should be fully utilized by the teacher so that they may serve the students of today and will also be available to serve the children of the future.

Recordings may be used for integrating subject matter with the total school program and varied activities such as dramatics, to develop the student's poise and overcome personality problems; English, to develop interest in good literature and poetry and foster habits of good speech; music, to acquaint students with various types of music and songs of other lands; physical education, dance instruction and sports, to develop rhythm in exercise, skill in games, or for teaching synchronized swimming.

School can and should be fun for the young, and the properly trained, alert teacher draws upon the vast reservoir of the old and introduces the new tools for learning—films, filmstrips, field trips, textbooks, references, newspapers, magazines, slides, flannel boards, pictures, exhibits, and others to make the school day come "alive" with meaningful experiences.

Teachers are in the enviable position of early and continuous contact with children and youth and of having the opportunity to give them the benefit of the enriching, stimulating audiovisual materials which will help them to develop to their full potential and thus nurture the nation's greatest assets—its young who are learning to be the citizens of tomorrow.

45. Field Trips

WILLIAM C. MILLER

"I'm sold on the values of field trips," the superintendent said, "but I wonder why 80 percent of the school journeys take place in May and June."

From William C. Miller, "Are Field Trips Worth While?" *Educational Screen and Audiovisual Guide*, XXXVIII (May, 1959), 245. William C. Miller is Deputy Superintendent of the Wayne County Intermediate School District, Detroit, Michigan. Reprinted by permission from *Educational Screen and Audiovisual Guide*.

Certainly when good weather comes, students and teachers alike yearn for the out-of-doors. Winter weather does limit some types of educational journeys but most field trips can be experienced during any season.

"If field trips are legitimate educational tools," the superintendent continued, "shouldn't visitation be going on throughout the year?"

Such questions are being asked more and more frequently with good reason. Because the field trip method is widely accepted, school journeys are becoming more common. Giving youngsters an opportunity to learn firsthand about their community rates high as a vital method of instruction; but some of the practices which go on under the name of educational field trips need objective examination. Outings which have as their primary purpose rewarding youngsters for good behavior, or trips which are not an integral part of a topic under study in the classroom should be subjected to close examination. School outings and picnics have a socializing function and there are opportunities for learning experiences, but such outings should not be labeled as field trips.

What questions should we ask ourselves to make certain we are utilizing the field trip method to the fullest? Here are some questions designed to help evaluate field trip practices.

Did the need for this field trip grow out of regular classroom work?

Is a field trip the best method of gaining the needed information? (Perhaps a motion picture could present the same information as effectively or resource people could be brought in at a great saving of time and money.)

Am I familiar with the place to be visited so that I know what will be seen? (A prior visit will help when it comes time to prepare the group. Contacting the place to be visited and informing them of the particular needs and interests of the group is also time well spent.)

Have I prepared the group for the field trip experience? (The group will profit most if they have specific information to look for and if they have discussed the most effective ways to observe and take notes.)

Was everyone able to see and hear satisfactorily during the field trip? Was time allowed for questions and did the questions reflect an understanding of what was observed?

Were the observations made during the trip discussed upon returning to the classroom and did the group engage in other follow-up activities?

By asking ourselves these questions we can properly evaluate our field trip practices. By having frequent and well-planned field trips, we can provide the best possible educational experiences for our pupils.

46. Bulletin Boards

HAZEL P. LUTZ

The bulletin board can boost ideas and sell them better than any other media used in our schools. Often, however, it becomes a catch-all for so many notices and "good" work that it passes unnoticed day after day. Newspaper clippings, which are almost impossible to read from a standing position, rows of identical class work, duplicated notices and unmounted pictures provide no incentive for the student to give it a second glance.

In order to be effective the bulletin board should:

1. Sell *one* idea at a time and do it dramatically, so that "he who runs may read."

2. Use short headings that involve the viewer by asking a question or stating a provocative fact.

3. Be built around illustrations, eye-catching and bold both in color and size and at the same time keeping them simple and uncluttered.

4. Contain an explanation or text that is short and clear and done in letters large enough to be easily read.

5. Have all material firmly anchored at all four corners. Flapping papers make for restlessness in the classroom. Common pins or tabs of masking tape are better for this purpose than shiny thumbtacks that call attention to themselves.

6. Control the direction and order in which the bulletin will be read. Movement should be from left to right rather than up and down for that is the way we read English. People, birds flying, planes, arrows, and vehicles all lead the eye to look in the direction in which they are facing.

7. Use one, or two colors at the most, for the letters, the background or the mounts to gain attention and unite the parts.

From Hazel P. Lutz, "Attractive Bulletin Boards Boost School Activities," *School Activities*, XXXIV (September, 1962), 12. Hazel P. Lutz, formerly Director of Art for the public schools of Manchester, Connecticut, is now School Service Supervisor of the Lutz Junior Museum, Manchester. Reprinted by permission of *School Activities*.

8. Have the whole arrangement balanced either formally or inform- ally so that the eyes stay within the frame of the bulletin itself.

Formal arrangements are easy to arrange by following this proce- dure:

a. Decide on a theme and select a title and materials to be used to illustrate it.
b. Prepare letters for a heading. Use one type of lettering for each bulletin, but try a new type each time it is changed. (Two days to two weeks is long enough to keep the same set-up on a school bulletin board.) Try *cut out* letters of construction paper, Con- tact paper or wall paper. Try *felt pen, lettering pen, brush* and *crayon.* Resist lettering in various free hand styles.
c. Mount your illustrations all in the same manner. *Inset, torn hole, free form opening, roll back, shadow box* or *foil covered frames* offer variety from the standard mount with its larger margin at the bottom.
d. Measure down the same distance on both sides of your board and place a common pin there. Stretch a piece of store string between the pins and use this to keep your letters straight.
e. Find the center of the board and mark it also with a pin.
f. Find the middle letter of the heading and place it so that it rests on the pin that marks the center. Work out from this point to the right and to the left. This will center the title with the same mar- gin on both sides.
g. Select the largest mounted piece and place it in the center.
h. Add other pieces to the right and left always balancing them in size. Have the space between mounts smaller than the width of the picture itself.
9. Be read.

Test your present bulletin board's effectiveness by reversing two of the letters in the title or pinning one illustration upside-down. If this seeming error is brought to your attention within fifteen minutes af- ter it was done your bulletin is working, boosting your teaching. If, however, a whole day passes without comment do take it all down and begin again.

47. The Chalkboard

ROBERT L. COARD

White blotches of chalk dust on suit, coat, or blouse that used to be thought of as a distinguishing mark of the teaching profession are seen with declining frequency these days. And in a way it is too bad. Grade school and mathematics teachers continue to make use of that valuable visual aid, the blackboard, but teachers of high-school English are perhaps allowing chalk and eraser to remain idle too much. Better nothing at all than a scrawny and feeble pair of items like "Ideals, attitudes," followed by an exhausted "etc." that we sometimes see chalked out apologetically in a corner of the blackboard.

True, the ubiquitous mimeograph and ditto make it profitless for language arts teachers to put tests, reading guides, exercises, and bibliographies on the board when they can be reproduced much more quickly and accurately by machines. Nevertheless there still remains a large area in which the blackboard may be utilized to great advantage.

Why not put your daily assignment on the blackboard at the beginning of each class period? Writing makes an exact man, Francis Bacon declared, and writing makes for precise thought as much today as it did in the Elizabethan Age. Objections and qualifications and more exact questions are possible if the assignment is given in writing. Extended explanation must, of course, accompany the assignment, but the student has something definite to record that he may refer to later. Any student arriving after the explanation is supplied with some inkling of tomorrow's work. The assignment written on the blackboard seems to afford a happy medium between the inexactness and looseness of the oral assignment and the inflexibility of mimeographed instructions necessarily prepared some days in advance.

As we teachers talk merrily along, we are all too prone to toss off the names of persons and titles of books, some of which we want the

From Robert L. Coard, "Whiten the Blackboard!" *Peabody Journal of Education,* XXXII (January, 1955), 234–236. Robert L. Coard is Associate Professor of English, St. Cloud State College, St. Cloud, Minnesota. Reprinted by permission of the *Peabody Journal of Education.*

baffled student to remember. But how can he when he has only a fleeting auditory impression of an unfamiliar word? If we write out occasional difficult names like John Dos Passos, Siegfried Sassoon, Erich Remarque, or Toussaint L'Ouverture, we increase the chance that the student will remember them when he encounters them again. Don't just recommend works like Mary Antin's *The Promised Land* or Edmond Rostand's *Cyrano de Bergerac.* Write them out.

Worth-while comment on spelling errors in that last batch of papers necessitates use of the blackboard. Why not give the students a snap quiz on ten or twelve selected misspellings? The right spellings could be ascertained immediately by having the teacher write in big bold letters the correct forms on the blackboard for all to see. Difficult parts of words like *reCEIve* might be exaggerated for emphasis. Homonyms too, bothersome twins like *principle-principal, their-there,* and *its-it's,* cry out for blackboard illustration. And why not a change of pace now and then by having some student come forward and taking over the job of explaining and providing examples?

When a teacher of English casually asks a question about geography, he is often horrified to learn that his auditors have no idea where Bavaria or Cyprus or Trinidad is located. Here is a situation that calls for blackboard use if no map is available. Even if one is at hand, the bare sketch is often more effective than the location of the spot on a detailed map. The construction of a spot map with a few simple lines—the *American College Dictionary* and the *Webster's New World Dictionary* have excellent models—will convey the required information more readily and thoroughly than any verbal explanation. Fortunately half of our states are simple boxes so that no intricate knowledge of lines and curves is needed. Some closely resemble other forms. If you are trying, for example, to locate the Spoon River Country of Edgar Lee Masters' *Spoon River Anthology,* sketch in a lop-sided vase to represent the state of Illinois, circle in the name Chicago in the upper right-hand corner, and pierce the middle of the vase with a line to show where the Spoon River Country lies. Thus the unknown has been speedily located by the known.

The learning value of maps and charts is probably consistently underestimated by all of us. Think how much more effective even a rough floor plan of a library is than a description confined to the spoken word alone. Incidentally in checking up on the results of the annual library tour, I find the drawing of a floor plan of the library a handy testing device. The card catalog, clipping files, *Reader's Guide to Periodical Literature,* and similar essentials must all be satisfactorily accounted for on the student's floor plan.

With a little ingenuity on the teacher's part, the blackboard can also be an aid in defining terms. If *Webster's New International Dictionary* employs 12,000 illustrations in its explanations, why can't we use a few? A big crown and a diminutive crown drawn side by side ought to bring out the difference between a crown and a coronet, the economy-size crown. Similarly a chalk sketch of a face with a colossal nose or immensely protruding teeth will make the class understand more readily just what a caricature is.

Pursue word study too with chalk and erasers. With your *phil* or philo meaning love to start with, assemble philander, philanthropist, Philadelphia, philosopher, philatelist, circling the appropriate roots for emphasis. Or with *pathos* meaning suffering or feeling, build up with the help of the class, pathetic, telepathy, sympathy, pathological, psychopathic, and apathy.

One word of caution. Be wary about falling victim to the disease that I call "blackboard blind." This ailment will cause you to stand in embarrassed silence before words like *recommend* and *prejudice* wondering how on earth you spell them. This hazard of temporary forgetfulness can occur with the most-innocent appearing words. Careful preparation involving a partial writing out of the material in a notebook previous to its employment in class on the blackboard is the only sure preventive. But don't be afraid to take a risk.

When I think of this question of using the blackboard properly, I am reminded of a teacher of linguistics I once had. With chalk a-splattering over the front rows, he would make words grow and diminish, separate and coalesce on the blackboard before our wondering eyes. At times he may have overdone this activity, but he had the right idea. Anyway a good screech of chalk rubbed the wrong way as you write on the blackboard insures wakefulness on the part of everyone.

48. Graphic Materials

JAMES S. KINDER

There are few, if any, instructional materials which have the flexibility, motivational power, and the outlet for creativity which graphic materials have. They are inexpensive and are suited either to group or individual work. Many of these materials are made by teachers and pupils.

Graphics have become practically a new science. They are a form of communication with great mass appeal. On every hand, we see a multitude of drawings, sketches, designs, diagrams, charts, graphs, arrangements of lines, forms, color combinations, exhibits, and displays. All these materials have at least one thing in common. They are functional art. They also have in common such general purposes as getting attention, clarifying ideas, presenting or "selling" ideas, illustrating or adorning facts or things which might otherwise be unnoticed or quickly forgotten.

Graphics are important to schools, teachers, and pupils. They have become just as noticeably important in business, industry, government, advertising, marketing, and in practically all walks of life. Anyone who reads the advertisements in street cars or subway trains is struck by the great amount of graphic materials consumed by the public. Government bulletins and reports which used to be dry-as-dust are now spiced with charts, graphs, and pictorials of intriguing variety.

Primitive man drew pictures before he developed hieroglyphics, visual symbols of things, and forerunners of the alphabet. In spite of the fact that language is a wonderful and powerful invention, and indispensable to modern civilization, man is still fascinated by pictures—handdrawn or photographic.

The term *graphics* embraces a large field which means *to give visible surface to a natural or an imaginary scene, object, or incident through*

From James S. Kinder, "The Use of Graphic Materials in Teaching," *Education,* LXXVII (January, 1957), 299–302. James S. Kinder is Professor of Education and Coordinator of Audio-Visual Services at San Diego State College, San Diego, California. Reprinted by permission from the January, 1957 issue of *Education.* Copyright 1957 by The Bobbs-Merrill Co., Inc., Indianapolis, Indiana.

the graphic arts. The word "Graphic" comes from the Greek, meaning *to write or to delineate by painting, writing, drawing, sketching, or diagramming.* The graphic arts have been practiced by etchers, engravers, and lithographers for years. New forms are being developed all the time. Charts and graphs date back to the use of mathematical principles of coordinates and Descartes' analytical geometry. In recent years, graphics has expanded to encompass much that is of a poster, cartoon, or line display character. Most of the material which goes onto the chalkboard, bulletin board, or feltboard is graphical in character.

Haas and Packer say, "Maps, charts, and diagrams have been named the 'spark-plugs' of visual training because they are easy to make and are effective devices for instruction. Extensively used in every type of industrial organization, by business concerns, in agriculture, and in many other types of instruction [schools], these teaching aids make dry often meaningless facts more understandable and interesting."[1]

DRAWING AND SKETCHES

Children like to draw, and most of them have an aptness for expressing themselves. Their drawings may be absolutely meaningless or grotesque to adults, but to the children themselves they convey a message. The drawings are explained in a manner that is perfectly logical and meaningful to them. Somewhere along the line from childhood to adulthood, people lose their ability to convey ideas by drawing. They become self-conscious, fear ridicule, and abandon this aspect of communication almost entirely.

Teachers who do not make satisfactory use of the chalkboard and other forms of room display, rationalize by saying that they can't draw, that they have no talent.

Some teachers shudder at the idea of teaching even the simplest drawing to children. They are embarrassed to use what little skill they have in their teaching, and it simply is not realistic to expect them to go back to school and take an entire art program. There are, for these people, many short-cuts, or types of "visual shorthand." One is the increasingly popular stick figure drawing. Anyone can develop a few skills with relatively little practice. A simple drawing primer or manual can be helpful. This is not a plea for an artist in every classroom, but for just enough skill to clarify ideas that crop up as a part of everyday learning experiences. Patience plus some practice and a knowledge of a few simple rules are all that is necessary to do satisfactory stick drawing.

There are certain mechanical aids to assist teachers who feel that

[1] Haas, Kenneth B., and Packer, Harry Q. *Preparation and Use of Audio-Visual Aids*, Third Edition, New York: Prentice-Hall, Inc., 1955, p. 93.

they cannot do freehand drawing. They may copy on glass or cellophane for slide projection or for use in an overhead projector. The opaque projector will enable the teacher to enlarge small pictures for copying on chalkboard or paper.

The method of proportional squares is also practical and within the abilities of every teacher. It will work equally well for making a poster, chart, or for reproducing many kinds of pictures on the chalkboard.

DIAGRAMS

A diagram is a drawing which makes use of lines and conventionalized geometrical symbols, but uses no pictorial elements. Because diagrams are highly condensed, they are usually quite abstract or symbolical. Often a diagram is difficult to understand unless the reader possesses a background for the interpretation. Yet, difficult as the diagram may be, it must clarify meaning or not be used.

Practically every curriculum can, and does, use diagrams at one time or another. Some fields would be hard pressed to get along without them.

Industrial arts, engineering, and shop work abundantly use diagrammatic drawings. Engines, flow of electricity, magnetism, vectors, stresses and strains, and all kinds of machinery and equipment can be explained best with supplementing diagrams. Architects, engineers, designers, and builders use blueprints as one of the tools of their trade.

In mathematics and science, diagrams play an important part. Schematic diagrams are widely used in physics, general science, botany, anatomy, astronomy, and chemistry. Attempts to illustrate the theory of probability, for example, will in all likelihood call for some sort of diagrammatic device.

Social studies, too, use diagrams, but somewhat differently. Here they help students get clearer pictures of relationships between social agencies, cultural patterns, functions of individuals, patterns of society, and the work of institutions. The interrelationships involved are often complex. Diagrams, charts, and graphs will help explain them.

CHARTS

Charts are defined as visual devices which combine graphic and pictorial representations for the purpose of summarizing, arranging, comparing, or contrasting data. The term chart is loosely used to cover many forms of graphics, such as graphs, some types of maps, outlines, diagrams, and even such forms as information in lists and tables. Among the words used to describe them are developmental, organizational, pictorial, progress, skill, tabular, stream, and experience. These charts are familiar to most teachers.

GRAPHS

Graphs are lines, diagrams, symbols, or pictures arranged to show quantity, development, function, or relationship. They are constructed upon definite mathematical principles; charts are not. The last decade and a half have seen an unusual interest in the use of graphs in business, science, government, and industry. Several splendid new types have been developed.[2]

POSTERS

The poster is one of the older graphic devices which is so common that it may seem unnecessary to include it. Yet, to omit it would be analogous to describing the human body without mentioning the eyes.

The purpose of a poster is to catch the attention of a passer-by long enough to impress a single idea on his mind. To do this, poster-making embodies such principles as:

> Simple structure
> One idea
> Accents in color
> Concise, pithy, apt slogans
> Bold, clear lettering
> Variety in motif
> Balanced (formal or informal) composition

In addition to the above principles, good posters require careful planning. A good poster usually relies on some sort of related symbol to help convey the idea cogently. For example, a travel poster may use a symbolized traveling bag, or a train, or an airplane. Size of poster is to a large extent determined by its purpose and its location. A commonly used size is 22″ × 28″. Letter sizes, too, vary—one-inch letters are suitable for close viewing, one and one-half inch for moderate distance, and two-inch letters for longer distances or for impressiveness or use on giant-size posters. Capital block letters, heavy and bold, seem best. Trick letters cannot be read easily and are confusing. Letters may be cut out of contrasting colored paper, or they may be hand drawn. In most instances, children should be encouraged to cut letters and designs from poster paper without detailed preliminary sketches or hand-drawn designs.

Posters, like bulletin boards, *should not be displayed too long.* If left up too long, a poster, no matter how good in the beginning, loses its effectiveness.

[2] Speer, Mary E., *Charting Statistics.* New York: McGraw-Hill Book Company, 1952.

CONSTRUCTION OF GRAPHIC MATERIALS

Commercial concerns make many kinds of graphic materials for sale. Schools are limited buyers of pre-fabricated graphics. They buy those complex charts and diagrams which they cannot make, but on the whole, they buy the raw materials and construct their own.

Although acceptable graphics can be made from wrapping paper and cardboard boxes, more artistic ones require better materials and supplies. The following list of materials and suggestions for construction should improve school graphics.

MATERIALS AND SUPPLIES

Drawing board
T-Square
Ruler
Masking tape
Soft pencil or charcoal
Drawing pencils (H& F)
Colored pencils or crayons
Inks and poster colors
Lettering brushes
Erasers; art gum
Oil paint
Triangles, 30°-60°-45°
Gummed or cardboard letters
Colored cellophane tape
Lettering and ruling pens
Construction paper (several kinds)
Detail paper
Corrugated display cardboard
Pantograph (in some cases)
Scissors
Paste
Dry mounting tissue

TECHNIQUES

Make graphic aids large enough to be seen easily by all members of the class.

Decide on a standard size and hold to it in most instances. It facilitates handling.

Present only one idea on a chart.

Leave plenty of open space. Artists say the open space should equal the filled-in space.

Use contrasts of dark on light or vice versa, or use harmonious color shades.

Enlarge when necessary by using the opaque projector or a pantograph.

Make a scaled working sketch in miniature before embarking on large graphics.

Use brief and crisp titles.

Put graphics in partnership with other learning devices—texts, pictures, films, trips.

CRITERIA

Simplicity
Readability
Manageability
Realism
Attractiveness
Appropriateness
Accuracy

School administrators might well consider making up "graphic kits" for teachers. These kits could be checked out for use at school or home. The cost to the school would be slight, but the advantage of having a complete kit of materials would be worth much to better instruction, because as Rachael Goetz says, "Good graphics tend to be more *noticeable*, more *memorable*, and more *action-stirring* than unadorned facts."[3]

Graphics, like clothes, should not be worn too long. They need to be changed; *they need variety*.

[3] Goetz, Rachael M., *Visual Aids*. Chicago: Administrative Service, 1954, p. 43.

49. Put It on Tape

I. KEITH TYLER

Seven-year-old Linda still used baby talk, largely from habit; the children and adults with whom Linda currently had contact all used normal speech. Her teacher recorded samples of Linda's speech for the child herself to hear. Within a few weeks marked improvement began to take place.

Discussion in a high-school "problems of democracy" class seemed to be getting nowhere. A few students dominated the discussion, which frequently strayed from the issue. The teacher tape-recorded an entire period's discussion and played it back for analysis. The students were able to see irrelevancies, technical mistakes of the student discussion leader, and the tendency of a few to talk to excess.

A sixth-grade teacher recorded portions of a phonics lesson, an oral-reading session, and the reporting on a "reading for information" assignment. At a parents' meeting later, these tapes provided dramatic answers to "What is the school doing about reading?"

Every fall, an instrumental music teacher for the elementary grades records a sample of each child's performance for comparison with a similar sample in the spring. In addition, he frequently records both individual and group performance for immediate analysis as a basis for remedial practice.

These are but a few of the almost infinitely varied uses to which tape recorders are being put in the elementary and secondary schools. Few teaching tools are of more practical usefulness, and none has greater versatility.

When we consider that tape-recording in the United States is only about 10 years old, the extent of its acceptance by schools has been remarkable. But most teachers do not yet have regular access to the tape recorder. Indeed, many are not even aware of the help it can give in day-to-day class work.

From I. Keith Tyler, "Put It on Tape," *NEA Journal*, XLVI (February, 1957), 98–100. I. Keith Tyler is Professor of Education in the Bureau of Educational Research and Service, The Ohio State University, Columbus, Ohio. Reprinted by permission of the *Journal* of the National Education Association.

WHY BUY TAPE RECORDERS?

Tape recorders are a good investment even in these days of heavy competition for the school tax dollar. They give major help with some of the more time-consuming aspects of analysis and drill as well as providing motivation for other learning activities. A tape recorder brings the neighborhood, the community, and the world into the classroom.

The tape recorder not only plays previously recorded material, as does a record player, but it has brought instantaneous recording into the ordinary classroom and home. An amateur can record the "moving stream of life" for temporary or permanent use. And this includes not only sounds, interviews, discussions, music, talks, and meetings, but radio programs and the sound portion of television as well.

FUNCTIONS OF THE TAPE RECORDER

Consider for a moment some of the functions performed by the tape recorder in teaching.

As motivation. The chance to record their own creative productions on tape is a powerful motivation to children. It stimulates the writing of original stories, poems, and songs. Even plays and dramatic skits growing out of units of work are motivated by the opportunity to record them on tape. New interest is taken in assigned reading when summaries can be recorded rather than written. And the improvement of everyday speech is motivated when boys and girls hear for themselves the speech practices which are interfering with their effective communication.

As a means of analysis. The tape recorder enables youngsters to record their proficiency in music, in speech, in discussion, in reporting, and in summarizing as a basis for analysis and improvement.

As enrichment. Radio programs can be recorded for use when desired. Programs from a tape library can be utilized. (One national tape library and about 30 state ones are now serving schools.) Interviews with authorities can be brought into the classroom when they will fit best into the unit of study. On-the-spot descriptions of places and events made by children, by the teacher, or by parents are frequently useful.

As a performance model. The tape recorder enables both individual and group learners to hear quality performance in speech, drama, and music. With a tape recorder, the teacher can supplement foreign-language teaching with recorded talks by visiting exchange personnel or recently arrived children from other nations, and with recordings made by the teacher on his own foreign trips.

As a reporter. Pupils can record summaries of reading, interviews, and investigations at the time they are made for reporting back to the whole group. Similarly one class or group can report its activities or findings to another.

Recorded classroom practice in such fields as reading, arithmetic, spelling, and music is far more accurate and convincing to parent and community groups than the teacher's account of these matters or even a specially staged demonstration.

As music background. The tape recorder can provide specially recorded background music for lunchroom and corridors, for industrial-arts shops and home-economics laboratories, and for rhythm activities or typing classes.

As instructor of shut-ins. Children forced by illness to miss school for considerable periods can be provided some of the lost school experience thru taped portions of classroom activities. Developmental lessons covering new material should certainly be recorded for their study. The shut-in, in turn, may request specific help and information on tapes he returns to the school.

As a means of testing. Specialists in test administration can record standard instructions and time sections and items accurately. Tests can then be given to a number of groups in precisely the same way. Or the teacher may wish to administer tests to varied individuals and groups within his class at different times as the slower or faster learners are ready to be examined. Finally, taped tests enable the teacher to work with some groups while other groups are being tested.

As an assignment device. In planning a day's work, the teacher can record various specific assignments for small groups within the class. As each group completes an activity, it can listen to the teacher's next assignment, and even re-hear it if necessary. This is easier for the teacher than writing out detailed small-group assignments and then having them duplicated.

As an administrative aid. The high-school radio workshop will make use of the tape recorder constantly in its operation as the school's closed-circuit radio station. Assembly talks and sessions of the student council can be recorded. Daily announcements over the speaker system can be wholly or partially recorded in advance, as can the principal's regular talks to the student body.

KINDS OF TAPE USES

The uses of tapes can be classified into temporary (used over and over) and permanent (saved for shorter or longer periods).

For temporary uses, five tapes per teacher using the machine might provide a starting point.

Permanent uses are relatively expensive because they involve tying up considerable quantities of tape. The number of tapes required for the permanent-library stock can be determined only on the basis of the availability of school broadcasts in the area, the availability of a "Tapes for Teaching" library unit, and the number of teachers likely to be recording significant community material. Perhaps 25 to 50 tapes for this purpose per machine might be added each year. For permanent student-record tapes, five tapes per teacher would be a good beginning.

OPERATING THE TAPE RECORDER

While a teacher may need to operate a tape recorder in the primary grades, this function should be turned over to pupils in the later grades when possible. Fourth-graders and above are capable of being trained to do this task responsibly and efficiently. In some elementary schools and in most high schools, crews or clubs of upper-grade pupils are organized to service the tape machines.

In any case, however, teachers today need to become acquainted with the tape recorder—its many uses and its operation.

Familiarity with the functions of a tape recorder and confidence in its operation should be developed in teacher-education institutions.

However, since surveys indicate that few teachers colleges are giving such training, the responsibility falls upon the school systems.

At least one session of the induction training of new teachers may well be devoted to an intensive exposure to various teaching aids, including the tape recorder. Experience ought to include actual handling of the machine as well as observing demonstrations of its uses.

HOW MANY TAPE RECORDERS?

How many tape recorders does a single school need? A suggested average for an elementary school is one tape recorder for each five or six teachers. In a general high school, the ratio might be one machine for each 10 teachers, but it must be expected that teachers in some subject fields will use the machines intensively while those in other fields will use them seldom or ignore them completely.

GENERAL SPECIFICATIONS

Any school preparing to buy a tape recorder should obtain informed advice on makes and specifications. Generally speaking, a machine for the classroom should include speeds of 7.5 inches per second, which is the speed at which most library tapes are recorded, and 3.75 inches per second, which is the speed most used for recording school materials.

A third speed, 1.87 inches per second, is useful only for recording conferences and summary material where voice quality, sound effects, or music is not involved.

For classroom use, the usual choice is a twin-track set, since twice as much material can be recorded on each tape—recording first on one edge of the tape and then on the other. Material for library purposes is usually recorded on only one track so that it may be played on a single-track machine. Material to be spliced and edited also has to be recorded on one track.

Obviously, a tape recorder for schools must be ruggedly built to withstand frequent use. It must be dependable and require a minimum of adjustment and servicing. It must be simple in operation—practically foolproof. For example, it should be virtually impossible to erase recorded material accidentally while trying to "play back" a tape.

More professional machines are, of course, necessary in school and commercial radio stations, in audio-visual centers, and in recording libraries. But the biggest need of the moment is to put the simpler machines to work aiding overburdened teachers with their instructional tasks.

50. Demonstrate and Teach
WILLIS SWALES, JR.

An ancient philosopher has said, "One picture is worth a thousand words." By implication, if the picture and words were both there then the importance of the event would be more clearly seen, more easily explained, and more readily understood.

To many science teachers memorizing a law, talking about a principle, and solving a problem are all with which they feel a need to be concerned. Their courses are generally boring to the student, and all that is learned is that which is needed for the immediate test.

If those same teachers were to demonstrate along with their talk, how much more meaningful and interesting their course would be!

A good science teacher, whether teaching physics, chemistry, biology, general science or any high school or grade school science, should be a good demonstrator for several reasons:

1. Science texts will not do all the teaching.
2. A good demonstration will shorten the time for learning and lengthen the memory of facts and principles.

From Willis Swales, Jr., "Demonstrate and Teach," *School Science and Mathematics*, LXI (February, 1961), 98–100. Willis Swales, Jr. is Chairman of the Science Department, Pascack Valley Regional High School, Hillsdale, New Jersey. Reprinted from *School Science and Mathematics* by permission.

3. An effective demonstration can do much to foster good thinking both of groups or of individuals.

The good teacher, or demonstrator, should of course realize that demonstration is only one of the excellent ways in which good science instruction can be accomplished. He will only demonstrate where appropriate. The demonstration will never be used as a substitute, nor will it eliminate other teaching methods.

The demonstration can open a student's eyes to a new world of understanding and logic. He can see scientific method and evaluation on one hand, and draw conclusions and absolute knowledge on the other.

A science teacher can easily say, "This is so." But that does not mean that he will be understood. With the demonstration the teacher may say, "See, this is what happens." He may say, "By doing this I may benefit all who learn from me. I will *tell* you that this is so. I will *show* you that it is so. You will *see* that it is so!"

The following suggestions should aid a teacher in becoming a demonstrator, or in giving a demonstration lesson:

1. Be sure that you are familiar with the demonstration. Go over it at least once prior to showing it to the class. In other words, rehearse it.

2. Explain the problem to the class beforehand. An understanding of what will happen will help in solving the problem later, and in the writing of the demonstration. After explanations, allow the students to make observations.

3. Be sure that the demonstration is visible to all of the students. Many classrooms are laid out in a way that this is difficult. A different seating arrangement might help.

4. Keep the attention of the students focussed on the demonstration table or close to it in the room. The background can be important, so a white surface, or if possible a black surface, should be used.

5. Use large size demonstration apparatus whenever possible. The advantage of this large size over small size is that attention will be further drawn to it. If large equipment is not available, small equipment is far better than no demonstration.

6. Allow students to help with the demonstration, if possible. Do not use the same students constantly, but choose different ones. This will lend interest to the experiment.

7. Never dictate conclusions of the experiment. A student's writing his own conclusions is a test of how effective your demonstration has been.

If a demonstration fails, the reason should be sought. This might be due to one, or several, reasons. If the demonstration succeeds, it may be well to point out several of the most common reasons why that demonstration might fail. These are typical reasons:

1. The demonstrator was not ready. He may not have his apparatus out or set up. He may not have tried the demonstration to see whether it will work. The solution to this failure would be to always rehearse the experiment before class time.

2. The demonstrator does not give enough time during the demonstration for recording data. A hurried experiment may do harm in moving too fast for a student to grasp an essential point. The ideal situation is to have enough time to repeat the demonstration, and make sure that the students have written the descriptions and numbers necessary to evaluate the experiment properly.

3. Perhaps the most common reason for failure, but the reason least seen by the demonstrator, is his own domination of the demonstration. Students should be assigned to do specific parts of it, with considerable responsibility for their technique. In the case where a student is wrong, and no classmate has caught the error, then it would be permissible to offer correction. The class should have the opportunity to correct the mistake of their contemporary. Once the student has done his part, he should draw his own conclusions. His demonstration report is the proper place to evaluate his conclusions, for him to see his errors, or to hear praise for his good work.

4. Students often do not have their attention focussed on major facts. A lesson in each science course on picking out the pertinent facts and applying them to the demonstration would be of value. These facts can also be used in the recall process. A critical analysis of the results, as well as unsolved problems, can be useful in later demonstrations.

Demonstrations are good teaching. A demonstration well planned and executed presents an easier, more pleasant, better understood science lesson. The time and effort could hardly be spent more profitably.

51. What Should Educators Expect of Television?

WANDA B. MITCHELL

The "post-sputnik" interest in science and mathematics, the President's proposal to aid education with scholarship funds, the crowded classroom, and the needs within the teaching profession itself have only served to make the public aware of what educators have known for some time: the need for the reappraisal and evaluation of teaching methods, of curriculum, of facilities, and of results. Educational television is only one of the areas being examined for its capacity to aid in this crisis.

The negative claims against television as a means of instructing pupils cannot be ignored. There are fears that an electronic machine may be substituted for the classroom teacher. Television, say some, can assist with only one small part of the learning situation: imparting knowledge or content; it cannot change attitudes or develop appreciation. Television, say others, can do nothing that a good teaching film, properly used, cannot do better.

On the other hand, the number of research projects reported in Dr. H. Kumata's *Inventory of Instructional Television Research* suggests that educators are sincerely seeking valid, documented data to guide their use of this medium of communication with the realization that it is just that: a medium through which either good or bad teaching may be transmitted, true or false information can be disseminated, challenging or boring ideas can be explored, ignorance or wisdom can flow.

Present evidence seems to indicate a few generalizations upon which educators can safely build their program:

1. Television can give every student a front row seat, bring students closer to the teacher and closer to objects. Army research indicates that televised instruction is very effective for explaining complex manipulations. South High School in Columbus, Ohio, uses television in the physics class to make charts and meters visible to those in the entire laboratory. Evan-

From Wanda B. Mitchell, "What Should Educators Expect of Television?" *The High School Journal*, XLI (February, 1958), 158–161. Wanda B. Mitchell is Chairman of the Speech Arts Department and Director of the Television Project, Evanston Township High School, Evanston, Illinois. Reprinted from *The High School Journal* by permission.

ston (Illinois) High School fastens the camera to the microscope to magnify the picture of bacteria to the size of a 31″ television screen. This same school uses the camera for magnification during the dissection of the frog and the grasshopper in biology classes.

2. Television can enable a teacher to handle larger groups; therefore, more students can benefit from the instruction of a superior teacher. At the University of Houston one professor instructs 800 students in biology. At Mt. Pleasant High School in Schenectady one teacher of advanced mathematics is made available to three sections of trigonometry and solid geometry by the use of television. By the use of television two senior typing classes are taught simultaneously by the chairman of the department at Evanston. At this same school the television camera makes the best teacher of poetry available to 120 seniors at the same time.

3. Television can enrich the learning situation and supply the classroom with otherwise inaccessible instructional aids. For example, teachers of the history of Iowa have the assistance of live interviews about many of the historically significant spots around the state, staged in front of rear projection slides presenting the actual scene in realistic pictures. French is offered to grade school children in Pittsburgh. A new orientation course for freshmen is offered at Stephens College. Teachers in Washington County, Maryland, received supplementary aid several hours a week from their closed circuit television studios in Hagerstown where a teacher devotes full time to the preparation and presentation of audio-visual aids, research material, dramatic and colorful units. Teachers in remote areas can "tune in" materials in art and music.

4. Television can provide uniformity where uniformity is desirable. If instructions for a standardized test are administered by one qualified person on television, a more uniform atmosphere can be created than would be possible when each teacher in each room gave the directions. When New York City gives tests for principals, the candidates observed the same schoolroom situation on television and for the first time in history are answering questions on the same learning situation rather than on several different scenes staged in different classrooms. Any classroom teacher who has explained how to write a term paper for five consecutive periods can see the advantage of presenting this information once for distribution by television to the five groups simultaneously.

5. Television can assist with the redeployment of teacher time and effort for more efficient utilization. For instance, when an Evanston High School teacher teaches three sections of English during one period, the two periods thus saved are used to have personal conferences with the students and to go over their papers with them. The team teaching made possible by television enables an instructor to present on television the units in which he is best prepared and best qualified while his colleagues have more time to prepare the units they will present. Students profit by the best teaching of a team of teachers.

6. Television can extend education beyond the walls of the school. Pittsburgh's high school courses are studied via television in a prison. Kine-

scopes of these same courses are used by the Army overseas. Television provides home study courses for credit at Chicago Junior Colleges, Western Reserve, New York University, Michigan State, University of Omaha, and Iowa State, to mention only a few.

7. Television can help with many non-instructional duties and thus free the teacher for the rewarding job of guiding boys and girls in a wholesome learning environment. Chicago Teachers College has saved one-third of the time required for registration by focusing a television camera on class cards so that students waiting in line can see immediately which classes are filled. A TV camera focused on the office records of any student enables any teacher to see those records without leaving her room and without removing those records from the files. If the evils of "Big Brother" can be controlled, supervision of parking lots, cafeterias, and study halls can be handled by television.

8. Television is an effective instrument for teacher training. No teacher is so good or so experienced that he cannot profit by observing the masterful teaching of an instructor who has been freed of all other responsibilities and who has the assistance of graphic artists, directors, and visual aids to make his lesson as effective as possible. TV cameras in an elementary classroom, remotely controlled by a college instructor in a teacher-training class, enables the class to observe a live teaching situation under the guidance of their instructor without disturbing the classroom situation. Kansas State Teachers College, Pittsburg, Kansas, and University of Minnesota's demonstration high school are two institutions using television in this way. Kinescope recordings of teaching and learning situations provide real material for evaluation and improvement. Evanston High uses a beginning teacher as the supervisor in the typing viewing rooms where she can observe the masterful teaching of the department chairman and at the same time gain experience in classroom management. Iowa State televises a special art education course on Saturday mornings as in-service training for elementary school teachers without their having to drive to the campus each week.

Instructional television is not a threat to teachers; it is a challenge to our imagination, our creativity, our ingenuity in adapting this medium to its proper place in the entire learning process. Television cannot and should not try to do everything in every subject matter area. The role of television in art is different from its role in Spanish. Its role in the elementary school is different from its role in a college. Its role in a small rural school is different from its role in a comprehensive urban school.

One thing is certain: educators dare not ignore television. Dr. Kenneth Bartlett, of Syracuse University, says: "Commercial television has proved it can sell *products;* educators must use television to sell *ideas.* Commercial television has proved it can motivate people *to buy;* educators must use television to motivate people *to think.*"

52. *Educational Television*

RAYMOND WYMAN

Classroom teachers have now been exposed to reports about educational television for more than ten years. They are familiar with much of the research. They know that television equipment and techniques can effectively convey or transport good films, demonstrations, drama, and other forms of presentation through receiving sets.

But many teachers are content with only fringe benefits from television. Their introductions give them away:

"Did you happen to see ... on TV last night?"

"Let's put away our regular work and watch ...."

"I wonder what is on TV right now...."

They have used television only as optional, supplemental, spur-of-the-moment, or enrichment material. Television has much more to offer the classroom teacher.

Direct teaching with television means that the classroom teacher has entered into a partnership with a studio teacher in order to do most effectively the assignment that is supposed to be done at the particular time. Partnerships exploit the particular talents, resources, training, and desires of the partners. Partners can do together what neither could do as well separately.

Education can conveniently be divided into three parts. The studio teacher does one part primarily, and the classroom teacher does the other two. No one person is most important. They are all essential.

Presentation is the one-way communication of facts, concepts, processes, relationships, and so on, through such devices as talks, films, slides, recordings, dramatizations, and demonstrations. Studio teachers can be supplied with the best environment, supplies, apparatus, resource people, and technical assistance to present materials to large groups of pupils. Studio teachers can look through the camera lens into

From Raymond Wyman, "Educational Television," *The Instructor*, LXXI, No. 10 (June, 1962), 53–54. Raymond Wyman is Professor of Education and Head of Audiovisual Services at the University of Massachusetts, Amherst, Massachusetts. Copyright 1962 by the F. A. Owen Publishing Company. Reprinted from *The Instructor* by permission.

the eyes of each viewer to make individual instruction out of mass instruction.

Another essential part of education is two-way communication, or interaction, between groups of students and between students and the teacher. Immediately following a presentation, the classroom partner can discuss, argue, question, test, reteach, and expand as necessary with individuals in the group until real understanding develops.

The third essential part of education is individual study, drill, experimentation, and application. This too is best done under the guidance of the classroom teacher.

With direct-teaching educational television, the classroom and studio teachers plan together as real partners for the educational outcomes desired. Goals for subjects and units must be established and agreed upon. Those parts that can best be presented over television become the studio teacher's lessons. Those parts that need discussion and study go to the classroom teachers.

Schedules, guides, and supplemental materials must be jointly prepared. Such work takes much preparation. During the term, the classroom teachers are in regular contact with the studio teacher through meetings, bulletins, study guides, and feedback sheets.

The classroom teacher introduces each new topic to be studied, relating it to past and future topics and to the experiences of the particular class. Questions are asked that will be answered by the studio teacher. New words are put on the chalkboard.

During the televised presentation, the classroom teacher checks sound and sight from a number of locations. She checks to see that very brief notes are taken or more elaborate work done if it was planned for. She actively learns with the children from the studio teacher, who has far more time and resources to obtain the latest and best information and techniques.

At the end of the presentation, the set is turned off and the aroused interests of the children are pursued. Children are eager to explain answers to their questions. They can discuss new or unclear ideas. They can ask questions. They can suggest and carry out dramas, exhibits, demonstrations, and field trips. They can search out additional material. They can interview parents or other adults. They can select, mount, and label tear sheets. Television that is worth using at all is worth adequate preparation and follow-up.

Many teachers do not have classrooms within range of an ETV station or closed circuit programs. However, commercial stations will sometimes be willing to broadcast an educational series during the regular school day if enough teachers will use it or if it has some general home appeal also. A few programs already scheduled by commercial stations during class time can be used for direct teaching—news, weather commentaries, public events.

Most of the good educational programs on commercial stations come when children are at home. The sponsors of some of these programs have done outstanding service to education by printing guides for teachers in advance. Although the planning, use, and follow-up activities are separated by some hours, there is still considerable value derived.

It will be far more fruitful for a teacher to plan good television viewing with her children than to decry the poor viewing that children often do. It is also possible for a teacher to improve family viewing, since parents will often view a program with their children.

With so much to be learned, so many to be taught, and with such limited resources, teachers need to make wide and good use of the television medium.

53. On the Differences Between Linear and Intrinsic Programing

NORMAN A. CROWDER

Many present discussions of programed learning do not clearly distinguish between linear and intrinsic programing. This is understandable in view of the history of the field, but it is quite unfortunate. Any attempt to view linear and intrinsic programing as mere technical variants of the same method, or to derive both techniques from the same basic rationale, seriously impedes an understanding of the field.

Linear and intrinsic programing have nothing in common historically, having arisen in different contexts and in response to different circumstances. They have nothing in common theoretically, but rather rely for their expected effectiveness on different rationales and make different and, in fact, diametrically opposed assumptions about the nature of the learning process. The materials produced following the different methods have only superficial similarities, and what similarities appear may be misleading, as will be discussed below. As a matter of fact, the

From Norman A. Crowder, "On the Differences Between Linear and Intrinsic Programing," *Phi Delta Kappan,* XLIV (March, 1963), 250–254. Reprinted by permission of the *Phi Delta Kappan.* Norman A. Crowder is Vice President and Technical Director of the Educational Science Division of U.S. Industries, Inc., 12345 New Columbia Pike, Silver Spring, Maryland.

common use of the word "programing" is coincidental, the word originally having been used in a somewhat different sense by writers of the two schools. It is the purpose of this paper to make these basic differences quite clear.

ONE PROBLEM, TWO DIFFERENT SOLUTIONS

The objective of both schools of programing is to produce materials that permit efficient individual study by a student independent of an organized study group and without the continuous intercession of a live instructor. Now, materials technically suitable for independent study, e.g., textbooks and reference materials, have been in use for many years. The educator may then well ask why proponents of programed instruction expect their materials to be more effective than are the conventional materials. The answers given by theorists of the two schools of programing are quite different. The linear theorist will describe a particular model of the learning process which he believes is accurate and general enough for practical educational use. He will then show how materials prepared by the linear method follow the requirements of this specific learning model, and hence should, in use, promote efficient learning. In the case of linear programing it is fair to say that the specific learning theory came first; the techniques used derive directly from the theory.

For intrinsic programing the situation is the reverse. The intrinsic programing theorist will not point to a specific learning model, but will rather describe a technique which, in common-sense terms, appears to permit inanimate materials to assume some of the educational functions that have previously required a live instructor, or tutor, for each student. Thus, while the linear programer is exploiting a particular theory, the intrinsic programer is exploiting a particular technique. The linear programer is, in effect, claiming to have discovered something about the learning process which he is putting to practical use with his materials; the intrinsic programer does not claim to have discovered something about learning, but rather to have developed a new technique that allows some rather old ideas about teaching to be more effectively implemented.

BASIC LINEAR THEORY AND TECHNIQUE

The learning model used in linear programing is basically a conditioning model. Briefly, it postulates that a desired change in behavior, defined as learning, can best be brought about by inducing and then rewarding the desired behavior, in much the same manner as a dog is trained. As a partisan of intrinsic programing, I would be decently diffident about drawing the parallel between linear programing and animal training were it not for the fact that the linear theorists place such emphasis on the derivation of their method from experiments with animals, and the parallel does serve to illustrate the technique. Thus the linear materials are designed to cause the student to emit the behaviors defined as the subject matter to be learned, piece by piece, rewarding each instance wherein the student emits the desired behavior.

The format of linear materials is by now familiar to most educators. Following a very short presentation of new material, the student is required to emit a response, usually the writing of a word. He then compares his response to the correct response (which he discovers by appropriate manipulation of the materials, such as turning to the next page) and, if his response matches the correct response, he feels thereby rewarded, and the act is thus "learned." *In linear programing, the student's response is considered an integral part of the learning process; the response is induced in order that it may be rewarded and learning thus occur.* In the strict application of linear theory the question of how the student is induced to emit the correct response is irrelevant; the important thing is to get response emitted in order that it may be rewarded and thus "learned."

Linear programs make no explicit provision for errors by the student, since errors are, by linear theory, simply irrelevant to the learning process. If a student makes an error, i.e., emits the wrong response, the program has at best wasted his time, at worst he may harmfully have practiced an incorrect response. Hence linear programs, if properly constructed, are refined to the point where errors occur very infrequently, and may be neglected. The task of a linear program is to get the student to emit, in response to the given stimuli, the responses that have been defined as constituting the behavior to be learned. An error on the part of a student is considered a fault on the part of the program.

From the above theoretical considerations, the characteristics of linear programs—very short steps, a high degree of redundancy and prompting leading to very easy "questions"—follow directly. The student response is ordinarily a "constructed" response, as it was early believed by the linear theorists that "thinking" a response could not properly be called "behavior" and thus could not be brought within the purview of the theory. "Thinking" is still a little awkward for the theory to handle, but experiments in which students, instructed to merely think the response, learned as well as students required to write out the response, have forced some reconsideration of this issue.

In summary, linear materials are built on the assumption that a conditioning model is appropriate for educational use, and the techniques employed are derived from that model. The student is confronted with a series of stimuli which, building from the presumed known or previously learned responses, cause him to emit new responses (or old responses to new stimuli); the emission of the desired responses is rewarded by the student's discovering that he was correct, and the desired responses are thus learned. Errors by students on a fully developed program are so few that their occurrence may be neglected.

BASIC INTRINSIC THEORY AND TECHNIQUE

Intrinsic programing makes no assumptions about the nature of the learning process that have not been common educational coin for some time. Furthermore, as suggested above, intrinsic programing is not a theory about how education should be conducted. It is a technique for preparing written materials that will accommodate quite a range of educational purposes. Accordingly, the technique will be described before the theoretical issues.

The technique is based on this simple fact: The student's choice of an answer to a multiple-choice question can be used automatically to direct him to new material; the student who chooses one alternative can automatically be directed to different material than that to which a student choosing a different alternative is directed. One use that can be made of the technique is to include in ordinary expository text questions that are automatically administered, scored, and appropriate remedial action automatically taken if indicated.

In the simplest "scrambled book" or Tutor Text (TM) format the student is given a short discussion of the material to be learned, followed by a multiple-choice question designed to test the point just discussed. Each answer alternative has a page number beside it. The student chooses what he believes is the correct answer to the question and turns to the page number given for that answer. If he has chosen correctly, the page to which he thereby comes will contain the next unit of material to be learned and the next question, and so on. If he has chosen an incorrect answer, the page to which he thereby comes will contain a discussion of why the answer chosen is incorrect, and, following this discussion, an instruction to return to the original question page to try again. He will not come to the next unit of new material until he has chosen the correct answer, of course, although in choosing incorrect answers he will come upon new discussion of the old material.

The pages in a Tutor Text are randomly arranged; that is, the page numbers given with the answer choices are not consecutive or in any other obvious order. Thus the student cannot ignore the question and routinely pass to the next page of material; he must commit himself to one of the answer choices, or else choose blindly, but he cannot ignore the question and pass to the "next page" of instruction, since the "next page" is not the sequentially numbered next page, but the page whose number is given with the right-answer choice.

The basic intrinsic programing technique, then, amounts to nothing more than the inclusion of multiple-choice questions in relatively conventional expository text and the use of these questions to continually check the student's progress through the material and to furnish specific remedial material as it is required. *In intrinsic programing the questions serve primarily a diagnostic purpose, and the basis of the technique is the fact that the diagnosis so made can be promptly utilized to furnish specific remedial material to the student.*

The inclusion of the question and its answer choices in each page of expository text brings about changes in both text style and format that the skillful program writer will use for a variety of auxiliary purposes. Thus the question may be used to draw the student's attention sharply to the key point of a paragraph; solutions to problems may be suggested by way of the answer choices provided with the question; answering the question may provide the student with useful practice with the concept involved, and so forth. I mention these auxiliary uses of the question to make the point that the material from which the student is to learn includes the expository text, the question, the answer choices provided, and the remedial material provided for each of the wrong answers. In other words, one does not prepare an intrinsic program merely by chopping up expository text into paragraphs and providing a multiple-choice question for each paragraph. However, the fact that a skillful writer will make the structural features of the format serve useful auxiliary ends, just as any competent craftsman will get the most from a technique, should not divert attention from the fact that the primary purpose of including the questions is diagnostic, the diagnosis being desired in order that prompt remedial action may automatically be taken.

BASIC DIFFERENCES IN THEORY

The basic differences in theory between linear and intrinsic programs should now be manifest. Indeed, it would be a shorter task to detail the similarities than to discuss the differences, since the differences cover almost every point of theory and technique. The linear theorist assumes that human learning is sufficiently well described by a conditioning model to allow the requirements of that model to be the overriding consideration in preparing educational materials. The intrinsic programing theorist considers the direct application of such a model to human learning to be naive. The linear programer assumes that the student will learn only those responses on which he can be given rewarded practice; the intrinsic programer does not pretend to know in detail *how* the student learns, but is interested in *whether* he learns. Hence one writes items to exercise the student, the other writes questions with a diagnostic purpose in mind. The linear programer is distressed if an item draws erroneous responses while the intrinsic programer regards a question that everyone passes as a waste of space.

The writer of intrinsic programs is no more committed to any specific theory of learning than is the writer of any other type of expository text. The writer may regard good expository writing as primarily an art; he may have very specific detailed rules he follows in writing; if he really believes that grossly redundant text with words left blank now and then communicates better than conventional prose, he could even prepare the expository part of the text in the form of a linear program. The distinguishing feature of an intrinsic program is not theoretical; it is the structural feature of including diagnostic questions throughout the exposition, and providing remedial material for those who fail the questions.

THE QUESTION OF SELF-PACING

It is often stated that all programs are self-pacing in the sense that the student proceeds through them at his own best rate. A moment's reflection will show that linear and intrinsic programs are self-pacing in entirely different degrees. A linear program is self-pacing in the sense that some students read faster than others, but all must read the same material. An intrinsic program provides different amounts and kinds of material for individual students, based not on prior estimates of the student's needs or on his self-evaluation as he goes through the program but on his demonstrated performance in choosing answers to the questions.

The matter of adapting programed material to the needs of the individual student is, of course, of primary importance in preparing material for individual use. The central feature of intrinsically programed materials—the fact that each piece of material seen by the student, whether it be new or remedial material, depends on his performance on the previous question—is intended to serve this end of adapting the material to the manifest needs of the individual student.

WHY SHOULD STUDENTS MAKE ERRORS?

It is a current shibboleth that "when the student makes an error, the fault is in the program." This is a seductive half-truth and as such proposes a solution that conceals the bulk of the problem. Certainly no one would propose to write materials systematically designed to lead the student into errors, and anyone would prefer programs on which no student made an error *if this could be achieved without other undesirable results.* To see what undesirable results we must concern ourselves with, consider how we would proceed to write a program on which no student will make an error. We can produce virtually error-free programs if we are careful never to assume knowledge that the most poorly prepared student does not have, never to give more information per step than the slowest can absorb, and never to require reasoning beyond the capacity of the dullest. The inevitable result of such programs is that the time of the average and better than average student is wasted, and what is more important, the subject matter itself, no matter how dignified and characteristically human are its antecedents, must be reduced to fragments appropriate to the conditioning model of learning.

It seems to me that the linear model makes the most pessimistic possible set of assumptions about the student. Material prepared in the intrinsic format, on the other hand, makes the most optimistic assumptions and lowers them only when and if the particular student, by making errors, demonstrates that he cannot learn from material written at a higher level of abstraction. It certainly seems to me that it is consonant with our educational goals that the pressure of the program should be upward, allowing the student to deal with the material on the highest level of abstraction of which he is capable, rather than downwards, forcing all students to plod through a path designed for the least able. We are free to apply such upward pressure in an intrinsic program because we can automatically make provision for those who cannot stand the pace.

THE QUESTION OF "RESPONSE MODE"

A great deal has been made of the presumed differences in the psychological process involved in constructing an answer in a linear program and those involved in choosing one of several alternatives to a multiple-choice question in an intrinsic program. Such discussion usually tacitly assumes that the function served by the question is the practice function considered important in the linear model, wherein the theory would predict that the constructed response would serve this practice function more efficiently. Experiments with linear programs have shown that multiple-choice questions in linear programs seem to work as well as constructed response questions, which would suggest that either the theory was wrong, or, what seems to me to be more likely, it simply did not describe accurately the function served by the question.

As I have indicated, I believe the practice consideration is irrelevant, particularly in intrinsic programs. We use multiple-choice questions for the purely practical reason that we think of the questions as primarily serving a diagnostic or testing function, for which the multiple-choice question is directly useful while the open-ended question is not. The choice of an answer to a multiple-choice question can be translated into a discrete physical act, such as turning to a particular page in a book, or pressing a particular button on a machine, whereby appropriate new or remedial material is automatically selected. In the present state of the art, no practical device that will respond differentially to written or open-ended questions is available, except in certain very specialized applications.

In any discussion of response mode, the question of whether having multiple-choice questions does not permit the student to practice errors is sure to arise. Again, the point is relevant to the training of pigeons, but it seems to me irrelevant for serious educational work with human beings. We expect the student to give the right answer to a question because he has understood the material he has just read on the point in question, not because he has given the response in question more often than he has given another response. For pure rote material the point may be relevant, but for most material of interest to educators there is presumably a reason behind the correct answer to a question, not merely a statistical history of frequency of responses.

THE QUESTION OF MACHINE *vs.* BOOKS

Nowhere does the confusion of linear and intrinsic programing produce more mischievous results than in the discussion of the relative merits of programs presented via "teaching machines" versus those presented in book form. In a linear program, the material is not responsive to the student's activity, i.e., each student comes to the same "next step" in the program, whether he has given the correct response, an incorrect response, or no response at all to the previous item. Since there is no control of the programed materials required in a linear program, it is hardly surprising to find that it seems to make little difference whether the material is presented via book or machine.

An intrinsic program, of course, varies the material presented to each student on the basis of the student's response to each question. It may be desired to direct the student to specific remedial material, through remedial subsequences, or even back through an entire lesson. All of this can be done in book form, or rather, one can suggest it to the student in book form; in the machine format, as in the AutoTutor® teaching machine, the desired excursions on the part of the student can be made automatic and mandatory.

The effect of the machine is to increase the responsiveness of the program; obviously it will not be of importance unless the programer has written a responsive program.

SUMMARY

Linear and intrinsic programing, while having some superficial similarities, are basically different in approach, intention, and rationale.

The linear technique is an attempt to adapt a simple conditioning model of learning to educational use; the intrinsic programing technique exploits the possibility of letting the student's choice of answers to questions included in the text direct him to new or remedial material as appropriate. The two techniques impose different restrictions on the program writer; the author has argued that the conditions imposed by the intrinsic programing format are consonant with a variety of desirable educational objectives, while the conditions imposed by the linear model are undesirably restrictive.

54. Future Classroom—an Educational Automat?

WILLIAM C. KVARACEUS

The embodiment of the ethos of our age may best be found in the automation processes and gimmicks exemplified by the vending machines (gum, soft drinks, newspapers, or pocket combs), the washing machines (clothes, dishes, even automobiles), and, on a more grandiose scale, the IBM installations. All these automatic devices save time and labor—and, of course, money.

Perhaps it is inevitable with the inroads made by the projector, record player, tape and wire recorder, TV screen, and teaching machine that the classroom of the future will take on more and more the efficient and economical appearance of an educational automat. If so, what is likely to be gained and what is likely to be lost to the young learner through the fast-growing trend toward this type of self-teaching process?

Three personal incidents, in one way or another, have accentuated the "teaching machine" or automation issue for me in recent weeks.

Motoring from Boston to New York City recently, I drove down the new Connecticut Pike—a multi-laned highway studded with toll stations. As I approached the first toll gate the big decision "correct change this-a-way and all others that-a-way" was forced upon me. Armed with the "right change" I fed the automatic register and as my coins clinked in, a most impersonal sign blinked out a mechanical "Thank You."

From William C. Kvaraceus, "Future Classroom—an Educational Automat?" *Educational Leadership*, XVIII (February, 1961), 288–292. William C. Kvaraceus is Professor of Education and Director of Youth Studies, Lincoln Filene Center for Citizenship and Public Affairs, Tufts University, Medford, Massachusetts. Reprinted by permission of the author and of *Educational Leadership*.

After two of these "Thank You's," I found myself driving through the stiles manned with humans rather than machines. Somehow I felt less lonely and more a part of a live universe hearing a human voice say, "Thank you"—even though in perfunctory fashion—and seeing a human hand take my change.

Walking across a well-known eastern university campus not long ago, I glanced in on a classroom (perhaps better described as a learning laboratory) and noted a number of students closeted in separate cubicles. They were all wearing earphones and were apparently listening to tapes. But there was no sign of a mentor around. If students are present, need there be a mentor nearby?

On returning home one evening, I was greeted by my daughter Jane, now in the fifth grade and in her second year of TV French: "Bon soir, Papa! Je m'appele Jeanne." "Merci," I answered, "mais tu parles comme une jeune fille Française." She had learned all her conversational French from a TV screen.

How depersonalized can the classroom be and what are the effects— immediate and long term, good and bad—of seeding the classroom with mechanical aids that enable or even insure effective self-instruction and learning? (The term "teaching machine" is much too controversial to be used in this discussion and makes too difficult a fair and objective consideration of this topic. Equating even a part of the teaching function to a mechanized gadget presents to many workers in the educational vineyard a threat to the worthwhileness of the human teacher and even to the teaching profession as a whole. In what kind of profession have we been engaged, if much or most of our function can be programmed more effectively on some mechanical gadget? Such a train of inquiry can interfere with a fair consideration of the real promise and the real problems inherent in auto-instructional devices.)

DEVICES AND THE TEACHER

The answer to the major questions that have been raised will come only through a consideration of two subsidiary queries: (a) What part of the educational process and product can be effectively programmed for self-teaching devices? and (b) What is the unique role and function of the teacher in today's classrooms?

Before considering these two essential questions we must recognize that the modern mechanized aids can hardly be considered "recent innovations." They have had their counterparts (and their critics) in earlier times and in less technological cultures. The abacus, the hornbook, the tachistoscope and the more recent paperback workbook were all devised to assist the pupil to engage himself in worthwhile learning experiences and, at the same time, to release the teacher from the class as a whole enabling him to apportion his time and energy more effectively.

What Can Be Programmed?

Accepting the mounting evidence that auto-instructional aids can and do abet certain types of learnings in certain subject areas, the basic issue does not center around the question, "Shall we use them?" Rather the issue turns on the more discriminating query, "When and how shall we use these aids?"

What we need to do at the outset is to review and set down a concise statement of the ultimate purposes of the educational processes and to mark out those particular outcomes which can now be programmed for machined learning. There is already some consensus that the self-teaching devices can handle learning outcomes which constitute factual material that can be itemized. Such learning product must be clear, simple and categorical; what is to be learned must be cut up into small, discrete but interrelated elements. Such learning generally falls at the levels of recognition and recall.

Unfortunately few personal, social, economic or political problems that are met in everyday living tend to be clear, simple or categorical. Furthermore the more crucial and far-reaching outcomes of learning will always be found at the level of interpretation, application, appreciation and invention. These levels are still outside the reach of most self-learning devices and thereby place a low ceiling on what is to be mastered.

Let us take a hard and realistic look at the nature and levels of the learning product that now preoccupy the combined human-teacher and pupil effort in most classrooms today. The impartial observer, on the basis of such observation, would be forced to admit that the self-teaching devices could be used to replace at least 75 percent (a subjective but conservative estimate) of the teaching function as played out in the typical classroom and reflected in the time-honored and time-worn ritual of lesson assigning, lesson hearing and lesson marking. This in itself is a most serious indictment of teaching in the school agency.

If learning product and outcomes of the school operation are viewed (as they must be) in terms of desired changes and modifications in pupil (and ultimately adult) behavior or in terms of new and desirable adaptations or ways of behaving, the limitations of what learning outcomes can be programmed become readily apparent. To know, to recall and to verbalize represent important and initial objectives of education, but they are seldom the ultimate goals. Living out the objectives of the school in play, at work, on the job, in the home and in community endeavors represents the real test of the educated person. Homes, neighborhoods and nations of the world do not so much lack "educated" persons who can pass or have passed advanced tests and examinations in the hard subjects so easily programmed as persons who can and do aspire to the *Summum Bonum* in the Judaic-Christian tradition as seen in the victory of the selfless as promised in the Ten Commandments and in the Sermon on the Mount. There is all around us today ample and tragic evidence, in the product of schools, that the factual teachings of the classrooms are falling on barren ground and among tares. Too few learners have been inspired to selfless behavior.

As Goethe pointed out at the turn of the 19th century, "A teacher who can arouse a feeling for a single good action, for a single good poem, accomplishes more than he who fills our memory with row on row of natural objects, classified with name and form." The young learner is much more than a memory drum on a 650 computer. He is a living, growing, feeling person. How he *behaves* is as important as what he can memorize and verbalize. Having looked at the unique function of the self-teaching aids, what is the unique role and function of the mentor?

Role and Function of the Teacher

What is the tutorial teaching that is promised as a solution to large-size classes and to the perennial problems of individual differences via the self-pacing auto-instructional aids? Will such teaching enable some strategic shifts in teaching role and function?

As a director of the learning process and as a "mediator of culture," the teacher plays many different roles:[1] he is a botherer, motivator or stimulant; he is a person who knows; he is a guide in the selection of learning activities; he is an evaluator; he is one who maintains order; he is the creator of a "moral atmosphere"; he serves as parent surrogate and character model. Some of these roles will be more affected by self-teaching gadgets than will others.

As "a person who knows," the mentor will need to know more. He will need to be more informed in learning theory and the communication processes. He will need to discriminate between content and to supplement programmed learning. And he will need to know each student's readiness for the various steps and types of programmed and unprogrammed learning. Even with a full bin of programmed concepts in his subject matter field, it is highly doubtful if the teacher's need to know subject matter will in any way be diminished. (One can almost see the phantom image of the teacher, trained only in machine methods, getting all his subject matter from the programmed library. This

[1] "Teacher's Role in American Society," *Fourteenth Yearbook of the John Dewey Society*. New York: Harper and Brothers, 1957, Chap. 6.

specter should keep the methods-baiters—Barzun, Bestor, Rickover, etc. —in a dither during the next decade.)

Anonymity

More crucial are those questions of role as they affect interpersonal relationships in the class and the growing threat of anonymity and impersonality if machine-oriented teaching means restricting the occasion and incidence of teacher-pupil and pupil-teacher interaction. Programmed learning must insure and enable more and deeper relationships between teacher and learner by releasing the instructor from time-consuming routines. In fact the introduction of auto-instructional devices should be justified on this basis as well as on learning increment.

Many of the current experimental studies of the use of self-teaching tools and techniques report that students "enjoy the experience of learning with auto-instructional devices." The teaching personality must be pale indeed if students prefer to relate to a machine. Perhaps these devices do have something in their favor. Unlike some mentors, the machines are infinitely patient and always rewarding via "positive reinforcement." They will never "take it personally" or "take it out on the learner" if at first he does not succeed. Machines may have the psychological advantage of not getting psychically involved. Few learners will be afraid to admit to the mechanized teacher, "I don't understand" or "I don't know"—phrases that bounce harshly off the sensitive ears of many human teachers. And in those classrooms where the climate is hardly safe or sanitary from a mental hygiene point of view, introduction of self-teaching devices may even help to neutralize the atmosphere. But, again, who wants to relate to a machine, especially since it does not seem to care?

When the novelty of levers, lights, and pushbuttons wears off, auto-instructional devices may have difficulty in attracting, interesting, and especially exciting the student to greater effort. As Anatole France once pointed out, "The whole art of teaching is only the art of awakening the natural curiosity of young minds for the purpose of satisfying it afterwards." This is the "botherer" or "motivator" role of the teacher. In stimulating, if not inspiring, the reluctant and recalcitrant learners (the Number Two problem of the teacher, according to a recent NEA study of working conditions in the classroom) the auto-instructional machinery may fail because many nonlearners, who now refuse to open their books, may refuse to turn the gadgets on.

Identification

In anticipation of this problem, any requisition for these devices should include a sizeable order for the model that comes with built-in handcuffs and leg irons that will be needed to hold many pupils at their machine-desks. Of course this may eliminate the post of "truant officer"—currently a very busy functionary in many neighborhoods in the larger urban-industrial centers. But that's the way it is with automation—it always means the elimination of some jobs!

Today through the intricate and intimate process of identification based upon a positive relationship between teacher and learner, many human mentors affect (and more could) the lives of children and youth and bring about significant changes or modifications in their behavior when they play out their role as parent surrogates and their role as creators of a moral atmosphere by presenting themselves as attractive and inspiring character models. If we assume that few learners will identify with the machine-instructor, we cannot at the same time assume that all learners will readily identify with their human mentors. But some youngsters do and more could and should identify with the teacher. It is the person (personality, if you must) of the teacher that is a paramount factor in improving the quality of the learning process. The teacher who has not himself achieved an emotional maturity and authenticity and who is hardly excited or interested in the teaching-learning drama in his field will not communicate to others the adventure, romance and battle-heat implicit on any learning frontier.

Instead of merely looking for a machine replacement, we should find for this instructor a better human replacement. The terrible reality that many youngsters face daily in the classroom confines them to close living with dull, listless and lukewarm personalities and the classroom becomes a place of boredom filled with never-ending and useless tasks that must be completed to keep the teacher happy or at least out of your hair. In contrast, perhaps the blinking and clinking machine looks exciting and contemporary to the bored learner. It is significant to note that after 12 years of association with teachers, very few high school graduates rush to fill in the ranks of the teaching profession and that such occupational selections generally represent second or third choices.

It has already been suggested that justification for using self-teaching equipment must stem from both learning increment and the fact that these devices can free teachers and enable them to play out their human relations function in a socialized classroom. Through this deskside function it may be possible to make what is learned on the machine and elsewhere significant and meaningful in life situations. "Trees and fields tell me nothing," Plato once observed. "Men are my teachers."

Auto-learning devices are here to stay. They will not revolutionize the classroom nor will they eliminate or even minimize the job and function of the human teacher. (Note, however, the "remedial instructors" had better retool in view of the research claims of some experimenters that "Total mastery has been exhibited by most experimental students." Perhaps, however, even these jobs are "safe" in view of the difficulties and complexities in the psyche and the culture and sub-cultures which frequently interfere with learning.) Karl Marx once expressed his concern for "intellectual desolation artificially produced by converting immature human beings into mere machines." To paraphrase him in the present situation, we should be concerned with the threat of emotional desolation that may be artificially produced by crowding the teacher out of the classroom and learning laboratory, thereby converting immature human beings into mere intellectual machines. Our vision is *not* "machines for making more machines."

PART THREE

PROFESSIONAL ACTIVITIES AND PROBLEMS

Introduction

It is sometimes disillusioning for the beginning teacher who is well grounded in teaching techniques and who believes that he understands a sound general approach to the teaching-learning process to discover that even this necessary background is not sufficient to prepare him for solving all of the problems that he falls heir to as a teacher. He discovers belatedly that the course in tests and measurements did, after all, include some vital information which needs to be recollected and put to use. Through experience, if in no other way, he learns that testing is more than a means of estimating achievement, it is also a method of teaching and learning. He soon perceives that the marking system is something to be endured and that the report card apparently is a subject for eternal study, change, and improvement.

He learns that it is for good reason that classroom discipline has been a perennial topic in the education journals for as long as they have been published and that his whole philosophy of education is reflected in his manner of controlling pupils and working with them. He recognizes that good discipline is more than good control over pupils and that what we think of as good discipline is also a means toward the ends of teaching and learning.

He soon becomes aware that he spends a considerable amount of time with administrators, supervisors, fellow teachers, salesmen, parents, contest chairmen representing civic clubs, guidance specialists, experts in reading, mathematics, and other fields, and possibly even social workers, physicians, and policemen. He discovers that all the problems of teaching are not solved in the classroom. Under some circumstances it is a relief to find that he does not face his problems alone and that there are a number of others standing by ready to help. But it is also true that the teacher's out-of-class contacts bring to light many out-of-class obligations which he may not readily accept but which inevitably become part of his professional life. He finds that he is expected to accept committee appointments, to join and be active in the affairs of professional associations, to support community affairs and charity drives, to direct extracurricular activities, and to take a part in the school-wide guidance and testing programs.

He must also, of course, keep up with trends in teaching his subject or subjects and, in addition, must learn to cope with administrative proposals for greater efficiency. Finally, he learns that the emotional climate surrounding education in his community does have a direct effect on his work in the classroom, even on the content of his courses and his manner of teaching.

The opinions which a teacher expresses about traditional problems such as classroom discipline, evaluation, and marking, and his practices in them, as well as his reactions toward new developments in his field or in professional education, tell others what kind of a teacher he is. The selections which conclude this book are concerned with some of the professional activities and problems that confront all teachers and that have a particular bearing on the methods of the classroom.

55. *Whose Standards?*

ARCHIBALD B. SHAW

One of the favorite pronouncements of the day is, "Standards must be raised in our schools and colleges!" When a principal, superintendent, or president makes some such avowal, he's publicly applauded. The pronouncement rings of progress, of improvement, of excellence. It rings loud. But does it ring true?

Too often, it has a hollow sound. It turns out that the standards he wants to raise are standards of expectation: admission standards, grading standards, standards of achievement, standards of conduct, stand-

From Archibald B. Shaw, "Whose Standards?" *Overview,* IV, No. 3 (March, 1963), 9. Archibald B. Shaw is Associate Secretary of the American Association of School Administrators and, at the time this article was published, Editorial Director for *Overview.* Reprinted with permission of *Overview* magazine. Copyright 1963 by the Buttenheim Publishing Corporation.

ards for graduation, standards for staying on for another semester.
Oddly, the standards are always solely and exclusively the student's
standards.

Perhaps there's a case for the dramatic dumping of students already
enrolled in the interests of new and higher standards. There must be a
case, or we wouldn't hear of so many colleges proudly flunking 30 percent or more of their freshmen. We wouldn't hear so much about the
high school "dropout." Whether or not the shakeup works may not be
so important as what it does to the victims and what it says about the
institution. We'd be very much surprised if setting standards for students alone can make an institution great.

When a youngster is accepted by a high school or college, there is
a two-way contract implied. The obligation on the student is clear. He
must meet requirements which are stated or clearly implied. But what
is the obligation on the school or college? Both as an institution and in
its people, it has, presumably, vastly more maturity, a clearer awareness of purpose, a longer history, broader experience, and greater resources than any of its students. Who then has the greater responsibility?
Whose standards do we start with when we reach for excellence?

Standards, like charity, should originate at home. We can think of
a few home standards that might profitably be re-examined: standards
of instructional effectiveness (especially for freshmen); standards of
resource availability (*Must* the top scholars, the richest libraries, the
most intimate classes be reserved exclusively for graduate students?);
standards of housing, both for students and program; standards of
cleanliness and beauty in the physical arrangements; standards of
human concern in the organizational and administrative pattern; standards of warmth and trust in the relationships among students, faculty,
and staff. The list is long. If we could choose only one to work on, we'd
start with standards of instruction.

We all know teachers whose "flunk list" is chronically long. They
take pride in this fact. They secretly scorn their colleagues who give A's.
They stand on the fiction that their particular subject is just naturally
harder for the ordinary person. It's difficult for them to see that it may
be their expectations which are unreasonable. It is difficult for them to
feel any real responsibility for the success of more than a few select
students. A parallel attitude may be held by many institutions.

This is a delicate and difficult business. Of course we want people
held to their top effort and helped to their top production. A hospital
counts on the active efforts of its patients. But if very many patients
were lost, a hospital couldn't, if it wanted to, get away with blaming
the patients for not trying or for being a pretty weak lot anyway. It
would feverishly study its own provisions and procedures. Shouldn't

schools and colleges be at least as accountable as hospitals? Shouldn't they measure themselves against their own goals and roles at least as vigorously and rigorously as do hospitals?

Excelsior! By all means, let's raise the banner. But let's be sure first that our own instructional and institutional standards are at the head of the procession upward. To one view, at least, only then can we, in good conscience, ask students to join the climb. That kind of standard-raising rings both loud *and* true.

56. *Practices in School Discipline*

LAWRENCE E. VREDEVOE

Three major trends outside the school are becoming more and more evident as creating problems of discipline within the school itself. These can be summarized as:

1. *The general breakdown in our society of agreement relative to moral and ethical standards of conduct.*

There is a growing confusion concerning attitudes toward right and wrong in both the national and local scenes which is affecting the behavior of students in some schools.

2. *The changing emphasis and attitude toward law enforcement.*

Today it appears that the enforcement agent or agency rather than the criminal or culprit goes on trial. This is becoming of greater concern to many school authorities.

3. *The explosion of population, its increasing mobility and concentration.*

One need but glance at the 51,000,000 below the age of 13 or ninth grade to recognize that the real impact of our increased birth rates has not yet been felt in our secondary school. Associated with this is the tendency of more and more families to change residences frequently and to concentrate in crowded industrial and commercial centers.

These three factors are also reflected in the growing tensions and instability of many homes. Lack of support by the home and community for the schools in their attempt to maintain good discipline makes the problem more difficult.

From Lawrence E. Vredevoe, "Practices in School Discipline," *The American School Board Journal*, CXXXIX (July, 1959), 19–21. Lawrence E. Vredevoe is Professor of Education at the University of California, Los Angeles. Reprinted by permission of The Bruce Publishing Company, Milwaukee.

During a ten-year study of school discipline—which included visits to over 800 schools in 32 states, interviews with more than a thousand administrators and teachers, and 4000 student-answers to questions relative to school discipline—certain factors and practices within the schools which effect the standards of discipline were noted. (The criteria for determining "good discipline" included: courtesy, respect for private and public property, conduct conducive to good working conditions or recreation, co-operation in maintenance of accepted standards and rules, and respect for adults, fellow students, etc.)

CAUSES OF GOOD BEHAVIOR

The factors and practices included:

1. *Alert, competent and positive leadership on the part of school administrators.*

Good discipline does not come naturally but as the result of continual alertness and competent leadership in administrative offices.

One school visited revealed administration which recognized no serious problems of discipline. However, 57 students indicated their greatest fear of being "shaken down" by certain members of a gang for lunch money. In another instance parents appealed to the police for assistance because a certain gang was dominating the activities in their high school. The administration had withdrawn so much from actual contact with the problem of discipline that it was unaware of what actually was happening.

In contrast to these and similar situations are those in which a good citizenship is being maintained in schools located in high delinquency areas and social tension centers. It was quite evident that in these schools the administrators and teachers were alert and competent. They worked constantly with students and parents in their attempt to keep high standards of conduct in their schools. School discipline was not left to a few members of the staff but all were expected to participate and were constantly reminded of their responsibility in maintaining it.

2. *An understanding of the adopted standards and rules, their origin, value, purpose, and their relationship to individual and group welfare and the educational process.*

Many of the rules and standards enforced in schools observed were of themselves unrelated and irrelevant to the primary objectives of the school or group activity. Others which were essential in contributing to a good "climate" or conditions in which to work and study were not understood by teachers in some cases, and students in others. An understanding and participation in formulating standards, rules and desired behavior patterns, and their acceptance by those involved is an important step in establishing better teacher-student relationship in school discipline.

3. *Emphasis upon self-discipline on the part of all individuals in the group.*

This may seem too idealistic but the majority in our democratic society demonstrate daily that they can be relied upon to practice self-discipline if the rules or standards are reasonable and understood. When the individual recognizes that observance is for the greatest good for the greatest number and he understands the essential purpose and values in certain behavior patterns, he can be depended upon to make a sincere attempt to adjust. This will be more true if the individual feels that he has had a part in determining the standards and rules.

Although the majority can be depended upon for self-discipline, the minority or often a very small percentage can make the situation most difficult. How to work effectively in such a way that the desired behavior pattern as well as good teacher-student relationship will occur is the problem which faces the majority of administrators and teachers. In reply to the question of "What gives you greatest concern or worry as you plan for your first teaching position?" asked in interviews with 3000 prospective teachers in the past four years, 2481 gave discipline as their greatest concern. Nineteen hundred seventy-four parents of 2400 who were critical of their secondary schools gave *lack of discipline as one of their basic criticisms.* One hundred four of the 140 selected administrators questioned as to chief reasons for failure to recommend re-employment or dismissal of teachers, gave top ratings to terms which could all be classified in the broad sense under *discipline*.

Critics of certain new courses, activities, and methods introduced in secondary schools seem to place great emphasis upon the apparent lack of "discipline" attributed to these innovations. Often the entire school's program is evaluated by certain individuals primarily by what they consider to be good behavior. Sometimes a careful analysis has revealed that a few nonconformists or problem cases have been selected by critics to use as a basis for judgment of the entire group. Credit for the majority who practice self-discipline is not given because of the few who misrepresent or overshadow the good discipline of the majority.

4. *Methods of dealing with discipline cases.*

Although the problem cases, according to the estimates of administrators, teachers, and students in the school represent only about three to five percent, they often consume a major portion of the class or activity time and the services of those responsible for guidance and student personnel. It is apparent that the constant trouble maker does not deserve or merit the class and activity time and services he now consumes in some schools. At the same time it is not possible to solve the problems by some methods now being employed.

Methods used to deal with discipline cases observed or discovered in the schools visited range all the way to use of the rubber hose, paddle, slapping, whipping, and other forms of corporal punishment to an attempt to ignore the individual. It was interesting that corporal punishment, legal or not, was found more frequently where men teachers were in the majority. Among the men teachers resorting to corporal punishment, other than administrators, were physical education teachers followed by those in social studies. In some schools where corporal punishment was illegal it was administered after giving students a choice of punishments. Interviews with 24 students who had received corporal punishment revealed that a majority preferred it because it was over with quickly. Three claimed they were used to it at home and school so they didn't mind. In another school where a choice was given, two students informed us that you were considered a chicken if you did not select corporal punishment.

It can be stated with little fear that any other study will prove that use of corporal punishment does not solve the problem of discipline. It quickly reaches the point of diminishing returns.

The one form of punishment which students generally dread most but is more difficult to administer is segregation. The trouble maker does not like to live alone and work with himself. When he is removed from contact with his gang, group, friend, or just others, he soon longs to be back with the group. The segregation which is most effective is that in which the student does not eat lunch with the others or has no contact between classes or at dismissal time. One student subject to this type of punishment said, "I got so damn tired of myself that I decided to behave." School authorities should have the right to dismiss the perpetual trouble maker after all other methods have failed. It would also help if facilities were available for *segregation* not *congregation* of these trouble makers.

This principle of *segregation* and periods of *living alone* might have a wholesome effect also in dealing with youth delinquents outside of the school. The present practice of the "bull pen" permitting delinquents to congregate and associate in our jails often breeds rather than deters crime. The "peer group" approval is often more influential than the threats or sentences of the courts.

No general procedure fits all cases but this study indicates that corporal punishment is not the answer. Segregation from others where possible seems to be most effective in the serious cases. It at least prevents the loss of time or services by the 95 per cent who are more deserving of our consideration.

Basic to the solution of the problem of school discipline is an evaluation of the school's program. Whenever the program was discovered to hold challenge for all groups, discipline was a minor problem. Too often our programs are geared to one, two, or three of the groups within the school but not all of them. When the program holds challenge for the gifted, superior, average, and slow learner, school discipline will become less of a problem. This requires competent administrators and teachers, adequate facilities, and community support.

STUDENTS RATING OF DISCIPLINE PRACTICES

Students questioned about the practices which they believed created the best relationships mentioned the following in the order of their frequency:

1. Interpreting the reasons and purposes of the rules
2. Fairness in enforcement
3. Treatment which recognized maturity of student
4. Consistency in enforcement
5. Enforcement without embarrassment whenever possible
6. Observance of the rules by teachers
7. Opportunity to participate in making rules in areas where students are capable
8. Elimination of waste of time of the many for the need to discipline the few. Students believe some teachers spend too much time during the class period with discipline cases which should be taken care of at another time.
9. Making the work so challenging that the students will be kept busy and interested
10. Conduct on the part of the teachers which demonstrates competence in dealing with adolescents. Teachers who can win the respect of their students.

CHARACTERISTICS OF DISCIPLINE TROUBLE-FREE TEACHERS

The following are the characteristics of teachers who have the least trouble with discipline in their classrooms:

1. Competent in teaching area
2. Knowledge of biological, sociological, and psychological characteristics of adolescents
3. Sense of security in position, administrative relations, and parental and public relations
4. Professional conduct, manners and appearance
5. Sincere interest in adolescence and teaching.

IN SUMMARY

In summary of observations and comments by teachers and students, it is evident that good discipline is essential to have good schools and it is to be found in many schools and classrooms today. Practices which bring about better relationships are those not so much related to the punishment of the transgressors but in the methods of development and interpretation of the standards and the rules. Good conduct and good citizenship should begin with the faculty members. Competence on the part of teachers who have a feeling of confidence and security is basic in developing good relationships with students. Whenever punishment or disciplinary measures are required they should be suited to the individual rather than the transgression. Fairness, consistency, and understanding should be characteristic of teachers in their treatment of disciplinary cases. Good discipline and teacher-student relationship is the result of intelligent, co-operative, continuing, and united efforts on the part of all staff members and student leaders.

57. *Evaluation as Teaching*

GEORGE H. COOKE

From time to time certain problems seem to come to the attention of people interested in testing. The use of questions as a device for encouraging thinking, research, and learning is as old as teaching. The questions posed in the following paragraphs do not represent all of the uncertainties of testing, and the discussions may not receive an A from the reader. It can be claimed, with little or no dispute, that at least one person gained insights by exploring his own experiences in an effort to formulate the questions and the discussions.

1. *How free are respondents to essay questions?*

The respondent is usually free to choose his own words. If the question demands a reproduction of certain knowledges, particular understandings or established relationships, the respondent is trapped. He realizes the teacher has a model on paper or a mental conception of the right answer. His aim then is to come as close to the model as possible. An essay question which has been stated with directions to guide the respondent, to identify clearly the desired approaches, the ground to be covered, is one which restricts the freedom of the pupil. The components of the answer are suggested and it becomes the task of the pupil to follow the outline. There is, however, a degree of respectability in such questions; one-third of the essay questions of a recent

From George H. Cooke, "What Is a Question but a Quest?" *Peabody Journal of Education*, XXXIX (March, 1962), 274–282. George H. Cooke is Associate Professor of Secondary Education, Kent State University, Kent, Ohio, and a member of the Advisory Committee of the Ohio Scholarship Tests of the State of Ohio. Reprinted by permission of the *Peabody Journal of Education*.

collection were of this variety. These restrictive essay tests have severe limitations in achieving the merits usually claimed for this form of educational measurement.

There may be a place for the restricted essay test but it should be realized that such questions are designed to measure sheer knowledge and memory rather than functional understanding. Such questions do not require pupils to organize answers or select their own method of attack.

The sincere protagonist of the essay examination will want considerable freedom for the respondents. The question itself will need to be a novel problem or one with a new approach to the topic or subject. The purpose is to see how the pupils can deal with a knotty problem. There may be many approaches open to the pupil. But the problem should afford an opportunity to demonstrate qualities, abilities, and understandings prized by the person who posed the question or topic. The pupils have freedom to show what they can do toward providing their own organization, their own sequence, their own selection of main topics.

The freer the respondents are, the greater is the problem of grading, but the reading of the answers will be more interesting and more revealing of pupil abilities than if the responses were restricted. A question of this nature will be a challenge to the superior pupil but baffling to the mediocre and difficult for those who do not write easily and fluently.

The degree and kind of freedom experienced by pupils is governed to no small degree by past experiences with a particular teacher. Some teachers may hope and expect an essence of the topic, or the use of certain terms or clichés. Other teachers might be pleased when pupils propose definitions of terms in the question, and state qualifications and criteria for their following statements. These same teachers will have respect for the courageous pupils who strike out into some heretofore unexplored area with a balanced attack on the problem. These teachers will seldom have an anticipated answer but are primarily concerned with how pupils attempt to answer the question. They will be interested in their style and level of sophistication, with the clarity of expression, with the sequence with which the pupils marshall and organize their knowledge and thinking. But it is true that different teachers have individual requirements for acceptable responses to essay questions, and wise pupils will recognize these differences in teachers.

2. *How critical are the "evils" of guessing and bluffing?*

In this troubled world of rapid changes there seems to be less certainty than ever before. Perhaps it is lifelike to guess, to estimate, to propose tentative solutions. The scientists call these shrewd guesses, hypotheses. The investor for quick profits on the stock market, the weatherman, the bridge player who attempts a finesse, in the final analysis, all make guesses or choices. It is true that such guessing is not blind, but this is likely to be the same on a test. Seldom will a pupil be found whose knowledge and understanding of a question is zero by any measurement.

Bluffing is another form of guessing, and it too is a natural reaction. When is there a speaker fully prepared for his platform obligation, or the professor who is completely ready for his class, or the plumber for his next household job? Instead these people and others attempt to meet their assignments to the best of their abilities. Pupils may not head directly toward an acceptable response, but they realize that if they start thinking and writing, these activities may lead toward a suitable response. In the essay response the teachers should be interested in the processes used by pupils in dealing with thought provoking problems. If the question is a novel problem, the teachers should expect some amount of fumbling toward an adequate response. Pupils may, like most of us, need to explore their mental resources, gather momentum and to a degree, evaluate possible approaches.

However, an essay test in some school subjects is not the place for vague, irrelevant obfuscations on the part of pupils. Pupils should receive credit for clear, concise replies and be criticized for failure to meet head-on the question. The terms guessing and bluffing are not very desirable terms in measurement and evaluation and seldom describe the real situation.

3. *How objective are objective tests?*

Objectivity in educational measurement refers only to the extent that performances, products, or tests may be graded with consistency. Objectivity refers mainly to scoring and grading. Misinterpretations are frequently made by the less sophisticated concerning this term. The naive may suggest that an objective test is a scientific product, or is an infallible instrument, or is one devoid of any human touch or foible.

It seems to be forgotten that teachers make the following decisions concerning objective tests: When shall the test be given? What is to be the nature of the questions? How many questions? Which will be acceptable answers? How important is the test? What will be the level of difficulty? These are not objective but are subjective judgments.

Seldom will a professional testmaker, let alone a classroom teacher, be able to construct a test and a key without having a number of questionable exercises or debatable answers. When test exercises are seriously considered by pupils, and if they are given the opportunity to criticize the questions and answers, there will be errors or weaknesses brought to the attention of the testmaker. These comments on the objective tests should not lead one to think that essay questions are beyond the same analyses and criticisms.

The question of objectivity in making choices and reacting to the problems of life is realistic. People who require an answer to a question will frequently admonish the respondent to be objective in his reply. Responses are always a product distilled from the total experience of the person being questioned. It is almost impossible to separate the intellect from the total background. This same condition exists when teachers grade responses to tests except when scoring a perfectly made objective-type test.

The most important choices in our daily living, and the decisions made by leaders at all levels cannot be reduced to making these choices in a purely objective manner.

Finally, there is no royal road for teachers or for any other leader to the perplexing problem of evaluating the efforts and the status of people. There is no escape from subjective judgment. There is no infallible set of balances by which the worth, the relative position, or the progress of pupils can be weighed or measured. Since teachers will be forced to judge pupils, considerable evidence should be available to afford adequate support for final decisions and judgments.

4. *Are essay tests diagnostic and projective techniques?*

If pupils are required to write on a good question and the replies are carefully reviewed, these outcomes are possible. The teachers are able to secure a general idea of the vocabulary of the pupils. The abilities of the pupils to write will be revealed. The degree to which pupils can recall and make good use of knowledge will be apparent in an essay test. Such a test may also bring to the teachers' attention certain personal attributes, e.g., creativeness, boldness, ingenuity, careful thinking, as well as the opposites of these qualities. In high school it is quite possible to find pupils who are unable to express their ideas or knowledge in a paragraph.

The nature of the question will be a factor in determining its projective values. If pupils are directed to feel free in their responses and there is a high degree of rapport in the class, emotional and intellectual reactions may be revealed. Pupils will respond with their personal beliefs and will tend to reveal their true feelings if their previous responses have been treated with sympathy and understanding.

Essay tests should result in a written record of pupils thinking their way through a problem. Their efforts should be of interest and concern whether the answers are acceptable or not acceptable. Good essay questions are directed toward a large chunk of subject matter and the replies will be an indication of their grasp of large ideas and concepts.

Furthermore, a properly marked test will have an abundance of comments by the grader. These comments should be clear and complete statements rather than a single word. Since teachers have encouraged the pupils to write their personal opinions and to reveal their true feelings, the teachers have an obligation to respond in similar fashion.

Diagnostic, intuitive, analytical reading of free response to a novel problem should provide new insights of pupils. Reading examinations in this manner supersedes the usual reading, more properly called, marking or correcting papers.

5. *Do classroom tests reflect the functional understandings of the subject or topic by the teacher?*

The answer is an unequivocal yes. This answer is as strongly affirmative for testing as it is for teaching and has the same limitations. The teacher who has a strong background, in all that this implies, ought to know what is important enough for a test question and what is of fringe importance. The teacher with a rich background should have within his own understanding the main principles and large concepts. These teachers should be able to devise test exercises which will probe the depths of knowledge and understandings of pupils. Teachers with keen subject matter insights are likely to be constantly thinking of problems and applications not only for teaching but for testing.

Teachers with an inadequate knowledge and understanding are limited to the superficial structure of the subject. Test exercises involving applications of principles to novel and everyday experiences will be less likely to originate with teachers who lack adequate background. Teachers who lack a functional understanding of a subject may not recognize a different but a right answer to an objective question or may not be able to follow the reasoning of a pupil who has made a choice which is different than the key. The same handicap may also prevent a teacher from perceiving the virtue and worth of a virgin approach to an essay question. In short, the pupils' responses may be beyond the intellectual scope of the grader. It is human to be suspicious or wary of an innovation. Thus these teachers may either miss the merit of a response or penalize the pupils because the answers are unforeseen.

6. *Are facts in an area of study to be considered of major importance?*

Yes, there is nothing more significant than important facts in an area of study. Most of these facts have been established through great efforts on the part of research workers. To some extent there is a negative feeling against mastery of subject matter or of the established facts. It should be apparent to all that facts do change just as thinking and understanding change, but at the moment the recognized knowledge and the accepted facts are the bases for thinking. Pupils with true understanding recognize the values of a rich background of significant facts. Pupils and others may object to the teaching and testing of facts. In a sense these objections point out to the discerning on-looker the superficiality of the alleged understandings claimed by learners.

Teachers need not apologize for teaching and testing for knowledge of facts. It is hoped that both teaching and testing will go beyond knowledge of facts. Facts are not unrelated to understanding. A test requiring knowledge of significant facts which are imbedded in meanings are valid materials for testing. Facts which have been taught as having rich implications in meanings and relationships are valid indications of understandings. This process is not complete proof of understanding, perhaps there is no complete proof, but such a process will provide the first step toward proof.

7. Have teachers and others made a fetish or god of consistency or objectivity in grading papers, performances, and products of learners?

Yes, as a result of the studies in the early decades of this century in this country and in England, objectivity in grading has been emphasized beyond its value. The discussion of question three provided a working definition of objectivity in grading. The scoring of pure recognition tests is almost one hundred per cent objective. In fact, a clerk or even a machine can score certain tests with complete accuracy and unimpeachable objectivity. Teachers cannot be limited to tests graded by machines if they wish to make a complete evaluation of the total growth and status of pupils. Even so, research workers have obtained high correlations among graders of English compositions by controlling the methods of grading.

Teachers are assumed to be persons of integrity and of good intentions but human. They read papers, view performances, and examine products. These same teachers exercise judgment, give consideration to the total situation, have insights and finally make records via marks, grades or comments. If such teachers are required to prove the accuracy of the grades and comments, there is little recourse except to reaffirm the qualities utilized. Just as a person decides to invest in a certain stock, when questioned as to whether his choice of stock was right beyond all doubt, he could only respond in terms of his experience, his judgment and his insights.

To require a teacher to regrade an answer to a true essay question, or to regrade a whole paper, is asking the impossible. While the papers do not change the teacher undergoes considerable change. It must be assumed that teachers grade the work of pupils with skill and integrity.

More confidence is needed by teachers in their ability to show good judgment in evaluative processes.

8. Have schools placed too much emphasis on classroom testing and on the total school program of measuring the many human qualities of pupils?

There are growing reactions against the rip-tide of tests forced upon schools and upon pupils. New tests are added to the programs and none is eliminated. Colleges and universities are overwhelmed by applicants and are forced to screen out those with less potential ability. Various foundations are searching for talented pupils and tests are the chief instruments of identifying them. The people in guidance work want more information in order to do more effective personnel work. Teachers are urged to use tests issued by state test bureaus and to be alert to the advantages of frequent checks in the academic progress of pupils. There are other pressures which have resulted in an over-emphasis in some schools of measurement to the detriment of or distraction from teaching and learning.

Schools should examine their total program of testing, grade by grade. Are too many tests given in a particular grade level? How much use is made of test results? Is it necessary to give the same tests to all pupils? Must all of the tests be given during school? Do teachers give tests as punishments or to keep pupils busy? Do the tests contribute to the welfare of pupils? Are the tests used to glorify the school or staff?

Tests used in the wrong manner may give unwarranted emphasis on intra-class competition. This is not to overlook the value and merits of competition but it should be controlled. All tests should not be used for the purposes of classifying, segregating, and ranking pupils. There are more significant values to a total program of evaluation. It is claimed that tests are needed to motivate or drive pupils to study and that tests offer proof of progress. Whether tests are good motivators depends more on the quality of the tests and their concomitant use than on the threat of a test. Perhaps teachers are looking for easy and quick methods to secure evidence of pupil growth and proof of teaching success.

Tests should be viewed as implements whose purposes are to aid in carrying out the functions of the schools. Like all instruments placed in the hands of amateurs, damage may be done not only to the stock but to the instrument or technique. Practitioners of tests and measurements who have thought rigorously about the field no longer believe in the power of a single test to perform miracles concerning the complex organization called man. But there is little doubt in the minds of these people concerning the values of a valid test as contributing to the solution of some of the educational problems.

9. *Do pupils learn while being examined in school subjects?*

Yes, if this were not true, one of the important values of testing would be lost. Pupils tend to learn whatever is given emphasis in the tests. The pupils are faced with test exercises and must search into their own resources for responses. The desired response may not be ready for use, but by thinking, by reorganizing their knowledge, and by reviewing understandings, they arrive at a response; thus new learning is created and emerges via a test response. Perhaps the question is a novel one which forces them to consider how they can use their organized knowledge in a new way. The pupils are required to consider the best means of analyzing the question; they must derive meanings from the terms of the question and mentally weigh their tentative solutions. This is also learning.

A test whether by intention or not tends to be a summation of the teachers' concepts of significant ideas. Pupils are or should be directed, encouraged and led to bring together in a test what was here-to-fore unrelated laws, facts, and sequences to a point of usefulness and to a level of understanding not previously achieved.

10. *Should teachers experiment with a variety of evaluative procedures?*

Yes, the best and final method of measuring progress or achievement has not been discovered or perfected. Teachers may believe that they have found the one and only way to do this important work. They should remember that teachers urge pupils to consider new and different approaches to problems in life. How could teachers ever do a better job in this respect than to demonstrate their own ability and interest in creativity than by trying out a new test question or devising a new measuring technique or modifying an existing one?

All pupils do not respond equally well to the same form of evaluation. There are hundreds of forms of the objective test and an unlimited number of ways of stating essay problems. Procedures for evaluating pupils should not be limited to pencil and paper tests but include products, performances, oral examinations, and observation of procedures in laboratory courses.

Many people are critical of questions, tests and evaluative procedures, but few do anything about improving the situation. A variety in the test questions or the evaluative techniques will be of interest for pupils and tends to develop a certain amount of desirable pupil adjustability. Further consideration of improving this part of teaching responsibility should contribute to the personal growth of teachers and advance the status of the teaching profession.

58. *Testing as a Teaching Device*

NICHOLAS A. FATTU

Experienced teachers have long recognized that testing was one of the most effective ways of insuring that a given educational objective would be mastered. Testing can help the teacher by giving him a means of effective study of the instructional process—its goals and its outcomes. Testing also can help the student by clarifying what is to be learned and by indicating the nature and extent of his progress in the desired direction.

The example below indicates how testing produced significant improvements in teaching and learning. To do so, testing went hand in hand with instructional planning, and the results of testing were constantly used to direct the planning of the course offerings.

Example:

Basic Engineering, a course for Navy enlisted men, was designed to prepare men for performance of various tasks in the engine room of a ship. Three-sevenths of the time in the course was devoted to classroom work and four-sevenths to shop work. Instructional units, requiring from one to five weeks, covered such equipment as diesel engines, refrigerators, boilers and turbines, pumps and valves, etc. Before intensive work in testing was started, it was noted that graduates seemed well-prepared in their academic work but lacked ability to do the jobs that required the technical "know-how" they had presumably learned in the shop. For instance, on a typical unit, diesel engines, it was observed that students could pass a pencil-paper test, but seemed to fail far too often on such tasks as operating the engine properly, replacing and timing an injector, etc. A comprehensive testing program was set up, as one of the tasks under NDRC Project N-106. Besides standardized pencil-paper tests of classroom performance, an intensive effort was made to develop performance tests of the shop skills. All tests

From Nicholas A. Fattu, "Testing as a Teaching Device," *The High School Journal,* XLI (December, 1957), 79–82. Nicholas A. Fattu is Professor of Educational Psychology, Director of the Institute of Educational Research, and Director of the Division of Research, School of Education, Indiana University, Bloomington, Indiana. Reprinted from *The High School Journal* by permission.

were developed through the joint efforts of a test specialist and the instructors in the course.

As performance tests were developed and used in one instructional unit after another, an interesting trend was observed.[1] When the performance test was first used, the average score was about 20 to 25 points out of a possible 100. As each successive class passed through the instructional unit, the scores continued to go up, until they stabilized (in the fifth to seventh successive class) at an average level of about 80 to 90 points. Thus trainees, in the sixth class through an instructional unit typically averaged 300 per cent or higher scores than those in the first class!

Since the performance tests covered the tasks that students had to perform later on the job, this meant that they were correspondingly better prepared for their jobs.

It is interesting to note that classroom learning did not suffer during this period. In one school, on a comprehensive standardized pencil-paper test of classroom learning, scores increased from a mean of 70.3 (before improved testing) to 105.5 (after). In another school the mean scores were 61.3 (before) and 101.5 (after).

It has been indicated that tests can have a powerful influence on learning if they are designed to attain the same goals as the teaching process. It should be added that testing can also produce undesirable results when badly used. The New York State Regents examinations, for a while, had the unfortunate effect of turning secondary schools into cramming schools directed toward the probable content of the next examination as revealed by past examinations. Such unwarranted control over the teaching process defeats the purpose of the examination and also puts a hurdle in the way of education itself.

Tests are effective teaching devices only when they are used as an integral part of the teaching process. When the teaching is planned, the measurement should be planned. The testing program must be as closely related to the objectives you are trying to achieve as is the instruction. Under these conditions tests can help the teacher in several steps of the instructional program:

1. They can help clarify the objectives to aim at or the changes to seek in students.
2. They can help determine what content and learning experience can best be used to attain these objectives.

[1] These data are taken from the author's notes. Some of the data are referred to in Gulliksen, H., "Intrinsic validity," *American Psychologist* 5:511–517, 1950; Stuit (40); Porter, R. B., and Fattu, N. A., "Test development in Basic Engineering," *Proceedings of the Joint Meeting of the Bureau of Naval Personnel, Standards and Curriculum Division, and NDRC Project N-106,* February 1945, pp. 70–75.

3. They can help determine an effective organization of the learning so that its effect will be cumulative.
4. They can help to appraise the effects of learning experiences—to find out where they have been effective and where they have not produced the results desired.

Although only step four is commonly associated with measurement, it is not possible to measure unless the major objectives have been identified *specifically* and defined in terms of *specific* phases of pupil behavior—knowledge, information, skills, interests, work habits, etc.

Instruction is most efficient when it is directed. An instructor needs to determine the objectives he aims at and to select those that can be reasonably attained.

Although careful selection and specification of objectives is recognized as important, actually many schools and teachers carry on their instruction without having a clear outline of the goals to be attained. Many find themselves using a particular instructional procedure or book because they have used it many years and accept it as useful without any clear notion of the underlying purpose.

It is entirely possible to carry on an instructional program for years without clearly specifying objectives. It is *not* possible to construct a valid achievement test, or to use one properly, without definitely clarifying the objectives that the test is to measure.

This imperative need of testing to have objectives stated in specific terms, rather than vague generalities, can stimulate the teachers to study the objectives and carry the analysis to a degree of definiteness that could not occur if the testing problem were not present. Educational measurement can help in selecting and clarifying educational objectives by stimulating the faculty to express these objectives clearly in terms of desired behaviors. When teachers focus their attention specifically on the goals, surprising clarification can arise. This improves instruction by giving it a definite goal rather than a vague one.

Testing also provides a means for obtaining data about student performance. These data can be used for making a rational choice of objectives. Testing helps in selecting content and learning experiences. By indicating level of student attainment, test data provide a basis for noting the rate at which students attain the objectives. This suggests the levels of content, instructional materials and procedures that are likely to be effective. Analyses of test results can indicate if failure to attain objectives was due to poor material or procedures. Test results thus provide a rational basis for continued improvement of course content and learning experiences.

In organizing learning experiences, the intent is to combine them so that their cumulative effect will be the greatest possible. Testing contributes to organization by stimulating teachers to inquire into the bases of organization. As with objectives, it is quite possible to teach without being aware of the organization in the program one is teaching. However, it is not possible to construct an effective comprehensive achievement test in a course without specifying the organization. This is a significant achievement, because one's organization of a course will not be improved, unless it is explicitly identified by the teacher himself.

Testing also can contribute to organization of instruction by providing a means of checking effectiveness of various alternatives in organization. This can separate those that are effective, and call attention to those that do not work.

Testing can thus contribute to the education of teachers in service. It stimulates the development of understanding of teachers by giving them a means of effective study of the instructional process and its outcomes.

Tyler has indicated that

> "Many of the present inadequacies of instruction are due to the common tradition in many schools of making no significant changes in the instructional program over the years, or the equally unintelligent practice in many other schools of making changes on the basis of current fads or personal whims of the staff.
>
> ". . . Educational measurement can have a profound influence in the improvement of instruction; but to do so, it must be viewed as an integral part of instruction, its planning must go hand in hand with instructional planning, and the results must be used continuously to guide the planning and development of the curriculum."[2]

[2] Tyler, R. W., "The Functions of Measurement in Improving Instruction," Chapter 2 in E. F. Lindquist (editor) *Educational Measurement*, Washington, D.C.: American Council on Education, 1951.

59. Report Cards and Marking

STANLEY E. JACKSON

In many communities across the nation committees are at work improving the school's report card. Sooner or later in the deliberations of these groups there usually comes a troublesome problem: What mark-

From Stanley E. Jackson, "Report Cards, The Marking Problem," *The National Elementary Principal*, XXXV, No. 5 (February, 1956), 27–30. Stanley E. Jackson is Principal of the Grant, Stevens, and Sumner Elementary Schools, Washington, D.C. Reprinted from *The National Elementary Principal* by permission.

ing system shall be used for the report cards?" The answer to this difficult question may be influenced by many factors, some of which are discussed here.

A committee for report card revision can be confronted with many diverse and conflicting recommendations for a marking system. Pressures from the community may demand letter grades such as A-B-C-D-F. Some teachers and parents may be insistent upon the use of checklists that will indicate "outstanding progress," or "needs much improvement." Others may suggest using a five-point number scale similar to the A-B-C letter grades. A few may favor a percent system. There may be those who believe there should be a less refined marking system with only "S" for satisfactory and "U" for unsatisfactory as the symbols used. With all these differing suggestions, it will not be easy for a committee to arrive at a marking system that will be acceptable to a majority. Faced with so many different types of marking systems, a committee will need some guides for determining which system will best meet its needs.

In arriving at a decision, four questions might be asked. First, *what purposes are marks assumed to serve?* This is an important question because it directs the thinking of individuals to basic ideas upon which intelligent action depends.

As purposes are revealed, a second question arises: *Do marks meet these purposes?* School marks and reporting should reflect the philosophy and curriculum of the school since the child is supposed to be evaluated on the basis of his growth within the curriculum built upon that philosophy.

When purposes have been enumerated and relationships between purposes, curriculum, and philosophy of education have been established, a third question comes to mind: *Which marking system best meets the purposes of this community?* Each community should decide for itself which marking system best meets its needs. The way the community looks at education, the curriculum in the schools, and the relationships of school and community will have a bearing on the answer to this question.

A fourth question should be posed for broadening and extending the thinking of all concerned in the matter of marking: *Are there better ways of evaluating the growth of children?* It might be discovered that marks are not absolutely necessary in pupil evaluaton.

Answers to the first question, "What purposes are marks assumed to serve?", will probably bring to light many viewpoints. People will vary in their ideas—both expressed and implied—as to purposes to be served by marks. Here are some of the purposes that are likely to be revealed. One purpose might be to give information for child guidance. Other purposes might be to show the achievement of the child in relation to his age peers, to his grade group, and to his ability. Some purposes might be to aid administrators in grouping and placing children; to give desired information to employers, schools and universities; to make possible the giving of rewards and honors as well as penalties and punishments; and to motivate children to do their best. Three other purposes, tho implied in some of the others, might be expressed this way: to aid communication between home and school; to provide a check for parents on what children are doing in school; to identify the child's strengths and weaknesses.

Answers to the second question, "Do marks meet these purposes?", will vary widely. There may be a response that marks meet their purposes in some instances and not in others. Other answers may indicate that marks meet the purposes they were designed to serve, with varying degrees of success. It is highly probable that there will be no single answer to the question.

We can understand why there will probably be no single answer if we take a look at a fairly typical school situation. Report cards in school system "X" are based upon a philosophy of education emphasizing academic achievement. In the report are listed specific outcomes of achievement expected in the three R's and other academic school subjects. A marking system of A-B-C-D-F is used since it is believed that each item on the report card is specific and objective enough to permit each mark given to be valid and reliable.

A critical look at specific pupil report cards soon reveals that the reason for the various items are difficult to interpret. For example, there is an item which says "Uses language well." The mark here is an "A." What does that "A" mean? Does it mean the child is excellent in *all* uses of language? Does this sixth-grader have an excellent creative vocabulary? Is his written and spoken language grammatically excellent? Is he excellent in communicating his thoughts in all circumstances? Does he write excellent letters and compositions? Furthermore, he is excellent by what standard: grade level, ability, others in his group, children his age in the United States? Analysis of the other items and interpretations of the marks soon make it obvious that one mark seldom represents a single outcome or several identical outcomes. It becomes doubtful if any mark tells adequately the level of achievement and progress a child has made.

Studies of teachers' marks have revealed that marks are affected by such factors as pupil interests, effort, degree to which child has grown, teacher prejudices and biases, pupil personality and attendance, as well as achievement. The more influences that are brought to bear in arriving at a mark the less reliable and valid that mark becomes. Pupil interest, effort, and achievement may be combined in the mark, together with many other factors. What, then, does a single mark mean?

The validity and reliability of a mark can be increased to the degree that the items marked are specific and objective. For example, the item on a report card under the general heading of "Typing" says "Can type 65 words or more per minute." If a child is rated "A" in this specific objective behavior outcome, it may be assumed that he can type 65 words or more per minute. The teachers in the school system can agree that in order for a child to receive "A" in this particular item he must meet the definite requirements specified by the item. Specific levels of competence are established for this item so that each teacher knows what represents "B" achievement (typing 50–64 words per minute), "C" achievement (typing 40–49 words per minute), and so on down the scale. Thus this particular item can be marked with reasonable accuracy by each teacher.

If marks are to have a high degree of validity and reliability, it would seem logical that the report card would have the kind of specific, objective items that would make this possible. A mark for each item would then mean about the same thing in any school, and any one teacher could mark a child with the same degree of accuracy as any other teacher. This would probably mean, tho, that a report card would be limited to only those items that lend themselves to specific, objective statements.

A careful examination of the intermediate-grade report card of school system "X" shows that the item listed under "Typing" is one of very few specific and objective statements. Other areas on the report card such as "Reading," "Social Studies," "Language," and "Science" do not have such exact statements to be marked. The marks given in those areas are open to many interpretations, and the validity and reliability of the marks are sharply reduced.

School system "X" assumes that its marks serve the purposes of evaluation and reporting. However, close examination has revealed that it is highly questionable if the marks really meet their purposes. When the meaning of marks is so uncertain, do they really have much worth?

School system "Y" has developed report cards that reflect a broader philosophy of education than that of school system "X." This particular school system does not use the A-B-C type of marking system, but there is doubt if the marks it does use are meeting their purposes. Here is the story.

School system "Y" believes that the school should not emphasize academic achievement at the expense of emotional, physical, aesthetic and social growth. It believes in helping each child become the best person he is capable of becoming, able to cope intelligently with the problems of living. The report cards have, of necessity, broad statements of behavioral outcomes in many areas of growth.

Over a period of years, school system "Y" tried several types of marking systems. At one time the percent system was used. Another time A-B-C-D-F marks were tried. Later, a numerical five-point rating scale was attempted. These marking systems were not successful. Attempts to use a refined rating system to rate meaningfully such areas of growth as citizenship, aesthetic interest and ability, physical growth and development, and social skills became almost impossible. Marks became vague and obscure in meaning in relation to the degree that the assigned items were specific and objective. Furthermore, there were few suitable tests in many of the areas covered on the report card to permit evaluation with a high degree of objectivity. A percentage marking system and a five-point rating scale became almost worthless because they were unable to convey accurate information. To repeat, the items to be marked lacked the specificity and objectivity needed for a refined marking system.

The school system decided to change from a five-point rating scale to a less refined one since the community insisted upon some kind of marking system being used in place of the unsuitable, refined scale. Now in use is "S" (satisfactory) and "U" (unsatisfactory). While these two marks are less refined and seem more suitable for the report card of school system "Y" than the five-point scale, this marking system, too, has been accused of not meeting its purposes. Rating systems of "S" and "U" or comparable symbols are believed to be too gross in meaning to be of much value.

It can be seen that marks do not seem to be meeting the purposes they are assumed to serve. Yet many communities are insisting upon the use of numbers or letters that are representative of a comparative rating scale. The community and school sometimes believe that the use of symbols is easily understood and conveys accurate information. This belief often turns out to be a delusion, a fallacy. A marking system does not necessarily mean what it purports to convey. Its value may depend upon what is being marked, who is doing the marking, and who interprets the mark. What often looks like a communicative bargain turns out to be a worthless product.

A fuller answer to the question, "Do marks meet their purposes?", would reveal further shortcomings. Some adults may insist that a marking system helps to motivate pupils. It is said that pupils work harder because of marks. Marks give the pupils definite knowledge of their progress. This may be true as far as it goes. A closer study often reveals that in the process of motivating and informing, marks also cause many undesirable results to be generated. Children may be learning to cheat while they are being motivated to achieve. They can be working for a mark rather than for the functional acquisition of the knowledge and skills the mark is supposed to represent. When pupils are of average or below average ability they may become frustrated because of the realization that the "A" and "B" or whatever are the symbols representing high achievement are out of their reach, no matter how hard they try to achieve. Children may be developing feelings of inferiority or superiority, depending upon the marks received. The motivation may prove to be highly superficial. Once the mark is removed, effort and achievement may sink, temporarily, to a low ebb since attention was being given primarily not to the tasks at hand, but to the extrinsic motivation.

Many individuals say that marks prepare pupils for the competition they will meet later in life. Is the kind of competition that is fostered by marks desirable? Competition is important, yes, but should it be the kind that may foster dishonesty, frustration, inferiority, superiority, and an unrealistic view of the pupil's ability? The justification of marks as a means of preparing children to face competition in later life seems highly questionable in the light of the undesirable attitudes and traits this kind of competition can foster.

There is a likelihood that marks may influence the emphasis on subject matter in the school to the neglect of the whole child. Achievement in subject matter seems easier to mark than most other facets of the school program. Furthermore, a subject-centered curriculum, together with marks, may encourage dull routine and uninspired teaching. Some teachers may hold marks over the heads of pupils as clubs and depend upon the mark for the stimulation of effort and achievement rather than upon the intrinsic worth of the school's activities.

A report card revision committee will have to come to its own conclusion as to whether or not marks meet the purposes they are assumed to serve. When this conclusion is reached, the committee will probably want to pass on to a third question: "Which marking system best meets the purposes of this community?"

If it is believed that the school's major function is to teach narrowly prescribed subject matter, regardless of the interests and abilities of children, a refined system of marking with narrow purposes may be more desirable than a broad, general system of marking. Furthermore, if the school believes that children are naturally disposed to resist all efforts to grow and develop along desirable lines, it may follow that a marking system is needed that will prod children to greater efforts. On the other hand, the school that believes in developing individual differences and in helping children become the best they are capable of becoming in a democratic society will probably find traditional methods of marking to be inadequate for the school's broad objectives.

In arriving at a decision as to what type of marks to use, a particular community must concentrate on its own needs and not be unduly concerned about what other communities are doing. Purposes can be clearly and definitively determined on the basis of the needs of school and community. The content of the report card and its marking system may be developed in the light of meeting those needs and purposes.

When there is dissatisfaction concerning the selection of a marking system, or when the marking system selected seems inadequate, it would be wise for a report card revision committee to answer a fourth question: "Are there better ways of evaluating the growth of children?"

Evaluation is a continuous process. The report card represents just one phase of the evaluation process. There are many other ways of reporting to parents. When these other ways are effectively utilized the report card with its marks can take its place as a summary statement in the process of evaluation. A report card can summarize the progress of the child at regular intervals for the benefit of the parent. This summary can help the parent do a better job in aiding the school to guide the child toward his best development.

Using ways of reporting other than a formal report card will help de-emphasize the importance commonly attached to marks. In addition to a regular report card, ways of reporting to parents may include planned and informal parent-teacher conferences, telephone calls, notes to parents, anecdotal records, cumulative records, summary statements, home visits and special meetings.

Personal conferences should be carefully planned and notes to parents should be carefully written in order to insure effective and friendly communication. Reporting should be positive and constructive, telling the parent not only the achievement and progress of the child but how and why the report is made. Reporting "months" might be better than reporting "days" so that teachers can have time to do a more efficient job of reporting to the parents of each child.

A committee for report card revision may conclude that report cards and marks will be with us for a long time to come. With this conclusion may come stronger efforts to develop better ways of evaluating and reporting to compensate for whatever deficiencies are found in the marks and report cards now used. Eventually, perhaps, the use of symbols will become unnecessary as the school is able to give to parents periodically a complete and effective analysis of the child's strengths and weaknesses, present evidence to support the analysis and then, as a result, give specific recommendations for the guidance of the child. Whatever the course, this primary aim in reporting to parents should be constantly before the committee as a guidepost: *to provide the information necessary for a sound working relationship between the school and the home in the guidance of the child.*

60. Considerations for Homogeneous Grouping
DOUGLAS E. LAWSON

INTRODUCTION

The entire history of education during the past century reflects many conflicting and confused opinions concerning the application of democratic principles in school operation and administration. Perhaps nowhere have the divergencies been wider nor the crosscurrents of ideas more confused and confusing than in the single area relating to grouping, classification, and promotion (or retention) of pupils.

Into this conflict have been thrown many pertinent and some rather irrelevant questions. Does a pupil fail—or is it the school that fails? Are differences in ability basic or do the faults lie with the environment and poor motivation? Does retention result in better, or poorer, learning in the succeeding year? Is the one-year-at-a-time system of promotion consistent with the facts of variation in growth patterns? Is it democratic to group pupils in accordance with their abilities? Do we have adequate testing devices to justify ability grouping? Can homogeneous grouping be justified even if no two children are identical in ability or learning capacity? Will special promotion cause social or emotional maladjustment of the child? Has our present grade-organization system outlived its usefulness? Are special promotions administratively feasible? Are they democratic? And, finally, if homogeneous grouping is to be attempted, what bases of differentiation will be used?

Various philosophical viewpoints hold that the *summum bonum* lies within an ultimate happiness for man, or that it rests with an ultimate "self-realization" of each child's spiritual being, or that only continuous growth and adaptation can be sought. In the light of these viewpoints it is important to ask how the various ideologies measure the validity of arguments for or against homogeneous grouping of pupils.

From Douglas E. Lawson, "An Analysis of Historic and Philosophic Considerations for Homogeneous Grouping," *Educational Administration and Supervision*, XLIII (May, 1957), 257–270. At the time of his death in 1961 Douglas E. Lawson was Research Professor of Educational Administration, Southern Illinois University, Carbondale, Illinois. Reprinted by permission of the A. M. S. Reprint Company, New York, Abrahams Magazine Service, Inc.

1. *The perennialist-idealist's stake in homogeneous grouping.* The perennialist-idealist, interested in classical cultural values, is apt to argue that first consideration be given to the "right" curriculum. To say that there is no "right" curriculum for all children is to destroy his faith in mental discipline, the child's will, and individual responsibility. It is to place in question all fixed educational values. If asked why the school should not differentiate groups of children and correspondingly differentiate curricular requirements to meet their individual needs, he is apt to reply, as did one early school committee, that the distribution of native abilities among children "is made by a higher power than our own, and that it is fruitless to confound the eternal distinctions of things" (*1*).

Or, disclaiming all responsibility for less capable pupils, he might agree with Nathaniel Thayer, who insisted that it was necessary "to be rid of those who stand at zero" and who happily predicted that "they will either take a hint from their own averages, and bid us good bye, or they will very quietly, and 'unknown to fame,' pass out at the end of their time. . ." (*2*).

Since, in the view of the extreme perennialist-idealist, there is a "right" curriculum which alone constitutes an education, his desire is to see that each child masters it at an appropriate age. Homogeneous grouping would deny that the same fixed values exist for all children or that certain curricular content is indispensable to the educated man. The mentally deficient child, perhaps, could be excused from the classical requirements and receive merely a form of training; but for those who would be educated, little of differentiation could be allowed.

Here is where the perennialist-idealist who opposed homogeneous grouping seems inconsistent with his own major aims—self-realization by the child and transmission of the culture. In the first place, he too seldom analyzes the term "self-realization." Basically it can mean nothing more than the child's ultimate development of all those potentials which make him a spiritual, social, or personal "self." It does not mean the development of potentials which the child does not possess. And a democratic philosophy should hold, not that all children have equal potentials (for this is patently absurd in the face of all research data on the subject), but that one child's potentials are as important for his own self-realization as are another child's potentials for his own self-realization. To deny full opportunity to the intellectually subnormal child for his own best development of whatever limited potentials he may possess is to strike at the very root of the real meaning of maximum self-realization. Yet it is the perennialist-idealist who often overlooks this very fact in his insistence upon fixed values in selected curriculum requirements. And, as a specific example, we have seen the child of poor mental ability in the abstract processes not only wasting the school's time and money in studying subjects beyond his intellectual capacity, but losing precious time which he might have devoted to developing those potentials that he could have developed. One sometimes wonders how the perennialist-idealist reconciles this obvious fact with his insistence upon rigidity and regimentation in what he calls the child's proper education.

And, as to the aim of cultural transmission, the traditionalist needs to be asked just who is capable of preserving and transmitting the thoughts of, say, Plato, Epictetus, Kant, Descartes, or Dewey? Surely he does not believe that such a function is for the average mind. The cultural heritage, at its best, is transmitted through good writing and good teaching. And this task is for the relatively few minds capable of interpreting the best from man's past thought. It in no way depends upon the formal education of average pupils. There are other levels of education for them if they are to realize individually their own best potentials. And this means a differentiated curriculum at each level of age and maturity beyond the level of learning the fundamental tools.

The perennialist-idealist, therefore, will best serve his own stated objectives of education by frankly admitting that there are no sacrosanct elements of education: for the only sacred thing in the school is the child.

2. *The pragmatist-experimentalist's stake in homogeneous grouping.* The pragmatic movement sparked what today is called "Progressive" education. The fact that the movement was a much-needed reaction against formalism and decadent traditions attracted all types of those persons, who, for one reason or another, were dissatisfied with the old system. Any reactionary movement is apt to make strange bed-fellows. Sane leaders of the movement soon found themselves surrounded by apostles who talked in strange tongues. Extremists, faddists, and happy seekers of the promised land flocked to the new doctrines. They were determined to clean up education; and some of them, in their own schools, nearly threw out the child with the bath.

Without footnote citations that might today embarrass enthusiastic writers who now may have reconsidered their earlier views, we might remind ourselves of some early pronouncements; to wit: "All activity is learning activity"; "There need be no curriculum"; "The only goal is adjustment"; "Children must never fail"; "The teacher is merely one of the group"; "All learning activity must be pupil-purposed"; etc., etc.

And from these views with their accent upon the child's happy adjustment came the doctrine that homogeneous grouping was the very enemy of the child's self-confidence and his sense of equality with others. This concept represented a sort of bliss-through-ignorance formula of child "growth." It was never the doctrine of responsible pragmatism but of the fringe-and-ragged-edge group of those who liked the sound of words without analyzing their meanings.

As the more extreme views finally were abandoned or modified, the American school began to show evidence of having acquired new skills in meeting the real needs of diverse groups of children. Motivation had lost much of its earlier brutality; much of the lock-step of earlier regimentation had disappeared; and schools that formerly had been staffed by teachers whose only job was to see that children studied, now hired personnel who had learned how to study the children. And throughout the entire philosophy of the new school there was a growing emphasis upon the democratic method, the individual-social needs that grow out of the child's basic impulses, and the continuity of total organismic development.

It seems surprising that among these new concepts and points of emphasis there should remain a distinct misapplication of the democratic principle. Yet the pragmatist, while emphasizing individuality of the child and properly insisting upon provisions to meet individual interests and needs, nevertheless often stands opposed to homogeneous grouping. He is apt to insist that there can be no such thing as homogeneous grouping anyway, because no two pupils are identical. Furthermore, he looks with suspicion upon standardized tests that purport to define among children the contrasting limits of their learning capacities. As to his first argument, it is enough to point out that the word "homogeneous" does not necessarily imply identity or exact equality of abilities. Both good usage and standard dictionary definitions indicate homogeneity where there is similarity, likeness, uniformity, or commensurability. And the pragmatist, insisting upon differences in interests and strengths of drives, should be among the first to recognize differences in potential learning abilities. Following, as he does, the doctrine of evolution, he should be first to recognize differences in native or absolute capacity, whether such differences are precisely measurable or not, and should welcome the attempt that is made to refine the instruments of measurement.

No one, more than the pragmatist, insists upon the democratic concept in education, its organization and its administration. It would seem that the pragmatist, then, would be attracted to a system which attempts to measure each child's potential and to place him in a group whose progress and capacities are consistent with that potential.

3. *The realist's stake in homogeneous grouping.* More perhaps than anyone else, the realist has recognized the better possibilities of homogeneous grouping. With the exception of those perennialist-realists who place extreme emphasis upon past culture *qua* past culture, there

is a tendency to measure curricular values in terms of their functional relations to the needs of the individual in society. The criterion frequently is stated as that of happiness for all human beings. And happiness is seen as being ultimately an individual condition contingent upon the learner's success in finding satisfaction for his basic social drives and achievement at or near his best potential for contributing to the happiness of his fellow beings. He requires recognition, success, acceptance, and a certain sense of security. These satisfactions he can find only when confronted with a learning situation that allows him to achieve comparably with his immediate associates and in line with his own peculiar aptitudes and interests. And these latter elements are measurable within ranges of significant statistical validity by use of standardized testing devices, whose results provide the basis for effective planning and guidance as steps toward intelligent grouping.

HISTORICAL CONSIDERATIONS

The simplest form of grouping is the traditional one which classifies pupils by chronological age, promoting them to a higher grade each year. Under this plan, those who were adjudged to have "failed" in the prescribed work of a course were retained at grade level for another year —in all subjects. The percentage of such failures often was high. For example, between 1850 and 1865 the percentage of students failing the admission examinations for two Philadelphia high schools dropped from 46.6 to 20.0 (3).

In Richmond, Virginia, the percentage of failure in the seventh grade in 1891 was 32.9 in the white schools and 41.2 in the colored schools.[1]

In the Baltimore schools of 1886, twenty-six percent of the third-grade pupils failed their final examinations.[2]

In Nashville, Tennessee, in 1889, seventeen percent of all pupils failed the work for the year.[3]

Examination of various reports published by the Chicago schools between 1880 and 1885 indicates that approximately thirty-three percent of all children failed to pass from one grade to the next during that period.

[1] Letter to the writer from Louis P. Weisiger, Director of Research, citing the twenty-second annual report of the superintendent of the public schools, Richmond, Virginia, for the scholastic year ending July 31, 1891 (p. 33).

[2] Letter from W. H. Lemmel, Superintendent of Schools, citing the fifty-eighth annual report of the board of commissioners of public schools for the year ending December 31, 1886.

[3] Letter from J. E. Nagy, Director of Research and Statistics of the Nashville City Schools, with calculations based upon figures found in the annual report of the superintendent of schools for the year 1888–1889, p. 53.

Some early reports show cases of children who had been retained in the first grade for as many as nine consecutive years!

As a reaction against the rigidly uniform requirements of the earlier years, a number of schools established "parallel curricula" at the second-ary level; but there appears to be little evidence of any successful at-tempt to devise ways of effectively guiding children in their choices; and at both the elementary and secondary levels the tradition of fixed standards of performance was largely retained.

Then came the decades from 1890 to 1920, with their unprecedented multiplication of high schools and their enrollments. No longer was secondary education reserved for the mentally gifted. It was for the masses. And the eventual result, greatly influenced by a number of converging influences from other sources, has given us today a school system which tries to serve several ideological masters simultaneously. Primarily, it tries to "provide for individual differences" while avoid-ing an "undemocratic" classification or grouping of pupils in terms of those differences.

The question of what to do with pupils of below-average ability was further complicated in the 1920's and 1930's by a number of rather extensive researches which cast serious doubt upon the effectiveness of failing and retaining pupils whose performance fell below expected levels. One of the more careful and complete studies was that of the Long Beach, California, schools during 1927 and 1928. Two equated groups of potential failures were used. These pupils were equated in terms of age, sex, IQ, MA, and CA. The experimental group of seventy-one children in grades 2A to 6B were promoted. The control group of seventy were retained. Achievement batteries were used both in pre-testing and in follow-up testing. It was found that, in general, children of normal ability gained more from trial promotion than from retention. That is, they apparently learned more during the following year, es-pecially if they were in grades above the third (4).

A Philadelphia study of three thousand, two hundred and twenty-one pupils in grades five and six showed that the percentage of failure per grade subsequent to grade 1A was lower in every IQ group for those pupils who had *not* been retained in 1A than was the subsequent per-centage of failure for those who had repeated grade 1A (5).

These results are merely typical of the findings reported by various investigative groups. A general summary of the pertinent research prior to 1950 appears in the *Encyclopedia of Educational Research* for that year (6). It indicates that, in general, retention does not result in significantly increasing the rate of learning among slow pupils; that it does not build better morale among pupils nor assure mastery of sub-ject matter; that it does not increase grade-achievement averages nor reduce the variations of achievement among individual classes; and that it does not improve the personality adjustment of the retained child (7). Similar findings from studies reported by various investigators who have examined available evidence from the numerous researches in the field indicate generally that, in a majority of cases, retention fails to improve the child's learning and may even cause subsequent learning to deteriorate. Consequently, by about 1930, many schools were seeking for something to take the place of failure for slow-learning children. Homogeneous grouping seemed to offer promise of aiding the solution of this problem.

The essential consideration which seems to have been chiefly responsible for initiating the movement to group pupils homogeneously was the desire to adapt curricular requirements to their capacities, special interests, and rates of learning. Unfortunately, a number of schools attempted such grouping on the sole basis of IQ tests (and sometimes group tests at that!), with no consideration of other factors. In some schools this plan meant nothing more than the putting of high IQ's of a given grade level in one room and the low IQ's in another, both groups being given identical assignments and being taught in the same way by teachers who had no specialized training for work with atypical groups. Such indifferent treatment of the problem was, of course, foredoomed to failure; and everyone, including the school janitor, recognized it for the farce that it was.

"Progressives," seeing how quickly the children themselves distinguished between the "bright" and the "dumbbell" groups, condemned not merely the misuse of intelligence tests, but many of them (as well as parents and the public in general) condemned the tests per se. They saw such tests as instruments designed to destroy the democratic concept of equality among children. A few of them even denied the very existence of the IQ. In addition, it was claimed that homogeneous grouping would make snobs and social misfits of the gifted children and would leave them unprepared for life in a world of heterogeneous population. And it was pointed out that children of diverse aptitudes and interests could work together in a single group by building their learning activities around meaningful projects and problems of living rather than following the traditional patterns of textbook study and class recitation. In regard to this latter claim, it should be stated that some schools were highly successful in demonstrating that the old memoriter learning was less than indispensable in some areas. Children of different abilities and potentials, working as a unit, learned to plan democratically together and to carry out many significant projects. By using integrated and fused experience units, they made firsthand studies of community resources; they built—and sold—real homes that were intelligently planned, skillfully decorated, and properly constructed; they studied local ordinances, sanitation conditions, recreational facilities, traffic hazards, and contrasting cultural patterns in their own communities; and they even investigated themselves, their habits, prejudices, and personalities. And all this (where the teaching was skillful and the guidance intelligent) was done by groups which embraced wide ranges of IQ, special interests, and backgrounds.

For a time it seemed that the new order of teaching, heralded as the "activity movement" and based upon "life needs," had found the answer to the problem of meeting individual needs without resorting to homogeneous grouping. Teachers would build learning situations' around large problems of sufficient scope to offer expression for every child's creative impulses and an outlet for all talents within the heterogeneous group.

Under skilled teaching and within certain areas of learning, the new theory exercised a wholesome effect; and good schools probably never again will return to an exclusive dependence upon textbooks, recitations, and inflexibly uniform achievement requirements. But the movement itself left some important questions unanswered. Being a reaction against traditionalism, it carried its practices so far to the left as to make a fetish of the activity concept and to neglect proper attention to some rather well established principles of learning. Under its spell, more than one teacher misinterpreted Dewey so completely as to believe that, if learning is an active process, then any active process promotes learning. And the movement threatened to run away with the schools completely until a few critical observers began to call for sober evaluation of some of the things that were being done. See, for example, *Fads and Fallacies in Present-Day Education* (8).

Thus movement and counter-movement, theory and counter-theory, have brought educational changes. But it does not appear that any complete solution has been found for the problem of meeting the individual needs of the mass of children while still preserving the desirable standards of performance for those gifted children whose learning capacities are markedly superior. It is in the hope that a number of educators will give a second look at the much-criticized theory of homogeneous grouping that the following viewpoints are presented here.

ESSENTIAL CONSIDERATIONS IN GROUPING

1. *Homogeneous grouping is not necessarily undemocratic.* Those who abandoned homogeneous grouping on the grounds that it violated the democratic philosophy seem to have ignored the fact that democracy in education means, or should mean, provision for each child to achieve at his own best level in accordance with his own individual po-

tentials. It is no more "democratic" to consider all children as having equal learning capacities and mental potentials than it would be to insist that all children have feet of the same size and must be given shoes that are exactly alike. It is true, and all major research supports the statement, that children are born with different physiological, emotional, and mental potentials; and, just as it is essential that each child have shoes that fit him, it also is essential that educational requirements be tailored to his capacities. Homogeneous grouping actually is an attempt to recognize each child's democratic right to an education that he can handle, to an education that will help him individually to achieve his own maximum of self-realization, happiness, and effective growth. Homogeneous grouping is the very antithesis of an autocratic regimentation and an imposed uniformity.

Intelligent clinical studies of children show that some need one dietary regimen while others need a different prescription. The same fact is true in educational prescription. No one accuses the medical prescriptionist of being undemocratic! The very heart of democracy in education is in the determination to measure each child's weaknesses and strengths—and to see that the requirements and the opportunities are consistently tailored to his needs. Properly conducted and with adequately skilled guidance, homogeneous grouping is a step in this direction.

2. *Homogeneous grouping is not impossible.* The term does not imply that children are identical. It implies that they are alike, that their abilities and talents are "commensurable," or that their potentials are highly similar. Under expert testing, interviewing, and try-out, it is possible for a competent staff to group pupils into classes of comparable learning capacity and interests.

Reavis, Pierce, and Stullken (9) have indicated three basic considerations for grouping or classification of pupils: (a) The guiding objective must be the promotion of total good or welfare of the learner. (b) Careful consideration must be given to the over-all efficiency of the school as a whole. (c) Grouping must be tentative and flexible rather than fixed and permanent.

Scientific grouping requires a diagnostic approach to the study of the individual. Such study must determine important facts about the child's (a) apparent mental ability, (b) special aptitudes, (c) basic social drives, (d) physical and emotional maturity, (e) educational age in the various learning areas, (f) health, (g) nervous stability, (h) personal and family history and attitudes, and (i) inter-personal adjustment factors.

3. *Intelligent grouping is not necessarily rigid and permanent.* Many opponents of homogeneous grouping appear to see it as a system which

permanently assigns a child to a specific classification from which there can be no escape. But under intelligent operation it is similar to the familiar plan used by any good teacher of beginning reading. Such a teacher customarily breaks a class into small groups, some of which are more advanced than others. Each group studies the materials which its members have not yet mastered. And when an individual child's progress justifies his being moved to a more advanced group, the teacher quietly shifts him. Thus a given pupil may move several times during the year from one group to another within his class. The sole purpose is that of seeing that each child works at his own best level and devotes his time to those learnings which he has not yet satisfactorily acquired but which careful guidance can enable him to acquire.

On a larger scale, over-all ability grouping attempts to accomplish the same result in each area of study or activity. And the learner may be shifted, say, from a slow group in mathematics to a more advanced group in that subject while remaining perhaps with a slow group in social studies or English. Flexibility is restricted only by the limits of administrative feasibility.

It has been claimed that, once the child is assigned to a slow group, he can have little opportunity to catch up with a faster group because he is out of contact with the things that the faster group has been learning. The fact is that, if he has the learning capacity and the desire to catch up with the advanced group, there need be no obstacle in his path. If both groups are taught by the same teacher, there should be no problem whatsoever, any more than there is in the case of the primary reading groups. And if the two classes are taught by different teachers, only the most remarkable lack of coördination and communication between the teachers should handicap the child's advancement.

In fact, it often can happen that a capable learner may need to be placed temporarily in a slower group in order to receive remedial attention after a period of illness or absence from some other cause. By remaining in the faster group, he might be permanently handicapped by having missed certain essentials which he now can get by working for a while with the less advanced group. After catching up with the work missed, he again may be ready to enter the faster group.

4. *Homogeneous grouping does not maladjust the child.* The claim that, by assigning a child to a group less advanced than others, the school causes him to develop inferiority feelings and to become maladjusted in his social relationships and attitudes seems to have little support. Research indicates that, in general, children tend to gravitate toward contacts with other children of similar mental and intellectual levels.

It is difficult to imagine anything more calculated to maladjust a child than to keep him continuously in a group with which he cannot compete. Here he meets constant failure. But if he is in a group of his mental peers, he finds success within that group. Success and the feeling of achievement are relative to the situation and the competitive demands that it creates. (In this regard some pragmatists should take notes from their own textbooks!)

5. *Homogeneous grouping can offer each child an optimum challenge for his best abilities.* Just as the slow child, unable to compete with his classmates, may become discouraged, so may the gifted child become bored in a heterogeneous group whose range of abilities extends far below his own level. The teacher often feels forced to pace the work to average abilities. It is true, as previously indicated, that in some areas of learning, large experience units may provide differentiated activity to challenge a wide range of learning capacities and interests. But it also is true that even the most imaginative and resourceful teachers find difficulty in planning such activities to cover all desirable learnings for a hetereogeneous group. Some subjects require drill more than others; and so do some pupils. Some require more reading. Some require more attention to fundamentals.

The best of well-planned and integrated experience units still leave out certain areas of learning which simply do not fit into the larger patterns and must be mastered separately. Here is where intensive study, drill, or practice can best be conducted by a teacher who has a group whose abilities are comparable.

Homogeneous grouping, then, makes it possible to challenge each child. A challenge soon loses its motivating force for the pupil who can never meet it with success or for the pupil who finds it too easy. Neither child continues to work at his best level. And not only the child, but society at large, is the ultimate loser. Under these conditions neither child can achieve his own maximum of self-realization. (And even here some perennialist-idealists should consult their own lecture notes.)

Research during recent years indicates a number of factors as being responsible for nonattendance of pupils, one of the more significant being the failure of the school to adapt itself to the needs of children. (*10*).

The child who cannot meet the inflexible standards of uniform requirements becomes a misfit in the school. It may be of significance here to note that the older schools, which failed almost universally to adapt their requirements to the individual differences of children, failed to discover and satisfy the real needs of many pupils who later proved themselves to be highly gifted. Herman H. Horne (*11*) has listed a number of those who were "misfits" in their early schools. The list includes Charles Darwin, Linnaeus, Napoleon, William Seward, Patrick Henry, Newton, Samuel Johnson, Swift, Wordsworth, Heinrich Heine, George

Eliot, Walter Scott, Hegel, Byron, Huxley, Schiller, Lowell, Gold-smith, Wagner, Goethe, H. W. Beecher, W. C. Bryant, Emerson, Pasteur, Thackeray, Shelley, Daniel Webster, John Adams, Gladstone, Coleridge, James Watt, Hume, Herbert Spencer, Ibsen, and others.

One wonders how many of these "misfits" might have been well adjusted to their school environments and learning requirements if, through clinical study of their individual aptitudes and abilities, their real needs and potentials had been discovered and used as a basis for such grouping as would have placed each child among others of more similar abilities and learning capacities.

Perhaps the school today, faced with the desperate need to cultivate the talents of its superior students, should take a second and very thoughtful look at the possibilities for homogeneous grouping.

REFERENCES

(1) *Annual Report of the School Committee of the City of Boston*, pp. 24–25. Boston, 1859.

(2) Nathaniel Thayer, In *Thirty-First Annual Report of the Commissioners of Public Schools of the City of Baltimore*, p. 197. Baltimore, 1860.

(3) *Thirty-Second Annual Report of the Board of Public Education*, pp. 105–106, 228–230. Philadelphia, 1866.

(4) Vivian Klene and Ernest P. Branson, "Trial Promotion Versus Failure," *Educational Research Bulletin, Los Angeles City Schools*, 8:6–11, January, 1929.

(5) *Report of the Division of Educational Research and Results for the Year Ended June 30, 1933*, pp. 35 et seq. Philadelphia, Board of Education, School District of Philadelphia, 1933.

(6) *Encyclopedia of Educational Research*, Passim, N.Y., Macmillan Co., 1950.

(7) Op. cit., p. 1123.

(8) Heinrich E. Buchholz, *Fads and Fallacies in Present-Day Education*. New York, The Macmillan Co., 1931.

(9) William C. Reavis, Paul R. Pierce, and Edward H. Stullken, *The Elementary School, Its Organization and Administration*, p. 141. Chicago, University of Chicago Press, 1935.

(10) Arch O. Heck, In *Encyclopedia of Educational Research*, pp. 1008–1009. New York, The Macmillan Co., 1941.

(11) Herman H. Horne, "Philosophies of Education," *Forty-First Yearbook of the National Society for the Study of Education*, Part I, p. 176. Bloomington, Illinois, Public School Publishing Co., 1942.

61. Instruction and Guidance in Education

HENRY WEITZ

I

In most schools, even in those fortunate enough to employ a well trained professional guidance counselor, the major guidance services are provided for the majority of the students by the classroom teacher. This is as it should be, for no one on the school staff, including the administrator and the guidance specialist, is in as strategic a position as the teacher to perform the three functions essential to effective guidance: (1) collecting the data necessary to the diagnosis of pupil needs, (2) providing the learning experiences essential to the acquisition of behavior required to meet those needs, and (3) evaluating the outcomes of guidance in terms of pupil adjustment.

Effective guidance demands these three functions, diagnosis, learning, and evaluation. The teacher is the only person in the school who can observe the student for a long enough period of time under more or less "normal" conditions to accumulate a sufficient body of data to permit an adequate diagnosis of the child's needs. The teacher alone can provide the conditions for learning, including repeated practice and reinforcement, essential to the acquisition of new behavior patterns. Only the teacher has an intimate enough understanding of the child's adjustment to be able to observe and evaluate outcomes of guidance.

Unfortunately, however, no matter how desirable it may be for the teacher to perform these guidance functions and no matter how strategically located he may be to do this, the fact of the matter is that most teachers are unqualified to play any but a minor role in any of these guidance functions not only because they are untrained in the important skills required of guidance workers, but also because they are almost entirely innocent of any understanding of the basic concepts which underlie the guidance function of education.

It is the purpose of this paper to attempt to define certain of the basic

From Henry Weitz, "Instruction and Guidance in Education," *The Educational Forum*, XIX (January, 1955), 169–177. Henry Weitz is Associate Professor of Education and Director of the Bureau of Testing and Guidance, Duke University, Durham, North Carolina. Reprinted by permission from Kappa Delta Pi.

concepts underlying the second aspect of guidance, namely, learning, in order that teachers may utilize the skills they already have more effectively to achieve the purposes of guidance. Little will be said except in passing, about the functions of diagnosis and evaluation, for in general, teachers will have received so little training in the skills related to these functions that they had best be left to the specialist. But the teacher should be a specialist in the area of learning unless he is no more than a repository for a mass of verbiage, and it is this skill which can be used to good advantage in guidance provided the teacher understands what guidance is and the ways in which it relates to instruction and contributes to education.

At the outset it is essential to understand what education is. Education may, perhaps, be best defined as the acquisition of behavior patterns in a contrived situation. This means, essentially, that the new behavior patterns to be acquired and the methods by which they are to be acquired are determined before the learning process is begun. For example, the arithmetic teacher decides that his class shall learn the multiplication tables. Standards of behavior acquisition are established before the learning process is undertaken. The behavior pattern, that is to say the student's response of "eight"? is predetermined to be the appropriate reaction to the stimulus, "How much is two times four?" The teacher also establishes the methods by which the response is to be acquired: memorizing, drill, repeated recitation, and reinforcement by verbal approval and grades. Thus the outcomes and the method of acquisition are predetermined in this kind of learning situation which we label *Education.*

Now not all learning is education, that is: contrived behavior acquisition. Much of what an individual learns is acquired without pre-existing goals, purposes, or methods. Thus, a child learns to love his parents although this outcome was not a predesigned goal for feeding the child. Little Johnnie learns that there are other children with the same given name as his, although no preplanned steps were taken to provide him with this knowledge or with new ways of responding to this knowledge. Much of the basic information we learn about the world around us and almost all of attitudinal and affective behavior is acquired in this unsystematic and uncontrived fashion. Thus most of an individual's acquired behavior, and by far the most important part of it is learned outside of an educational situation.

Furthermore, not all education takes place in the school. The fact of the matter is that most education, that is, most learning involving fairly clearly predetermined goals and methods, takes place outside of school. Basic motor skills, such as walking, balancing, running, self-feeding, and the like are taught in the home. These essential behavior patterns are taught by parents and agemates using extremely simple and consequently extremely effective contrived learning situations. Basic language skills and quantitative concepts, fundamental ideas of honesty, cooperation, analysis, and organization as well as their related attitudes are all established as part of a child's reactional repertory during the early years of his life before he comes in contact with the school.

Relatively few entirely new modes of behavior are acquired by the child through the educational efforts of the school. Literature and grammar are merely refinements of and generalizations from the basic language skills already acquired by the child. Mathematical education would be impossible if the child did not come to school already well trained in the concepts of "oneness" and "manyness." History is merely the extension of the child's understanding, acquired outside the school, of events in time and the interrelationship of these events. Thus education in each instructional area is dependent upon the educational experiences acquired by the child outside the school. An understanding of this concept of education should make teachers less willing to assume the responsibility or credit for the "total education of the *whole child.*" Accepting the school as merely one element on the educative process places both the school and education in a more realistic perspective.

The discussion thus far may seem to suggest that in education the learning situation is contrived by someone other than the learner himself. This, of course, is not so. Goals of learning and the methods by which these goals are to be achieved may be determined and frequently are determined by the learner himself. Although the education of young children is usually carried on under the supervision of adults, as the individual matures, he assumes more and more responsibility for establishing his own goals and methods of learning. The adult in our society is reasonably free to select what he shall learn and the ways in which he shall learn it, and children, too, have considerable latitude in the matter of education.

The child decides that he would like to learn to swim. He then follows a rigorous learning program in order to acquire this behavior pattern which he has established as his goal. The outcomes and the methods of achieving them were established by the learner himself. Here education appears to be under the complete control of the child himself.

Mastery of the multiplication tables, on the other hand, presents the opposite picture. In most instances, the child has little understanding of what the multiplication tables are at the time he is expected to learn them. The good teacher will make adequate preparation for this piece of instruction by filling in enough background material, in terms of meaningful illustrations so that the child can feel that the mastery of this piece of behavior is worth while. In this way he is "motivated" to accept the teacher's outcomes of learning as his own. He has some notion, if only a vague one, of where the learning process is leading him. No matter how skillful the teacher is in evoking student interest and participation, this educational experience may still be said to be contrived by the teacher.

II

Educational experiences, then, are of two kinds. On the one hand, there are learning activities in which the goals and methods of learning are contrived by the learner himself and, on the other hand, there are those which are established by agents other than the learner. Few educational activities can be clearly designated as belonging to one or the other category. Most contrived learning situations are made up of complex interrelationships between the two elements of self-direction and external direction. The adult who decides to learn a foreign language is externally limited, among other things, by the foreign languages available to be learned, the structure and form of the language he selects, the learning materials at hand, and the attitudes of his social group toward foreign language study. His acquisition of this foreign language behavior pattern is modified by the social framework in which he finds himself. Thus, although the major emphasis is upon self-direction here, the educational experience is not an exclusively self-directed experience.

Similarly, a learning activity planned by someone other than the learner can not be an exclusively externally-directed experience. Thus, a sergeant training his men in markmanship can establish standards of performance and methods of learning for them, but he can not anticipate any high degree of mastery unless the men accept the outcomes as behavior patterns appropriate to their own survival.

We may say, then, that education is the acquisition of behavior in contrived learning situations. In some instances the learning goals and the process of learning are controlled by the learner; in other instances they are externally controlled; in most educational situations there is a dual control of the objectives and methods. In any given educational experience, however, external or internal direction is emphasized. It is this emphasis in a given learning situation which has important implications for education in the schools.

Education as it takes place in the schools may be thought of as constituting two separate functions: (1) instruction and (2) guidance. In the first, instruction, emphasis is placed upon the external control of the learning process while in the second, guidance, emphasis is placed upon the self-directed aspect of the learning process.

The instructional and guidance functions of education may be differentiated with respect to other factors as well as the degree of emphasis upon self or external direction of the learning process. Instruction and guidance may be differentiated in terms of value standards thus:

1) Instruction may be defined as a process of assisting students to achieve adjustment within the framework of *society's* value standards.

2) Guidance may be defined as a process of assisting students to achieve adjustment within the framework of *their own* value standards.

Adjustment is a key concept in both of the above definitions, yet it need not concern us greatly at this point since it retains the same meaning in both instances. It is enough to say that for the purpose of this discussion, adjustment is defined as a state of the organism characterized by a relative freedom from tension, a feeling of satisfaction, and an attitude of self acceptance resulting from or accompanying a particular behavior segment.

III

The source of *value standards* is the element which differentiates these two functions of education. In the case of instruction, the value standards are established by the society; while in the case of guidance, they are established by the student himself.

Value standards may be defined as the goals or objectives toward which activity (of an individual or a society) is directed. Value standards differ from society to society and from individual to individual.

Each society requires of its members that they have a pattern of value standards which will contribute to the maintenance and development of that society. In order for any society to achieve its value standards, it is essential that its members acquire a body of skills and hold a system of beliefs and attitudes which contribute to the attainment of those value standards.

It is important to note that the value standards of any particular society derive from the structure of the society and not from the wishes or influence of any individual or small group of individuals. The internal structure of a society and its interactions with other contemporary and historic societies will determine its values. Thus, even in a dictatorship, the approved modes of behavior of its constituents derive from the internal interrelationships among the constituents and from the interactions between the dictator society and its contemporary societies. The dictator, himself, and his immediate advisors become merely vehicles for the expression of these interrelationships and structures. The dictator, himself, is as much a product of the structure as any other member of the society, and his very existence depends upon the continuation of the structure. When the structure is impaired, as in the case of Italy during World War II, the value standards change, with resulting attitudinal and behavioral changes, and even the dictator perishes at the hands of the society he appeared (erroneously) to have created.

The structural pattern of a society, and hence its value standards, grows out of the natural environment in which it becomes established, its experience derived from its history, the peripheral pressures of other societies and cultures, and the physical, psychological, and philosophical growth which is generated from the interactions of its constituents.

A democracy such as that found in the United States derives from its structural pattern certain value standards which are essential to its maintenance and development as a democracy. These ultimate goals, in turn, require that citizens of a democracy acquire a system of behavioral patterns which will facilitate the achievement of these value standards.

In a democratic society, the value standards which serve as objectives toward which the society is striving would include the "perfect states" of the following: individual freedom coupled with individual responsibility, majority welfare with the protection of minority rights, material and intellectual honesty, the reward of individual effort limited by a code of "accepted practice," and the like. Individual and group behavior which facilitates the achievement of these goals is valued highly while behavior which does not contribute to their achievement is, in general, disapproved and thwarted.

Instruction then consists of informing students about these societal values and training them to cherish and to strive to attain them. Skills which make the attainment of these standards possible are also taught. These skills would include: (1) the ability to communicate ideas and feelings by means of a variety of media including verbal, quantitative, graphic, plastic, tonal and pantomime language; (2) the ability to analyze problems by means of induction, deduction, intuition, and similar processes and (3) the ability to organize ideas, events, circumstances and the like. These three basic skills, communication, analysis and organization, are essential to the attainment of the value standards in a democratic society. These three basic skills and the value standards they are designed to attain form the content of instruction. The subjects which are taught, English, mathematics, science, history, and the like, are simply media for presenting this socially essential course content.

While in each society, the value standards are fairly clearly discernible and identifiable, they are, at the same time, sufficiently flexible, especially in a democracy, to permit individuals to interpret them in terms of their own behavioral history and to select as their own those which appear to be most meaningful. The implementation of society's goals may take a variety of forms; thus, so long as an individual's value standards are not markedly incompatible with those of his society, he is capable of making satisfactory adjustments.

Just as a society's value standards derive from its internal and external structure, so an individual's values derive from his natural environment, his physiological efficiency, his psychological structure derived from experience, and the peripheral pressures of his contemporaries and antecedents. Since these factors form different configurations for different individuals each individual develops somewhat different value standards. The following are illustrative of the kinds of individual value standards which develop in a democracy: prestige, power, material acquisitions, security, affection, acceptance, opportunity for social contribution, acquisition of knowledge, health, identification with the laws of God or nature, satisfaction of curiosity, and the like. In most individuals, several of these values are operative at the same time.

Guidance, then, consists in providing experiences designed to aid students in gaining insight into their own value standards and in acquiring those behavior patterns which will make the attainment of their goals a possibility. In general, the skills and attitudes essential to the attainment of society's values are the same as those required for the achievement of individual goals. The emphasis and the media used to exercise these skills and attitudes, however, will differ from individual to individual.

Guidance and instruction, then, differ in two major ways. On the one hand, they differ with respect to the goals they seek to attain and, on the other hand, they differ with respect to the degree of self-direction in the learning process utilized to achieve the goals. These differences have important implications primarily for the teacher, but also for the administrator and the guidance worker.

IV

In the school, education comprises both instruction and guidance. The teacher has a dual responsibility. On the one hand, he is required to act as a representative of society and to provide experiences which will aid students in acquiring behavior designed to achieve the values of a democratic society. On the other hand, he must provide experiences designed to facilitate the attainment of the student's own goals. In order to meet both responsibilities adequately, the teacher must be a master of the techniques and arts of each.

Effective instruction requires that the teacher be able to interpret the needs of society in terms of the subject medium through which he proposes to train students in the essential skills and attitudes. This means that the teacher of history, or science, or mathematics, or physical education must view his subject not as an end in itself, but simply as one medium through which the society's goals may be achieved. Having made his interpretation of society's values (in a sense, this involves *diagnosing society's needs*) the teacher should be prepared to apply all the methodological skill at his command to provide learning experiences through which students may acquire the behavior essential to meeting the needs.

Effective guidance follows a similar pattern although here the emphasis is somewhat different. *Student's needs* are first diagnosed. Steps are then taken to provide an atmosphere within which a student may undertake a more or less self-directed learning program through which he may acquire those behavior patterns essential to the attainment of *his own value standards.*

Both processes, guidance and instruction, involve: (1) diagnosis of needs, (2) providing experiences through which adjustive behavior may be acquired and (3) the evaluation of the behavioral product. In instruction, the teacher will, for the most part use group methods of diagnosis, teaching, and evaluation, while in guidance, individual methods will need to be used. Both processes may be carried out simultaneously in any classroom, by individualizing instruction.

Now most teachers are fairly skillful in group instructional methods and many teachers can use individual learning experiences effectively to achieve the purposes of *instruction,* but few are aware of the ways in which individualization of instruction can achieve the purposes of guidance and can utilize the self-directed learning process which characterizes guidance. The following outline of procedure may prove helpful in this connection.

It must be assumed at the outset, for the purposes of this discussion, that the following two conditions are met: (1) the objectives of the course the teacher is offering and the specific behavioral outcomes for each unit of the course must be clearly defined before the teaching is started. (2) The diagnosis of student needs must be thorough and meaningful to the teacher. Since the first condition involves simply effective pedagogy, there is no reason to believe that the good teacher would be unable to fulfill it. The second condition will, in general, require the assistance of a guidance specialist in interpreting the mass of diagnostic data a teacher is capable of collecting.[1] This condition is not so easily fulfilled and the degree to which it is not fulfilled will serve as a limiting factor on what is accomplished in instruction and guidance.

The diagnosis of the pupil should reveal his major value standards and his major needs in terms of behavior acquisition. It is important at this point to emphasize an attitude on the part of the teacher which

---

[1] Weitz, Henry. "Semantics in Diagnosis," *The Journal of Counseling Psychology,* Vol. I, No. 2 (Spring, 1954).

is basic to the success of the guidance process. This attitude may best be labeled *acceptance*. The teacher must accept the student's values and needs as they are so long as they are not incompatible in some major way with society's values. So long as the student's values will not bring him into marked conflict with society, the teacher cannot question them even though they may be markedly different from his own.[2]

The student's value standards and need should now be examined (with this acceptant attitude) and compared with the course objectives in order to determine which of them is capable of being met through the particular course. Not all of any child's needs can be met in every course. The teacher should then examine those needs which can be met in the course and determine which if any can be met in terms of the expected outcomes of a given unit being taught. The most important needs, in terms of the student's total adjustment, are then selected for special attention during the unit.

The instructional unit is now introduced to the whole class. It is emphasized that this unit has a dual purpose (1) to aid students to acquire new skills (these are enumerated) which will make them more effective citizens in a democracy and (2) to provide them with an opportunity of acquiring some special skill related to the main aspect of the unit which they feel will help them personally to achieve their own life goals.

Most students will soon find ways of adapting the learning experience to their own ends. They should be encouraged in this. Those who find some difficulty in making such an adaptation should now be interviewed. Their major needs will be discussed in the course of the interview and possible ways of meeting them through the unit will be suggested. Thus each student will be motivated to undertake an individualized project which will at the same time contribute to the child's mastery of the essential social skill being taught in the unit and aid him in adapting that skill to his own needs and values. Adequate time should be provided to permit the child to accomplish this.

Most important to consider in arranging these individualized projects is the utilization of a child's strengths in overcoming his weaknesses. Thus a child with considerable art skill and interest but with little mathematical talent may be encouraged in a mathematics class to work with more mathematically sophisticated students in designing posters to illustrate mathematical principles. Or a shy child with some clerical skills might be encouraged in a history class to act as secretary of a student committee, thus gaining in self assurance in a group of contemporaries who will accept her for a special skill she has.

This approach to individualizing instruction has been used with

[2] Weitz, Henry. "Helping Children through Understanding," *The Educational Forum*, Vol. XVIII, No. 1. (November, 1953).

teachers enrolled in a course entitled Guidance Functions of the Class Room Teacher offered by this writer. The teachers are asked to work with case summaries of high school students. With the aid of the instructor they identify the diagnosed needs of the student and plan special projects to meet these needs within the framework of the content and objectives of units of instruction in their own teaching specialty. This writer is impressed with the insight, resourcefulness, and ingenuity teachers can exercise in providing guidance experiences for students once they understand the purposes and methods of guidance. The scissors, pastepot, and notebook approach to student projects, so dear to the heart of the subject matter oriented teacher, disappears. Hours of copying from encyclopedias and almanacs into note books (which is so often labeled "research" by the social studies teachers) is exchanged for vital experiences in interpersonal relationships designed to influence the acquisition of behavior essential to the child's achievement of his own values. Many of these teachers report that this approach applied in their own class rooms has paid rich dividends in both student and teacher adjustment.

During the past twenty or thirty years, guidance workers have been examining the problem of whether guidance should be concerned with vocational adjustment exclusively or with the total adjustment of the student. As of this time, the question appears to be resolved, or to be in the process of being resolved, in favor of the latter position. Now this has resulted in many changes and even a few improvements in the activities of guidance workers and teachers.

This change has also resulted in the identification of guidance and instruction in the minds of many educational workers with the result that both the guidance and instructional functions of education have become diluted. The development of measurement programs and record systems, the establishment of courses in "life adjustment problems," and even reorganizations of the school transportation system or the order of serving in the cafeteria line are now labeled for the purposes of administrative reporting or public propaganda, Guidance. While all these activities may, and probably do contribute to the improvement of educational services in general, they probably contribute little or, at least, less than they could to the guidance function of education. Yet many of these activities could make a contribution to the guidance services of youth if the goals, and limits, and methods of guidance were clearly understood by those who direct our educational programs. It is hoped that the material contained herein has in some small measure contributed to this understanding.

62. How Many Extracurricular Activities Are Enough?

HARRY C. McKOWN

How many extracurricular activities are enough? Because this question immediately brings up important correlative questions it cannot be answered satisfactorily in a paragraph or two.

"Enough" for whom?—the participant, his parents, his school, his community? No one answer can be given for all of these. What might be "enough" for the participant might not be "enough" to satisfy his parents, school, or community in case he is, say, an outstanding athlete who wants to "do better" academically by participating less. Or he might satisfy himself, his school, and his community, but not his parents, or even satisfy one parent and dissatisfy the other.

However, here we assume that the question refers to the student (and his participations within the school) only, and that the general idea is to "strike a happy balance (whatever that is) between his curricular and extracurricular participations." So "enough for what?" (this "happy balance" business) emerges. And this can be answered only on the basis of a consideration of what the school and its curricular and extracurricular activities are supposed to do to the student.

Quite obviously, a student cannot be promoted or graduated on the basis of his extracurricular participations. These he must achieve in his curricular activities. So a facile answer to the original question would be—participation is "enough" up to the point where it begins to handicap curricular progress.

But up springs another question—just what is meant by handicapping curricular progress? For example, is a potential "A" student "handicapped" when, because of his activity participations, he makes only

From Harry C. McKown, "How Many Extracurricular Activities Are Enough?" *School Activities*, XXXIV (February, 1963), 183–184. Harry C. McKown is Editor of *School Activities* and has long been recognized as a leading authority on the extracurriculum. First published in 1937, the third edition of his general volume, *Extra-Curricular Activities*, was published in 1952 by The Macmillan Company, New York. Dr. McKown has also written separate books on school assemblies, school clubs, the home room, the student council, commencement, and leadership. This article is reprinted by permission of *School Activities*.

B's? Naturally, this question concerns the relative value of the student's possible "A training minus activities" and his possible "B training plus activities." And this leads in turn to the most basic of all pertinent questions—just what is the main purpose of the secondary school?

Now *if* the main purpose of the secondary school is scholarship, then anything that decreases the student's scholarship can be considered detrimental. *And* activities must then be considered as having motivational value only.

However, we cannot accept scholarship as the main end and aim of secondary education because (1) the community which supports it is composed of citizens, not scholars, and (2) the good scholar is not necessarily the good citizen (although many people, even some teachers, cling to this thoroughly illogical and unprovable view) any more than the good citizen is necessarily the good scholar. The main goal of the secondary school is good citizenship. And the academic classroom is not a setting for the development of this; good citizenship is not its main business.

Nor can extracurricular activities be justified on the basis of their motivational effects; these are important values but are not the main purposes of activities. These activities must and can be justified on their own important educational contribution.

Extracurricular activities provide many opportunities in which the student participates in as important-and-real-to-him citizenship settings as those in which the adult as a contributing member of his community participates. His is a miniature but none-the-less vital democracy.

In student council, newspaper, assembly, athletic and safety activities, in projects, drives and campaigns, and as officers, committeemen and members, the students help to promote the general welfare of the school. All these represent actual citizenship in natural and vital settings. In the classroom the student works for himself; in activities he works for his school—and benefits himself, both directly and indirectly.

Incidentally, just here is the main objection to awarding a school letter for high scholarship—the scholar "fights" for himself while the athlete or other activity participant "fights" for his school. Of course the scholar should, can be, and is rewarded by honor listings, prizes, scholarships, programs, and other public recognitions. But a school letter? *No*—unless he participates for the school in interscholastic academic contests or similar events.

Further, even within participations there may be "enough," "too much" and "not enough." His participations may not represent full development of the student's specialized abilities. If he, say, has unusual ability in both dramatics and music but splits his attention between the two, both developments suffer. Even here, however, it is conceivable that participating and achieving one-half in each might be more desirable than full participation and achievement in one only. Broadening might be preferable to deepening.

To emphasize, there can never be a rigid rule which will apply equally to all students because no two of them are alike. What is "enough" for one—due to his abilities and potentialities—may be "not enough" or "too much" for another.

At least an academic answer to the question of "how much?" is the "enough" is represented by the quantity and quality of participations—both curricular and extracurricular—which help to discover, develop, and capitalize the student's abilities and potentialities; "too much" and "not enough" when these activities are so over-emphasized or under-emphasized, either singly or in total, that profitable discovery, development, and capitalization do not occur.

Just who decides how much is "enough"? The student? His parents? His teachers? His activity sponsors? His guidance officer? All of these have had some experience and their judgments should be and can be capitalized. All of their judgments taken together and intelligently equated on the basis of their own experiences, interests, prejudices, ignorances, and stubbornnesses will help to arrive at a justifiable answer. No one of them alone is competent to give the final answer.

Frankly, we are of the opinion that there is relatively little over-participation because no intelligent student, teacher, sponsor, guidance officer or administrator would fail to recognize and limit it. And, especially in larger schools, there are various kinds of "point systems" which, based upon their relative importance, time and efforts required, etc., limit a student's participations.

Finally, we believe that the recent and persistent hysterical blather of Sunday-supplement writers, penny-a-paragraphers, publicity seeking ignorants, sensationalists, and other self-appointed "experts" about "fads and frills" presents a badly distorted picture of the purposes, place, organization, and administration of extracurricular activities—and student participation.

63. Parent-Teacher Conferences

HAROLD J. MAVES

Parent-teacher conferences are increasingly used today for pupil evaluation. Report cards are criticized for the unreliability of the marks given by teachers as well as for the unreliability of the interpretation of marks by parents. Furthermore, the effect of marks on a child's efforts is likely to be temporary. The parent-teacher conference makes possible the pooling of significant information about a child and allows for the planning of his future development by two persons vitally concerned—the parent and the teacher.

In Richmond, California, where parent-teacher conferences have been a part of the instructional program in the elementary schools for over five years, an extensive study of the conferences was recently completed. The analysis was based on tape recordings of sixty actual conferences held during one of the regularly scheduled semiannual conference periods. Attending these conferences were parents and teachers of a representative sampling of children enrolled in the fifth grade.

During the research it became clear that the performances of parents and teachers in the conferences could be separated into two groups. One group consisted of "high-level" performances, the other of "low-level" performances. Performances were judged in relation to sets of items in six categories, namely, "Teachers' Aims for Conferences," "Parents' Aims for Conferences," "Outcomes of Conferences for Teachers," "Outcomes of Conferences for Parents," "Topics Occurring in Conferences," and "Topics Stressed in Conferences." Once these criteria had been determined, it was possible for the analyst to separate the protocols into two contrasting groups.

The reliability of the judgments involved was determined by obtaining the extent of agreement between the judgments of two accredited judges and the judgments of the analyst on the six sets of categories.

From Harold J. Maves, "Contrasting Levels of Performance in Parent-Teacher Conferences," *The Elementary School Journal*, LVIII (January, 1958), 219–224. Harold J. Maves is Principal of the Washington Elementary School, Berkeley, California. This school is the University of California Demonstration school. Reprinted from *The Elementary School Journal* by permission of The University of Chicago Press. Copyright 1958 by The University of Chicago.

The percent of agreement was high, ranging from 88.9 to 96.5, and indicated a high level of reliability in the analysis of the semantic content.[1]

This article gives a résumé of the factors which primarily contribute to the contrasting levels of performance in conferences and presents illustrative excerpts from each group of conferences.

ESTABLISHMENT OF RAPPORT

The establishment of rapport appears to be the main factor contributing toward achievement of a high level of performance by the participants of parent-teacher conferences. Rapport is generally established early in the conference and is maintained throughout. In the successful conference characterized by good rapport, there is free exchange of information. Although the initiative is generally assumed by the teacher, a comfortable working relationship exists, and contributions are freely made by both participants.

After an exchange of introductory conversation, the teacher generally starts the conference by selecting one of the child's strong points and then continues to focus attention on the child throughout the conference. Although there may be some general conversation and personal visiting, the conference is basically purposeful. Even though a child has a marked academic or behavior problem, discussion of the problem does not prohibit a high level of conference performance once rapport has been established and is maintained.

The opening of one high-level conference on school progress is eased by the mother's statement, "Mike met me at the door and said that I should see his arithmetic paper for today because that was at least one paper that was all right." After mutual laughter, the teacher follows the cue offered by the parent and shows other examples of work in arithmetic and in other subject areas which are "all right." The teacher frequently interjects incidents about the child with an introductory phrase such as, "One of the things I wanted to tell you which is so nice about Mike. . . ."

In another conference stressing child behavior, there is some general conversation about the mother's employment. This introductory conversation was prompted by the teacher's remarks of appreciation for the mother's arranging to get time off from her work. The teacher then mentions that the child's improvement in relation to others in the class stands out above all else. The teacher states, "Norma used to take too much care of the children in the room, and they didn't like it. She now has several good friends in the room and that, in itself, is an improvement. Last year Norma was umpire for all differences of opin-

[1] Bernard Berelson, *Content Analysis in Communication Research.* Glencoe, Illinois: Free Press, 1952.

ion on the playground and in the classroom, but now she gets her attention in better ways."

The mother wishes to know how the teacher has achieved this and is told that it is because the child has earned the respect of her peers. The teacher relates how the child has been given extra duties, such as keeping records and acting as classroom librarian, and thereby has obtained the attention she desires. The mother reciprocates by relating that Norma is having tennis and swimming lessons to aid in developing poise and grace. When the mother elaborates on the child's reaction to the lessons, the teacher, with an occasional interjection, encourages the recounting of considerable background information. The conference closes with a summary of the child's progress in social growth. At the end, when the mother questions, "In other words, you think she'll be all right?" the teacher says, "Oh, yes, she's doing nicely, and she's such an attractive girl."

In a conference depicting a low level of performance, where it is evident that rapport has not been established, the participants do not engage in introductory conversation upon meeting. The teacher introduces himself to the mother and asks her to be seated. He presents the mother with a guide sheet of the check-list type and, without allowing her any time to go over it, opens the conference by reading the items aloud and indicating how he has checked them. Once during the report the teacher abruptly says, "Now, I don't want to do all the talking. You do some."

"Dave seems to be doing all right," responded the mother.

The teacher continues reading the list and, at the end, says, "I shouldn't do all the talking, you know. Do you have any questions?"

The mother replies, "No, I guess not. The same things are checked as last year."

Although the teacher had indicated that the child was shy and was retarded in his reading and arithmetic, there was no specific planning for improvement. The teacher gained no insight from parental reactions or contributions. The teacher's final statement was, "I believe our plan for the year should be to bring him out of his reticence."

DOMINATION IN LOW-LEVEL CONFERENCES

In conferences of low-level performance the discussion is frequently dominated by one of the participants. The free, comfortable working relationship manifested in high-level conferences is not evident.

These conferences are most frequently dominated by teachers. This condition stems from the belief of the participants that it is the teacher's responsibility to give a report to parents. As part of the total study of conferences, parents and teachers were asked to state their aims prior to the conferences. These statements indicated that teachers considered their primary function was to make a report to parents. Parents indicated that their primary aim was to obtain a report from the teachers.

The domination by one of the participants occasionally results when one or the other participant is put on the defensive. Direct, inept questioning by the teacher often fails to elicit a response from the parent and leaves the teacher in the dominant role. Frequently the low-performing teacher adheres rigidly to a conference guide sheet, gives a report, and fails to engage the parent in discussion, as in the last conference reported above. While a guide sheet is employed in conferences of both levels, its use is more flexible in the high-level conference. Domination by the parent may give the teacher an insight into home relations and the history of the child, but it usually gives little or no direction to the conference.

One parent-dominated conference begins with a discussion about a note which the parent had sent to the teacher sometime previously and which the teacher had misplaced. The mother engages in a long discourse regarding an illness in the family, and the attendant hardships, which had been explained in the note, and it is some time before attention is turned to the child. The teacher listens but makes little attempt to direct the discussion. The mother places herself on the defensive and dominates the conference throughout. Her lengthy accounts of the home background and the child's problems offer insight for the teacher but give no helpful direction to the conference. Many areas related to sibling and peer relations are considered, but there is no common planning for co-operation in the correction of the child's behavior problem.

On several occasions the parent states, "If you have any suggestions, I'll be glad to go along with you." In response to this the teacher cites instances of the child's behavior at school or agrees with the mother that the child's difficulty with her peers is a tit-for-tat situation. There is no reference to obtaining help from specialists. The conversation appears to leave the participants with a feeling of hopelessness. The teacher tells the parent that the child needs to learn the multiplication tables, and the mother defends her child by saying that the tables were not taught to the girl while she attended another school. There is a similarly ineffectual discussion about the need for improvement in spelling. The conference concludes with the parent's request that the teacher write her a note if she has any suggestions.

A teacher dominates another conference by adhering rigidly to the check-list type of guide sheet. In opening the conference, the teacher explains the check list and says that, by using it, he will certainly cover everything. In the beginning, when he mentions that he feels the child's health is good, the mother agrees and says, "That's all right, and I feel that her school work is better now than at the beginning of the year, but she needs to practice the multiplication tables." The teacher says, "I've got something down here on that" (obviously pointing to the place on the check list), and returns to the earlier point of discussion. Thirty-nine specific items are classified under four headings of adjustment and growth on this check list, and the teacher indicates how he has evaluated the child's performance for each of the items on a three-point scale. Occasionally he gives an illustration to emphasize a point, but he allows for virtually no interjection by the parent and encourages none. After running the gamut in fourteen minutes, he asks the parent if there are any questions or comments. There are none. The parent is given a copy of the check list, and the conference is closed.

USE OF ILLUSTRATIONS AND PLANS FOR FUTURE DEVELOPMENT

High-level performing parents and teachers give more specific illustrative incidents in reference to a point of discussion than do low-level performing parents and teachers. High-performing teachers use more samples of the children's work to illustrate past achievement and to aid in planning for improvement in a specific area.

In conferences having a high level of performance, there usually is evidence of the interpretation of some phases of the school program in light of the child's present status or grade level. There is usually evidence of planning for the child's future development. The teacher may describe his plans for the individual or the class, or teacher and parent may work out an agreement for concentrated teamwork in some area.

In one conference of high-level performance, the mother furnishes insight into family life by telling how the father aided the pupil to learn the multiplication tables by inventing a game using casino rules; how the boy voluntarily reads since he has been selected chairman of a social-studies committee; how this reading has led to discussions at home, including one on religious freedom in the New England colonies; and how the mother and her son together got an "excellent" mark in spelling one year. There is a discussion of the child's writing and arithmetic, which are in need of improvement, followed by the making of a plan for improvement. The teacher gives the mother a folder of work but does not discuss all the papers in it. She refers only to items pertinent to the discussion and thereby makes them meaningful.

Another mother is interested in knowing the place of oral reading in the school. The teacher gives examples of its use in the classroom, such as reading phrases which answer questions, reading sections to prove a point, and reading for audience situations. At this point the teacher volunteers the information that the child is near grade level in reading achievement. A discussion of the child's need for reading and also for studying spelling at home closes the conference.

One teacher begins a high-level conference by telling the mother that her son has considerable ability and by showing her samples of the child's work. Although the teacher begins rather abruptly by telling the mother that the boy is immature in his work habits, he gives her a frank account and qualifies it with evidence. For example, the teacher shows a test paper in which the child did poorly and states, "I really jumped all over Bob that day." He then presents the next test paper, pointing to the marked improvement. Because the child failed to assume the responsibility for completing work while having been on traffic-patrol duty, he was removed from the patrol. When he mentioned to his mother that he had quit, his younger sister said, "You mean you got fired." His reply was, "No, but I knew I was going to be!" It was agreed that he should be reinstated on the patrol if his work continued to improve. When the mother had told her son that he would have to begin to do better work so he would be successful in college, he had said he might go to reform school and that "wouldn't cost her anything." The mother and the teacher agree to attempt to interest the child in current school projects and to place renewed emphasis on participation in those sports in which he excels.

Low-level performing parents give few specific illustrative incidents, and the teachers use few or no samples of children's work. These conferences give less evidence of interpretation of the school program and less evidence of planning for the child. In the main, the low-level conferences are mere verbalizations of a report, as evidenced in the inflexible illustrative excerpts noted previously.

USE OF COMMENDATION

In the high-level conferences teachers more frequently commend the children and express pleasure with having them in their classes. In these conferences, parents more readily extol the teachers, and both groups of participants make voluntary commendation of the conferences themselves.

Commendation of children or of conferences is not evident in the low-level performances. In the latter type there is some criticism of the conferences by parents and teachers. During one low-level conference a parent volunteers, "I think the parent-teacher conference is too time-consuming to be regularly scheduled. I prefer a report card, and, if a conference is necessary, it will be asked for anyway." Although teachers do not openly criticize the conferences during the participation, the brisk manner of one teacher during a low-level conference is apparent. In stating his purpose, he remarks, "A conference is expected of me by my superiors, so I give one. There is no point in this one at all."

In the course of the conferences, high-level performing teachers extol children and conferences with such remarks as:

Thank you for coming. I think these conferences are wonderful opportunities for both of us, don't you?

Mark is a champ in my book.

Raymond is a fine boy, and so considerate.

She's an excellent student.

Marcia and I have become close friends.

I get nothing from a report card, but the conference is as much for the child and for me as it is for you.

High-level performing parents make these remarks:

Sharon finds school interesting and stimulating because of you.

It takes a lot more than just nature. The teacher next year won't have as much trouble because Frank had you this year.

She likes you, and that's important. Teachers are so important to her.

I admire you teachers. I don't know how you can wrestle with so many children at one time.

The P.T.A. is fine and it's nice to visit with you there, but the conference is so much beyond that. I feel it is just for me.

During these four years that I've come for conferences, I've never been in doubt as to just where my daughter stood in school. I didn't feel that way when we only had report cards.

CONCLUSION

When criticisms of parent-teacher conferences are based on the characteristics of conferences representing a low level of performance, it is clear that the criticisms are justified. The lack of communication between the participants and the failure of common planning for the child are all too apparent.

Conferences which are representative of a low level of performance can be improved with freer exchanges of information by the participants. The teacher must avoid direct, inept questioning which fails to elicit responses from the parents and leaves the teacher in the dominant role. The items on a guide sheet should be limited in number and should not be adhered to rigidly. Only a few points should be discussed, but these should be stressed. Specific illustrations and examples of work should be used to make the discussions meaningful, and purposeful planning should be done jointly by the teacher and the parent.

It is evident from the characteristics of parent-teacher conferences representing a high level of performance that the conference is more than a pupil-progress report. It is an experience in co-operative human relationships. It offers an opportunity for communication between two persons vitally responsible for guiding a growing child in meeting his needs and the demands of democracy.

Advocates of improved public relations for schools state that even the most casual contacts tend to influence the public attitudes toward schools, favorably or unfavorably. The parent-teacher conference, which can be used in any community, is a dynamic potentiality for continuous publicity, educational interpretation, and co-operative endeavor. The conference must, however, reach a high level of performance if it is to be of the most value.

64. *Team Teaching: A Review*
STUART E. DEAN

Of all the ideas to come out of the current reappraisal of the ends and means of the elementary school, one of the fastest to capture both professional and public attention is the idea of team teaching. In the ordinary meaning of language the term suggests merely a kind of cooperation among teachers; but in the meaning it is now being given, it is much more. It is a way of organizing a school, a way of utilizing staff, a way of using space and equipment. It is, in short, a considered and pointed response, from the organizational angle, to the nationwide cry for quality in education.

Because the term "team teaching" has come to mean so much, most of us are not clear on what it does mean; its meaning depends all too much on who is speaking—or listening. Until we can arrive at some degree of consensus on a definition, we can at least consider how the idea grew and why, what claims are being made for it, and how it is working in practice.

From Stuart E. Dean, "Team Teaching: A Review," *School Life*, XLIV (September, 1961), 5–8. Stuart E. Dean is the Specialist for Elementary School Organization and Administration with the United States Office of Education.

BEHIND IT, PROBLEMS AND QUESTIONS

Nearly every change in the schools, now as always, is in response to the demands of the times. Our times are full of change—social, cultural, technological, economic, and international—and it has driven us to scrutinize the fundamental values of a free and universal public education. We are also in one of those recurring cycles of disenchantment with the structural organization of the school which periodically send us into fresh debate on the virtues of the present pattern— a pattern which for us in the elementary school today is usually influenced by what we call "the self-contained classroom" (a term which can mislead but which means no more than a classroom in which a number of pupils at the same grade level are taught nearly every subject by the same teacher).

Much of the present querulousness over the self-contained classroom is the result of the growing interest in subject matter—the call for more science, more mathematics, more languages—and the growing worry about the talented student, who many fear will be a heavy loser if his teacher has to spread himself too thin over too many subjects and too much diversity in pupil ability. As the stress on academic achievement has increased, the doubt has grown that one teacher can teach all subjects to all children with equal effectiveness and skill; and from that doubt there is only a step to the conviction that the subject-matter specialist has become necessary in the elementary school and that some way must be found to narrow the spread of capability in the group of pupils with which a teacher works.

The age-old questions about class size also have arisen: How large a group can a teacher handle effectively? does not the optimum number vary with the circumstances? are there not some subjects that can be taught just as effectively to many at a time as to few—and some that cannot?

And at the same time concern has grown over certain circumstances that make the teaching profession less than attractive to many talented and creative persons. Much attention has been spent on finding ways to relieve teachers of the endless clerical nonteaching chores laid upon them in most schools, and on devising an organizational pattern that will make it possible to promote to positions of leadership—and to remunerate financially—those teachers who show extraordinary skill and ability.

NO ONE DEFINITION

There are only a few definitions of team teaching available, and none of them say quite the same thing. Taken together, however, they suggest that for some of these questions and problems team teaching may have an answer. In effect they suggest that team teaching can take various forms, but that whatever its variations it is essentially a way of organizing the instructional program which is applicable at either the secondary or the elementary level. Teams may work "vertically" through the school, i.e., at all grade levels in a single subject or closely related subjects; or they may work "horizontally," i.e., at one grade level but in several subjects. For example, all teachers of the language arts may work as a team with all pupils from grade 7 through grade 12. Or all teachers in, say, grades 5 and 6 may work together, each one taking the chief responsibility for classes in his special field and probably doing most of the teaching in it but working always as a member of the team.

Even a small team has a leader, and many large teams have a hierarchy of levels that bestows different titles on its members—titles like "team leader," "master teacher," "senior teacher," "regular teacher," and "intern." Many teams also include nonprofessional people, such as aides and clerks to assist the teachers.

Team teaching as it is being defined today is certainly more than a group of teachers who have amiably agreed to work together. The heart of it seems to be an almost unprecedented kind of unity: members of the team plan together, collaborate constantly, communicate without restraint, and share sincerely and selflessly. Working together they can revise procedures and revamp programs to meet the educational needs of their pupils. In a sense the movement toward team teaching may be considered something of a revolt against the organizational restrictions of the past and a sharp reminder to all and sundry that the purpose of school administration is to serve the educational process, not to control it. One project director says: "We are questioning the status quo."

NEW, YET OLD

Is team teaching new? Yes—and no. The term itself is new; it first appeared in *Education Digest* in 1957. And there are inescapable signs of newness in current literature and in practices developing in some schools. History, however, reminds us of other forms of elementary school organization that begin with the same goals as team teaching —the Platoon School, the Winnetka Plan, the Pueblo Plan, to mention a few. The Cooperative Group Plan, formulated in the 1930's by J. F. Hosic, who felt the same disquietude about elementary school structure that impels us to experiment today, is probably the most recent prototype; in this plan, small groups of teachers together organized the work for a group of children within a range of not more than three grades, and each group had its own chairman who also served in a supervisory capacity.

It is generally agreed, however, that the first recorded project in team teaching was begun in 1957 at the Franklin School in Lexington, Mass. This is one of the projects sponsored by Harvard University's School and University Program for Research and Development—SUPRAD—a program aimed at bridging the gap between university research and school practice.

The Franklin School project has been followed by many others in scattered parts of the country. Estimates of the number and substance of these experiments vary, but it seems fairly reasonable to say that they are to be found now in at least 100 communities, in both elementary and secondary schools.

Some of these projects have been much written about, in both professional and popular publications—for example, the projects in Norwalk, Conn.; Flint, Mich.; Baltimore, Md.; Jefferson County, Colo.; Evanston Township, Ill.; Ft. Wayne, Ind.; Newton, Mass.; Montgomery County, Md.; and Palo Alto, Calif. Some are linked with universities, such as Harvard, Chicago, Stanford, and Wisconsin. A great many of these have been encouraged and assisted by the Commission on the Experimental Study of the Utilization of the Staff in the Secondary Schools, appointed by the National Association of Secondary School Principals and supported by the Fund for the Advancement of Education.

HOW ONE SCHOOL DOES IT

The very flexibility that characterizes team teaching makes it hard for any one to draw with firm lines a picture of how, precisely, a team works; it makes it in fact impossible, for no two teams are likely to work in the same way. That they do not is reenforcement for the point of view that team teaching is more of an organizational idea than a set of procedures and practices. It is moreover an idea which a group of teachers must understand and accept—to which they must in fact commit themselves—before they can work as a team; an idea which they must also adapt to their own personalities and abilities and to the personalities and needs of their pupils.

Claremont, Calif., has published a booklet which describes how its team-teaching project operates. But anyone who examines this project as an example should first remind himself that the Claremont way is not necessarily typical. From project to project teams differ both in the number of their constituents and in the way these constituents complement each other. In general, however, the following summary of the

Claremont plan may be considered a reasonable review of how a team in an elementary school is organized and how it works.

Pupils. For each team there are about 150 to 200 pupils, drawn from a particular age or grade group. For more flexible grouping of pupils and easier movements from one level to another, the school may be divided into 3 parts: early elementary, middle, and upper. But whatever arrangement the school makes for flexible grouping, the pupils assigned to each teaching team form a distinct group within the school organization.

Faculty. Each team has 5 to 7 classroom teachers with both general and special abilities. The school tries to select teachers who have already specialized, or plan to specialize, in certain subjects in the elementary school curriculum. Some team members also specialize in certain skills, such as giving tests, interpreting results of group testing, and giving remedial instruction. Teams meet regularly to exchange ideas, share information, clarify their purposes, and organize their programs. They decide on the size of each instructional group and how the specialist will handle it.

Team leader. The team leader, who is either elected or appointed, assumes responsibility for the way in which the team works and gives it leadership in improving instruction and guidance. He receives an additional stipend; and from time to time an auxiliary teacher relieves him of teaching, to give him time for his added responsibilities.

Auxiliary teacher. The auxiliary teacher is a substitute teacher assigned specifically to the team. He not only substitutes for teachers when they are absent but also teaches approximately 20 full days a year to give teachers time for planning. His service makes the schedule more flexible; and, since he is a member of the team and attends all meetings, he is able to preserve the continuity of instruction in a teacher's absence.

Teacher aide. The teacher aide does some of the clerical and routine work connected with teaching, such as correcting tests and marking papers, arranging for field trips, supervising study periods, and giving makeup examinations. Sometimes he tutors individual pupils or works with small groups, and does research for teachers on curriculum problems.

Citizens. The team draws on citizens with special skill and knowledge. Scientists, mathematicians, story-tellers, children's librarians, artists, musicians, travellers, and others help the team enrich the curriculum; for example, they instruct small groups and lead discussions, either during school hours or at regular sessions after hours.

Intern teachers. Intern teachers are an integral part of some teams.

At the same time that they are being introduced to actual teaching, they are giving support to seasoned teachers.

BUILDINGS TO MATCH

The Claremont plan of team teaching—in fact any plan of true team teaching—obviously needs special arrangements in both space and equipment. Several observers already have commented on the limitations and restrictions the traditional type of school facility imposes on a full-scale program. "Conventionally constructed school buildings," a SUPRAD report says, "with their rows of equally sized self-contained cells divided by immovable partitions do not meet the needs of most effective team operation."

What kind of school will it have to be? One thing, for certain—a school with flexibility built into nearly every cubic inch. A number of actual and proposed plans for elementary schools and junior high schools can be found in *Schools for Team Teaching*, published by the Educational Facilities Laboratory; but the Laboratory does not say that they are final solutions to the problems posed by the team teaching. It calls them experiments, planned for an experiment, but goes on to say that "both the educational idea and the schools planned for it represent new and adventurous thinking, attempts to meet this country's mounting educational challenge." Among the schools it describes are the Estabrook Elementary School in Lexington, Mass., and the Dundee Elementary School in Greenwich, Conn.

Whether schools that fit team teaching cost more to build than the usual kind of school has not yet been determined, but informed estimates say they do. Robert H. Anderson of Harvard University, who directs the Franklin School project, says, "It is hard to predict whether the radically different buildings needed for team teaching will be more expensive. . . . My guess is that they will cost about 10 percent more than 'standard' obsolete buildings, although an ingenious acoustical invention could conceivably reverse the cost picture." Arthur D. Morse, in his *Schools of Tomorrow—Today*, says that team teaching will raise the cost of operating a school, but not because of the building: "Although the new building will feature versatility, it will cost approximately the same as the traditional school. But team teaching with its upgraded salary scales is likely to add 10 or 15 percent to the cost . . ."

TOO SOON FOR EVALUATION

The team-teaching idea has been in practice for so little time in so few communities that conclusive evidence of its effectiveness has not had time to accumulate. After all, the oldest project, in Franklin School, is only 4 years old.

And it is out of Franklin that most of the evaluation has come. Dr. Anderson's subjective summary indicates that team teaching is not "disadvantageous" to children, that its results warrant further experimentation and refinement of proceedings. As far as its effects on pupils go—in growth of personality, in adjustment and achievement—he thinks them "no less satisfactory" than the effects in a more traditional setting. He has found no evidence that children suffer emotionally or academically or in any way feel "lost" in the process. The reactions of the teachers have been favorable. Parents of the children, according to Mr. Morse's report on Franklin School, seem more willing to express satisfaction than "the cautious officials of SUPRAD." Almost all say that their children enjoy their team-taught schooling and benefit from it.

The next logical step, obviously, is to put team teaching to the test. Plans for investigative studies and research projects are already being discussed in a number of quarters, and some proposals have been submitted to the Office of Education for inclusion in its cooperative research program. In due time, no doubt, more objective bases for judging the worth of team teaching will be at hand; but present evaluation is almost entirely in the realm of personal opinion and speculation.

Opinions and speculations, however, despite their shortcomings as a body of evidence, are highly worth reviewing: many of them come from men and women renowned for their sound judgment; many have been formed against a background of long professional experience. That some of them are diametrically opposed should not disturb anyone: this is healthy evidence of the questioning and weighing that must go on until such time as research puts an end to uncertainties.

CLAIMS AND QUESTIONS

Opinions about team teaching are not sharply divided into two camps. Some of the proponents are as ready as the critics to point out practical problems and raise provocative questions; and many of the critics concede that team teaching promises much, at least in theory.

Among the advantages being claimed for team teaching are these:

It is good organization. As a plan of organizing for instruction, it preserves the virtue and avoids the weakness of both the self-contained classroom and its opposite number, departmentalized instruction; it makes it possible to have every subject taught by a specialist, yet it preserves the interrelatedness of subjects and learning. It makes the most strategic use of each teacher's knowledge and skill, accommodates different levels of teacher responsibility and competence.

The pupil profits. The pupil, having the academic advantage of being taught each subject by a teacher strong in it, is more likely to find scholarship attractive, to be challenged to work to capacity. His interests, abilities, and needs are more likely to be discovered when he is taught by two or more teachers working closely together than when he is taught by one teacher working more or less alone; and the flexible grouping and regrouping that characterizes many team-teaching programs provides more realistically for pupil differences than straight "ability" grouping. The quality of instruction that a pupil receives during any one term or school year does not depend on the competence of a single teacher.

The staff profits. The teacher gets more professional and personal stimulation when he works on a team than when he works in isolation. There is better communication among staff members, more motivation for continuous curriculum improvement, more cooperative planning. Because the team places a premium on unusual ability and skill and on exceptional qualities of leadership, it encourages teachers to grow professionally.

The school profits. There is more opportunity for flexible schedules and efficient use of space, materials, and equipment; in other words, the administration is encouraged to respond to changing needs rather than to be restrictive. Well-qualified teachers are more likely to be attracted to the school. Because the team has room for different levels of teaching ability, it makes it easier for the school to peg teachers' salaries to professional skill and leadership; easier, too, to provide inservice training for inexperienced teachers.

Among the many questions being raised in connection with team teaching are these:

What are we talking about? Does not the present loose application of labels and terms lead to a possibility that the basic concepts of team teaching will be misused and abused? If, before we have precise definition and full understanding of team teaching, we leap aboard the bandwagon, do we not run the risk of missing entirely its idealistic purposes?

Are the assumptions sound? On what basis have we judged inadequate the present methods of school organization and instruction? Can we safely assume that all teachers are qualified by temperament and training to work effectively as members of a team? Is the theory valid that some things can be taught more efficiently to large groups? Are we certain that children learn more from a subject-matter specialist than from a generalist?

How do we surmount the practical difficulties? How can we get enough teachers specially trained in subject matter and team relationships? Enough skilled and gifted team leaders? How will we meet the increased salary and operating costs? How serious are the limitations of our present school buildings for housing this sort of program?

Could team teaching become form without substance? Does not history suggest that our schools have a tendency to become so preoccupied with innovations that they make them the ends rather than the means they were conceived to be? Should not team teaching be evaluated on the basis of its contributions to classroom practice and not judged on the basis of administrative efficiency, popular expediency, or the glamor given by publicity? Is there not an ever-present danger that we will overemphasize organization and, in so doing, distort our sense of the educational values of the elementary school?

65. *Merit Rating of Teachers*

EDMUND H. THORNE

More and more opposition is being voiced to across-the-board salary increases and the lock-step type of advancement that characterizes the conventional teachers' salary schedule, based solely on degrees earned and years of service.

Many boards of education want some other basis for differentiating salaries. They are seeking some plan that will enable them to reward superior service. In an effort to find a way, they hopefully look to their superintendents and teachers to come up with mutually acceptable plans.

In many places, the pleas of the board either fall on deaf ears or are opposed. Administrators and teachers alike have been reluctant to depart from the comparatively safe and traditional basis for building salary payment plans. Teachers are afraid that a merit type of schedule may be used as a device for retarding the development of adequate professional salary schedules. Both teachers and administrators are fearful because of previous unsuccessful attempts, most of which took place with the introduction of ill conceived plans several decades ago.

Past failure is no excuse for abandoning further consideration and

From Edmund H. Thorne, "Teacher Merit Rating Really Does Work!" *The Nation's Schools*, LXIV, No. 5 (November, 1959), 70–71. Edmund H. Thorne is Superintendent of Schools in West Hartford, Connecticut and a member of the editorial advisory board of *The Nation's Schools*. This article was prepared from a talk given at a workshop on merit salary schedules held at the School of Education, Syracuse University. Reprinted by permission of The Modern Hospital Publishing Company, Chicago.

research. We know that *merit plans can work* and, in fact, *are working successfully* in many school systems today.

The installation of any merit plan should be considered as a calculated risk and developed with utmost caution. Boards of education cannot expect a plan to succeed by forcing it on an unwilling staff. On the other hand, progress cannot be made if professional educators refuse to consider the issue, examine the known facts, and experiment with new concepts of salary payment.

Nothing is to be gained by defending the status quo. There is no reason to believe that the conventional preparation-development type of schedule is best. Teachers and administrators should have to encourage, develop, try out, and evaluate new concepts. In so doing, the profession may discover ways whereby we can pay outstanding teachers salaries equal to the best in other professions. As we increase the ceiling of opportunity, we should be able to recruit more able minds into teaching. By paying for superior work, we can retain many talented teachers who now leave for higher salaries in other lines of endeavor.

Those interested in developing schedules that incorporate some form of merit can profit from the conditions that have contributed to success or failure elsewhere. I believe the following principles and practices will help to ensure successful development and operation of a merit plan:

1. *A merit pay plan is not likely to succeed unless a good basic professional salary schedule is maintained.* It is an illusion to think that introduction of merit pay will correct an inadequate basic salary plan or that it can be used as a scheme to reduce teachers' pay. Compensation for meritorious service should be something "over and beyond" an already good schedule.

2. *The merit concept must be applied to all administrative actions involving personnel,* including initial selection, evaluation for tenure, advancement on the schedule, and promotion within the system. The professional administrative staff must be free to operate the school system on a merit basis and also be free from outside interference by politically-minded board members or others who may try to exert pressure or control.

3. *The prime principle underlying the plan should be the improvement of instruction.* Instruction is the chief function of the school and what happens to children in the teaching-learning process is all-important. Any plan for increasing the ceiling of opportunity should result in the recruitment and retention of superior teachers. Merit incentives are justifiable only to the extent they reward top service.

4. *A merit salary program should not be adopted until after sufficient study,* and then only upon thorough understanding and acceptance of a substantial majority of the staff. The climate for develop-

ment is important. Teachers themselves must be involved in the process. The staff must be open-minded and willing to examine evidence and give careful study to all proposals; it should not be forced to develop a plan under pressure. Failure is inevitable if an unwilling staff adopts, prematurely, an unsound program impossible to administer.

5. *The plan should be adapted to local conditions.* There is no assurance that a successful plan in one school system can be transplanted to another. The philosophy behind the plan and its method of operation must be worked out by those concerned.

6. *It requires the complete understanding and support of administrative personnel, board and public.* Because the superintendent, the principals, and other administrative officers will be responsible for the administration of a plan, it is essential that the procedures proposed will be workable. In addition, the board of education will have to appropriate the necessary funds to operate the program. Consideration should also be given to informing the public and enlisting its understanding and support.

7. *Well defined standards of evaluation should be agreed to and understood by those to be evaluated.* The key to the successful operation of a merit pay schedule is judgment based on evidence. Teachers should know the criteria by which they are to be judged. They should know where they stand and should be aware of their strengths and weaknesses. Opportunity should be given, through conference, for teachers to review the facts.

8. *Extra merit awards should be commensurate with the value placed on superior service.* They should be large enough to offer a real incentive. It is ridiculous to go through the process of selection only to offer a paltry sum to those chosen.

9. *Teachers must have confidence in the competence and integrity of the administrative staff* or others responsible for evaluating teachers for merit pay. Programs are most successful where good teacher-administrator relations exist. Staff harmony in the school system is essential. Inasmuch as many principals and superintendents are not skilled in evaluation technics and procedures, an inservice workshop in this important area might well be held.

10. *Sufficient administrative and supervisory personnel should be provided* to ensure adequate time for evaluation. Boards of education cannot expect already overworked superintendents and principals to do an adequate job in administering a merit plan without offering them sufficient administrative help. It is more difficult to evaluate teaching service and relate it to the salary schedule than it is automatically to advance teachers on schedule in terms of credit earned and years of service.

11. *Final selection should be entrusted to more than one person.* Rotating membership on a representative committee is more acceptable because it tends to minimize individual prejudice and bias.

12. *Teachers should be given the right to appeal.* They should know wherein they failed to measure up to established criteria. Procedures should be established for review by an appeal board, the superintendent, or the board of education.

13. *Merit awards should be based on predetermined criteria and not on percentage quotas.* A teacher who is eligible and qualified should not be denied a merit award because of some arbitrary limitation.

14. *Adequate safeguards should be established to provide continuity of program from one year to the next.* Merit awards cannot be offered one year and skipped the next. Except in unusual situations, thoroughly understood by the staff, failure to grant merit awards because of budget limitations will weaken staff morale and confidence in the merit program.

15. *Plans should be made for the continuous reevaluation.* In spite of how carefully a plan is developed, imperfections will appear. A procedure should be established for periodic review and modification in the light of new experience.

16. *Provision should be made for informing new staff members on the philosophy behind the merit plan,* its application, and the rights and obligations of all for whom it is intended. This is especially necessary in a growing school system where many new teachers are added each year. A plan can be well conceived and approved by a staff and later lost because of failure to maintain understanding and support by new members joining the faculty.

66. Secondary Education and the Current Educational Debate

OVID F. PARODY

There is a great debate raging in American educational circles. You know the many issues as well as I do, therefore I shall not bore you with

From Ovid F. Parody, "Secondary Education and the Current Educational Debate," NASSP *Bulletin,* XLIII, No. 251 (December, 1959), 81–85. Ovid F. Parody is Chief, Secondary Schools Section, United States Office of Education. Reprinted by permission of the *Bulletin* of the National Association of Secondary-School Principals, Washington, D.C. Copyright December, 1959.

an enumeration of them. However, I would like to abstract from this debate one major theme for our consideration. It goes something like this: "The American secondary school needs to raise its academic standards so pupils will have to work harder to excel." Now some of us are in agreement with this directive and have already moved ahead with plans to readjust our school programs accordingly. And perhaps this is what we should all do, but first I think we should give it some thought because I am convinced that, if we give the public what it is asking for, they will not get what they really want or need. Therefore, I propose that we spend some time thinking together about this proposition. I think we can break it down into three parts for analysis:

1. The raising of standards
2. Getting pupils to work harder
3. The idea of excelling

RAISING STANDARDS

Now let us turn to the first point—the raising of standards. When we begin to think about standards, we note that the nature of standards differs according to the purposes for which they are used. First there are standards which are used for the purpose of raising quality through a process of selection and elimination. A life-insurance examination is a good example of this type of standard. An applicant is examined by a physician and is passed or failed according to certain predetermined standards. Another illustration of this type of standard would be the New York State Regents Preliminary Examinations which are given at the end of the eighth grade. These have to be passed before a pupil can be admitted to the high school. Obviously standards of this type serve to raise the quality of the group selected because people below the predetermined standard are not accepted.

However, there is another type of standard which is used when we have to select and distribute people without the possibility of elimination. The annual health checkup would illustrate this type of standard. We go to our doctor and he examines us and reports on our strengths and weaknesses and suggests a health program appropriate to our needs —a little more of this and a little less of that, generally a little less of that. Another example of this type is the eighth-grade examinations which a counselor uses for guiding a pupil in program making. Standards of this type do not improve our quality of health or scholarship, but they do aid in making a more purposeful distribution of abilities.

This point is obvious, yet it needs to be emphasized, because it seems to me that, in the educational debate, these two types of standards are constantly being confused. Colleges can raise the level of academic achievement simply by raising their standards of admission, but the secondary schools can't do this, and yet the public seems to think that it can. High schools can raise the standards for admission to certain subjects or courses of study, but this does not raise the general scholastic levels of the school—it merely redistributes the abilities already there. We have to accept the fact that, as a matter of broad social policy, our secondary schools are deliberately non-selective.

Let me give you a typical example of this confusion. Some time ago, Fred Hechinger, an educational writer, said in the *New York Times,* "The raising of standards for the great mass of students would mean a spectacular improvement in the country's total reservoir of skills." Now I ask you, would it? This confusion in regard to the nature of standards reminds me of the girl who was asked how high she liked her heels. Her reply was 6:2. But you may not agree with this analysis. You may think it is just a splitting of hairs and dealing in sophistries. You may think that the public is right in demanding that we raise standards, especially to challenge the gifted and superior to work up to their capacity. And this moves us to the second part of our analysis—"to make pupils work harder."

GETTING PUPILS TO WORK HARDER

Will the raising of standards make people work harder? Perhaps so with some of our more talented youngsters who may have been coasting along. But the deeper and more significant question to raise would be, Why were they loafing? This brings us into the area of human motivation, where we find that the social scientists have been doing a lot of research in this area. Their answers are not complete, but they do provide us with some guidance. They tell us that people will work harder and more constructively if certain conditions are met. Among these conditions are the following:

1. People need to be known and understood.
2. People need to be recognized and respected as individuals.
3. People need to be allowed to assume responsibility; that is, in planning and establishing goals.
4. People need to be kept active along their lines of interest.
5. People need to feel secure and be dealt with firmly but kindly.

These are some of the conditions which have to be met if people are to work hard and well. I am sure that you could go on and add others from your own experience in working with people. The problem has shifted from the mere manipulation of external standards to the much more significant and complex problem of developing a school culture which will facilitate human growth because it is organized to serve human needs.

We should be clear as to just whose needs we are working on. A friend of mine visited a private school recently. When he stepped into the corridor, he met a boy who was cackling like a chicken. When he met the headmaster, he said, "That boy——." "Oh, yes," interrupted the headmaster, "I know, he is very disturbed." "But isn't there anything you can do?" asked my friend. "Well, yes . . . I guess so," mused the head master, "but you see we need the eggs."

Another point to be considered in regard to motivation is that school motivations do not exist in isolation from the larger society of which the school is a part. In the long run, school goals have to be in harmony with cultural goals. This brings us to the third part of our problem—"What does it mean to excel in our society?"

THE IDEA OF EXCELLING

In a society where the meaning of success is clearly spelled out, school goals are relatively easy to arrive at. Under such circumstances, the values of the culture set in motion prevailing winds and establish direction flags which guide behavior in the desired direction. This was the case for many years in America. Our national growth was keyed to the concept of individual success; our cultural hero was the business tycoon—the rugged individualist who came up the hard way. But today we have a more corporate society and the picture has blurred. Instead of the rugged individualist, we hear more about the organization man—the conformist in the grey flannel suit. In addition, the problem of our national survival in competition with Russia in the Space Age now dominates the world scene. Formerly we held to the view that if each man followed his own self interest, the national welfare would automatically be provided for. Now we have to equate self interest with the national interest.

It is charged that the public schools are neglecting talent in what should be a pursuit of excellence. The pursuit of excellence is certainly a worth-while goal, but the very nature of a pursuit of excellence makes for a neglect of talent. The best we can do is to help pupils make a wise choice of the talent which they want to pursue to excellence as they judiciously neglect other talents which might be developed. If a youngster spends a large part of his time on science in a superior group, is he neglecting his other talents?

Admiral Rickover neglected whatever talents he might have had for becoming a professor of history when he became a naval officer. And Professor Bestor neglected whatever talents he had for becoming a naval officer when he became a professor of history. And both Professor Bestor and Admiral Rickover have become critics of the public schools largely because both of them have neglected whatever talents they had for becoming students of the behavioral sciences.

This is to say that it is not possible to develop fully all of the talents of any individual; therefore, it is even more impossible for a school system to develop fully all of the talents of its students. A school system, to pursue excellence properly, will have to function through a guidance process which wisely develops certain talents and at the same time judiciously neglects others.

In summary, the American secondary school is under pressure to make students work harder by raising academic standards. The general assumption seems to be that, if students work harder on tougher subjects, we shall solve the educational problems of the Space Age. I think that this is a dangerous over-simplification of the problem which is likely to deepen our confusion and add to our frustration. We need to rely more on wisdom drawn from our democratic philosophy and the psycho-social foundations of education as we attempt to guide the growth of individual boys and girls.

Of course the person who doesn't subscribe to the raising of intellectual standards in our high schools as the one-shot quickie solution to our educational problems leaves himself open to the charge of anti-intellectualism. On the contrary, I believe that the true anti-intellectual is the person who seeks to promote scholarship, but ignores the mounting scholarship of the social sciences which teaches us that:

1. Man does not learn with his mind, but with his whole organism—body, mind, and emotions. The way he feels about what he learns is just as important as the knowledge he learns.

2. Man does not learn in school alone. He is educated by his total environment—home, school, and community. It is impossible to separate in-school and out-of-school learnings, and frequently the out-of-school learnings are more dominant than school learnings. Education is not the same as schooling.

3. Each man is unique. Each person draws different meanings from the same experience. Teaching is not the same as learning.

4. Men do fail, but their failure is due more to poor interpersonal relations rather than lack of scholastic challenge.

Many other insights could be listed, but this is sufficient to indicate that any approach that is confined to working on the intellect alone through the single agency of the school is doomed to defeat. The really intellectual approach is a cooperative one involving the home-school-community. I hope, therefore, that we can look upon the present emphasis on raising intellectual standards as the beginning of a continuing search toward a more adequate program for our social democracy as we enter the Space Age.

"What is a good high-school education?" asks Dr. Conant. Then he goes on to say, "A meaningless question to my mind unless you specify the pupil, his environment, his capacities, and his ambitions." If our problems appear to be overwhelming, I think we can take heart from reviewing the history of our profession which clearly shows that periods of educational controversy and debate have always been followed by creative educational advances. Therefore, if we can continue to meet our problems from day to day with intelligence and courage, we can move forward in the faith that the Bestors and Rickovers of today will be followed by the Horace Manns and John Deweys of tomorrow.

INDEX OF SUBJECTS

INDEX OF NAMES